UNIVERSITY OF WESTMINSTER

German Writings
before and after 1945

The German Library: Volume 84

Volkmar Sander, General Editor

GERMAN WRITINGS

BEFORE AND

AFTER 1945

E. Jünger, W. Koeppen, I. Keun,
A. Lernet-Holenia, G. von Rezzori,
E. von Salomon, A. Schmidt

Edited by Jürgen Peters

CONTINUUM
NEW YORK · LONDON

1 9 MAY 2003

2002

The Continuum International Publishing Group Inc
370 Lexington Avenue, New York, NY 10017

The Continuum International Publishing Group Ltd
The Tower Building, 11 York Road, London SE1 7NX

The German Library is published
in cooperation with Deutsches Haus, New York University.
This volume has been supported by Inter Nationes, and a grant from
the funds of Stifterverband für die Deutsche Wissenschaft.

Printed in the United States of America

Library of Congress Cataloging-in-Publication Data

German writings before and after 1945 : E. Jünger, W. Koeppen, I. Keun,
A. Lernet-Holenia, G. von Rezzori, E. von Salomon, A. Schmidt / edited
by Jürgen Peters.
    p.   cm. — (The German library ; v. 84)
    ISBN 0-8264-1405-2 — ISBN 0-8264-1406-0 (pbk.)
    1. German prose literature—20th century—Translations into English.
I. Jünger, Ernst, 1895– II. Peters, Jürgen, 1940– III. Series.
PT1308 .G47   2002
838'.910808—dc21   2002000373

Contents

Introduction

Fascism, and German fascism in particular, apparently has permanent tenancy right in Hollywood. The SA and the SS, their "ranks tightly closed," march through the trivial mundane mythology of the Western world. One's experience again and again while watching the films: they're walking into the trap of fascism. Its self-portrayal was theatrical and cinematic, speaking to that readiness for identification in the viewer without which Hollywood would have remained an insignificant suburb of Los Angeles. Literature proves itself at a distance: the distance of the author to his material, the distance of the reader to the work.

One of the central questions of modernity, formulated by Robert Musil, involves the recountability of reality. Even if this interrogatory formulation has since proved to be a sly trick that served to render reality capable of being properly narrated only under the aspect of its unrecountability, the question of the ability to portray German fascism nevertheless remains. It poses itself literarily and morally because literature, when portraying the particular, makes possible generalizations that, perhaps, can pardon crimes. For centuries, morality has not been an aesthetic criterion. Yet, in this particular case, it is: portrayal is the provision of meaning—and of that which is meaningless.

Ernst Jünger was born in Heidelberg in 1895. He was an officer in World War I and the author of a 1920 bestseller, *In Stahlgewittern (In Storms of Steel)*, about his experience at the front. Jünger was antidemocratic, antibourgeois, and nationalistic. In

1941, he was in Paris at the Hôtel Raphaël as a member of the Occupation force, protected by leading members of the Headquarters. Jünger lived in the ambience of the collaboration, which made innumerable encounters of the most pleasant sort possible. And the smooth "solution of the Jewish question." Jünger's official task, as his highest superior in Paris described after the war, was to observe the "underground struggle between the Party and the Wehrmacht." Most of all, he observed himself by pursuing life in Paris. And by writing in his diary, the publication of which was inconceivable under National Socialism.

Born in Vienna in 1897, Alexander Lernet-Holenia was an officer in World War I. He was a recipient of the Weimar Republic's most important literary award, the Kleist Prize. In 1934, he became known to a wide audience as the author of a novel, *Die Standarte (The Standard),* which dealt with the downfall of the Austrian double monarchy. Lieutenant Lernet-Holenia was a member of the Greater German Army that attacked Poland on September 1, 1939. He was soon wounded. Lernet-Holenia wrote a novel, *Die blaue Stunde (The Blue Hour),* which intertwined his own war experiences with the invented fate of an officer named Wallmoden. The novel appeared in 1940–41, now under the title *Mars in Aries,* as a serial in the illustrated magazine *Die Dame.* After being approved by the Supreme Command of the Wehrmacht, it was published in a large printing by the "aryanized" S. Fischer publishing house of Berlin and, at the last minute, banned through the intervention of the Ministry of Propaganda in July 1941.

Ernst von Salomon, born in Kiel in 1902, was the product of a cadet school. He then became a member of the Freikorps and a member of nationalistic secret organizations whose view was antidemocratic, antibourgeois, and nationalistic. Salomon belonged to Captain Ehrhardt's legendary Organisation Consul (OC). Salomon participated in the murder of Foreign Minister Walter Rathenau and sat in prison from 1922 until 1928. The publisher Ernst Rowohlt discovered the author. Salomon had success as the author of autobiographically inspired writings. In 1945, he was interred by the United States for fifteen months as one of the "erroneous arrestees" as he was called upon his release. In 1946, the denazification of Germany's western zones began. Questionnaires with 131 questions were distributed. Everyone had to provide the most detailed information about his life: family relations, voting patterns, finances. Ernst von Salomon used this questionnaire as an opportunity to present his life, especially at the time of the Third Reich. He remained antidemocratic and nationalistic. His antipathy toward the bourgeoisie has a discretely self-ironic effect. The book appeared in 1951 and became the Federal Republic's first belletristic bestseller. By the end of 1952, nearly a quarter million copies had been printed.

Born in Berlin in 1905, Irmgard Keun became a star upon publication of her first novel, *Gilgi, eine von uns (Gilgi: One of Us)*, in 1931. Her second book, *Das kunstseidene Mädchen (The Artificial Silk Girl)* followed one year later. *Gilgi* was then made into a movie. Her books were banned after 1933. Irmgard Keun emigrated in 1936. She lived in Belgium, Holland, France, Austria, Poland, and the United States. In 1937, *Nach Mitternacht (After Midnight)* appeared in the important exile-publishing house Querido in Amsterdam. The novel was translated into Dutch, Danish, English, Norwegian, Russian, and French in the following two years. In 1940, Keun returned to Germany. She managed to get by in hiding until 1945. Perhaps she was also protected by the rumor—spread in 1940—that she, like Walter Hasenclever, had committed suicide in exile. *Neue Literatur,* edited by the Nazi bard Will Vesper, remarked about this: "For all guilt comes home to roost on earth."

Wolfgang Koeppen, born in Greifswald in 1906, was feature-article editor of the *Berliner Börsen Courier* from 1931 to 1934. He published the novel *Eine unglückliche Liebe (An Unhappy Love)* in 1934 and *Die Mauer schwankt (The Wall Shakes)* one year later. In 1934, Koeppen went into hiding in Holland. He returned to Germany in 1938, being accepted, upon application, to the Reich Chamber of Literature. He worked as a screenwriter without ever leaving any footprints in the history of film. In 1951, he achieved success with the novel *Tauben im Gras (Doves in the Grass),* which was immediately recognized as a literary event. *Das Treibhaus (The Hothouse,* 1953) and *Tod in Rom (Death in Rome,* 1954) followed.

Born in Hamburg in 1914, Arno Schmidt was a clerk in a business, a soldier from 1940 to 1945, and then a prisoner of war. He lived in northern Germany (Cordingen, the Lüneburg Heath) from 1946 to 1950. His first publications, after *Leviathan* (1949), appeared in 1951: *Brand's Haide (Brand's Heath)*, and *Schwarze Spiegel (Black Mirrors)*, and in 1953 *Aus dem Leben eines Fauns (From the Life of a Faun)*. These three novels form a trilogy that Schmidt entitled *Nobodaddy's Kinder (Nobodaddy's Children)* in 1963.

Gregor von Rezzori was born in Czernowitz, Bukovina, in 1914. He was a Rumanian citizen. Rezzori moved to Berlin in 1940 and was the author of three dime novels that were partially published in illustrated magazines, including *Dame*. After 1945, he became an editor at Nordwestdeutscher Runkfunk (Northwestern German Radio). With the appearance of the anecdotal *Maghrebinische Geschichten (Tales from Maghrebinia)* in 1953, Rezzori instantly became very popular within a brief time, but from then on had to continue fighting during his lifetime against the preconceived notion that he was nothing but a jester. His appearances in films, including two by Louis Malle, seemed to confirm this image.

The texts collected here—and this is their common feature—are by authors who lived in the Third Reich. When addressing the issue of the period of National Socialism, these works present and engage the authors' own experiences. Yet they are not only testimonies of the time. Reading these texts, one will ask oneself to what extent their respective authors also thought of themselves as perpetrators.

Next to Gregor von Rezzori, there is hardly a German-language writer who, throughout his or her entire life, conjured up in a comparably intense manner the absence of Jews in everyday life—a loss that, for him, was a loss of homeland. Growing up in Czernowitz, he experienced as a child what he put in his narrator's mouth in 1958 in *Hermelin in Tschernopol (The Hussar)*: [we did] "not make the usual discovery *that Jews are also people,* but rather just the opposite, *that people are also sometimes Jews.*"

In *Denkwürdigkeiten eines Antisemiten (Memoirs of an Anti-Semite)*, first published in 1979—"Löwinger's Rooming House" was taken from this book—Rezzori gathers together individuals whom he allows to speak in dramatic prose. Anti-Semitism may interest the political scientist as an ideological phenomenon and the psychologist as a prejudice, but an author questions it in everyday life. The book is comprised of the life stories of men who are confronted with anti-Semitic prejudices without always being able to draw the correct conclusions from them. For this reason, too, the reader here learns more about the origin and effect of anti-Semitism than elsewhere.

"Löwinger's" is not a spectacular story. The authors gathered together in this volume have avoided tying the history of their time to large-scale political constellations or figures. They have set temporal and spatial limitations. They have stuck mostly with what appears small: with daily experience.

For Arno Schmidt, this is the key to literary representation. It is logical that, already on the first page, he allows his narrator to formulate that life experience which determines his writing style: the technique of repeatedly dividing the text into recommencing breaks, which by now has become the trademark of Schmidt's prose: "My life?!: is not a continuum!"

Literary figures are always primarily artistic figures. How things actually are or were in reality never determines their literary value. This authenticity is always a purely literary one, to measure by aesthetic standards alone. This does not rule out their simultaneously going back to their creator's autobiographical material. The author runs the risk that his or her own experience will overly determine his or her work, that the work will not muster enough resistance against the author. The heroes then become rogues; they acquire no life of their own. The writer, then, does not create the distance to his heroes that makes them into figures within a constellation of figures for the reader. Heroes so constructed invite either identification or resistance. Schmidt repeatedly fell into this temptation. In his early prose works, especially those that deal with National Socialism as well as the postwar period, he is successfully able to convey the hobbyhorse-riding and criticism of the time—especially in the trilogy *Nobodaddy's Children*.

The hero, Düring, is one who thoroughly lives his petit bourgeois values. He enjoys the raptures of normality and is not disinclined to tell a dirty joke. He tends toward know-it-all judgment. And he calls a profound affinity to the values of education his own (a trait that he shares with his creator). With Düring, Arno Schmidt—perhaps against his will—created a figure who precisely portrays the everyday complacency that made (and makes) fascism possible. Düring is a collaborator, a person who steers his way through. He shares this with all his contemporaries, upon whom, though, he looks down—without allowing his arrogance to be noticed. With such people, a state is made.

The world of *Faun* is comprised of quotidian chatter, polemic-fascist rags, speech and action shaped by tradition, sex (and talk about it); there are no clear fronts between good and evil, no one is really guilty, no one innocent. Stupidity rules, and he who describes the stupidity of others—Düring—is, in so doing, the owner of a very special stupidity: that of pride which comes before the fall. Here is everyday life in a small town in 1939, Lower Saxony. Nearby, impossible to overlook, is the Bergen-Belsen concentration camp, as well as a munitions factory.

Schmidt tidies things up—literarily. In his writing style, distanced and unbeholden to realism, he can nonetheless realistically portray terrible events. This distinguishes his text from those of so many of his colleagues, regardless of how well their writing might have been intended.

Wolfgang Koeppen did not report about his experiences in the Third Reich. His novels are set in the Federal Republic of the recent present. Literarily, he worked out his experiences in the Third Reich as follows: time and again, he portrays in his books the aspect of historical continuities, especially that of fascism. This brought upon Koeppen—at the time, during the cold war—the charge of being a communist sympathizer, a nest befouler. Ernst von Salomon described this reaction to *Hothouse* as follows: "Koeppen's book is directed, if it is directed at anything whatsoever, against a mentality, and this mentality has also always reacted, as it almost always does, with almost the same furious vehemence, with almost the same phrases and with almost the same penetrating compulsion to appeal to state power to protect interests."

Koeppen's third postwar novel, *Der Tod in Rom (Death in Rome)*, the first of its two parts is presented here, then places this question of the German tradition at the center. Koeppen sends a West German family to a family gathering in Rome for a few days. Perpetrators, collaborators, and victims of the Third Reich meet here. Koeppen the narrator does not work with omniscience. Using inner monologue—highly organized prose that works through means of free association—he reconstructs the consciousness of the individual in brilliantly crafted portraits.

Koeppen's prognosis is grim. Two sons have learned from history. One is a priest, the other a musician and homosexual. Only the conformist, ambitious brother Dietrich, will produce offspring. "He was powerless against the drive, but it drove him powerfully to the mighty."

Ernst von Salomon, characterized up to this time by a rather traditional writing style, uses the form of the Allies' questionnaire as an opportunity to tell his life story in discontinuous form, chopped into bits. If the course of the story is determined by the questions provided, Salomon also sees to it that the story coheres. One of Salomon's strengths is the punch line. Perhaps anything that could not be brought to a head remained untold.

Salomon's problem: belonging to the right spectrum politically, he must ask himself the question to what extent he (and his buddies) share responsibility in what happened in Germany without his participation. Salomon's ideological trick is to define himself as a Prussian. The Nazis have dissolved the land of Prussia, they have broken with Prussian traditions. Next to historically exculpatory passages, though, stand incredibly terse depictions of everyday life in the Third Reich. Salomon laconically describes the gatherings of German writers, chatter on the street, the gradual seizure of power in the state.

Since his appearance at the Nuremberg War Crimes trial, from which he emerged a star, Albert Speer had a very wily relationship with the Third Reich. He pleaded—quite generally—guilty, but claimed to have known about nothing in detail. This is not the strategy of the narrator Salomon. He depicts moments, experiences, and discussions about the fate of the Jews in Germany. A longer passage is presented here. In it is tested, within the confines of rather sophistic argumentation, the not untypically German notion that "more is happening to us than the Jews." This was formulated after the Nuremberg Laws of 1935 had "excluded the Jews from participating in the political life of the German people," before the Final Solution had been decided in January 1942. Salomon here defines himself as someone who will succeed in somehow keeping himself apart: "Now, since every action is a crime under these circumstances, the only thing that remains is to do nothing." A few pages later, he formulates his—late—discovery of 1944: "My attempts to live an individual life, a life on my own terms, without obligation to a community, had failed."

Literature presents reality in the sphere of the "as-if." As if the fictitious were real: in the text. Literature shares this with advertising and propaganda. To be sure, writers do not lie because they cease being writers if they propagandize for a cause. Ernst von Salomon crossed this border in the final, broadly conceived part of *Questionnaire*. Here, the suffering in the U.S. camp is depicted in detail. It is written at once grippingly and entertainingly. As far as the book—which does indeed speak about the National Socialist extermination camps, but does not and cannot describe them—is concerned, Salomon now awakens, as a summary, the suspiciously sensationalistic impression that the truly terrible camps of this period were those of the occupation forces. Composition and ethics have come into conflict here.

Irmgard Keun and Alexander Lernet-Holenia are the two authors who published their texts during the Third Reich. For Keun the emigrant, the antifascist tendency is clear without her ever being in danger of plunging into propaganda. In *Nach Mitternacht (After Midnight)*, Keun uses the picaresque literary technique that she developed in her first two novels. She chooses a somewhat foolish yet always lovable girl who reports about everyday events in the first person, and who thereby gains genuine knowledge with the help of her lack of understanding. If her first novels were set in the normal insanity of everyday life in the Weimar Republic, Grand Politics now enters the scene. The heroine,

Sanna, is less loosely playful than her predecessors. The topic of fascism has become menacing in its madness, such as in the demand that authors write about *Blut und Boden* (blood and earth): "The purpose of the soil consists in writers' having to sing its praises in order to avoid coming up with stupid ideas and considering what is happening in the cities and to people." Concerning Adolf Hitler's appearance in Frankfurt: "Perhaps the Führer later thought that the people thronged him in love. But, as Führer, he will be too smart to believe it. A thousand times as many people come to the Carnival Parade in Cologne and sit on street lamps and the highest roofs and break their arms and legs and they don't care about anything."

With its somewhat apocryphal title, Alexander Lernet-Holenia's novel *Mars in Aries* alludes to impending war. One can only speculate about the reasons for its having been banned. It is apparent that he opposes one of the most important statements about the outbreak of the war. Hitler had declared before the Reichstag on September 1, 1939: "Since 5:45, fire is being returned! And from now on, bomb will be answered by bomb." In the novel, though, the carefully planned deployment of the Greater German Wehrmacht is described, from the viewpoint of an Austrian. It is shown that the Poles are completely surprised, that resistance remains only sporadic. In addition to all this, Lernet-Holenia corrects the official start of the war to 4:45. At least to the Wehrmacht censor, it did not seem worthy of criticism that German soldiers in this novel pass swift judgment on resistance by the civilian population: "They were led to execution."

With the story of Officer Wallmoden, Lernet-Holenia outlines a game with different levels of reality. The private story of its hero, who loses himself in dreams and visions, appears beside the real events of the German attack. Since nothing is certain, the description of the crab migration given here could also be a vision of the hero.

Lernet-Holenia makes use of a literary trick here. It is common in dictatorships. (In *Marmorklippen* [*On the Marble Cliffs*], Ernst Jünger does nothing different.) Events are turned into a puzzle, allegory is intended to render the author—and his book—unassailable. Such allegories flourish in protection of a taboo, and they usually pass with its passing. Yet the gait of the crabs remains recognizable as the movement of armored troops. On the eve of World War II, the hero of the novel sees this army marching from east to west, be it as beaten German or victorious Russian forces.

Ernst Jünger enjoyed a privileged position in the Third Reich. Adolf Hitler himself played host to him. Jünger did not even join the Reich Chamber of Literature, yet was able to publish—albeit under supervision. For example, *Blätter und Steine (Leaves and Stones)*, a collection of essays from 1934, bore the note in 1942: "For sale only outside the Greater German Reich." In *On the Marble Cliffs*, an allegorical story set in the Middle Ages, Jünger deals with a dictator named Oberförster, behind whom Hitler can be seen.

The novel seems contrived and is rather colorless or concocted. Jünger's particular literary forte is the diary, beginning with *In Storms of Steel*. In addition, Jünger is a brilliant essayist. He is an original cross-thinker. But one who does not directly express his feelings; he expresses them in a form worked out in writing.

In the words of his colleague Gottfried Benn, who also fled to the protection of the Wehrmacht, Jünger lives a "double life." On duty, he is the courageous officer who is working on a resistance pamphlet that he distributes internally; the censor who undertakes the risk of not turning in careless letter writers. Next to this, the private man Jünger, who, as a flaneur, reserves the right not to have to wear a uniform: no Nazi sympathizer, no resistance fighter.

The everyday life of a privileged man in occupied Paris; the officer as flaneur; Ernst Jünger in the traditional role of the writer who must sit enthroned over everyday life; the diary as actual reality; Jünger in the role of one who does not want to explain anything to the reader—an enormous number of people, artworks, novels, and streets populates the book. All this is entirely aside from the "subtle pursuits" to which Jünger the bug enthusiast devotes himself. What person, what insect is hidden behind what name? This is either of no import or, rather, the reader himself or herself must worry about it. Jünger's expeditions through antique stores and intellectual history assume prior knowledge that only Jünger calls his own.

On May 26, 1944, he is confronted with an officer's brutal behavior. The man blusters that he will deal with deserters himself. Jünger notes that he is seized by a "type of nausea." It remains unclear whether he is complaining about human rights or, rather, like a Prussian, wants to know that proper channels are being kept. Or is it the disgust that he has for the type of officers who steadfastly cling to obedience while honor goes down the drain? And now he formulates the program that characterizes his diaries. He aspires to attain the distance of the scientifically trained observer: "However, I must reach a point from which I can watch things such as the nature of fish in a corral reef or of insects in a meadow or also like the physician watches the sick person." This is a literarily legitimate position. It affords Jünger the distance that he needs in order to be able to write. Perhaps it made it easier—or possible—for him to survive. The paragraph concludes: "Whoever is not involved in the conflict should thank God, yet he is not yet for that reason fated to be a judge." In this manner, Jünger maintains aesthetic distance by situating it in everyday life. For himself, this might have worked out.

The lives and writings of the authors gathered together here were and remained shaped by German fascism. Even when they did not always expressly write about this topic. For this reason, it seems best to arrange this volume thematically. The manner in which the authors dealt with their experience of the Third Reich is presented here. This came at the cost of the authors' appearing to have written only about this single topic.

It is nearly impossible to present several novelists within the confines of a single volume. It was possible to include an entire text only in the case of Schmidt. Although only sections of novels could be selected, they are unabridged. In the cases of Wolfgang Koeppen and Irmgard Keun, I have chosen the beginning—as an invitation to further reading. This was not suitable in the cases of Ernst von Salomon and Alexander Lernet-Holenia. Here, I have selected a central passage unabridged in itself. Only in the case of Ernst Jünger were three passages chosen; these are separated by asterisks. The diary form, especially of this type of diary, seemed to allow for this.

I owe Volkmar Sander thanks for advice, assistance and encouragement. With great effort, Daniel Theisen initiated this volume. With even greater effort, Evander Lomke brought it to the light of day. I thank them both, as well as Lance Garmer for his thoughtful translations of the introduction and author biographies. Columbia University Press is the future publisher of Ernst Jünger's diary, *Strahlungen,* which is excerpted here. I thank the Arno-Schmidt-Stiftung in Bargfeld for its friendly support. Kai Bachmann is responsible for the notes (unless marked "Transl.") and biographies.

J.P.

ERNST JÜNGER

From The First Paris Diary and The Second Paris Diary

Paris, 18 July 1942

Architectural dreams in which I saw ancient Gothic buildings. They stood in abandoned gardens; not a soul comprehended their significance in the midst of these solitudes. And yet in a mysterious way they seemed to me even more beautiful; they revealed a character that is also peculiar to plants and animals—transcendent nature. Thought: this they added for God's benefit.

In the afternoon at the photographer Florence Henri's. Beforehand, right at the corner, I rummaged in books. There I acquired among others *Les Amours de Charles de Gonzague* by Giulio Capoceda, printed at Cologne in 1666. Inside an old ex libris: "Per ardua gradior," which I now endorse on the opposite side with my "Tempestatibus maturesco."*

Yesterday a number of Jews were arrested here for deportation—first the parents were separated from their children, so that the lamentation could be heard in the streets. I must not forget for an instant that I am surrounded by unfortunates, by the most sorely afflicted. What sort of human being would I be otherwise, what sort of officer? The uniform obliges us to grant protection wherever possible. Yet one has the impression that to do so, one must—like Don Quixote—join issue with millions.

Paris, 19 July 1942

In the afternoon at Père Lachaise. I roamed about with Charmille among the tombs. Now and then, without looking for

---

*"Per ardua gradior [. . .] Tempestatibus maturesco": Through tribulation I stride [. . .] In tempest I mature. From the Latin.

them, we lit upon famous names in the labyrinths of the necropolis. In this manner we found the stone of General Wimpffen, with a sword enwrapped in a banderole bearing the word "Sedan?" The question mark on a tombstone was new to me. Then Oscar Wilde, to whom a wealthy female reader had erected a monument, in poor taste—one sees the guardian angel that shades it poised beneath the weight of massive wings in perpetuated torment. Beside a mossy path overarched with green that descends like a road of oblivion amidst dilapidated monuments, the tomb of Cherubini, crowned by an urn with a serpent coiled round its foot. Next to it Chopin's, with its oval medallion of marble.

This cemetery is especially beautiful in the parts that have gone to ruin. Here and there, from overturned stones, flash words of consolation, like *Obitus vitae otium est.** Thought of the legions reposing here. No spaces suffice to harbor their ever growing armies; for this a different principle is required. There is room for them in a hazelnut.

A being is touched with the dark scepter and then disappears: there is no greater miracle in the world. It cannot be compared with birth, which is only the budding of life as we know it. Life lies in death like a little green island in a dark sea. To investigate this, and be it only on the shorelines and fringes of surf, is true science, compared to which all physics and technology are mere trifles.

Took byways back to the city. The winged spirit of the Bastille with its torch and the links of broken chain it holds in its hands awakens in me a sense, more compelling with each viewing, of extremely dangerous and far-reaching power. It gives at once the impression of great swiftness and of great calm. One sees the Genius of Progress raised aloft, already inflamed with the triumph of future conflagrations. Just as the plebeian and mercantile spirits united to lay its foundation, thus it combines the violence of the Furies with the astuteness of Mercury. This is no longer a symbol; it is a veritable idol, surrounded by that aura of formidable power which has radiated from such brazen statues since ancient times.

**Obitus vitae otium est:* Death is life's peace. From the Latin.

Paris, 21 July 1942

Finished Lautréamont, *Préface à un livre futur.* To deepen my impression of this author, I am going to read his complete works, which are collected in a single volume. Anticipated in this preface is a form of modern optimism, *also* without God, yet different from the optimism of progress in that it enunciates a consciousness of perfection rather than a utopian view of it. This gives the diction a kind of metallic purity, a technical brilliance and sureness. Here reigns a style devoid of pain, as on some beautiful, swift, and tenantless ship that is propelled not by electricity but by consciousness. Doubt is eliminated like the resistance of air—the True and Good resides in the elements and then becomes visible in the construction.

In our era this state of mind is more pronounced, already early in the painters, for example Chirico, in whose work the cities are depopulated and the human beings are forged from sections of armor. It is the optimism that machine technology produces and which it cannot do without.

It must resonate even in the voice of the announcer who reports that a capital has been laid in ruins.

Paris, 22 July 1942

This afternoon I called on Picasso. He lives in a spacious building whose storeys now serve as lofts and storerooms. This house in the Rue des Grands-Augustins plays a role in the novels of Balzac, and it was there that they brought Ravaillac after he murdered the king. In one of its corners rose a narrow winding staircase with steps of stone and old oakwood. Tacked to a narrow door was a sheet of paper on which the word ICI was written in blue crayon. After I had rung the bell, the door was opened to me by a short man in a simple overall, Picasso himself. I had met him once before briefly, and again I had the impression that I was looking at a magician—an impression enhanced on that occasion by a little pointed green hat.

Apart from a small flat and some storage closets, the domicile consisted of two capacious lofts, the lower of which, it seemed, he used for sculptural work, the upper for painting. The plaster floor was bricked in a honeycomb pattern, the yellow-washed walls buttressed by dark beams of oak. Also beneath the ceilings ran black ribs of oakwood. The premises seemed to me well suited for work; they had the fecundity of old attics in which time stands still.

First we looked at old papers downstairs, then ascended to the upper story. Among the paintings that stood there, two simple female portraits struck my fancy, and then, above all, a stretch of seashore that seemed to blossom before my eyes in ever greater intensities of red and yellow. While regarding it, we talked about painting and writing from memory. Picasso asked me what real landscape was to be looked for behind the *Marble Cliffs*.

Other pictures, such as a series of asymmetrical heads, struck me as monstrous. Nevertheless, such an extraordinary talent—whom we have seen devote himself for years and decades to such subjects—must be granted an objectivity of vision, even if it eludes our own perception. Ultimately it involves something not yet seen and not yet born, experiments of an alchemistic nature—in fact, several times he used the word *retort*. Never was it so compellingly and so eerily plain to me that the homunculus is more than an idle invention. The image of man is magically prefigured, and few suspect the terrible profundity of the decision the painter makes.

Although I tried more than once to steer him onto this subject, he was evasive, perhaps deliberately:

"There are chemists who spend their entire lives exploring the elements hidden in a lump of sugar. Well, I'd like to know what color is."

On the influence of his works:

"My pictures would have the same effect if after finishing them I wrapped them up and sealed them without showing them to anyone. They are essentially manifestations of an immediate nature."

On the war:

"The two of us, as we sit here, would negotiate peace this very afternoon. In the evening mankind could light the candles."

Paris, 23 July 1942

Began the Book of Esther, where Herodotus's old world of pageantry is still in full bloom—in the very first chapter, with the feast that goes on for months at Susa in the Asiatic palace of

Ahasuerus, who reigned over a hundred and twenty-seven kingdoms from India to Ethiopia. Whoever appears unsummoned before him must die, unless the king holds out the golden scepter to him as he does for Esther. From this terrible realm of magic only the Jews have survived to our day—it is the serpent of ancient life turned to bronze. At times I have seen this very clearly—for example, in the demeanor of a Polish Jew I observed at Silesian Station in Berlin. Thought: "Thus you must have stood once beneath Ishtar's Gate at Babylon."

In my mail the letters are multiplying in which surviving relatives tell me of readers who have fallen in battle. It is often as though the dead were suddenly present—voices of readers in tenebris.*

Visit from Kurt, from whose person I borrowed traits for Biedenhorn.† One might call him a kind of Falstaff, in whom indulgence is coupled with a sense of power. He is back from the East, where he commands a tank company. He carries his official seal in his pocket in order to issue at will courier passes, railway tickets, ration cards, and whatever else he chooses. Thus equipped, he stretches out in reserved compartments, together with the pilfered contents of his "courier baggage," over which he then has the conductor stand watch. When in hotels they do not immediately come running, he demands in a thundering voice room, service, wine, so that the proprietors apologize in a tremble. If he wants to gain entry to an off-limits area, as today to the commissary of the Military Academy, he will not attempt it with a finesse, but will first inspect the guard to find something he can reprimand, then he requisitions people to carry the merchandise that he buys up. All this gives him material for amusing anecdotes later over wine.

I had a long chat with him at the Raphael—for one thing, his conversation has a cynical, certainly, but elemental intensity, for another, he is representative of a type. It would seem, too, that he has immediate insight into our state of affairs. He considers it old-fashioned of me, one of my vagaries, that the injustice of this world still offends me. We shall never eradicate it. And here I

---

*in tenebris: from the dark. From the Latin.
†Biedenhorn: the rough but good-natured mercenary leader in *On the Marble Cliffs*—represents the typical "Mauretanian" or "Landsknecht"; cf. footnote on the following page.

discover a delicate trait in him: the solicitude of the strong man for the weaker, which I strike him as being. This solicitude is specific: he would not feel it if I were with him under fire or in an attack on one of the wielders of power, things with which he is familiar as an old OC-man. On the other hand, it would sadden him to see me perish through "kindheartedness." Politically he has notions such as prevail in herds of big game—one must avoid the royals and seek to feather one's nest apart as long as they are powerful.

I asked myself while we talked so pleasantly about the course of events whether he was not still preferable to those officers who rigidly cling to obedience while honor goes to the devil. As opposed to the sham idealism that continues as if things were in order, the *Landsknecht** represents a genuine type—one feels it: he was, is, and will be in all countries and all periods, and he has nothing to do with those living corpses. As danger increases he is more in his element and becomes more indispensable.

Paris, 24 July 1942

The beautiful images that appear before closed eyes between sleeping and waking. Today, a honey-yellow agate shot through with mosses of sepia brown. It slowly floated past, like a flower falling in an abyss.

The red flowers that one occasionally sees in the windows of dark rooms. They are like light accumulators scintillating in the sunshine.

Paris, 25 July 1942

The tiger lily before me on the table. As I contemplate it, the six petals and six stamens drop from it all at once like a magnificent garment that is pitilessly unripped, leaving only the dried up pistil with its fructifications. In an instant I perceive the force that so plucks the flower. Oh, gather fruit betimes, so swift are the Parcae's shears.

---

*English "Lansquenet," originally a German mercenary foot soldier of the 16th and 17th centuries (Holy Roman Empire); now means "trooper," "foot soldier." Jünger uses the term to denote a specific type ("Typus"), a combination of grittiness, nonchalance, and knightly valor.

Afternoon in the Quartier Latin. There I admired an edition of Saint-Simon in twenty-two volumes, a monument of historiographical passion. His work is one of the crystallization points of modern times.

Tea at the Doctoresse's. Afterward, we went to Valentiner's, who had invited us to dinner; there besides him des Closais. Conversations about Picasso and Léon Bloy. Des Closais told an anecdote about Bloy which, though I do not believe it, I quote, because it gives a notion of the abysmal and probably not unmerited hatred that the literati feel for this author:

"According to his custom, he had also asked Paul Bourget for money, without avail, and then publicly affronted him. Some time later, Bourget received another letter from Bloy requesting an immediate loan of five hundred Francs on the grounds that his father had died. Bourget puts the money in his pocket and betakes himself in person to Montmartre, where Bloy lives in one of the dubious hotels. From his room, to which Bourget is shown by the porter, comes the sound of music, and when he knocks Bloy answers the door unclothed; one sees naked women and on a table cold cuts and wine. Bloy, cynical, asks Bourget in, and he accepts the invitation. First he lays the money on the mantle and then looks around him.

"Monsieur Bloy, you *did* write me that your father died?"

"I take it you're a pawnbroker?" Bloy replies, opening the door to an adjoining room in which his father's corpse is lying on the bed.

What makes the story particularly suspicious is the location, which is not exactly one in which a person is apt to die. Even so it is strange that in Bloy's numerous journals there is scarcely ever mention of his father, although they otherwise overflow with detailed descriptions of his family.

Bloy, asked on his deathbed what he felt in the face of death: "Une immense curiosité."

That is very beautiful. Invariably he disarms with powerful sallies.

Then about celebrities. The Countess Noialles, who had invited Marshall Joffre:

"How dull it must have been before the Battle of the Marne!"

The concierge served up the dishes, and each time he presented one he clicked his heels. He had fought in World War I as

Nettoyeur* in an assault party; in hand-to-hand combat, a German bit off his thumb. He forbids his wife to call the Germans "Boches"—"I have the right to say Boche, because I fought against them."

Paris, 26 July 1942

In the afternoon at the cemetery of Montparnasse. After a long search I found the tomb of Baudelaire with its tall stele surmounted by a bat with huge nocturnal wings.

In the midst of dilapidated graves I lingered for a long while before the stone of Napoléon Charles Louis Roussel, who died "an artist" on the twenty-seventh of February 1854 at the age of nineteen and a half years. Above the ledger, which his friends had contributed, lay a chalice that had fallen off its pedestal; the invading moss seemed to gush forth from it like a verdant stream of life.

I am always moved by the mystery surrounding these sepulchres of unknowns in a sea of tombs. They are like traces in the sand which the wind will soon obliterate.

At the Raphael I read *Der Theodor* by Heinrich Hansjakob. It seems that this storyteller's gift that springs from the common people is all but exhausted today. With it the very humus of literature will be lost, the mossy flora at the roots and at the foot of the stocks, and the hierarchy of descriptive endeavor in general. Then it grows drier in the crowns as well.

Last night I dreamt of a beautiful serpent; its mail was a brilliant steel-blue and had labyrinthine wrinkles like a peach stone. The animal was so large that I could scarcely fit my hands around its neck; I had to carry it for a long time, since no cage was to be found.

Thought: I should like to build it a beautiful garden, but how can I manage without charging admission fees?

Paris, 27 July 1942

A surprise arrived in the mail today: the proofs of Friedrich Georg's *The Greek Gods,* published by Klostermann. Although the ideas and images were already familiar from our conversa-

---

*Mopper-up.

tions in Überlingen, in print they made a powerful impression on me. Marvelous the way ancient and modern concur here—age-old phenomena are fathomed in the workings of time. One can sense that the German mind approached them over a long period, step by step, and that they in their turn came to meet it. The mythical world and mythical earth is always present; it is like the abundance that the gods conceal from us—we wander as beggars amidst inexhaustible treasures. But the poets coin them for us.

Paris, 28 July 1942

The unfortunate pharmacist on the corner whose wife was just deported. Such good-natured souls would never think of resisting, or even defending themselves with arguments. Even when they resort to suicide, they do not choose the lot of free spirits, who withdraw into their last stronghold, but they seek out the night as frightened children their mother's arms. It is appalling to what extent even young people have become blind to the suffering of the defenseless; there is no feeling for it. They have grown too feeble for the chivalrous life, indeed they have lost even the plain decency that prohibits ill-treatment of the weak. On the contrary, they glory in it.

Just now, after having written these lines before lunch, I went to see the good *potard** to give him a prescription that the Doctoresse had written for me. While he was preparing it, he made me a present of a little piece of soap, as if he had sensed that I had just been thinking of him with sympathy. I must never forget that I am surrounded by people who are suffering. This is far more important than all military glory or literary fame, than the empty acclaim of a youth that is pleased with whatever strikes its fancy.

Then in the Rue du Faubourg Saint-Honoré, at the antiquarian bookstore with the lame proprietress, where I glanced through the *Voyage on the Nile*, illustrated by Carl Werner in 1870. It does me good to look at pictures especially when I am out of sorts.

*   *   *

*Colloquial French expression: *one who owns or works in a pharmacy.*

Paris, 1 September 1943

More and more frequently I find myself having to enter two symbols in my address book, namely †: dead, and ♀: bombed out.

As to the latter, Dr. Otte writes me from Hamburg that on the thirtieth of July his pharmacy was destroyed along with the entire fish market, with everything he had inherited from the days of his great-grandfather and the rooms in which he kept his Kubin archive. He has set up a provisional pharmacy in a cigar store: "Anything but leave Hamburg! Here I will live or go to my ruin."

In the evening I had dinner with the President, who told me about concentration camps in the Rhineland in the year 1933, with many details from the realm of the flaying pit. I feel, to my regret, that the knowledge of such things has begun to affect my attitude, not towards the fatherland certainly, but towards the Germans.

Paris, 4 September 1943

Yesterday, as we entered the fifth year of the war, intense melancholy; went to bed early. Once again I am dissatisfied with my health, but this is less troubling to me since I formed an idea of it. My growth reminds me of a rootstock that vegetates beneath the earth, often nearly withers, and yet occasionally in the course of the years, nourished by the mind, puts forth green shoots, flowers, and fruits.

Further in Huxley, whose dry nonchalance makes the reading rather difficult. One passage I found noteworthy in which he points out that the influence of the seasons, the seasonal disposition of life, diminishes with increasing civilization. He cites, for example, that in Sicily there are twice as many births in January as in August. It is true; periodicity decreases over time. It is a kind of attrition, a kind of wearing away through rotation. By the same token, the difference between ordinary days and holidays is fading; every day is fair-day in the city. We still find reminders that morals used to change from month to month—on the banks of Lake Constance it is generally understood that husbands and wives show indulgence toward each other as long as the carnival lasts. But the waning of periodicity is only one side of the phenomenon—the other lies in a corresponding acceleration of rhythm. The oscillations grow shorter, but at the same time more frequent. The end result is our world of machines. The machine moves at a furious pace, but it is wanting in periodicity. Its oscillations are numberless, but regular, vibratory, uniform. The machine is a symbol, its economy is an illusion—it is a kind of prayer wheel.

While I slept my spirits improved—I found myself in a garden where I was taking leave of Perpetua* and the child. I had been digging there and uncovered with my spade a small cavern in which a dark snake lay sleeping. As I was about to leave, I mentioned it to Perpetua, afraid that the child could be bitten by the animal while playing, and for that reason went back again to kill it. But now I discovered that the garden harbored numerous snakes—great tangles of them were sunning themselves on the *terrazzo* of a dilapidated pavilion. I saw dark red, blue, and other specimens that were mottled black and yellow, black and red, and black and ivory. As I began to fling them across the terrace with my walking stick, bunches of them stood erect and nestled against me. I realized that they were harmless and therefore scarcely took fright when I saw my little son, who had followed me unnoticed, standing at my side; he took hold of the animals around the middle of the body and carried them, as if it were lighthearted play, out into the garden. The dream cheered me; I awoke with fresh courage.

As we learned this morning, the English have landed on the southwestern tip of Apulia.† During yesterday's raid on the city, the quarters around the center were hit for the first time, including streets I love like the Rue de Rennes and the Rue Saint-Placide. Two bombs also fell in the Rue du Cherche Midi, one right near Morin's bookshop, whom I immediately called, and one across from the Doctoresse's apartment.

Afternoon in the Quartier Latin, first visiting with an unknown reader named Leleu, who in a tubular letter had requested an interview. He turned out to be a traveler in textiles from Lyon and received me in a tiny room of a rundown hotel. After I had sat down on the only chair and he on the bed, we

---

*Perpetua: This refers to Jünger's first wife, Gretha (1906–60), whom he married in 1925. They lived in a former parsonage in Kirchhorst outside Hanover.
†It may be that Jünger means Calabria.

became absorbed in a discussion of the situation during which he vented ardent but vague velleities with a communistic bent. It reminded me of the years when I myself used the shears of abstraction to cut life up into paper flowers. How much precious time is wasted in this manner.

Then at Morin's; on the way there I viewed the damage in the Rue du Cherche Midi. The beautiful soft stone of which the city is built had already been gathered in great white piles in front of the wrecked houses; curtains and bedclothes hung out of the vacant windows, or a lonely flowerpot still rested on their sill. These bolts out of the blue had struck small tradespeople and all the simple folk that live above their shops in the old jumbled flats. I also stepped into the Doctoresse's house and, since she is away on travels, had myself let into her apartment to see that everything was in order. As in nearly all the houses, the window-planes had fallen out of their frames, but otherwise nothing was damaged.

During these errands, another lone plane began circling over the center of the city, surrounded by bursts of flak, without an alarm sounding or the people on the streets being disturbed.

The worst depredation that Kniébolo* has visited on the nation is his depredation of justice—that is to say, he has robbed the German of the possibility of being right, of feeling that he is in the right with respect to the injustices that are being inflicted on him and continue to threaten him. To be sure, the German people as a whole have implicated themselves through acclamation—it was the dire, dismaying undertone that was heard beneath the storms of triumph and orgies of jubilation. As in so many instances, Heraclitus hit the mark when he said that the tongues of demagogues are sharp as butchers' knives.

Paris, 5 September 1943

Again weak health; I have also grown appreciably thinner. There are two reasons for this: first, the sedentary city life, after a certain time, is detrimental to me, and secondly my spiritual being is like a lamp that burns rapidly. I decided to apply the only remedy that promised success: long walks, and I began with the one

---

*Jünger's sobriquet for Hitler; diabolic association is obvious.

that took me from the Étoile via the Cascade to Suresnes, and from there along the bank of the Seine, across the Pont de Neuilly, back to the Étoile.

A spell of Subtle Hunting at the edge of the pond in Suresnes. The plants on the big refuse dump that has collected there—paradise for nightshade. I searched in vain for the thorn apple, but in return I discovered for the first time in open country the poison berry from Peru, Nicandra. It had settled in rank, rambling bushes on the south slope of a hill of rubble and bore, next to the five-pointed stars of its yellow and black speckled chalices, little still-green lampions. I never saw it so robust on garden soil—as it is, many species of nightshade recall those existences that no education furthers because they thrive best in the ruins and on the rubbish heaps of society.

On the Quai Galliéni swarms of anglers; one of them had just caught a rudd the size of a little finger which, with a tender "viens, mon coco"* he gingerly coaxed over the smooth sheet of water onto the bank. Kingfishers, marvelous to behold, whirred over the loamy water with a delicate, languorous trill. Rest in a little church that rises from the faubourg like a country ruin. On the Quai National, on a decrepit barracks, a tablet commemorating the composer Vincenzo Bellini, who died there on September 23, 1835. As I read it, I thought of the creative individual's sacrifice and his role as stranger in this world. Here, too, congregations of anglers who, squatting in boats or on quay stones, conjured tiny silverfish from the water. An angler is a refreshing sight—he is master in the art of comfortably stretching time, of relaxing it, and therefore one of the countertypes of the technician.

Impatiens noli tangere, the snapweed, the balsamine or touch-me-not. Whenever I have walked in the woods with women, I have found them susceptible to the tactile charms of this plant. "O, ça bande." There is turgor in these seed-slings, and extreme vital tension, ready to fire and elastic. I have seen tropical species in conservatories, almost grandeur naturelle. In my ideal garden I would plant them in the beds that encompass the jolly statues of Priapus—them and many another droll weed as well.

---

*French slang for "my pet," "my darling."

I do not contradict myself—that is a temporal prejudice. Rather I advance through different layers of the truth, of which the one currently uppermost subordinates the others. From an objective point of view the truth becomes simpler in these upper layers, just as, from a subjective point of view, in the upper layers of thought, the subordinating power of the idea increases. Viewed atemporally, this truth is like a ramified rootstock that gathers in ever robuster strands, and then, where it breaks forth into the light, merges in a single eye. That will be, I hope, at the moment of death.

Further in Huxley. There is still a great deal of abstract thought, of purely constructive intellection in his style. Occasionally, sporadically, like grains of gold in soap, his genius condenses to images of material power. For example, the observation that struck me today: that human economy gravitates toward the exploitation of defunct life, to the coal beds as remains of primeval forests, to the oil fields, to the guano coasts and the like. Railway lines and shipping lanes converge on these sites, immigrants settle there in swarms. Viewed by a distant astronomer by some time-lapse process, such a spectacle would resemble the stir of a swarm of flies that has scented a giant cadaver.

In such images the author delves deeper, touches strata in which the intellectual superiority of our century lies, as compared with the preceding one. It is the difference in the light that no longer appears as pure oscillation, but also in corpuscular form.

Paris, 6 September 1943

Continued the Appeal.* I notice during this work an exertion that is difficult to describe. A sentence seems clear to me—I could write it down. Nevertheless, its recording is preceded by an inner struggle. It is as if there were needed for this venture a drop of some special essence that can only be obtained with great effort. But oddly enough, the wording mostly conforms to the original conception—while I also have the impression that in passing through this tension it has changed.

Further in Huxley. Then I dreamt at length of a sojourn at a farmhouse as a guest—yet the only detail I could remember in

---

*This refers to Jünger's work *Der Friede (Peace)*, which is substantively in agreement with the officers' right-wing resistance against Hitler.

the morning was that I had entered a room on whose door there was a plate inscribed with the word *astuce*. "Aha," I thought on waking, "it must have been a kind of parlor, since *astuce* means "haughtiness." Just now, as I consult the dictionary, however, I see that this word is translated with "wiliness,"* "cunning."† And that fit the situation.

Paris, 7 September 1943

I repeated the woods-and-water tour in the company of Jouhandeau, who told me that the onrush of images and ideas so completely absorbs him that he is at work almost without interruption. And indeed I had found him at our meeting place, a bench on the Étoile, studiously writing, immersed in his notes. I have the impression that the tremendous calamity afflicting the nations releases spiritual energies that impinge, in ever more powerful waves, in ever mightier vibrations, on our finer perception. Our heads are encircled as spires in a thunderstorm are encircled by swarms of pigeons and jackdaws; legions of spirits seek a place of repose.

I showed Jouhandeau the plants on the rubble tip and learned from him another name for the mullein: "Le Bon Henri."

Paris, 9 September 1943

This morning came the news of Italy's unconditional surrender. While I was contemplating the large map of the Mediterranean, the sirens sounded again and I headed for the Raphael. There I finished my reading of the Apocrypha and with it my reading of the Old Testament, which I began two years ago, on 3 September 1941. I have now read the entire Bible and am thinking of going back and rereading the New Testament with the Vulgate and the Septuagint at hand.

The two books are complementary in a marvelous way. They tell the story of man, first as God's creature and then as God's son. The open, unfinished character of the Book would seem to call for a Third Testament: *after* the Resurrection, emanating from the Transfiguration. In fact, this is adumbrated at the end

---

*Arglist.
†Verschlagenheit.

of the Bible, in Revelation. The supreme endeavor of Western Art might be construed as an attempt to frame this testament; it shines through its eminent works. But one might also say that each of us is the author of the Third Testament; life is the manuscript, and out of it unfolds the text's higher reality in the unseen, in the realm beyond death.

Stepping to the window I caught sight of two bomber wings flying low over the city in wedge formation, while the antiaircraft guns fired.

The beautiful passage at the beginning of the additions to Esther with which Artaxerxes' letter to the one hundred and twenty-seven vassal princes from India to Ethiopia and their ministers opens. And yet these words introduce an order to shed blood. It is a pattern that still prevails today.

In the evening at Jouhandeau's we looked at poems of the 16th and 17th centuries—notably the "Sonnet" by Mellin de Saint-Gelais with its gracefully recurring "Il n'y a pas," whose loops are then knitted together in the final verse. It reminded me of the beautiful "Trost-Aria"* by Johann Christian Günther, in which the word *Endlich* is repeated in the same manner.

> *At last the aloe blooms,*
> *At last the palm tree bears fruit,*
> *At last, at last will come one day.*

Also noteworthy are Saint-Gelais's last words. The doctors were holding a consultation at his bedside, quarreling about his illness and how best to treat it. After he had listened to their dispute, he turned his face to the wall with the words: "Messieurs, je vais vous mettre d'accord"† and expired.

Further in Huxley. His prose is like a net of finespun glass filaments in which occasionally beautiful fish are caught. Only these stick in my mind.

Paris, 10 September 1943

Dreams during the night of which I have retained only fragments. Thus to characterize a bad painter I said: "When he couldn't sell his pictures, he drew unemployment benefits."

---

*Consolatory air.
†Sirs, I am going to reconcile your differences.

Upon awakening I thought of the volumes of my journal that I burned along with some early works and poems. Certainly the ideas in them were imperfect, often naive, but over the years one grows milder in one's self-criticism as well. We must put some distance between ourselves and our works and must also change in order to view them more justly, more objectively. This circumstance reminds one of fathers who are dissatisfied with their sons for no other reason than that they resemble them, but who are then on good terms with their grandsons. Perpetua also deplored my autodafé, which followed upon a house search in the spring of 1933. If I recall, they came looking for letters from the old anarchist Mühsam, who had formed a childlike affection for me and who was later murdered in such a gruesome manner. He was one of the finest, most kindhearted human beings I have ever met.

Contact, attachment must be very important in this world. I can tell by the pain we feel at missing an encounter, which stays with us for a long time, indeed forever. For instance, that little black tentyria on the parched cattle track by Casablanca where a stunted fig tree stood. How annoying not to have caught the little creature. Then particularly in the erotic domain—all the missed opportunities, the failed rendevous. Here we must be neglecting something that reaches beyond the physical sphere, when in our hunter's existence we fail to "get our shot in." It is that we did not make the most of our talent. No doubt this also has its place—limited though it be—in the great cosmic allegory.

Thought: perhaps at the moment of contact a light flashes in unknown realms.

With respect to the perception of historical realities I am one step ahead—that is to say, I perceive them a little sooner, a little before they appear. This is not favorable for my practical existence since it puts me at variance with the powers that be. Nor do I see any metaphysical advantage—for what difference can it make whether my insight bears on today's situation or on one of its later developments? On the contrary, I strive for a spiritual marriage with the moment in its timeless depths, for it alone, and not duration, is the symbol of eternity.

Evening at Florence's. Also there Jouhandeau, who had passed a sleepless night because he heard that his name was on an execution list. As he told of his worries, he had something of a little boy who has just been booked by a policeman.

Paris, 11 September 1943

In the mail a letter from Carl Schmitt, who is one of the rare minds capable of an impartial view of the situation, about Bruno Bauer's *Russia and the Germanic World*.

"Tocqueville had a perfect grasp of the situation as early as 1835. The conclusion of the second volume of *Démocratie en Amérique* remains the most magnificent document of the 'Decline of the West.' " Then about Benito Cereno and the reference made to him by Fabre-Luce at my inspiration. "Du reste: Ecclesiastes 10.1."

In the daily letter from Perpetua, who liked the dream about the snakes: "I also sense that this secluded spot is your true source of strength and that you will return here to accomplish your task."

The adventure of these years lies in the fact that there is no issue in sight. Not a star twinkles in the lonely night. This is our horoscopic, our metaphysical situation; the wars, civil wars, and engines of destruction appear as secondary, as temporal décor. The problem we have to solve is the overcoming of this world of destruction, which cannot be achieved on the historical plane.

At the National Archives in the afternoon, where Schnath showed me a number of documents in which the histories of Germany and France meet. Down through the centuries, particularly in the papal chanceries, a high parchment culture flourished. When favors were granted, the seal hung on a silk ribbon, otherwise on a strip of hemp. The monks whose duty it was to affix the seal had to be illiterate, Fratres barbati, for the better guarding of secrets. Especially fine parchments were won from the skin of unborn lambs.

Walk through the depositories, in which there is food enough for generations of archivists and bookworms. The National Archives are housed in the rooms of the Hôtel Soubise, a mansion of the old Marais that shows the energy and unaffectedness the nobility still possessed at the time of its building.

Then a desultory stroll from the Rue du Temple through the old quarters as far as the Bastille—among the street names were many that amused me, for example the Rue du Roi Doré and the Rue du Petit Musc. I bought grapes and offered some to the children who were sitting in front of the doors. Nearly all refused or regarded me suspiciously; man is not accustomed to receiving things as gifts. Then at the bookstalls on the quays, where I purchased several pictures of tropical birds.

Further in Huxley. There I came across the following observation: "Everything that happens is intrinsically like the man it happens to." That is also my view—it is not fortuitous that on the occasion of a murder we appear as the murderer, as the victim, as witness, as policeman, or as judge. Nor does the environmentalist theory contradict this perception; rather it can be incorporated into it en bloc. Our environment is a characteristic of our species, like the form and color of the mussel and snail shells in the world of mollusks. Just as there are a great many "petit gris," there are many proletarians.

Hence the enormous importance of working on our inner self. We shape not only our destiny, but also our world.

K. has the consistency of a pumpkin into which one jabs a finger: first hard, then soft, then hollow.

P., on the other hand, is like a peach: first comes the pulp, then the hard stone, which in turn encloses the soft kernel.

Paris, 12 September 1943

At midday to see the sculptor Gebhardt in the Rue Jean Ferrandi. Conversation about the troubles in Italy, in which this war has put forth some very new and strange blossoms. The two great elements, war and civil war, are interfusing with explosive intensity. At the same time scenes have occurred that have not been witnessed since the Renaissance.

Then about France. Here too hatred is increasing unremittingly, but more in secret, as in stagnant waters. Many people now receive little coffins in the mail. It is part of Kniébolo's role to discredit good ideas by emblazoning them on his shield. For instance, that of friendship between the two countries, for which there is so much to be said.

Returned by way of Saint-Sulpice; I stepped inside the church for a while. Among other details I was struck by two giant shells that served as stoups. Their wavy rims were adorned with a metal trimming, their mother-of-pearl bed was the color of the honey opal. They rested on pedestals of white marble, of which the one was embellished with marine plants and a large sea-crab, the other with a cuttle-fish. It all was alive with the spirit of water.

Reflection there before a mediocre painting of the Judas kiss: the sword that Peter draws he must have worn all the time—are we to infer that Christ allowed him to gird it on? Or did he wrest it from Malchus before striking him?

Paris, 13 September 1943

News came this morning that Mussolini was liberated by German paratroops. There was no mention of location or circumstances. The war is becoming increasingly dramatic. If things drag on in Italy, it will very likely come to large-scale massacres, as in Spain. Man is caught on the horns of a dilemma.

Telephone conversation with Schnath about Count Dejean and the possibility of examining documents relating to him. I would like to include in my short works a series of essays on the men and books that have helped me in life, as a monument of gratitude.

As Horst just now informs me, General Speidel's beautiful house in Mannheim is in ruins. Immediately afterward, a courier coming from Russia handed me letters from Speidel and Grüninger as well as a detailed report on the battle of Bjelgorod. Grüninger suggests that the paladins' entry through the Brandenburg Gate on white steeds can scarcely be reckoned with; for one thing, nobody knows how long the Brandenburg Gate is going to be standing, and for another, the color white is dying out. That is true, but then the stakes against red are higher on the blue field.

Further in Huxley, where I found the following excellent observation: "One should never formulate one's knowledge of coming evil; for then fate would have a model, as it were, on which to shape events."

This describes the phenomenon that is popularly known as "jinxing" and which today millions indulge in. Our prefigurations, our immersing ourselves in details of a calamitous future, in a word, *fear,* destroys the delicate layer of well-being and assurance that protects us. This is particularly dangerous in a situation where the knowledge of the means of sustaining and preserving this layer is largely lost, above all, the knowledge of prayer.

Paris, 14 September 1943

Telephone conversation with Marcel Jouhandeau. *"Je vous conseille de lire la correspondance de Cicéron—c'est le plus actuel."** Yes, one returns to it again and again. Wieland wrote almost the same thing after Jena and Auerstedt.

Paris, 15 September 1943

Slight fever during the night. Dreamt that I was crossing luxuriant marshes on the lookout for insects. From a tall mouse-ear or water fennel I plucked a few exquisitely metallic species—they were buprestidians, as I discovered to my astonishment.

"A most remarkable find—constitutionally they are completely adapted to the dry heat of the sun, so foreign to the paludal and aquatic world."

Thereupon the voice within:

"But these are transitions, confirmations in a foreign element. These species have shifted with the fennel to a moist habitat, and the fennel, by virtue of its height, partakes of the sun's blaze. Think of Prometheus."

In reality, nothing is more explicable than the exception—in fact, exception and explanation are directly connected. The rule—much the same as light—is inexplicable, invisible, and shines only on what opposes it. Hence one is right in saying that the exception proves the rule—one might even say that it alone makes the rule visible.

Here lies the intellectual fascination of zoology—in the study of the prismatic deflection that invisible life undergoes in the infinite multifariousness of its organization. What delight I felt as a boy whenever my father revealed such a secret to me. All these singularities form the arabesques on the setting of the great mystery, of the invisible philosopher's stone which is the object of our search. One day the setting will cease to glow and the stone will shine forth in all its splendor.

---

*"I recommend you read Cicero's correspondence—it is most topical."

Lunch at the Doctoresse's. Then strolled through different quarters and streets of the city, with a short rest in the church Saint-Séverin, whose exterior and interior moved me deeply. The Gothic is not just architecture there; it has retained its radiance. I was having dinner in my room at the Raphael when at around twenty minutes to eight the sirens sounded the alert. Soon there came the sound of intense fire; I hurried up to the roof. There my eyes were met by a spectacle at once terrifying and magnificent. Two large squadrons were flying in wedge formation, from northwest to southeast, over the heart of the city. They had apparently already dropped their loads, for in the direction from which they came clouds of smoke rose in billowing masses, darkening the firmament. It was a calamitous sight and I knew at once that down there at this moment hundreds, perhaps thousands of people were suffocating, burning, bleeding to death.

Before this dismal curtain the city lay in the golden light of sunset. The glow of evening struck the planes from below; the fusilages stood out like silvery fish against the blue sky. The tail fins in particular seemed to capture and concentrate the rays; they sparkled like Roman candles.

These squadrons flew low in glittering wedges over the outskirts of the city, while clusters of white and black cloudlets accompanied them. I saw the specks of fire around which—first sharp and minute like heads of pins, then gradually dissolving— the globes of smoke gathered. Now and then a plane fell burning from the sky, very slowly and without a plume of smoke, as a golden orb of fire. One plunged darkly toward the ground, twirling like a leaf in autumn, leaving a trail of thick white smoke. Still another was torn apart as it went down. A huge wing hovered for a long time in the air and something sepia-brown and bulky fell with increasing velocity—here a man was plummeting at the end of his smoldering parachute.

In spite of these hits, the formations held their course without swerving to the right or left, and the linearity of their movement gave the impression of awesome power. Add to that the loud drone of the engines, which filled the expanse and sent flocks of pigeons anxiously fluttering around the Arc de Triomphe. The spectacle wore the two dominant features of our existence and of our world: strictly rational, disciplined order and unbridled elemental force. It was at once a scene of sublime beauty and of demonic power. For some moments I lost track of what was happening, and my consciousness dissolved in the landscape around me, in the perception of catastrophe, but also of its underlying significance.

Huge conflagrations, whose centers merged on the horizon, glared more intensely as darkness fell. Then flashes followed by explosions convulsed the night.

Further in Huxley, whose lack of composition is tiresome. Essentially he is an anarchist with conservative memories who has taken up position against nihilism. In this situation he ought to make more use of images and less of ideas. As it is, however, he only seldom realizes his true strength as an author.

He uses an excellent image to describe the impersonal, inextricable quality of sexual relations: a tangle of snakes whose heads are raised in the air, while below their bodies are intertwined in writhing confusion.

Film, radio, the whole mechanical sphere will perhaps help us achieve a better knowledge of ourselves—a knowledge of everything we are *not*.

*   *   *

Paris, 11 October 1943

Plans of mass annihilation can only succeed if there are parallel changes in the moral sphere. The human being must further decline in value, must become metaphysically indifferent, for wholesale destruction as we know it today to graduate to total annihilation. Like our entire situation, this contingency is also anticipated in Scripture, not only in the description of the Flood, but in that of Sodom as well: God expresses it by agreeing to spare the city as long as ten righteous persons are found living within its walls. This is also a symbol of the enormous responsibility of the individual in our time. One person can be the warrantor for untold millions.

Paris, 14 October 1943

I descended to a tomb, to the coffin of my grandfather, the teacher of boys. In the morning I consulted a dream-book and found in it under "tombeau": *longévité*. This is one of the shallow interpretations by which these books distinguish themselves. To descend to the tomb of an ancestor is more likely to mean that in difficult situations one seeks advice that as an individual one cannot give oneself.

In the mail a letter from a young soldier, Klaus Meinert, who has written me before about my little treatise on vowels.* This time he informs me of a discovery he has made concerning the symbolic value of the old Roman capitals:

A, he says, represents spaciousness and elevation. This is demonstrated most simply by the sign ∧: two distant points converge at the zenith.

E is the phone of nonspatiality, of abstract thought, of the mathematical world. This is signified by three monotonous parallels, ≡, joined by a vertical.

I is an erotic sign, a lingam, and evokes associations of blood, love, fervor.

O, as light-sound, is the embodiment of the sun and of the eye.

U, or as the ancients wrote it: *V,* is the earth-sound that plunges into the depths. It is also plain to see that it is the opposite sign to the *A.*

His work pleased me, for it betrays a good eye. I also thought of the conditions under which it was written—during marches, on night watches, in bivouac. The young people cling to the spiritual elements of life as to a constellation that is sighted where all hope is lost. How seldom are they furthered in this their finest instinct.

Horst, who is sitting with me at the table, received word that his aged father was fatally injured in the raid on Münster. There were ghastly circumstances involved. It seems that the bombings are mounting in intensity. The damage wrought in Hanover in the night between the ninth and tenth of October was considerable; hundreds of thousands of people are said to have lost their homes. Still no news from Perpetua!

In the afternoon, conversation with a Captain Aretz, who once visited me in Goslar as a student. We discussed the situation

---

*Cf. Jünger's essay *"Lob der Vokale"* ("In Praise of Vowels") in *Blätter und Steine (Leaves and Stones)* (1934).

for a long while. He suggested that I did not know the frame of mind of the twenty- to thirty-year-olds, who believed only what they read in the newspapers and had never learned anything else. He seemed to regard this as favorable to the consolidation of the existing regime—whereas in fact precisely the opposite is the case: one need only change what appears in the newspapers.

Paris, 16 October 1943

Reflected upon the machine and where we went wrong. As a product of pure masculine intellect, it is like a beast of prey whose dangerousness man did not immediately recognize; he thoughtlessly reared it in his home, only to discover that it cannot be domesticated. Curiously enough, when it was first employed, as locomotive, the results were good. The railroad, either entirely or partially under state control and strictly regulated, has over the past hundred years provided innumerable families with a modest but adequate existence—a railroad man is generally content with his lot. The engineers, officials, and workers enjoy within this framework many advantages of the soldier and few of his disadvantages. We would be better off now, if the domain of the power loom had been treated in the same way, if it had been organized constructively from its inception. To be sure, a special circumstance comes into play in the case of the railroad—namely its spatial character, the fact that it is an extended system. It has the property of attaching to itself a great number of existences, only half of which are bound to technology, while the other half is rooted in organic life, as for example the signalmen and gatekeepers with their simple but healthy way of life. From the very beginning, each of the technical occupations should have been allocated a plot of land, and were it only a garden, since every life is dependent on the earth as all-nurturing mother and in times of crisis finds refuge in her alone.

Technology is like a building that was erected on insufficiently explored ground. In a hundred years it has grown to such huge proportions that any change in the whole, in its master plan, has become exceedingly difficult. This is particularly true of those countries in which it is furthest advanced. Herein lies Russia's advantage, which is now becoming apparent and for which there are two fundamental reasons: it had no technological past and it possessed ample space. Of course, it immediately underwent enormous destruction of resources and human life, but that for reasons extraneous to any plan.

The ravages inflicted on our fatherland may have one positive aspect: they may mark for us a new beginning in circumstances that seemed irrevocably shaped. They create a situation that surpasses Bakunin's wildest dreams.

Finished the first volume of *Causes célèbres,* published at Amsterdam in 1772 by M. Richet, former barrister at the parlement. There I found in the description of the Brinvilliers trial the sentence: *"Les grands crimes, loin de se soupçonner, ne s'imaginent même pas."** That is quite true and derives from the fact that a crime increases in magnitude, the more it rises above the level of instinct and the more intelligent it becomes. In equal measure the evidence disappears. The greatest crimes are based on combinations that from a logical point of view are superior to the law. Moreover, crime increasingly shifts its focus from the deed to existence itself, reaching degrees at which it dwells in pure realization, as the abstract spirit of evil. In the end one even loses interest—evil is done for the sake of evil. It is celebrated as a rite. Then even the question *"Cui bono?"* is no longer relevant—there is only *one* power in the universe that benefits from it.

In the evening Bogo came by the Raphael with Husser. In this age so poor in original minds, Bogo appears to be one of the acquaintances about whom I have thought the most and have been least able to form an opinion. I used to believe that he would go down in the history of our time as one of its intellectually subtle yet little known figures, and today I believe that he will accomplish more. Above all, a great many, perhaps even the majority of the intellectually alert young people of the generation that grew up in Germany after the First World War were exposed to his influence and often passed through his school, and I have almost always observed that the encounter left its mark on them.

He was returning from Brittany after prior sojourns in Poland and Sweden. According to his old whimsical custom, he began to prepare for the discussion by unpacking various objects, an array of carved pipes with tobacco pouch and cleaners, then a

---

*The great crimes, far from being suspected, cannot even be imagined.

skull cap of black velvet with which he beautified his long since bald pate. All the while he regarded me with a sly, searching expression, but with a certain complacency, like one who expects a revelation or two and himself has some pleasant surprises up his sleeve. I had the impression that he chose his pipes as the progress of the conversation required.

I asked after some acquaintances, for example after Gerd von Tevenar, who died recently, and learned that he, Bogo, had buried him. About Aretz, however, who visited me the day before yesterday, he said: "I married the man." With this he confirmed a suspicion that I have entertained for some time, namely that he has founded a church. He is currently at work on the dogmas, having already made great headway with the liturgy. He showed me a collection of hymns and a cycle of feasts, "The Pagan Year," which comprises a system of correspondences between gods, feasts, colors, animals, foods, stones, and plants. In it I read that the consecration of lights should be celebrated on the second of February. It is sacred to Berchta, whose symbol is the spindle, whose animal is the bear, and whose flower is the snowdrop. Her colors are fox-red and "snowy"; the present that is given on her feast is the pentagram. The prescribed food is herring with dumplings, to drink: *Seehund,** and as pastry *Klemmkuchen*. On the other hand, for Shrove-Tuesday, which is celebrated in honor of Freya, I found tongue, champagne, and doughnuts.

We reviewed the situation. Here Bogo was of the opinion that after the Biedenhorns had not been able to blow up Kniébolo,† this was now the task of specific circles. He intimated that he would perhaps be forced to prepare and initiate the matter himself—as a kind of Old Man of the Mountain, who sends his young followers into the palaces. As he conceives it, the fundamental problem in politics today can be formulated as follows: "How does one get inside the top security zone for five minutes with weapons? As I listened to him elaborate the details, I realized the predicament Kniébolo is in, who today is being stalked and attacked from many sides by his own hunters.

---

*"Sea dog," "seal," a Frisian bitter.
†Refers to German officers' preparation to kill Hitler. The attempt failed on July 20, 1944. At the High Command's urging, Jünger was subsequently discharged from the Wehrmacht in October of that year.

On the whole, I thought I observed a change in Bogo that seems to me characteristic of the entire elite: essentially, he is pressing forward into metaphysical spheres with an elan that was acquired rationalistically. This struck me already in Spengler and may be considered an auspicious sign. Speaking summarily, the nineteenth century was a rational century, whereas the twentieth is primarily cultic. This has been the lifeblood of Kniébolo's career, hence the total incapacity of liberal intellectuals even to begin to understand his position.

Then he spoke of his travels. In this connection, certain secrets. I was especially shocked by details he reported from the ghetto in Lodz or, as it is now called, Litzmannstadt. He had gained admittance there on a pretext and conferred with the headman of the Jewish community, a former Austrian lieutenant. One hundred and twenty thousand Jews live crowded together in this cramped enclosure, toiling for the armaments industry. They have built up one of the largest factories in the east. That means, as long as they are indispensable they enjoy a certain reprieve. Meanwhile increasing numbers of deported Jews stream in from the occupied territories. To eliminate every trace of them, crematoriums have been built near the ghettos. The victims are brought there in vans that are alleged to be an invention of the head nihilist Heydrich—the exhaust fumes are funneled into the interior, which within seconds becomes a death chamber.

It seems there exists yet a second manner of slaughter: before incineration, the victims are lined up naked on a huge iron plate that is then charged with high-voltage current. One had recourse to these methods because it turned out that the SS men who had been assigned to shoot the victims in the back of the neck were suffering nervous disorders and finally refused. To run these crematoriums one requires little personnel; evidently a breed of diabolical masters and attendants ply their trade there. So that is where the multitudes of Jews disappear who are deported from Europe for "resettlement." This is the setting in which Kniébolo's nature reveals itself perhaps most clearly and which even Dostoevksy did not foresee.

Those destined for the crematoriums must be named by the headman of the ghetto. After long deliberation with the rabbis he picks out the old people and the sick children. Among the old and the infirm many are said to volunteer—in the end, such atrocities always redound to the glory of the persecuted.

The Litzmannstadt ghetto is closed off—in other, smaller towns there are ghettos that consist merely of a few streets inhabited by Jews. There, evidently, Jewish policemen who were charged with the capturing of victims also seized some Germans and Poles who were passing through the ghetto and turned them over without anyone ever hearing from them again. Above all, this is reported of Volga Germans who were waiting there for allotments of land. Of course they assured their tormentors that they were not Jews, only to hear in response: "That's what they all say here."

It is said that in this ghetto no one begets children except members of the most pious sect, the Chasidim.

The name *Litzmannstadt** shows what sort of honors Kniébolo is capable of bestowing. He took the name of this general renowned for great victories and linked it for all time to a carrion pit. It was clear to me from the very beginning that his marks of favor were what we had to fear most and I said with Friedrich Georg:

> *It brings no glory*
> *To fight in your battles.*
> *Your victories are contemptible*
> *As defeats.*

Paris, 17 October 1943

In the afternoon at the Théatre de Poche, which has just been reopened in the Boulevard de Montparnasse. Schlumberger had invited the Doctoresse and me to see his play *Césaire.* Also given was Strindberg's *Storm,* whose atmosphere, already ghostly by the agency of time, was heightened by the play's being staged in this house. It was performed in fin de siècle costumes that had been unearthed from old wardrobes; also a telephone—at the time, no doubt, an extraordinary novelty on stage—was in the style of the period.

---

*By Hitler's decree, the Polish province of Posen, with Lodz as its capital, was incorporated into the German Reich on October 8, 1939, and renamed after General Karl Litzmann (1850–1936), who had served with distinction there in World War I.

Afterward at tea the Doctoresse said: "One recognizes the work of geniuses by its mathematical character: the problems are divisible and come out even. There is nothing left over.

There is a certain truth in this judgment, although it takes into account only one of the two sides of the creative imagination. On the other side, namely, the results are distinguished precisely by the fact that they do *not* come out even—there is always an indivisible quantity left over. That is the difference between Molière and Shakespeare, between Kant and Hamann, between reason and language, between light and darkness.

To be sure, there is also a small number of minds that are at once divisible and indivisible. Among others, Pascal and Edgar Allan Poe, and Paul in antiquity. Where language as a blind force informs the luminous elements of thoughts, palaces gleam on the faceted crystal of night.

* * *

Paris, 23 May 1944

It was announced this afternoon that General von Seydlitz has been condemned to death.* The sentence was pronounced in absentia. It seems his activity fills Kniébolo with apprehension. Perhaps the Russians have a general on their side who is the equivalent of our Niedermayer. At the same time, an address was read in which the Army's Field Marshals affirmed their loyalty to Kniébolo; it was written in the customary phrases. I believe, it was Gambetta who asked: "Have you ever seen a courageous general? Every petty journalist, every working-class housewife can muster more courage." They are chosen precisely for their ability to hold their tongue and carry out orders; a further recommendation is senility. That might work in monarchies.

In the evening at Madame Didier's, whose sculpture is progressing. Once again I had that sense of Promethean, demiurgic creation, a phenomenon I find uncanny—particularly in the kneading, stroking motions where the material takes form as if by conjuration. The artist comes nearest to the great creative cosmic forces and it is *his* symbols that testify, even in a world of graves and ruins, to a life that was once exuberant.

---

*For having capitulated at Stalingrad against Hitler's order.

Paris, 25 May 1944

Visit from Wepler, who was passing through and with whom I spoke once more about the death of the Poppy Flower. The older and the young friend of one departed. It took her death to bring us closer to each other.

Paris, 26 May 1944

Early in the morning, departure for Sissonne. I had not been back there since 1917. In Laon recent bombings had destroyed the area around the railroad station, but the cathedrals and the upper city were nearly intact. The cities and paths of our destinies that we tread again and again—in what pattern is our journey upon this earth inscribed? In wondrous arabesques and flowers, perhaps?

We were busy on the drill ground because irregularities had occurred in one of the Caucasian battalions. To get there we used a wood-gas car that was mounted with a stove at the rear. Now and then we stopped to add wood, which we did well-concealed on account of low-flying planes. The burned-out cars that lined the road did much to intensify our vigilance. In fact, the submachine guns we now hold between our knees on such excursions attest that things have gotten nastier.

I must change maxims; my moral attitude towards people is gradually becoming too taxing. For example, vis-à-vis the battalion commander, who declared that he would have the first captured deserter taken before his troops and then "dispatch" him with his own hands. At such encounters I am seized with a kind of nausea. Yet I must reach a state where I can view such things as one would view the behavior of fish around a coral reef, or of insects on a meadow, or even as a doctor examines a patient. Above all I must realize that these things are law in the lower spheres. There is still weakness in my aversion, too great a stake in the world of destruction. One must penetrate the logic of violence, guard against euphemism and sentimentality like Millet's and Renan's, and no less against the infamous role of the philistine who from the safe rooftop moralizes about the participants in an atrocious brawl. He who is not involved in the conflict might thank God, yet this does not entitle him to play the judge.

This occupied my mind as I stood beside Reese while he addressed a speech to the foreign troops. They were drawn up around us in an open square, in German uniforms, on whose sleeves the tribal emblems gleamed. Thus a mosque with two minarets and the circular inscription "Biz Alla Bilen. Turkistan." Reese spoke slowly, in short sentences which an interpreter translated.

Our position in the middle of this square appeared strange to me, like the position on a chessboard that intelligent moves have prepared, among them moves of ethnographic finesse.

We ate with the German officers, who gave the impression partly of technicians, partly of mercenary chiefs—the eighteenth and twentieth centuries have merged in pseudomorphs that are difficult to classify. Where theory peels, pure violence emerges. There is no court martial; the commanders have the power of life and death. On the other hand, they must reckon with being murdered some night together with their officers if their men desert.

In Boncourt we then drank a tumbler of vodka with the Russian company commanders, while the Turcomans and Armenians gathered in a great ring. They squatted there for hours chanting monotonous airs; now and then individual dancers or pairs leaped into the circle and expended themselves to the point of exhaustion.

In the meantime I managed to slip away for a half-hour of Subtle Hunting. I encountered for the first time in nature the blue-green Drypta dentata, a creature of exquisite elegance. The Italian Rossi, a physician at Pisa, assigned it its name in 1790.

Paris, 27 May 1944

Air raid warnings,* bombers over the city. From the roof of the Raphael I saw twice in the direction of Saint-Germain enormous burst clouds billow into the sky, while squadrons flew off at high

---

*Jünger's detractors quote the following passage. In 1982, Jünger spoke about this to the news magazine *Der Spiegel:* "So, the English bombers come in 1944. . . . I go to the top floor and watch the air attack. And maybe I'm looking through a champagne glass. It's a fraternal drink with death. It's *anarch*. It's the man who doesn't care at all about the people up there who want to cause fear or about the people on the ground who are afraid, but the man who's standing comfortably at the window and looking: the strawberry crystallizes."

altitude. Their target was the Seine bridges. The nature and se-
quence of the operations directed against supply lines point to a
first-rate mind. During the second wave, at sunset, I held in my
hand a glass of burgundy with strawberries floating in it. The
city with its red towers and domes lay stretched out in breathtak-
ing beauty like a chalice that is overflown for deadly pollination.
Everything was spectacle, pure power, affirmed and exalted
by pain.

Paris, 28 May 1944

Pentecost. After breakfast I finished Revelation and have thus
concluded my first entire reading of the Bible, which I began on
September 3, 1941. Before, I had read parts of it, including the
New Testament. This endeavor I might call meritorious, particularly since it stemmed from my own resolve and prevailed
against many a resistance. My education tended in the opposite
direction; from early childhood my thinking was influenced by
the precise realism and positivism of my father. Every teacher I
had of any calibre abetted this. The religion teachers were mostly
boring; with some I had the feeling that the material embarrassed
them. Holle, the subtlest of them, hinted that the vision of Christ
on the water could be explained as an optical illusion; the region
was known for its ground fog. The more intelligent of my comrades, the books I admired were tuned to the same key. It was
necessary that I pass through this sphere, and I will always carry
traces of it in me. Above all, the need for a logical foundation—
here I mean not so much demonstrability as the testimony and
presence of intellect, whose light should always be in evidence.
The goals can only lie ahead. That distinguishes me from the Romantics and serves as beacon on my journeys through the upper
and nether worlds: in my spaceship, in which I dive, sail, and fly,
in which I sweep through fire-worlds and realms of dreams, I am
always accompanied by navigation instruments that were fash-
ioned by science.

Paris, 29 May 1944

Excursion to the Trois Vallées. It was a hot, radiant day. How
lovely it was in the quiet thicket, beneath the foliage of the

bushes and their shimmering patches of cloudless sky: pure Present. "Linger awhile. . . ."*

The wisterias and the way their woody coils appear to consume the bars of the garden fences. At a glance the eye takes in the substance that has been molded over decades.

The ruby-wasp Chrysis on a grey wall—with its metallic silky green thorax and brilliant raspberry-red abdomen. This little creature seems to concentrate the sun's rays like the focus of a burning-glass. It lives wrapped in fine, quivering ardors.

The tree-frogs, and the way the beating of the scythes incites them to sing in chorus.

"He wanted to ride horseback on a fiddle"—a saying that is used to characterize someone foolhardy.

Evening with the Président. During these Pentecost holidays, five thousand people have been killed here in France in bombing raids. Among other things, a crowded train was hit that was bound for the races at Maisons-Lafitte.

The Président told of a *Gefreiter*† who itches to take part in executions. He generally aims at the heart—but when the man who is to be shot arouses his displeasure, he aims at the head, which then flies into pieces. It is a subhuman trait: the will to rob one's fellowman of his face, the will to disfigurement.

At whom does he aim in this manner, I wonder? Probably at those who come closest to the image of man, at the upright, the kind, the noble.

"Soldiers, aim at the heart, spare the face!" cried Murat as he stepped up to the wall.

Incidentally, two mornings ago a twenty-six-year-old captain was shot here, the son of a Stettin ship owner, for having dropped the remark that headquarters ought to be struck by a bomb. A Frenchman close to Laval reported it.

Paris, 30 May 1944

Lunch at Madame Didier's. Conversation with her nephew, a child of five years, whom I found very engaging. The other day the little boy was taken to mass for the first time and witnessed the administering of the Sacrament. When asked what the priest had done:

---

*Cf. Faust II, 11,582: "Verweile doch. . . ."
†The American equivalent would be a private first class.

"He served out vitamins."
"Il a distribué des vitamines à tout le monde."

Vaux-les-Cernay, 31 May 1944

With the commander in chief in Vaux. Despite the intensely hot weather we lit a fire in the evening to purify the air. Seated around the fireplace, besides the General, were the Professors Krüger, Weniger, and Baumgart.

Generals are usually energetic and obtuse, that is to say: of that active, coordinating intelligence which every better-than-average telephone-operator possesses and to which the masses render stupid admiration. Or they are cultivated, largely at the expense of brutality, which belongs to their métier. Thus there is always a lack somewhere, either of will or of mental vision. The combination of energy and culture such as was seen in Caesar and Sulla, or in modern times in Scharnhorst and Prince Eugene, is extremely rare. That is why generals are mostly drudges who serve as tools.

As for Heinrich von Stülpnagel, who is also called "the blond Stülpnagel" to distinguish him from other generals of this old military family, he bears princely traits such as befit his proconsular rank. These include the appreciation of quiet, of leisure, of influence exerted on a small intellectual circle. All this is very different from the agitation that is otherwise met with in general staffs. His aristocratic nature inclines him to judge men according to their inner worth. His life recalls that of a scholar, and in fact during long periods of illness he acquired a vast erudition. He seeks the company of mathematicians and philosophers, and in history it is ancient Byzantium that fascinates him. It is certainly correct to say that as commander in chief he has led well, as statesman he has negotiated well, and as politician he has never lost sight of our situation. All this makes it easy to understand that he was an opponent of Kniébolo's from the beginning. But he is tired, as I discern from one of his gestures that often repeats itself: he is given to running his left hand along the small of his back as if he were propping it up or righting his posture. At the same time a look of apprehension comes over his face.

Conversation about the Stoics and their maxim: "In certain situations it becomes the worthy man's duty to depart this life."

It seems that the general is in intimate correspondence with his wife about this and other matters of ethics.

Began reading the translation of the New Testament by Hermann Menge, which Pastor Damrath gave me as a present.

Then leafed through Georges Migot's *Essais pour une Esthétique Générale,* a little volume in which I was impressed by some observations about symmetry. This is a subject on which I have often meditated in recent months. This author attributes to the Egyptians an asymmetrical bent and adduces among other examples their partiality for heads in profile. What the mirror image is in the visual arts, repetition is in music. The symmetrical impulse, he says, is a subordinate tendency—hence more aptly applied to form than to content, as in the case of those pendants in painting in which the size of the picture, the frame, and perhaps even the motif could be identical, but not the actual style. For the rest, the observations remain marginal and not especially precise. Symmetry is an enormous subject. When I have some leisure, I would like to venture into it by two lines of approach—namely, by exploring its affinities to freedom of will and the erotic sphere. It was the contemplation of insects and the description of an hermaphroditic butterfly that gave me the idea.

Paris, 31 May 1944

Before starting back, I went for a swim in the lake, then engaged in some "Subtle Hunting." This spring I have fallen entirely under its spell again.

Lunch at Madame Didier's. She put the final touches on the bust and then wrapped it in moist cloths for safekeeping in the cellar since she is going to visit Hendrik de Man in the mountains.

Apropos the style of the polytechnician: *Entscheidung* becomes *Entscheid*—that is, first it is spuriously masculinized, and secondly it is removed from the depth of deliberation to the surface of raw volition.

Paris, 1 June 1944

Luncheon at Florence's. After the meal a brief conversation with Jules Sauerwein,* who had just arrived from Lisbon, about the possibility of peace and its framing.

---

*Jules Sauerwein (1880–1967), French journalist.

In the evening, discussion of Stalingrad with the President and a Captain Uckel. It seems there was filming going on there right down to the final hours, specifically by units from a propaganda company. The films fell into the hands of the Russians and are allegedly shown in Swedish newsreels. One part of the dismal proceedings takes place in the tractorworks, where General Strecker blew himself up along with his staff. One sees the preparations, see how the men who do not belong to the staff leave the building, and then the gigantic explosion. There is something automatic about this impulse to record to the bitter end; a kind of technical reflex manifests itself, similar to the twitches of the froglegs in Galvani's experiment. Scientific motives are also involved. These are not monuments that one leaves to posterity or to the gods, and be it only in the form of a cross that is hastily bound from willow twigs, but rather documents of mortals for mortals and nothing but mortals. Extremely gruesome and actually the Eternal Return in its bleakest form: this incessant dying in the icy expanse, in monotonous repetition—demonically evoked, without sublimation, without a trace of grandeur, without consolation. What glory is there in this?

The captain was of the opinion that the films ought to have been burned beforehand—but to what purpose? They are technicians' communications to technicians.

Then about photography in general. The President recounted a scene he had observed as an eyewitness in "Dreesens Hotel" by Godesberg. Kniébolo, descending the stairs, was greeted in the lobby; among other things, a little girl presented him with a bouquet of flowers. He bent down to receive it and to pat the child on the cheek—at the same time he turned his head a little to the side and called in a dry voice: "photograph!"

Paris, 6 June 1944

Yesterday evening to see Speidel in La Roche-Guyon. The trip was complicated on account of the destruction of the Seine bridges. We started back around midnight, thus missing by an hour the arrival at headquarters of the first bulletins about the landing. News of it reached Paris this morning and caught many by surprise, particularly Rommel, who had been absent yesterday in La Roche Guyon, having left for Germany to celebrate his wife's birthday. This is a flaw in the overture of such an important battle. The first paratroopers were sighted after midnight.

Numerous flotillas and eleven thousand planes took part in the operations.

This is undoubtedly the beginning of the great invasion that will make this day historical. All the same, I was surprised, precisely because there had been so much speculation about it. Why now, and why here? These are questions people will talk about far into the future.

Reading: *The Story of Saint Louis* by Joinville. Husser, whom I visited the other day in his new apartment in the Rue Saint-Placide, gave me extracts of the work to take with me. In certain scenes, such as the landing of the crusaders at Damietta, one sees humanity at its most glorious. Materialistic historiography apprehends in things only what it is able to see. It does not know the manifoldness that alone gives the weaving its color and pattern. This also is part of our task: the rediscovery of the multiplicity of motives. It demands a firmer objectivity than the positivistic.

Paris, 7 June 1944

Evening stroll with the Président. On the Boulevard Amiral Bruix, two heavy tanks had halted en route to the front. The young crews were sitting atop the steel colossi, in that mood on the eve of battle, that cheerfulness tinged with melancholy that I remember so well. About them, almost palpable, was the aura of death, the glory of hearts that have assented to the flames.

How the machines receded, how their intricacy disappeared, and at the same time they became more elemental, more significant, like the shield and lance on which the hoplite leaned. And how the boys sat on the tanks, eating and drinking, heedful of one another like bride and bridegroom before their wedding feast, as at a spiritual repast.

Paris, 8 June 1944

At lunch Florence absented herself for a telephone conversation and said when she came back: "La Bourse reprend. On ne joue pas la paix."*

It seems that money has the finest antennae after all, and that the bankers' judgement of the situation is more scrupulous, more exact, and more prudent than that of the generals.

---

*The Exchange is recovering. One doesn't wager on peace.

In the afternoon I received a visit from Dr. Kraus, the ballistics expert. Conversation about my physicist brother and his work on continued fractions and prime numbers, then about Cellaris, who is still in prison, but for whom, as for many thousands of his fellow sufferers, the hour of freedom will soon arrive.

Then about the so-called new weapon and its trial launchings. Kraus reported that recently a projectile, after an unexpected loop, landed on the Danish island of Bornholm, what is more, as a dud, which by evening the English had already photographed. They were able to study the electromagnetic guidance system and promptly erected in the south of England a generating station of enormous power to drive the projectiles off course. The talk about this weapon affords a good illustration of how destruction is the polar force of Eros. The two forces would seem to share a certain common ground, like positive and negative electricity. Thus the whispering at home is very similar to the whispering that surrounds the salacious joke: No one is supposed to talk about it, yet at the same time Kniébolo hopes that rumors, carefully nurtured by him, circulate from one ear to the next. The whole thing is utterly nihilistic, redolent of the flaying shed.

Paris, 11 June 1944

Once more from Saint-Cloud along the Route de l'Impératrice to Versailles. And again my sunbath in the little glade among the chestnut bushes. On each of these walks I think to myself: this could be the last.

Paris, 12 June 1944

Visited Husser, in whose apartment I want to stow some files and perhaps even put up for a few days. This is my left stronghold in the Quartier Latin. The Doctoresse occupies the center, while the bookdealer Morin holds the right position. Friends won are worth more than gold.

I am reducing my baggage to a minimum. Kniébolo and his gang are prophesying speedy victory, very much like the Anabaptist paladin. On what figures' heels the rabble treads, and how universal the *ochlos** has become.

Translated by Hilary Barr

Ochlos: Greek for "mob."

ALEXANDER LERNET-HOLENIA

From Mars in Aries

The surrounding clouds had risen above the horizon. The sun was gone. It was half past five. Wallmoden had a tent built for himself next to the street. The tent was placed on the rounded back of a strip of field. Straw was laid in the tent. Wallmoden rummaged through his things and prepared, for the night, a candle, then he tried to sleep. But just then, the straw began to stir at a particular spot. A field mouse seemed to have made its way into the tent, probably from below, through one of the tunnels which mice build in the ground. Wallmoden kicked with his heel at the spot where it was rustling, it was quiet for a while, then the mouse stirred again. The tent walls began to rock to and fro. A wind had come up. The air hissed around the tent. It seemed "afraid," like at Azincourt.* Wallmoden looked out, or rather, he stretched his head out of the tent, lying on his back, the wind drove the clouds over the entire sky, but then rent them asunder. Dust was blowing, it became evening. The clouds were gray, the Tatras seemed bathed in purple tints.

The restless wind continued to shake the tent walls. The tent was small, its color greenish-gray, it looked like the inside of a rocky crevice. In the tent, it was still warm, outside it had, due to the wind, become considerably cooler, clouds blew in and blew out.

A motorcycle sidecar brought food. Afterward, it remained quiet for a while. Then Wallmoden heard another motorcycle

---

*Cf. William Shakespeare, *Henry V,* Prologue: "the very casques / That did affright the air at Agincourt. . . ."

coming, and a voice asked for him. It was Kaufmann's messenger. He approached the tent and brought the news that the order to assemble had come.

The sentry group had to halt until the squadrons were nearby. Wallmoden had the tent struck, set out for the valley in which the vehicles had converged, and ordered that the unit prepare its things.

The people began to pack, and meanwhile it became dark. A half moon stood between fleeting clouds in the sky and sent down violet-colored, almost morbid light. The land all about shimmered like blackish silver. The Tatras, in the distance, were still just discernible, a shadow at the edge of the world.

Wallmoden sat a while on his automobile, then he turned back to the street. He remained standing a few moments on the street; afterward, he made off in the direction of the forest. To the advance group, he had to walk about ten minutes. The street dipped at first, then it rose again. The wind had stopped blowing.

The group lay to the right of the street in a ditch. The people spoke with one another or slept, two sentries held watch. From here to the forest, it was still about five-hundred paces. Wallmoden walked on slowly. The street lay dusty in the moonlight, the edge of the forest already rose up like a wall. In front of it lay a bridge that led over the stream. But just before the bridge, a dark strip that Wallmoden otherwise would not have noticed stretched straight across the street.

That is to say, the strip, or the band, stretched across it rather somewhat diagonally. It could not at all be immediately seen what it actually was. It seemed to move, and although it was blackish, it glittered a bit here and there.

Wallmoden stopped, now all was again completely quiet, only in the sky did the wind chase the clouds. But, in this stillness, Wallmoden heard a noise that was so quiet that he needed several moments to make himself believe that he really heard it.

Or rather, it was not so very quiet as it was indistinct, it seemed to be composed of a vast number of tiny noises. It was a continuous, barely noticeable grinding, abrading, and scraping. It was coming from the band that lay over the street.

Wallmoden walked several steps toward it, stopped again, then again went several steps and discovered that the band was, in fact, moving. But not until he had come right up to it did he see what it was.

The band had a width of two or three feet and was moving not only over the street, coming out of the right ditch and leading into the left one, but it was also moving within itself. It continuously rose and sank a little, rustled and scraped. Indeed, it even seemed as though it were clanking now and then with a light, metallic tone. As if a bundle or rather a strip of chains lying next to one another were being drawn over the street, it crawled across. Yet the chains did not consist of links, but rather of animals crawling along. It was crabs that they consisted of. The crabs were migrating.

It would have been natural to have laughed at the sight or to have called over the unit and to have had as many crabs gathered as possible, or to have done both at once. But Wallmoden did neither. Rather, he was afraid. He was afraid mostly because something immediately occurred to him (and perhaps had already begun to occur to him even before he had recognized with certainty what it was that was crawling along before him)—he was afraid because it instantly entered his mind how he, bent over the bridge railing with Rosthorn, had spoken of how crabs can also migrate. And it seemed to him—silly as he found it—that he himself had caused this migration. He was completely foolish to believe that the crabs that had been in the stream could have been, so to speak, given the idea that they could migrate by the discussion whose witnesses they had become. Yet he was not able to dispel the feeling that there could be some connection. Perhaps it was the other way around: he had had the discussion only because the crabs had already been determined to migrate. He was afraid that it had already gone so far with him that he had felt this. And he was generally afraid that they were migrating.

He could not have said why. Most of all, he had actually not believed that they could really migrate. Now he saw it before him. But he did not understand why they were going over land. They moved westward, thus in the direction of the Black Arva. He would have understood it if crabs, in order to go from one river basin to an entirely different one, had made land marches—over a watershed, for instance. But the ones here did not at all—at least so it seemed—want to go to the basin of another river. They would have had a considerably easier time simply swimming down their stream until they had arrived at the spot where the stream flowed into the Jelesna Woda. For it did, in fact, flow into the Jelesna Woda, or rather it actually seeped into a marsh on the border over which Wallmoden and Rosthorn had walked in the afternoon. The crabs would have easily gotten over the marsh, to the river, and could then have continued on their way without difficulty, in the water, up to the Black Arva.

Yet if it was quite unclear why they were not swimming in the water, but rather marching over land—for what reason were they marching at all? Why, if they certainly were not soldiers, did they subject themselves to the unpleasantness of this night march that seemed quite difficult for them? For they made progress only very slowly. Wallmoden remembered having owned a certain toy as a child, a bear, that one could wind up and that then moved forward step by step and snapped to the left and right with its mouth. Before each step, a preliminary and strenuous humming of the clockwork sounded from the bear until it finally, very hesitantly, took the step, and the short, dry snapping of the mouth, turning to and fro, sounded intermittently. In a quite similar way, the crabs were moving onward.

It is commonly held that crabs always do only the so-called crab walk, that they thus move only backward. But a crab very rarely moves backward. Usually, it walks, if only very slowly, forward. On the other hand, it can swim backward very briskly by beating forward with its tail. The crabs, raising their heavy claws in front of them, were crawling across the street not significantly more quickly than snails. They were moving the machinery of their many legs with great ponderousness, and, with each step, they lifted their bodies, then lowered them again, like icebreakers at work, and remained lying on the ground for a moment until the next step was made. The scratching of their legs made a soft, but thousandfold noise, and their bodies now and again also hit and scraped one another. Indeed, individual crabs had pinched their claws on the tails of their foreamblers and had let themselves, at least to a certain extent, be dragged. Wallmoden could not see how long the entire column was. There were thousands of crabs, how could one have known that there were so many in the stream! They came from the darkness of the field at the right and crawled into the field at the left, into the darkness. They were migrating from east to west.

Among them were small ones and large ones, tiny ones and huge ones, indeed, gigantic ones of a sort that one otherwise never laid eyes on nor ever caught, apparently they stayed in the streams, in places to which one never came, or indeed in some subterranean inlets. The march—scraping and grinding, rattling and clanking like a squadron ready for battle—moved onward, a sum of innumerably many movements, and seemed unstoppable, it was as if it were a single animal that was crawling across the street, the feelers touched, the eyes stared, and the shells shone in the moonlight. As Wallmoden bent over the crabs and looked at them, words that he knew went through his mind, but even if it was he himself who had them in his ear, it yet seemed as if Rosthorn were reciting them to him:

Et apertus est puteum abyssi, et exierunt in terram. *
And he opened the pit of the abyss and they went out onto the
   land.
   *Et data est eis potestas, sicut habent potestatem scorpiones
   terrae.*
And unto them power was given, as the scorpions of the earth
   have power.
   Et similitudines eorum, similes equis paratis in proelium:
And their shapes were like unto horses prepared unto battle:
   et super capita eorum tamquam coronae similes auro:
and on their heads were (as it were) crowns like gold:
   et facies eorum tamquam facies hominum:
and their faces were as the faces of men:
   et dentes eorum, sicut dentes leonum erant:
and their teeth were as the teeth of lions:
   et habebant loricas sicut loricas ferreas,
and they had breastplates as it were breastplates of iron,
   *et vox alarum eorum sicut vox curruum equorum multorum
   currentium in bellum:*
and the sound of their wings was as the sound of chariots of
   many horses running to battle:
   et habebant caudas similes scorpionum,
and they had tails like unto scorpions,

---

*The quote is almost verbatim from Revelation, Chapter 9, Verse 2 ff. The Latin is untranslated in the original.

et aculei erant in caudis eorum.
and there were stings in their tails.
Et ita vidi equos in visione:
And thus I saw horses in the vision:
et qui sedebant super eos,
and them who sat on them,
habebant loricas igneas, et hyacinthinas, et sulphureas,
had breastplates of fire, and of jacinth, and brimstone,
et capita equorum erant tamquam capita leonum:
and the heads of the horses were as the heads of lions:
et de ore eorum procedit ignis, et fumus, et sulphur.
and out of their mouths issued fire and smoke and brimstone.
Et ab his tribus plagis occisa est tertia pars hominum de igne,
et de fumo, et sulphure,
And by these three the third part of men was killed by fire and
by the smoke and brimstone,
quae procedebant de ore ipsorum.
which issued out of their mouth.
Potestas enim equorum in ore eorum est, et in caudis eorum.
For their power is in their mouths and in their tails.
Nam caudae eorum similes serpentibus, habentes capita:
For their tails were like unto serpents, having heads:
et in his nocent.
and with these they do hurt.

Translated by Lance W. Garmer and Josephine R. Garmer

ERNST VON SALOMON

From The Questionnaire*

This happened while the Olympic Games were taking place in Berlin. That was a good time, wasn't it? The city was decorated with unusual gaiety, the ladies wore pretty summer dresses, very agreeable young girls in simple white tunics handed the laurel or oak-leaf crowns to the victors, and each time a German won a gold medal the proud new German flag was hoisted by sailors in white dress uniforms. The streets were filled with foreigners. The cases that contained the anti-Semitic paper, *Der Stürmer,* had disappeared from the walls, as had the notices on the park benches which forbad Jews to sit down. We all had occasion to feel more or less satisfied. The revolution was over,† wasn't it? The Olympiad was a gateway between us and the outer world which had now been opened; we could not as yet step through it, but the world could and did come to us, which was after all a beginning. Germany, it was plain, presented herself as the land of order, tradition, and justice. The law was once again in force, even the Nuremberg Laws, those fatuous, infamous, wretched laws; but they were laws, after all, weren't they? And as such they placed a limit on the atrocities of despotism. And so great was the importance which Hitler attached to justice that he needed two Ministers of Justice: one was the National Minister of Justice, Dr. Gürtner, an old and experienced official; the other, in the full vigor of his prime, was Minister Frank, the President of the Academy of German Law, whose task it was at long last

---

*The questionnaire asks more than fifty questions about "membership in organizations." Salomon summarizes questions 41 through 98. This text begins in the middle of his response. The Olympic Games took place in Berlin in 1936.
†Refers to the national revolution that, in the opinion of many German nationalists and Salomon alike, remained incomplete due to Hitler's seizure of power.

to codify the German legal system. And Frank set to work with a swing.

This valiant Munich lawyer had every reason to wish to get this job, than which none more suitable could have been found for him. Now he was confronted with the task of conjuring a basic concept of law from out of the National Socialist Weltanschauung. He had long enough thundered against Roman Law; his qualification for his new job was that he had always held Roman Law to be a distortion of the substance of German justice. Now he was to show what he could do. It was a job to make the doughtiest man think twice, particularly if he stopped to examine this National Socialist Weltanschauung—it was not the sort of task that I should have been eager to tackle and, in the American phrase, I was prepared to eat my hat if it were successfully done. To view the law, not as a series of eternal statutes, but as the variable norm of so variable a phenomenon as race—for does not every poultry breeder know that race is always the culmination and never the starting point of a development? And can its limits be fixed either chronologically or spatially?—but still, to work! Let it be said in Frank's honor that he was, according to the doctor, sweating with anxiety and worry. Hitler, it seems, regarded Frank's exertions with contempt; for him justice was just an institution designed to spin cobwebs across his path. Himmler, too, despised Frank's efforts. His task was to guarantee peace and order, to safeguard the vitality of the National Socialist revolution. He despised Frank, but this did not prevent him from casting an occasional sidelong, though well-meaning, glance in his direction from behind his uncompromising spectacles: he recognized Frank's obvious inability to draw the actual consequences from the situation as given. Himmler did draw them, and there emerged from this something which Dr. Luetgebrune* called the "sumptuary laws."

Himmler was indeed a very different type of man from Roehm, at whose side he had once stood outside the wire entanglements surrounding the Munich War Ministry on a November day in 1923.† Himmler could be relied on not to indulge in explosive excesses, whether of a personal or of a political nature.

---

*Right-wing star attorney in the Weimar Republic as well as Salomon's attorney.
†Refers to Hitler's failed putsch of November 8 and 9, which was put down at the Feldherrnhalle in Munich. In 1933, the NSDAP declared these as holidays.

According to the judgment of all who knew him he was an honest family man without worldly ambition, an exact worker, strict with himself and with others and strictest of all with his colleagues. He was not the man to mount a white horse and charge some hypothetical enemy. He sat in his unusually tidy office. He only reluctantly appeared in public. He never made speeches to the masses. At the most he would occasionally address the most intimate circle of his fellow workers on some curious subject such as the "people's sovereignty." He was beyond dispute very far from being an unthinking soldier, and in this he was the exact opposite of Roehm. He was a moralist, though his morality had no connection with his solid Catholic upbringing at Landshut in Lower Bavaria. But one important card was missing from his hand—a legal basis from which to orientate himself. The law had not been scrapped, it had simply been temporarily suspended by the Authorization Act. Dr. Gürtner's penal code was still in force, though it only treated the individual in his quality as a private person, and according to the National Socialist *Weltanschauung* the individual had been transmuted into a political creature, had been completely politicized. Meanwhile Frank was simply unable to lay the egg of his new "German" justice. This was all of no immediate concern to Himmler, whose task was the safeguarding of the National Socialist state. But what does a good employee at the Chancellery do in such a situation? He looks for a precedent—and Himmler found one in those "sumptuary laws."

It was thus, with all the contempt of an old jurist, that Dr. Luetgebrune described the Military Penal Code. This code did not lay claim to any moral, any philosophical or any metaphysical basis for its laws. It simply asserted a state of crisis, the condition of war or of the preparation for war, and it declared unambiguously: "Such-and-such is allowed and ordered while such-and-such is forbidden, and to do it involves such-and-such punishment, and that's that." Furthermore, military law breaks every other law.

Himmler found in this "precedent" the answer to his own position as well as to that of the country. The country was engaged in liquidating the revolution, which is another way of saying that it was still in mid-revolution. It would remain in this condition until a "German justice" had come into existence. Until that day Himmler would apply his sumptuary laws—and his logic, in the circumstances, is hardly open to question.

When man emancipated himself from God, might he not have guessed that one day, by an inevitable process, things would emancipate themselves from him? To whom should the blame be apportioned for all that had happened? How could it come about that everyone was guilty, which means of course that no one was guilty? That beneath the slogan of the triumph of will all will was rotted away?

There I sat, in the back room with the curtains drawn, while outside the glass smashed and tinkled, telling a trembling young woman of things that had been.

The telephone rang shrilly. It was Axel. He told me the synagogues were burning. From his balcony he could see the glow of the fires. I thought that Axel would now produce his political platitude, his insurance. Instead he said:

"Please make a careful note of this. Early tomorrow morning it will be announced on the radio that the German people, infuriated by the criminal action of the Jew Grünspan who shot the Councillor attached to the German Embassy in Paris, rose spontaneously and set fire to the synagogues. I assert here and now in the most solemn terms that I have never risen spontaneously, that I have never committed arson. Since the Reichstag fire arson* has been a capital offense, to be punished by hanging."

I said:

"Yes, yes. Good. I'm sitting here quite quietly with Ille,† too, discussing this and that. I'll call you in the morning."

But Axel did not ring off. He said, pronouncing his words with icy clarity:

"It is extremely interesting. For years these people have announced officially that it was not their intention to attack the Jewish religion, that they were simply fighting against the danger of contamination by the Jewish race. They have even published laws to this effect. Are the synagogues places of worship or are they institutions for racial interbreeding?"

---

*On February 27, 1933, the parliament in Berlin burned down. On the basis of an emergency decree, the NSDAP was subsequently able to neutralize political opponents and sentence a communist to death in a show trial.

†The actual Ille Gotthelf (b. 1912) is behind this figure. According to the Nuremberg Race Laws (1935), she was considered a "full Jew." She lived together with Salomon during the time of the Nazi regime; he passed her off as his wife.

I said:

"Yes, I know all about that. But at least the burning syna-gogues* cast a clear light on our situation." And I rang off.

I told Ille what Axel had said. I went on:

"Why are Axel and I not standing in front of the synagogues with outstretched arms protesting and accusing at the top of our voices? Because we know that what we might say would have no echo? That's not the reason. It is something far worse. We are in reality already dead. We can no longer live from within our-selves. Everything that is happening about us is not the product of the internal life of those who are doing it; it is the product of a collective. And a man who will not accept and believe in that collective is dead. The collective always acts unconditionally. It also demands our unconditional faith and acceptance. But this collective has not gathered us up into itself, it has atomized us. Atomized fragments cannot constitute a community, but only an explosive mass. Ernst Jünger said once that the saint on a pillar, the stylite, presented socialism in its most accomplished form. That is certainly true: the deliberate act of the individual for the sake of a solitary solution must also, always and inevitably, be an act of solidarity. I have never recoiled from true solidarity, or from a collective society. But this collective is now destroying it-self, it is a false collective. It offers the individual no chance to perform his deed of solidarity."

I said:

"This collective is a *reductio ad absurdum* and that is the greatest crime that it can commit. I know, of course, what is hap-pening to the Jews. Were I not myself a witness I should still know, for it has been announced often enough what would hap-pen. The burning synagogues simply show that it is happening now. The appalling thing is that nobody can help 'the Jews,' be-cause any attempt to do so simply increases their peril. The ap-palling thing is that we cannot help ourselves, and far more is happening to us than to the Jews. And far more is happening to the collective than is even happening to us."

---

*In this paragraph, Salomon jumps ahead approximately two years to the night of November 9–10, 1938, the Reich-pogrom night against the German Jews. The personally motivated assassination by Hershel Grünspan or Grynszpan (b. 1921) of a German diplomatic official in Paris gave the NSDAP a reason to instigate the pogrom. The legend of the "spontaneous uprising of the German people" was subsequently circulated.

I said:

"Last winter I had occasion to come home by streetcar 176. I was standing on the front platform. Besides the driver three were also two SS people there. Then an elderly lady got on. Suddenly the two men began to talk filth. It began with one saying: 'Terrible stink of garlic here!' and you can imagine how it went on from there. The old lady tried to open the door leading to the interior of the car. It was only then that I realized the men's filth was directed at her. Now I am not accustomed to let old ladies be insulted in my presence, as you know. Maybe it's an old-fashioned atavism, but there you are. What should I do. Set upon the two oafs? That would have been just stupid. Do nothing, as though it were no concern of mine? That would have been cowardice. I was interested by the alternatives, and I tried hard to think of a third solution. Of course! The simplest! I helped the old lady in her attempt to open the door. It would not move. I called the conductor and he walked the length of the swaying car. I shouted through the little hole in the door that he should open it. He shouted back that in winter that door had to be kept closed. I bellowed through the hole that he must open it at once, an old lady was here in need of help. The conductor cried that she would have to get down at the next stop and reenter the car by way of the back platform. While I was still arguing with the conductor I suddenly saw the old lady's face, only a few inches from my own. She was looking at me with undisguised hatred, a hatred that came from her sensation of complete helplessness, the worst sort of hatred there is. And I understood: of course! This woman wanted, more than anything else in the world, to avoid attracting attention. To be conspicuous might mean anything, martyrdom, death. And I, it was I who was creating this danger. It was I, not the two SS oafs, who just stood there grinning spitefully though in silence. The car stopped, and the old lady hurriedly got off. It was not my stop but I followed her. I wanted to help the old lady, I wanted to try to explain why I had behaved as I had done, I don't really know what I wanted, I was acting 'spontaneously.' The old lady did not get back on to the other platform. She disappeared into the darkness. I walked home along the Kurfürstendamm and I thought as intensively as I could—there must, there must be a third solution. And if there is in fact none, which was preferable: to behave like a fool or to act like a coward?

"At the corner of the Clausewitz Strasse there stood a lamp-post. Near the lamppost I saw, hanging on a tree, a piece of cardboard as big as a poster. I walked up to it and read: 'The seamstress Frieda Junge, who lives at Weiz Strasse 14, commits racial infamy with the Jew Victor Aaron.'

"There it was, written on the poster. Not far from the lamp-post stood an ordinary policeman. Now then, here was a chance. I decided to be a fool and not a coward. I ripped down the poster. Immediately the policeman came up to me. He asked:

" 'Are you authorized to remove the poster?'

"I said:

" 'No. But it's a piece of filth.'

"The policeman said:

" 'Quite agree. That's why I'm here, to nab the fellow who keeps hanging them up on this tree. There are special columns for posters at the street corners.' He went on: 'If you've nothing to do with it, go on home. And give me the poster, I'll stick it up again so as I can catch the fellow. If this goes on anybody will think he can just come here and stick posters to this tree.' "

I said to Ille:

"But if this is the truth: if the provocation of the Reichstag fires served to destroy communism but also, and simultaneously, destroyed the actual legitimacy of the party's road to power: if the events of June 30 ended the revolution but simultaneously created the police state instead of the people's society: if tonight the true central point of the party, its racial doctrine, has been reduced to an absurdity and the Jewish problem has really been transformed into a German problem: if at the same time we are all atomized, isolated, incompetent, sterile, without any direct connection with the now discredited collective—and that is perhaps the most monstrous aspect of the whole process; the hope of our age, the real objective of civilization, the constructive element for the future, the collective discredited by its own most fanatical exponent—if this is the truth, then what remains?

"Now since in these circumstances all action is crime, all that remains is to do nothing. It is at any rate the only decent course. And it is also the most difficult thing in the world, a sort of Gandhi-ism without Gandhi. The individual solution has here a solitary constructive force. It is really the most difficult course of all, and it looks so easy, doesn't it? All honor to him who can follow it—as to myself I am not so sure whether I can or not. In any case I'm going to take a bath now, and shave, and put on clean clothes, and have breakfast—and then I'm going to see Meissner."

Ille drew herself up:

"Surely," she cried, "you're not now. . . ."

I said:

"I am. I have an appointment. And apart from that I'm curious, I want to know what's happening. For my health's sake. I want to know what's going on, so that I can talk about it. That's my psychotherapy; without it I can't rid myself of my complexes."

Ille said a great deal more, but she laid out a clean shirt for me. She filled my wallet with documents proving my identity, all that I possessed. She complained, as I could well understand, that Grünspan had simply walked into the Paris Embassy and shot the Councillor, and everybody had wondered how the man had succeeded so easily in entering the building; I was to be sure to show everyone I met in the New Chancellery my membership card of the Chamber of German Writing;* if anybody asked me my name I was to mumble indistinctly, because if a sentry heard it he was certain to shoot me dead on the spot.

In the streets the sun was shining and it was a clear, cold day. To my surprise I suddenly felt in an excellent humor. There seemed to be something to the methods of the psychoanalysts after all. The first person I saw was my friend Kurt Heuser. He had gone to Africa as a young man, where he had been a farmer. In the solitude of the bush he began to write, short novels with an African setting. Back in Germany he had given up writing literature and had turned to film scripts. Now here he was, striding as fast as ever toward me, wrapped in his fantastically aged overcoat—tradition had it that he had worn it in the bush, and it always had one button missing.

"What do you know!" he cried, and went on at once. "Funniest thing just happened to me. Imagine, I had no idea what was up. I wanted to come into town"—he lived out by Lake Stölpchen—"and I noticed there seemed to be great crowds in the Ku-Damm, you know, the sort of people you don't normally see

*Department of the Reich Chamber of Culture under Goebbels. Every author had to join it or was excluded from it—which amounted to official professional debarment.

there. Difference struck me right away. Then I saw the glass—and then all of a sudden the crowds moving! There's a man running toward me and other men running after him. The man—he's bleeding from the head, great drops of blood falling from his black hair—he's staggering but he keeps on running, straight toward me. There's hundreds of people about, but it's me he's running to. And I feel damn proud that I'm the only one he trusts. He runs up to me and he damn near kisses me, crying: 'Save me! I'm a Persian!' "

Kurt Heuser said:

"I stopped a passing cab. To begin with the driver said he wouldn't take us. The gentleman was bleeding and who'd pay to have his taxi cleaned afterward. I shouted at him: 'Go to the Persian Embassy.' At last he drove off, and just in time too. As for my Persian, do you know who he swore at? Me! He could only blubber, but he kept whining away at me as though it were all my fault. 'I, non-Aryan!' he suddenly shouted: 'What do they imagine? I'm a Persian! If I'm not Aryan who is? Where did the Aryans come from if not from Persia?' "

I laughed and Kurt Heuser said:

"Now tell me, what do you make of it?"

I said:

"I don't know, I'm no expert on the subject, but I think he's right, your Persian. The Indo-Germanic tribes at least are supposed to have originated in Persia."

Kurtchen said:

"That's not what I meant. Can you understand all this business? They've just got over one world crisis, they've just won everything they could possibly want at Munich by saying that they would abstain from all acts of violence—and now this! They're just slapping the world in the face once again. Can you understand it?"

I said that I could not. He cried, in desperation:

"It's so incredibly stupid!"

"Yes," I said, "it is. But stupidity is the norm."

He stared at me and then, with an expression of dread on his face, he said:

"You know, I think that he is an evil man."

It was quite clear to whom he was referring. I had never before heard Kurtchen Heuser speak anything except good of any human being. If he now described a man as evil, then something unheard of must have taken place within him.

I hailed a cab.

"Where are you going?" asked Kurt.

I got into it and said to the driver:

"The New Chancellery!"

I looked back, for I did not intend to miss Kurtchen's completely bewildered expression.

An SA man of the Feldherrnhalle unit was standing outside the New Chancellery, his legs well apart. On his chest he wore an oval shield, suspended by a chain about his neck, which gave him a thoroughly martial appearance. As I approached the steps he stamped to attention and flung out his right arm in a salute. I raised my hat, thinking with satisfaction that he must have taken me for some important foreign diplomat. I said politely:

"I wish to see the Minister of State, Dr. Meissner."

"This way, sir," he said, and directed me toward the main entrance. Hardly was I through it before an SA man sprang out of an alcove, stamped to attention, and flung out his right arm. I said, with somewhat more assurance:

"Herr Minister Dr. Meissner!"

"This way, sir," he said, and directed me toward a flight of stairs covered with a red carpet. I climbed the stairs. On the first landing an SA man sprang to attention, banged his heels together, and flung out his arm, straight in my face. I said, gruffly:

"Minister Meissner!"

"This way, sir," he said, and directed me toward large double doors that were standing open. Through them I could see a long, well-lit corridor, carpeted in gray. I entered it and a gray little man in a simple, gray livery came up to me. In a soft and sympathetically attuned voice, he asked:

"May I take the gentleman's coat?"

I handed him my overcoat, in the pocket of which were all my identity papers, and my hat. He hung them on a peg in a small recess behind one wing of the double door. Then he said, bowing politely and in a mild tone:

"Whom shall I announce?"

This was the moment to start destiny boldly in the face. I announced my name loudly and clearly. Destiny's expression did not alter.

"One moment, please!"

He disappeared through the first door that opened off the corridor. He returned at once, saying:

"The Herr Minister asks the gentleman to be so good as to come in."

It was just as easy as that. I entered a big room, filled with the light of day. The Minister had already risen to his feet and was walking toward me, his hand outstretched. He wore a simple gray suit without any emblem in his buttonhole. He said:

"I am very pleased to meet you in person."

So he had read my books. He went on at once:

"Is this your first visit to the New Chancellery?"

I said:

"I never set foot in the old one either, Herr Minister."

He laughed and I glanced about the room. Opposite the big, dark, flat-topped desk—on which lay no papers; so that I received the impression I was intended to receive, namely that for the time being the Minister was prepared to devote his entire and undivided attention to me—there hung a large portrait of Hitler. He stared intently at the desk, as though to watch carefully what Meissner was up to there. On another wall there was a large portrait of Hindenburg. The old gentleman's expression was rather tight. There was also one of Bismarck. But the fourth wall, the wall by the door, was blank. I glanced that way and said:

"You're a picture short."

The Minister gave a hearty laugh. There was an expression of satisfaction on his ruddy, healthy face beneath the already whitening hair as he said:

"Yes, one short. This is my office; the portrait of President Ebert, for whom I have a very great respect, hangs in my home. There it occupies the place of honor."

He had an agreeable voice and spoke with a South German intonation.

He offered me a chair and sat down himself behind his desk. I said:

"Herr Minister, I am engaged in assembling material for a history of the German postwar."

He smiled courteously and said:

"I know. A fine and very necessary undertaking."

Now how did he know this?

I determined to go straight to the heart of the matter and said:

"Herr Minister, during the course of my researches I have come across a rumor—forgive me mentioning this, Herr Minister—a rumor that you were appointed head of the Presidential Chancellery because you once brought the late President Ebert a sack, a sack containing a million marks."

The Minister laughed heartily. Then he leaned back in his chair and laughed again. At last he said:

"Yes, yes. You know, Dame Rumor always spreads stories which contain a proportion of truth. The proportion is usually small but it is invariably there. I'm only too pleased to tell you the real story."

During the Great War, he said, he was a lieutenant with the field railways, working on the staff of the Chief of Army Railway Services, General Groener. When, toward the end of the war, Groener succeeded Ludendorff as Chief of General Staff, he appointed as his successor in charge of the Eastern Front railways, with headquarters at Kiev, young Lieutenant Meissner. The task confronting Meissner was stupendous. There were still half a million German troops in the East, dispersed throughout the vast area from Reval to Rostov-on-Don: the task was to get them home at the very time when revolution had broken out in Germany. Kiev was in a state of chaos. The military governor had already packed up and gone; Poles and Bolsheviks were fighting for control of the Ukraine, while the Cossack chieftain, Petljura, was struggling to secure the independence of his country. Everywhere guerrilla bands and partisan groups fought one another, while among them were scattered, often at great distances from one another, small German units whose one desire was to get home. All that remained intact and was still in working order was the German military rail network—and indeed, Meissner said not without pride, the repatriation of the German armies in the East was successfully completed almost without incident.

Meissner said:

"I reserved an armored train to take out myself and my staff and the last of our security troops. The train had already got up steam, ready to leave, and all the jobs connected with my appointment had been completed. All that is, save one. I had to go and say good-bye to Petljura. I went alone. I was the last German in the town."

Meissner said he had worked well with Petljura. Petljura knew that he had to thank the presence of German troops in the town for a great deal, and he was very sorry to see us go. Indeed Petljura's position was highly dangerous. In three great columns Polish, Bolshevik, and Allied forces were moving on the Ukraine. Petljura had only a few reliable troops at his disposal. They might have been enough to cope with any one of the approaching columns, but certainly not with two, let alone all three. So the farewell, though hearty, was tinged with sadness. Meissner finally said that they had nothing more to discuss—apart from the question of the compensation to be paid for German property left behind in the Ukraine. Petljura did not immediately understand. "What do you mean?" he asked. Meissner said, good-naturedly, well, there were the railway installations, the tracks and sleepers and telegraph poles and bridges and stations . . . all German property. "But," cried Petljura, "you can't take that stuff with you!" "No," said Meissner, "we can't take it with us. But we can destroy it."

Petljura was horrified. "If you do that I'm lost!" In fact without the one communications system still intact in a vast territory menaced by guerilla bands he would have been lost. "Then pay for it," said Meissner. "But I haven't got any money!" "Then write out a bill of sale!" said Meissner.

And Petljura did so. He signed bills of sale for tracks and sleepers and bridges and telegraph poles and stations and smashed trucks. Meissner had all the papers already drawn up, and Petljura signed the lot.

Meissner tucked the bills of sale into his sleeping bag and made his way to the station. But the armored train had already left.

So Meissner procured himself a sleigh, packed his sleeping bag full of bills of sale on board it, sat down on top of the bag, and in a journey of several weeks' duration drove straight through a country in the full ferment of revolution and civil war, over the snow-covered Carpathians, through a Czechoslovakia seething with its newly acquired independence, and so arrived in Germany. Once there he began to search for some authority to which he could hand over his accounts. But there was none. No such authority existed any more. The Demobilization Commissioner was not competent to accept them, nor were the Soldiers' Councils. So Meissner went on to Berlin. He tried to reach the provisional head of the Republic, the President of the Executive Council, Ebert, the most important of the "people's representatives." But Ebert was unapproachable. Ebert hurried from one conference to another. When Meissner had tried for the eighth time to obtain an interview, Ebert's assistant, the Social Democrat Wels, threatened to have him thrown out. "We're desperate," said Wels: "We don't know whether we're coming or going. The President is attending an important conference. With an Allied commission that wants to take possession of our property in the Ukraine. It's a matter of millions that we haven't got and need. And now you force your way in and ask for an interview with the president." "It's because of the Ukrainian property that I'm here," said Meissner, pointing to his sleeping bag. Wels sent him in at once to see Ebert. And Ebert presented the Allied commission, which regarded itself as the legal successor to the Ukrainian State and which wished to take possession of all German property there located in exchange for Ukrainian corn, with Petljura's bills of sale. These totaled slightly more than the actual value of the property. The commission left without entering into an argument about the small discrepancy involved. And Ebert asked Meissner what position so admirable an official would like to fill. Then Meissner told the president of his vain attempts to find an authority capable of handling so confusing, and yet politically so important, a contingency as that which had brought him to Berlin. He proposed to Ebert that such an office be created, and added that he felt it should function in the closest proximity to the supreme head of the country.

"And so," said Meissner, "by order of the late and highly respected President of the Reich I was installed in the Presidential Chancellery." He laughed heartily. "The sum in question was considerably in excess of a million, but it was all in the form of bills of sale."

I thanked the Minister as best as I could for the information he had given me, and he got to his feet. But before wishing me good-bye he asked me if I should care to be shown over the New Chancellery. I did not move as I said:

"Thank you. Today I'm more interested in smashed windows."

Meissner stopped smiling but did not become in any way less friendly. He said calmly:

"There's been more smashed than you know."

I cried:

"But one day it'll all have to be paid for! And who's to pay . . .?"

Meissner looked at me calmly. The pupils of his eyes had shrunk to pin points. He said:

"Well, in the first place there is the insurance."

This was a thought which had not occurred to me. I said:

"But can you? Will you?"

Meissner said:

"Then there is the reinsurance. And the underwriters are abroad."

I said bitterly:

"But is there nobody . . . to put a stop to this lunacy . . ."

He said:

"There are people who are trying, at least. It's hard to do anything about a fatality. It just has to be paid for."

I cried:

"This is no fatality, it's a crime!"

Meissner said:

"Crimes are always fatalities. You, I think—must—grant—me—that." He said: "But one can try to bring about a decent solution to the results of a fatality. One can try to ensure a decent solution, and that is the only thing one can do. And one must do that and meanwhile hope that others are doing likewise."

When I reached home Ille was not, as I was accustomed, waiting for me at the door with a big glass of brandy in her hand. She was standing in a smoke-filled kitchen, with pieces of sooty ash floating about her head. She was streaked with grime and was blowing on a pile of red ash that glowed in the dustpan. She stared at me from red-rimmed, inflamed eyes.

"What's up?" I cried.

She looked at me and sobbed:

"I've burned the papers!"

I was taken aback.

"What papers?"

Ille said, between her tears:

"The ones in the trunk. The blank signatures."

I laughed and helped to wash the rest of the ashes down the sink. While she was cleaning her face and hands, she said:

"Now tell me all about it. Start: 'Well, when I got there they'd all arrived already . . .' "

I told her about Kurtchen Heuser and his Persian. I told her about Meissner.

When I had finished I got my brandy and Ille said:

"What terrible times these are we live in." She said, "I was born in 1912. I wish I'd died in 1912, at the age of seventy." She sighed and went on: "And the fashions of the eighties would have suited me so well!"

I laughed and contradicted her:

"Look, there's one thing you can't deny. The times we live in are interesting if nothing else. I think this is probably the most interesting period in the history of the world. Never has a generation undergone so many and so diverse experiences as ours."

Ille said:

"You're quite right. But, you know—don't be angry with me—but I'd rather just read about it."

99. Have you ever sworn an oath of secrecy to any organization?

I don't know.

100. If so, list the organizations and give particulars

I have never sworn an oath of secrecy to any organization, except possibly on the occasion of my being commissioned in the Army. This is only assumption on my part, but I imagine that there must be a clause relevant to the subject somewhere buried in the articles of war.

Private individuals have of course frequently requested that I treat information divulged by themselves as confidential. On such occasions I have always requested with insistence that they refrain from recounting to me any information that is an embryonic anecdote. I have never felt that my discretion could really be relied on if I were offered the opportunity of telling a good story with a point to it.

101. Have you any relatives who have held office, rank, or post of authority in any of the organizations listed from 41 to 95 above?

I refuse to answer this question.

102. If so, give their names and addresses, their relationship to you and a description of the position and organization

It is only with difficulty that I can deny myself the pleasure of answering these two questions. I could, by so doing, reveal some extremely curious facts. But I shall not. I regard these two questions as perfidious.

I am aware that this omission constitutes an offence against the regulations of Military Government which renders me liable to prosecution and punishment. I can only hope that Military Government will, for its part, deny itself the pleasure of prosecuting and punishing the one person in all the world who has really taken its Fragebogen seriously.

> *103. With the exception of minor contributions to the Winterhilfe and regular membership dues, list and give details of any contributions of money or property which you have made directly or indirectly to the NSDAP or any of the other organizations listed above, including any contributions made by any natural or juridical person or legal entity through your solicitation or influence*

I have always entrusted the administration of my financial affairs to members of my household belonging to the female sex. During the period 1936 to 1945 Ille had the pleasure of dealing with my income and outgoings. On May 6, 1945, she informed me, with apparent satisfaction, that since 1942 she had consigned all communications from the NSV or any other branch of the NSDAP, requesting contributions for Winter Relief or similar causes, to the wastepaper basket, unanswered. Apart from normal taxes, she had since that date refused to contribute in any way to the state or to the party organizations. In the most solemn terms I told Ille of my disapproval concerning her behavior in these matters. Ille's financial activities, like my own, were never based on practical considerations. But whereas I valued money primarily as a means for enabling its possessor to avoid situations of a dramatic nature, Ille chose to regard it as the starting point, the trigger mechanism, of just such situations. Thus it was her custom on the days when money was being collected for the Winter Relief—and avarice was not the cause—to buy a single small 20-pfennig badge which she would then stick into a little fur cap, especially purchased for these occasions. She did this with a purpose. When a uniformed man stopped her on the street and rattled his collecting box at her she could, with a most significant gesture, quietly tap her forehead. As soon as I heard of this I naturally put an immediate stop to such goings-on. On another occasion, it was Police Day, Ille appeared bedecked from head to foot with the emblems that were sold by the collectors. Her whole coat was covered in them. She jingled and clattered with every step she took. And she did this solely for the pleasure of seeing weighty and formidable police officials kneel down before her in the public street in order to affix yet one more emblem—the little, porcelain figure of a policeman—to the hem of her coat. I put a stop to this, too.

All the same, Ille once had the satisfaction of seeing me, who always made such an effort to behave so correctly, in the same sort of situation from the consequences of which I was forever, and so vainly, attempting to save her. I have a marked dislike of being disturbed while at table. So on those days when collections were being made I customarily urged Ille to prepare our meals in our home. If, however, I yet found myself compelled on such a day to eat in public, it was my habit to buy a complete set of emblems from the first collector who approached me and to construct a pile of them before my plate. I relied on this producing a sensation of shame in subsequent collectors who, I hoped, would in consequence allow me to eat on undisturbed. On one occasion we were sitting with numerous friends in the restaurant belonging to Max Schlichter, the late brother of my friend Rudolp Schlichter, the painter. This was a day on which emblems were being sold in aid of the Winter Relief, and each emblem was a little glass head of a "great German." Hitler's head sold at a higher price than did those of, say, Bismarck or Frederick the Great or Luther or Kant. I had piled up the whole series in a heap of blue glass before me. Nevertheless a much-decorated SS man approached the table. I pointed at the emblems before me, remarking:

"I've enough already."

The SS man was not to be dismissed as easily as this. He said that he had a number of other glass emblems depicting the Führer. I said angrily:

"I've enough of the Führer, too."

It was only when I saw the SS man start that I realised what I had said. Nor was that the worst part. Henny Porten, the well-known German movie actress, who was seated with us, leaned across the table in her naïve and impulsive fashion, took my hand, and said loudly:

"Oh, how right you are!"

But it was far from right. The SS man stopped collecting and immediately left the restaurant. From then on the atmosphere at our table was positively hectic. Only Ille had blanched somewhat, while I wondered whether the restaurant possessed an alternative exit. It did not. Since a number of total strangers took the opportunity to express their admiration of my courage, I had no alternative but to order a second helping of dessert in a somewhat cracked voice; and I never have cared for crêpes, either. But the SS man did not return, neither alone nor with companions armed to the teeth.

Of course I had no way of supervising how the money collected for Winter Relief was in fact spent. On the other hand I had no way of knowing how the money collected as taxes was spent either, but I paid mine just the same.

104. Have you ever been the recipient of any titles, ranks, medals, testimonials, or other honors from any of the above organizations?

No.

105. If so state the nature of the honor, the date conferred, and the reason and occasion for its bestowal

Not applicable.

106. Were you a member of a political party before 1933?

No.

107. If so, which one?

Not applicable.

108. For what political party did you vote in the election of November 1932?

In November 1932, the period of "loss of civic rights" to which I had been condemned in 1922 had not yet expired. I was therefore not entitled to vote. Apart from that, I was abroad in November 1932.

109. In March 1933?

Nor did I vote in March 1933. As my answers to questions 1 to 131 of this *Fragebogen* have, or will have, shown, I have a strong bias, both moral and intellectual, against voting at all. I have never voted. In view of the fact that on the one hand the secrecy of the ballot box is supposed to be inviolable, while on the other an official *Fragebogen* such as this can ask questions like 108 and 109, I regard it as unlikely in the extreme that I ever shall vote.

110. Have you ever been a member of any anti-Nazi underground party or groups since 1933?

Yes.

111. Which one?

Master Group Imming.

112. Since when?

Since 1933.

113. Have you ever been a member of any trade union or professional or business organization which was dissolved or forbidden since 1933?

Even memory has its limitations. I have always limited my recollections to such facts as interest me. I cannot answer Question 113. I have forgotten.

114. Have you ever been dismissed from the civil service, the teaching profession or ecclesiastical positions, or any other employment for active or passive resistance to the Nazis or their ideology?

No.

115. Have you ever been imprisoned, or have restrictions of movement, residence or freedom to practice your trade or profession been imposed on you for racial or religious reasons, or because of active or passive resistance to the Nazis?

Yes.

116. If you answered yes to any of the questions from 110 to 115, give particulars and the names and addresses of two persons who can confirm the truth of your statements

It is after a close scrutiny of my conscience, rather than of my memory, that I have reached the conclusion that since 1933 I did in fact belong to an illegal opposition group. I have called it a master group because from its fertile soil many another opposition group was to spring. I do not even think that I am exaggerating when I state that the existence of this master group alone was responsible for the construction of the whole massive machinery of totalitarian terrorism. Since this master group could not obviously, in view of its extremely dangerous nature, flaunt an official name, I shall, for reasons of simplicity, just refer to it as "Master Group Imming."

In Paris stands the statue of Madelon. The French, who fought with such remarkable bravery in World War I, erected this statue as a gesture of gratitude to the womanhood of France. At armistice celebrations Madelon's song is to be heard more often than the Marseillaise, a powerful paean of homage to the good genius of France, to the mother of victory. A graceful and yet strongly built girl is Madelon, with her pert little nose beneath a steel helmet worn at a rakish angle—every Frenchman knows her statue. Hardly a Frenchman, however, knows that other statue, to the father of victory, Clemenceau, *le Tigre,* battling his way forward into the teeth of the storm while the wind snatches at the folds of his voluminous bronze cloak. The enviably mature people of France know well the menaces and dangers inherent in victory. It is not Napoleon whom they revere but Jeanne d'Arc, not Clemenceau but Madelon.

We Germans are not without our own fondness for memorials of victory. But apart from the uncommonly solid and allegorical figure of Germania who, with sword and buckler, may perhaps awaken all the emotions save only affection, we have never thought to see the good and brave genius of our race in the form of the German woman. Yet it is German womanhood that may justly claim to be honored as the true embodiment of our country's heroism during World War II.

It thus seems right that the great and otherwise nameless master group of the opposition should be called after a woman, an unknown woman, good, brave and honorable, loyal and true, and who always seemed to me the very personification of the resistance. Her name was Frau Imming.

Frau Imming was my charwoman. When, one day in the spring of 1939, I entered my kitchen and said: "Frau Imming, have you heard the news? German troops have entered Prague!" she replied in her Berlin accent, amid the rattle of the pots and pans: "I don't want Prague. I want butter."

"You see," Frau Imming said to me on one occasion, "I'm a Social Democrat. My old man was always a Social Democrat too. Same for me. In my house we're all Social Democrats and always have been. And we're going to stay that way."

Her house was in a block of workers' flats in the Heidelberger Strasse, which lies in the extreme eastern suburb of Berlin, Treptow. She was the porter of this building, a great red stone barracks of a place, with many entrances and a passageway leading to the back courtyard, where there was a factory. Three times a week Frau Imming came to us in western Berlin. It was a long way. Ille reckoned that the journey to our place and back must take her a good three hours, although Frau Imming never asked us to pay her fares. When Ille drove me to or from my post-war archives at Friedrichshagen she always tried to arrange the trip so that she could give Frau Imming a lift home. Frau Imming enjoyed these rides immensely. If the top of the car was down she would sit, not next to the driver, but in the center of the back seat. There she would fold her arms over her uncommonly well-developed bosom and glance proudly from side to side. Ille had to drive up to the very center of the apartment block and there play a regular tattoo on the horn. Frau Imming would never leave the car before all the inhabitants of the building were looking out of their windows.

"You see," she said, "you've got to do it. Else my people here won't believe what a fine lady and gentleman I work for."

"But, Frau Imming," said Ille, "have you told the people in your house that we're very far from being Social Democrats?"

" 'Course," said Frau Imming. "They know all about that. But they don't mind about your husband. He was a cadet, and it's his education. He just don't know any better. But our own people what go over to the other side, them we don't fancy. And when the day comes we'll show them, every one of them."

On one occasion, when I had had to leave Berlin for a couple of days, the doorbell rang, and since both Frau Imming's strong, red arms were plunged in soapy water, Ille went to answer it herself. On the threshold stood a man with beetling brows who announced:

"Secret state police!"

Ille was terrified. With trembling knees she led him into her room. The official asked:

"Does a certain Frau Imming work for you?"

When Ille said that that was so, he asked her what sort of a woman Frau Imming was. Ille hurriedly described her character at great length and in the most glowing manner: loyal, industrious, conscientious. The official listened to all this, an expression of skepticism on his face, and finally said:

"Are you aware that this Frau Imming is a dangerous agent?"

Ille was not aware of this, and she hastened to speak of Frau Imming's mental qualities in the most derogatory terms: simple, stupid, says the first thing that comes into her head, totally incapable of understanding politics. The official said:

"Are you aware that in a hardware store Frau Imming said: 'I could hit myself over the head with that mallet there for having brought three sons into the Third Reich!' "

Ille, more or less in despair, said she could not imagine such a thing, but that she would herself ask Frau Imming at once. She called Frau Imming in. Frau Imming came, drying her hands on her blue apron. Ille said, with careful emphasis:

"Frau Imming, this gentleman is from the secret state police."

Frau Imming glanced at him and said:

"Well?"

Since the direct method did not seem particularly fruitful, Ille tried the indirect approach. She spoke of evil persons, gossips who repeat everything they hear, changing it slightly so as to give a sinister interpretation to completely innocent remarks. She presented Frau Imming with every possibility of explaining away the allegation. She practically put the words into her mouth. Then she said:

"Of course it's quite impossible that you could have spoken in so ridiculous a way. But this gentleman has been informed that you said, in the hardware store, that you could hit yourself over the head . . ."

"Could too," said Frau Imming promptly. " 'Course I could. It's my head, isn't it? What I do with it is my own business."

The man gazed at her without a flicker of expression. Ille hastily turned toward him and once again attempted to overwhelm him with a flood of words:

"You see what a simple, foolish person she is? Of course she didn't mean what you think she meant. It was just a silly expression of hers." She promised the official that she would speak seriously to Frau Imming. "You see, I can explain things to her. She listens to me." And she offered to guarantee that in the future Frau Imming would abstain from such idiotic chatter. The official then left. Before going he said:

"For the time being I shall not order her arrest, but I'm warning you!" And he repeated, with unpleasant emphasis: "I'm warning you!"

Then Ille gave Frau Imming a thorough talking to, while Frau Imming stood solidly before her, twisting her apron between her fingers. After a half hour's intensive explanation, Ille ended with the words:

"Now I hope you understand how you've got to behave in future."

"That I do," said Frau Imming. She wiped her nose with the back of her hand and said loudly: "In future we'll find some place else to buy our soap."

During this period I received a long series of anonymous letters. Rowohlt too, got such letters, and after he had read them he used to throw them into his wastepaper basket. But one day a man with beetling brows appeared at his publishing house and proceeded to interrogate Rowohlt. The police, it seems, knew that he was receiving such letters and he was emphatically told that he was failing in his duty if he did not hand over all correspondence of this sort to the police authorities immediately on receipt. I could only assume that the police must also be aware that such letters were being sent to me too. I therefore handed over these anti-National Socialist leaflets, the contents of which were generally foolish in the extreme, to the police. When Frau Imming heard of this, she said:

"Not the envelopes! It's the envelopes they're after, because of the postmarks. And I'll give the letters a good dusting before you send them, in case of fingerprints."

I was informed by the police that I must hand over the envelopes too.

"What shall we do now?" I asked Frau Imming. Frau Imming knew. She said:

"You just tell them I open all your letters for you and I throw the envelopes away and then I burn them. That's the way they do it in all high-class offices."

Frau Imming was keenly interested in the contents of these letters. I remember one that contained shattering information to the effect that Hermann Goering had given his Emmy some valuable jewelry, while Goebbels and the famous film actress . . . Frau Imming said:

"We've got nothing against Hermann."

"Because he was a cadet?"

"That's right. It's education. But as for that Goebbels! We'll know what to do with him. We'll hang him up in a cage at the Brandenburg Gate, and everyone going by will have to spit on him!"

During the war my work compelled me to live in Munich. Only occasionally did Ille visit Berlin, for the purpose of paying our taxes and so on. Ille informed me that as soon as Frau Imming heard Ille was in Berlin she would come to see her, bearing on her back a sack of potatoes. In Berlin, for obvious reasons, the workers' quarters in the east were better supplied with food than was the western sector of the city.

"But they can't fool us that easy," said Frau Imming. "In hard times we've all got to stick together."

Her potatoes were noticeably larger and better than ours.

Ille experienced a number of the Berlin raids. Each morning after a raid Frau Imming would come to our apartment to make sure everything was in order. "You know, madam," said Frau Imming, "you can't help respecting the fine ladies. I've seen them carrying buckets of water into burning buildings. With rings on their fingers and painted nails and all I've seen them do it! Down my way my people just sit in the cellar and leave it all to the air-raid warden up on the roof."

In her house Frau Imming was the air-raid warden.

Ille laughed and said to me:

"Imagine, after the last raid Frau Imming came around, and she was in quite a state. She banged about with her pails and mops and at last she said: 'That Churchill, he ought to be hung up in a cage by the Brandenburg Gate and everyone going by should be made to spit at him!' "

Frau Imming was a barometer.

When Ille returned from her last trip to Berlin she was extremely upset. We were living by that time at Siegsdorf, in Upper Bavaria. I met here at the station. She seemed to be at the end of her tether.

"Our beautiful Berlin!" she sobbed. "It seems like cowardice, like running away, for us to live here in complete safety. But I can't stand it any more, I can't go back, I'll never be able to go to Berlin again." She burst into tears. "There's nobody left."

I asked:

"Is our house still standing?"

Ille said:

"Our house is still standing. I think Frau Imming's dead."

"What do you mean?" I cried. "What . . .?"

Ille said:

"I'd told her she shouldn't come anymore. With the alarm sounding day and night you never can tell . . . but she kept on coming. The last time I sent her straight home. I'd noticed she seemed worried and was hurrying over her work. Less than a quarter of an hour after she'd left the alarm went. It was frightful, but the house was all right. Next day they telephoned me from the butcher's shop in the Heidelberger Strasse: Frau Imming hadn't come home. I went to the police and the security-assistance people and the fire service. No one knew anything. And still no sign of her at her home. She must have gone into some air-raid shelter that got a direct hit. The people in her house tried to find her everywhere, to identify her corpse. I—I couldn't do it."

At home Ille had some consecrated candles. She was strongly inclined to Catholicism. I took one of the candles into my room and lit it. I did not want Ille to see its flame; she had told me of those lights which Frau Imming had called "Christmas trees." I had no Catholic inclinations. But no heart is immune to the spirit of Upper Bavaria.

And that is how it came about that in a peasant house in Upper Bavaria a consecrated candle was burnt for Frau Emma Imming, charwoman, of Berlin-Treptow, Heidelberger Strasse 4, member of the Free Thinkers' Union and of the Society for Burial by Cremation.

Approximately eighty percent of the German nation belonged to Master Group Imming.

Translated by Constantine FitzGibbon

IRMGARD KEUN

From After Midnight

1

You can open an envelope and take out something which bites or stings, though it isn't a living creature. I had a letter like that from Franz today. "Dear Sanna," he writes, "I want to see you again, so I may be coming to Frankfurt. I haven't been able to write for some time, but I've been thinking about you a lot. I'm sure you knew that, I'm sure you could feel it. All my love, dear Sanna, from Franz.

What's happened to Franz? Is he ill? Maybe I should have got straight on a train and gone to him in Cologne. But I didn't. I folded the letter up very small and put it down the neck of my dress, where it still is, scratchy in between my breasts.

I feel tired. Today was so eventful, and such a strain. Life generally is, these days. I don't want to do any more thinking. In fact I *can't* do any more thinking. My brain's all full of spots of light and darkness, circling in confusion.

I'd like to sit and drink my beer in peace, but when I hear the words World Outlook I know there's trouble ahead. Gerti ought not to go provoking an SA man like that, saying the soldiers of the Regular Army, the *Reichswehr,* have nicer uniforms and are better-looking too, and if she absolutely had to pick a military man of some kind she'd rather a Reichswehr soldier than a Stormtrooper. Naturally, such remarks act on Kurt Pielmann like a swarm of angry hornets, stinging him badly—and though the wounds may not be mortal, he'll still turn nasty. I can tell.

Yes, Kurt Pielmann is suddenly looking very sick, and he was so cheerful just now you could almost feel sorry for him. After

all, he got another pip three days ago, and he came from Würzburg to Frankfurt today specially to see Gerti, and the Führer.
Because the Führer, no less, was in Frankfurt today,* to gaze
gravely down on the people from the Opera House, and attend
a tattoo put on by men who've recently joined up again. I'm
going to stand us all another round of beer, by way of a distrac-
tion. I hope I've got enough money.

"Waiter!" The place is frantically busy this evening. "Waiter!
Oh, Herr Kulmbach, would *you* call him, please? You can make
yourself heard better. And do drink up—yes, four more export
beers, please, waiter, and—" But he's off again already.

"Could you by any chance spare another cigarette, Herr
Kulmbach?" I don't want Herr Kulmbach to hear Gerti talking
to Kurt Pielmann in such a dangerous way, so I keep chattering
away at him, anything that comes into my head, just to keep his
mind off them. I listen to my own babbling with one ear, while
with the other I hear the row brewing up between Gerti and Pielmann.

If I stop talking for just a moment, there's such a roar of
voices around me that I feel tired enough to drop.

We're sitting in the Henninger Bar. There's a smell of beer and
cigarette smoke, and a lot of loud laughter. You can see the lights
of the Opera House Square through the window. They look a
little dim and weary, like gaudy yellow flowers which finally feel
like folding up and going to sleep.

Gerti and I have been out and about since three this afternoon. I've been friends with Gerti ever since I came to live in
Frankfurt. I've been here a year now.

Gerti looks lovely, sitting there with her breasts all blue. Well,
not actually her breasts, of course, only the dress over them, but
she always looks as if she doesn't have anything on. In Gerti,
however, that doesn't seem at all indecent, because she carries
herself and talks in such a bright, lively way, she doesn't act at
all mysterious. Her thick, fair hair shines, her bright blue eyes
shine, her face shines with a rosy glow.

I don't shine at all. I expect that's why Gerti likes me so much.
Even though she says I could look very good, I just don't know

---

*On May 19, 1935, in order to dedicate a section of the Reichautobahn. "Re-
cently joined up" refers to the reinstitution of mandatory military service on
March 16 of that year.

how to make the best of myself. Gerti and Liska both go on at me about it, and I'm sure they honestly *would* like me to make the best of myself. I would too, but I can never quite manage it.

When I look in the mirror before I go to bed at night, I sometimes do think I look very pretty. I like my skin, because it's so smooth and white. And my eyes seem large and gray and mysterious, and I don't believe there can be a film star in the world with such long, black lashes. At times like this I feel like opening the window and calling out to all the men in the street to come and admire my beauty. I could never really do such a thing, of course. Still, it's a shame if someone's so often at her prettiest when she's alone. Or perhaps I'm only imagining it. At any rate, when I'm with Gerti I feel small and pale and peaky. Even my hair doesn't shine. It's a kind of dull blond color.

I shouldn't have ordered those beers—now Herr Kulmbach is following them up with a round of kirsch. Herr Kulmbach is a waiter in the "Squirrel," and when waiters go out to other bars and restaurants they almost always order lavishly.

"Here's to you, Herr Kulmbach!" "And the Führer!" Today is a wonderful day, says Kulmbach; today has been a very special experience for the people of Frankfurt.

A couple of SS men at the next table glance across at us and raise their glasses, whether to Gerti or the Führer I'm not sure. Perhaps they're drunk and are raising their glasses to everyone in the world, except, of course, Jews, Social Democrats, Russians, Communists, the French, and suchlike people.

I am busy telling Kulmbach I've been in Frankfurt for a year. I was born in Lappesheim, on the Mosel. "That's my home, and of course you never forget your home, do you, Herr Kulmbach?" I'm nineteen now; Gerti is a little older. I got to know her through Liska, because Liska works with handicrafts, and Gerti's mother and father have a handicrafts shop in the best part of Frankfurt. Gerti helps in the shop. My father has a public house in Lappesheim, and three vineyards, though they're not in the very best position. In summer, when the vines are in flower and there's a gentle breeze, and the warm sun is shining, the whole world smells of honey. The Mosel is a happy, sparkling snake of a river, with little white boats on it letting the sunbeams pull them downstream. "And the mountains on the opposite bank, Herr Kulmbach—well, you have to cross on the ferry and get quite close before you realize they *are* mountains. Seen from our pub, they look like great green curly heads, all warm and friendly, so you want to stroke them. But when you get near them you don't find any soft green curls, you find tough trees covered with leaves. And if you climb the mountain you come to the Hunsrück range. It's colder up there than down by the Mosel, and the people are poorer. The children look pale and hungry. The flowers aren't so brightly colored up in the mountains, and they're much smaller—it's the same with the apples and pears, and there are no vines at all."

I think of the mountains that look like nice, curly green heads from a distance, and they make me think of my hands. I kept on rubbing Liska's marvelous skin cream in, thinking that would make my skin wonderfully silky, but Algin's got a magnifying glass, and when I put one of my hands under it I got quite a shock. A freckle on my hand looked like a cowpat. Who wants to look at a thing like that? Magnifying glasses ought not to be allowed.

My name is Susanne. Susanne Moder, but I'm called Sanna. I like it when people shorten my name, because it shows they like me. If you're never called anything but your full baptismal name, you are often rather unpopular.

Franz could say it more lovingly than anyone. "Sanna." Probably because he thinks in the same slow, soft sort of way. Will he really come? Does he still love me? In a minute I'll go to the Ladies and read his letter again.

I wonder what his mother's up to now? Horrible Aunt Adelheid. Something ought to be done about her; why didn't I do it? As a child, I certainly *would* have paid her out somehow, and it wouldn't have been any laughing matter. That cow. When you grow up you accept things much more meekly, you go soft. We always got our revenge for shabby treatment as children, and quite right too!

Aunt Adelheid is totally uneducated, but she puts on amazing airs. She had several reasons for disliking me. In the first place, she disliked me because my father sent me to secondary school in Koblenz. He was in favor of children getting some learning. I'm not all that keen on learning, myself; didn't have the right sort of head for it. But Algin did, and you only have to look at him to see where learning will get a person.

Algin Moder's my stepbrother, and a famous writer, and seventeen years older than me. His real name is Alois, but he changed it off his own bat, because Alois is more of a name for a humorous writer, which he isn't.

When Algin's mother died, my father married again. His new wife had me. My mother died young too, but my father couldn't help it, he was always good to his wives. Then he married for the third time, a sandy-haired woman from Cochem. Well, being a man *and* the landlord of a pub, my father can't manage without a wife. This one's still alive. She's all right, but naturally she loved her own small children more than the two of us left over from the previous marriages, and being a bit stupid and not very pretty she was determined that at least she'd rule the roost. I didn't feel really happy in Lappesheim after she came.

Anyway, the whole place could be too small for me in the long run. I'd far rather live in a city. You're not supposed to say that kind of thing these days, on account of World Outlook and the government. Right-thinking people don't prefer cities or think they're nicer than the countryside. And all the poets nowadays write things saying the only kind of Nature you must love is your original natural background. They keep building bigger and bigger cities all the same, and laying main roads over the redolent soil. The point of the redolent soil is that poets have to sing its praises so as to avoid thinking any stupid thoughts, like what is going on in our cities, and what's happening to the people. You also need the redolent soil for making films about country life which the public do not flock to see. Heini once explained all this to me and Liska. Liska is in love with Heini. I don't always understand him myself, but that doesn't make *me* fall in love with him.

Anyway, I don't think the provincial governors, the Gauleiters, and high-up Ministers would much fancy spending the winter in Lappesheim, when the Mosel's full of poisonous-looking yellow mud, and mist weights down on the whole valley so thick you can hardly breathe. It's always dark, and you stumble over holes in the roads. The only way to stand it is if you have some kind of business of your own, and you're always thinking how to improve it. Or if you have a husband and children to annoy you, which at least is better than being bored to death. I don't want to spend my life there, and neither does Algin, though he carries on in the stories he writes these days as if a right-thinking person ought to clasp every cowpat to his breast.

When I was sixteen, I went to live with Aunt Adelheid in Cologne. She has a stationer's shop there, in Friesen Street. She's my dead mother's sister, and it was my mother who let her have the money for the shop. Aunt Adelheid either has to pay me back some of that money every month or let me live with her free. This was another reason for Aunt Adelheid to dislike me. I'd never have stuck it out there as long as I did—two whole years— but for her son Franz. It is hard to believe he's her son; she doesn't love him, either. I helped Aunt Adelheid in the shop. I love selling things, and everyone says I have a gift for getting on with customers.

When the Führer came to power, Aunt Adelheid went all political, and put up pictures of him, bought swastika flags and joined the National Socialist Women's Club, where she got to meet a good class of person as a German wife and mother.

Then there was an air-raid drill, held in what used to be the Young Men's Christian Association hall. Aunt Adelheid went regularly, taking me along, and she made sure everyone else in the building went too and didn't wriggle out of it. She was nearly the death of frail old Herr Pütz, who lives on the top floor.

Old Pütz is a pensioner, leading a quiet, peaceful life on his own. He has nicely brushed white hair and walks with neat, tottery little footsteps. Aunt Adelheid made him come to air raid drill. That day we had to put on gas masks, which practically smothered you, and then run up a staircase. Old Pütz stood in a dark corner, all shaky, holding the gas mask in his thin little hands and no doubt hoping nobody would notice him. But Aunt Adelheid's beady black eyes noticed him all right. He had to put his gas mask on, and Aunt Adelheid chased him up the staircase ahead of her. Up in the loft he collapsed. Everyone was horrified, though you could only tell from their fluttering hands and agitated footsteps, because there were no human faces in sight, just hideous masks. Pütz's crumpled body lay there on the floor in his one good, dark blue Sunday suit, and we could hear him breathing stertorously inside his mask. Aunt Adelheid had put the mask on him wrong, and it was difficult getting his head out again. I thought he was going to die, but he recovered, very slowly. It was like a miracle.

"Pütz," said Aunt Adelheid, "I hope you realize you should be thankful to me? But for me you'd have been done for in a moment of serious danger." "Just le me die in my bed," Pütz whimpered in a voice like a mouse's squeak, "just let me die in my bed." "Pütz," said Aunt Adelheid sternly, "you have failed to understand the new Germany. You have failed to understand the Führer's will for reconstruction. Old folk like you must be either ignored or forced to see where their welfare lies!" Later on, Aunt Adelheid campaigned successfully to be made warden of the building. That means that if there's a genuine air raid she gets a gun, and everyone in the building is under her orders. And she has the right to shoot anyone who disobeys her.

A thousand enemy aircraft wouldn't frighten me as much as Aunt Adelheid with a gun and the power to give orders. There will be no need for any enemy airman to drop a bomb on Aunt Adelheid's building in order to kill the people inside, because Aunt Adelheid will do the job for him in advance. Unless Schauwecker murders her first, that is. He's another enthusiastic Nazi, and lives on the first floor. He looks like a great fat, yellow sponge, and he is stage manager at the City Theater. He used to be a member of some sort of organization which got him his job. Then he was going to be sacked, because he was always feeling up the actresses with walk-on parts—he was in charge of them, and could go into their dressing-room—and doing really disgusting things, and he wouldn't even leave children alone. I know him; he's an old pig. I was always afraid of meeting him out in the street at night on my own. He wasn't sacked, just given a warning. But on account of all he'd suffered he became an anti-Semite.

He has a tearful wife, and three children who are all in the Hitler Youth movement. He's much respected in the Party because he knows a whole lot about the actors and the other people working at the theater. And *he* was dead set on being warden of the building, and he would have been too, but for Aunt Adelheid. However, Aunt Adelheid had witnesses to the fact that when a man came round selling lottery tickets in aid of the Winter Relief programme, he had said, behind the man's back, "I've no intention of buying any of that fool's trash." This amounted to sabotage of the Winter Relief effort, and Aunt Adelheid had only to inform on him, so she was well able to scare Schauwecker into letting her be warden. He'll get his own back when the war comes and everything's in confusion.

Then Aunt Adelheid did something really horrible, something which might have been the death of *me*. After that I wasn't going to stay on at her place, and I went to Algin in Frankfurt. He'd been to see me in Cologne, and he'd always been nice to me. Thank goodness he was glad to have me, and I stayed.

Algin's been all over the place, even Berlin, where he wrote for the newspapers. Then he began writing books, and one day he became really famous. There were reviews of his books in all the papers. They're novels. One is about a woman who steals things from a department store, but she's a good person all the same, it was just that there wasn't anything else she could do. She gets badly treated by one man, he's a cashier, and then she has an affair with a waiter, but that doesn't turn out well either.

Algin used to send copies of his books to Lappesheim, and we looked at them, too. When November came and the vintage was over and the tourists had gone home, my father used to read half a page every evening. But I don't think he ever got to the end of any of the books.

They even made a film of one of Algin's books, and it was shown in Koblenz. Father and I and six other people from the village went to Koblenz specially to see it. When we were in the cinema we felt just as if the place belonged to Algin, and all the film actors too, and he was responsible for the whole thing. Even the little torches the usherettes carried. The posters outside said, in big, bold letters, "*Shadows without Sun.* From the celebrated novel by Algin Moder." We never really stopped to think if we liked the film, we just felt pleased and very proud, particularly my father. He didn't say anything, but you could tell how proud he was because he took us all into the Königsbacher Bar afterward and spent quite a lot of money.

After that he put the book on the little table by the counter in the pub, where he always puts the newspapers, so that his customers could see it. There was an article about Algin in one newspaper, with a photograph of him, and Father had it handsomely and expensively framed and hung it over the settle in the bar.

Algin sent home suits and dresses, and woollen waistcoats and expensive cognac for Father, who knows a thing or two

about liquor. Father sent Algin the biggest salmon he caught in
the Eltzbach, and the best vintage years of our wine. All the vil-
lagers envied us Algin, and the old Forest Supervisor went so far
as to tell Father, "Moder, you should be a proud man! Your
son's made good." Perhaps my father would have been even pro-
uder if Algin had made good as a general, Father himself being a
veteran of the Stahlhelm corps,* but obviously the times just
weren't right for Algin to get to be a general.

So my father had to content himself with the splendid things
the newspapers printed about Algin, all down there in black and
white. He *was* content, too, and proud. He even made some
sharpish remarks about Father Bender, the only person in the village who had read Algin's book, and who said that when God
had endowed Algin richly with gifts and talents it was poor
thanks to Him to deny the giver of such gifts.

Father Bender's in protective custody now, for thrashing the
parish council chairman's son because the parish council chairman's son made use of the church wall instead of a tree or a lavatory. The boy is high up in the Hitler Youth, and as well as being
parish council chairman his father's an old campaigner, and used
to lead a detachment.

Algin's book is not on the little table by the counter any more,
because the National Socialists put it on a black list. Its trouble
is that it's demoralizing and offends against the basic will for reconstruction of the Third Reich. That's what they said in the
Nazi newspaper in Koblenz. My father wasn't a National Socialist to start with, but he was all for a basic will for reconstruction.

Also, he had to think of his customers, so he hung a picture
of the Führer over the settle instead of the framed article about
Algin. It annoyed my father to think of Algin writing banned
books, after he'd laid out good money on his education. After
all, said my father, you have to show respect for the Führer, and
the national emblem, and if Segebrecht, who keeps another local
pub, has landed himself in a concentration camp then it's entirely
his own fault. Segebrecht can certainly carry an amazing amount
of drink, but he *will* keep putting it back, and it was one day

---

*Also known as the League of Front Soldiers, which was founded in 1918 and
became a front-line opponent of the Weimar Republic. It was subsumed by the
SA in 1933.

when he was drunk that he painted a swastika on his lavatory floor. When Pitter Lambert came into the bar and asked what the idea was, he shouted at the top of his voice, "To show all the assholes what they've gone and elected, that's the idea." Well, no good's going to come of that kind of thing.

Anyway, Algin *had* made good, as everyone had to admit. I used to think it must be wonderful, and I'd have loved to be brilliant and successful too, but now I wouldn't really, not any more, because things can go wrong so quickly, and you never get much fun out of any of it in the long run, either.

When Algin was first famous he thought he'd go up in the world a bit, and he did, and now it's a burden to him, one he can't shake off. Since the new government banned one of Algin's books, he has to be scrupulously careful what he writes, and he doesn't earn much money any more. His entire life, his whole working day from morning to night, is spent making enough to pay for his apartment and the furniture. Because when he was first famous he rented an apartment with lovely big rooms on the main Bockenheim Road, where the most prosperous people in Frankfurt have always lived, and lovely lush magnolia trees bloom in the front gardens in spring.

Then Algin married Liska, because she's so tall and lovely that even women who don't like her say she really is quite something. He also married her because she admired his divine gift for language, and because you need a wife as well as an apartment if you're going up in the world. They furnished the apartment with expensive rugs and cushions, and furniture which is so low it makes you feel somebody sawed the legs off the chairs and tables one cold winter and fed them into the stove. Although the apartment has central heating. Alcoves have been built into some of the walls for books. Algin saw this apartment as a magnificent stage setting for a theatrical show performed by himself. He wanted people to come and applaud, and be aware that Algin was playing a leading part.

Algin isn't happy any more. Liksa isn't happy any more. I love them both. When I came here they gave me board and lodging just like that, and now I'm running the household for them. All Liska can do about the house is create chaos and stuffed toy animals. She used to work with handicrafts in Berlin, and she still does. It even earns her a little money. Her soft toys are silly, daft—but amusing and appealing too.

Oh dear, now Herr Kulmbach's ordering yet another round of kirsch. And I've got an incredible amount of work to do to-morrow, because tomorrow evening is Liska's big party.

Gerti called for me at noon today, because she was going to buy a pink blouse and wanted me to come along to the shops and tell her which suited her best. Even Liska says I have good taste in clothes, and people are always wanting me to knit them sweat-ers. Actually I can knit fast, and well. If I really do marry Franz, I can always earn us a little money by knitting. However, here in Frankfurt I've been moving in circles which are quite different from anything Franz is used to. I mix with high-class, rich, intel-ligent people here. Franz wouldn't know what to say to them.

Well, anyway, we were out in search of a blouse, Gerti and myself. We looked in Goethe Street and the Zeil. Then Gerti said why didn't we go and have a coffee in the café in the Rossmarkt, so we did. Jews sometimes use this café, because unlike nearly all other bars and restaurants, it doesn't have a notice up saying JEWS NOT WELCOME.

The better class of Jews mostly stay at home anyway. If they do want to go out in public there are still three cafés in Frankfurt they can visit. These happen to be the three best cafés, which is hard luck on Aryans, who are afraid of going there too, with good reason. The good reason is that the Nazi paper, the *Stür-mer,* will write about them if they do and call them lackeys of the Jews. And if they have official positions they get sacked. Only a very few brave Aryans dare go in, people without jobs to lose.

Similarly, a few brave Jews venture into the Rossmarkt café. They drink light beer which they don't really like, so as to look inconspicuous and Aryan. Whereas in this particular café Aryans don't happen to drink beer.

Gerti said why didn't we have a vermouth with our coffee, and then another one, and I was her guest. She kept looking at the door. Her neck must have hurt from all that turning to look. She was hoping Dieter Aaron would come in.

Goodness knows how often I've told her, "Gerti, don't make yourself and Dieter unhappy." Dieter is what they call a person of mixed race, first class or maybe third class—I can never get the hang of these labels. But anyway, Gerti's not supposed to have anything to do with him because of the race laws. If all Gerti does is simply sit in the corner of a café with Dieter, holding hands, they can get punished severely for offending against national feeling. Still, what does a girl care about the law when she wants a man? And if a man wants a girl, it's all the same to him if the executioner's standing right behind him with his axe, so long as he gets one thing. Once he's had it, of course, it is not all the same to him any more.

I don't mean that Dieter Aaron is a totally unacceptable sort of mixed-race person. He's polite, and nice, and young, with soft, brown, round, velvety eyes. He's never been very energetic or competent, and his father has never been happy about him. Old Aaron *is* very competent, and rich, and he has a fine, grandly-decorated detached house with a garage. He sells curtains and furnishing fabrics abroad. Gerti says it's an export business, and Jews can run export businesses; they aren't banned. So old Aaron has no problems with his business although he is a full Jew. However, he doesn't like people to call him a Jew. He says he's not a Jew, he's a non-Aryan.

I've sometimes been invited to the Aarons' with Algin and Liska, and Algin almost always quarrels with the old man. Because Algin is against the National Socialists and old Aaron isn't. Old Aaron thinks the Nazis have put the German mentality in order and saved him from the Communists, who would have taken away all he has. He never has any trouble in big, grand hotels; indeed, he gets excellent treatment, and they even offer him a chair at the Revenue offices. There are some very inferior riffraff among the Jews, he says, so he can understand anti-Semitism, and as for the armed forces, there are some fine fellows among *them*, it's a pleasure to look at them. Frau Aaron is not Jewish. She is dry and hard as old straw, and she dominates her husband. Young Aaron is of mixed race because of his non–Jewish mother, who loves him so madly it's practically indecent.

Dieter is in love with Gerti, but he's scared stiff of his mother. He used to work in a chemicals factory, a job obtained by much effort and expense on his father's part, but now he can't do it any more. Nobody knows what will become of him. For the time being, he drives his father to business meetings and takes the Dobermann out for walks. He also goes looking for Gerti, and she goes looking for him.

And then the pair of them sit in a bar looking at each other, the air around them positively quivering with lovesickness.

Everyone in the bar must notice; no good can come of it. They just live for the moment, and cause the air to quiver, and don't stop to wonder what next. Gerti thinks the good Lord will help them, because she's so beautiful, and the good Lord is a man. Dieter thinks, by turns, what his mother thinks and what Gerti thinks. Also, he is afraid of his father.

Sometimes Gerti and Dieter do try to plan for the future, but then they look into each other's eyes, and all thought fades away. Sometimes I keep them company, so that the impression they make in the bar won't be quite so dangerous. I don't like doing this, and I always feel very foolish. I could weep with the worry of it. They're both so pretty and so nice, and they may be hauled off to jail tomorrow. Why are they so crazy? I can't understand it. Other people dance, but they can't. The radio is playing string music, soft as a feather bed. Bright light shimmers in the wine. The wine is sour, but they are drinking hot, bright radiance. I long for Franz, and Gerti's voice grows thin and faltering. The proprietor of the place keeps glancing at us—perhaps he knows Gerti from her parents' shop and he'll inform on her tomorrow. Dieter's well known in Frankfurt too, through his father. There are people wearing Party badges at the next table—oh, dear God, we must get out of here! We must find another bar, and yet another, and some time disaster will strike.

Perhaps the two of them wouldn't love each other so much if they were allowed to. However, there's nothing more idiotic than wondering why people love each other when they *are* in love.

So when Gerti and I were sitting in the Rossmarkt café this after-noon, she thought Dieter might turn up because she'd been there with him once or twice, around this time in the afternoon. They hadn't made a date. All the same, Gerti was nearly weeping with fury because Dieter didn't come in. Now she won't see him again until tomorrow, at Liska's party; the Aarons are invited. And then they will have to be very careful, because of the old Aarons and because of Betty Raff. And I'm not sure that all the other guests are entirely safe, either.

Gerti wanted to have one more vermouth. She suddenly looked dead and drained. The way a woman looks when she's been waiting with all her might, waiting and longing, and all for nothing. Gerti did not want to buy a pink blouse any more, and anyway there wouldn't have been enough money left. We decided to go home without the blouse. It was five in the afternoon. There was turmoil around the Opera House. People, and swastika flags, and garlands of fir, and SS men. The place was in confusion, all excited preparations, much like preparations for the handing out of Christmas presents in a prosperous family with quantities of children. You get used to feverish celebrations of something or other going on all the time in Germany, so that you often don't stop to ask what it is this time, why all the fuss and the garlands and the flags?

Suddenly we felt cold. We were in a hurry to get home. But the SS wouldn't let us cross the Opera House Square to get to the Bockenheim Road. We asked why not; what was going on? But the SS are always arrogant and inclined to put on airs. This lot had nothing better to do than stand around, but they still couldn't find time to answer us. Possibly their minds were working away so frantically that they could only manage to give a contemptuous shrug of their military shoulders.

Gerti's eyes went dark as coal with rage. I know her in that mood: it makes her dangerous, and then of course she's the greatest danger of all to herself. So I asked one of the SS men again, sweet as sugar, very humbly, as if I thought he was one of the greatest rulers of Germany—well, that's the way men like a girl to treat them.

So then the SS man said the Führer would be coming down the Mainz Road to the Opera House at eight. If we wanted to get to the other side of the square we'd have to go round. Yes, of course the Führer was coming! How could I have forgotten? After all, little Berta Silias was due to break through the crowd with flowers, and Frau Silias had talked of nothing else for days.

It was beginning to rain. People were gathering in the square, more and more of them all the time. It looked quite dangerous, as if they'd crush each other to death. Everyone wanted to see something, some of them may not even have known what there would be to see, but all the same they were risking their lives.

Possibly the Führer thought, afterward, that the people had come flocking up out of love for him. No, being the Führer he'll be too clever to think that. Thousands more people join the carnival parade in Cologne, and clamber up on lampposts and high rooftops, breaking arms, legs, anything—they don't mind. It's just a kind of sport: they're proud to have got a good viewpoint, so they can say, and believe, they were in the carnival. And classy people always want to have been at something classy—like Press balls and first nights. But as those things cost a lot of money, there isn't usually such a dangerous crush as in the enormous crowds of people who don't have any money and can only go to shows that don't cost them anything.

We reached the Mainz Road. It was officially lined the whole way down by SA men, who always look broader than usual on these important occasions. Mostly they don't have anything much to do these days, and go about looking as if they've shrunk a bit. Kurt Pielmann and Herr Kulmbach, for instance, resent the fact that there isn't a campaign on any more. Today, however, they could form an imposing cordon, which puts new life into them.

A thin, gray man with a bicycle was going on angrily about not being allowed through. He had finally got a new job, he said, and he had to be on time. Unpunctuality could mean bad trouble for him. And even if his employers did realize he couldn't help being late, they might still be angry with him. Life's nearly always like that: you put difficulties in a person's way, and a slight aura of something dubious and unpleasant still clings to him whether it is his fault or not. "Look, be reasonable, will you?" a fairly high-up SA man, drinking coffee from his flask, told the thin, gray cyclist. "Don't bleat on like that! Just you be thankful to the Führer for his high ideals!"

"That's right," said the thin, gray man, "the Führer gets to have the ideals and we get to carry the can." His voice was trembling; you could tell his nerves were worn to a shred. The people who'd heard him were struck dumb with alarm, and the SA man went red in the face and could scarcely get his breath back. All at once the gray man looked utterly broken, extinguished. Three SA men led him away. He didn't put up a struggle.

His bicycle was lying on the ground. People stood around it in a circle, staring in nervous silence. It shone dully in the rain, and had a subversive look about it; nobody dared touch it. Then a fat woman made an angry face, flung her arm up in the air in the salute of the Führer, said, "Disgusting!" and kicked the bicycle. Several other women kicked it too. And then the cordon opened and let us through.

The Esplanade Café is diagonally opposite the Opera House. It has pansies flowering outside it in summer time, and its customers are nearly all Jews. Gerti and I ought to have gone on down the Bockenheim Road, but there was a cordon blocking that road off too, so we went into the Esplanade. The first thing I did was phone Liska, who said that was all right, she'd make a bit of supper, and Betty Raff could lend a hand too. Gerti rang her mother. Her mother said Kurt Pielmann had come from Würzburg and would be meeting her in the Henninger Bar about nine this evening.

Kurt Pielmann's in love with Gerti and wants to marry her. His father has put a lot of money into Gerti's parents' shop. If he takes it out now, the business will fail. You can't help understanding them and seeing their point. I persuaded Gerti to keep the date with Kurt Pielmann. She can be friendly to him, after all; that doesn't mean she has to marry him, and she certainly does not, *not* have to kiss him. With a man like that, all she has to do is say she's glad there are people like him around, and she'd like him to tell her about National Socialism and introduce her to a wonderful world of ideas. And she isn't mature enough yet to be the lifelong companion of a National Socialist and old campaigner, but she would like to improve her mind until she is, and the way he can help her is by sending her constructive literature. The likes of Kurt Pielmann will be sure to send her the constructive literature, if only because then he can believe he's read it himself. I know about this sort of thing through my father, and Aunt Adelheid, and a good many other people too. They find reading far too much of a strain, far too boring. You can bet your sweet life they haven't read *Mein Kampf* from beginning to end yet. Not that I have either. But they've bought it, and glanced at it now and again, and in the end they believe they've read the whole thing.

Heini once said, "People either buy a book and don't read it. Or they borrow a book and don't give it back, and still don't read it. Or they give it back without reading it. But they've heard so much about the book, and gone to all that trouble buying it or remembering to return it, they really do feel they know it inside out. So they're familiar with the book without ever having read it." This way, he said, thousands of Germans had read Goethe and Nietzsche and other poets and philosophers without going to the bother of really reading them. Look at it like that, and our Führer has something in common with Goethe.

Gerti and I sat in the Esplanade while the place got emptier and emptier around us, quite deserted. All the Jews were leaving. Speeches came roaring out of the loudspeaker like a storm. The café was full of them: speeches about the Führer who would soon be here, about a free Germany, and about the enthusiasm of the crowd. Two elderly ladies came in, thin and neat, looking like spinsters of slender means, maybe small-town schoolteachers on a visit to the city. They ordered coffee and apple tart with cream. Just as they were about to start eating, the Horst Wessel Song came over the radio. The old ladies put their spoons down, stood up and raised their arms. You have to do that, because you never know who may be watching, who may denounce you. Perhaps they were afraid of each other. Gerti and I stood up too.

The radio fell silent for a moment. A waiter came over and asked Gerti if she wanted to see it all from a balcony. Since we were stuck there, of course we did want. We went up and down in the lift with the waiter; all the balconies were crammed full of people. But in the end the waiter found a balcony where he could squeeze us in. He wasn't interested in seeing anything himself.

I was half sitting on a fat man's lap; I couldn't make his face out properly, but his breath was like a greasy, smelly ball that kept flying into my face. There were elegant ladies and gentlemen sitting behind us, keeping still and paying attention as if they were in a box at the theater. Gerti herself said she felt as if we'd been given free seats for a show, only we didn't really fit in, and we weren't dressed for the occasion.

Over to the right of the Opera House Square, where it's almost like a park, a black sea of people had gathered, moving back and forth in slow waves. A dull sort of light shone over them. Several SS men were bustling about the cleared square in an excited manner, frantically waving their arms about. But still nothing happened.

Now and then SS men carried fainting women out of the sea of people, so the wait wasn't too boring for the spectators in the balconies.

Then, suddenly, cars came down the road—fast and quiet as downy feathers flying. And so beautiful, too! I never saw such cars in my life before. So many of them as well, so many of them! All the Gauleiters, and high-up Party men accompanying them, drove up in those cars; it was splendid. They must all be enormously rich. When I think of Franz, and I imagine him living for a hundred years working from morning to night—always supposing he *had* work—and not drinking or smoking all that hundred years, doing nothing but save, save, save—well, I work it out that even in a hundred years he still couldn't buy a car like that. Maybe in a thousand years. But who lives to be a thousand years old?

I enjoyed seeing the beautiful cars; they looked like marvelous, shiny, racing beetles seen from above. And all the people down below, who must have been worn out with waiting by now, were enjoying themselves too, because something was finally happening, although only the people at the front of the crowd could see any of it.

Shouts arose in the distance. *Heil Hitler!* The roar of the crowd came surging up, closer and closer, up to our balcony—widespread, hoarse, a little weary. And a car drove slowly past with the Führer standing in it, like Prince Carnival in the carnival parade. But he wasn't as funny and cheerful as Prince Carnival, and he wasn't throwing sweets and nosegays, just raising an empty hand.

A little sky-blue ball came rolling out of the dark ranks of the crowd and into the street, making for the car. It was little Berta Silias, who'd been chosen to break through the crowd, because the Führer often likes to be photographed with children. But he can't have felt like it this time. Berta was left standing there, a solitary little speck with a huge bouquet of flowers.

The Führer had passed. Some SS men were kneeling round little Berta, lights were flashing, photographs were being taken. Well, Berta may get into the paper after all, even if it's only with some SS men and not the Führer. That will be some small consolation to Frau Silias.

Men who were currently famous were getting into position on the long balcony of the Opera House, with much ceremony, bowing politely to each other. They waved to the crowd too.

They weren't really doing anything of interest, but you were allowed to look at them.

Gerti's opinion was that you didn't get much fun out of looking at these eminent men, the eminent men must get far more fun out of having all of *us* looking at *them*.

On the other hand, there were ladies on our balcony in ecstasies because they could recognize one General Blomberg, and

Göring too, because Göring had a touch of red on his jacket, and we all know from photographs that he likes to wear stylish suits. Though by now he's really so well known he doesn't need to make his mark by wearing striking clothes.

Algin sometimes has a visitor, a young actor who can't get parts, who has to make a good impression by his appearance, so he wears very expensive ties, and pigskin gloves so bright you can see them a mile off. But Göring already *has* a part, in his own way. Then again, however, even established film stars can never let up—they have to keep showing their public the latest thing in fashion and elegance. I expect someone like Göring is obliged to think hard all the time, if he's going to keep offering the German people something new. And men like that have to find time to govern the country as well. Personally, I can't think how they do it all. Take the Führer: he devotes almost his entire life to being photographed for his people. Just imagine, what an achievement! Having your picture taken the whole time with children and pet dogs, indoors and out of doors—never any rest. *And* constantly going about in aeroplanes, or sitting through long Wagner operas, because that's German art, and he sacrifices himself for German art as well.

Well, fame always demands some sacrifices. I read that once in an article about Marlene Dietrich. They say the Führer eats nothing but radishes and rye bread with cheese spread. That's another sacrifice to fame. Hollywood film actresses sometimes eat even less, because they mustn't get fat. And they don't drink or smoke either, so as to keep their looks. Liska sometimes diets till she's quite ill, just to lose weight.

I can well imagine our Führer wanting to have a particularly slim, handsome figure, what with being photographed all the time and appearing in newsreels and Party Congress films. And maybe he'd like to show up well in contrast to Göring, and Dr. Ley, and a number of other ministers and mayors, who have all got noticeably fatter. You can see that any day from their pictures in magazines.

Anyway, there were these eminent men in the flesh, standing on the Opera House balcony. The balcony, with them on it, was illuminated; everywhere else was dark. The lights in the square had been turned off so that the Army would show to good effect. The Reichswehr men wore shiny steel helmets, and they were carrying blazing torches. They did a sort of ballet dance with these torches, to the sound of a military band. It was a tattoo, and also a historic moment, and it looked very pretty.

The world was big and dark blue, the dancing men were black, moving all together—faceless, silent, dark figures all in time. I once saw some African war dances in an educational film. The African dances were rather livelier, but I did like the Reichswehr's dance very much too.

Translated by Anthea Bell

WOLFGANG KOEPPEN

From Death in Rome

1

Once upon a time, this city was a home to gods, now there's only
Raphael in the Pantheon, a demigod, a darling of Apollo's, but
the corpses that joined him later are a sorry bunch, a cardinal of
dubious merit, a couple of monarchs and their purblind generals,
high-flying civil servants, scholars that made it into the reference
books, artists of academic distinction. Who gives a damn about
them? The tour group stand in the ancient vaults, and gawp up
at the light falling on them like rain through the only window,
the circular opening in the cupola that was once covered with
bronze tiles. Is it golden rain? Danaë succumbs to the approaches
of Thomas Cook and the Italian Tourist Board; but without
much enthusiasm. She won't lift her skirts to receive the god into
her. Perseus won't be born. Medusa gets to keep her head and
moves into a swish apartment. And what about great Jupiter? Is
he here in our midst? Could he be the old fellow in the Amex
office, or the rep for the German-European Travel Agency? Or
has he been banished to the edge of town somewhere, is he in the
asylum enduring the questions of nosy psychiatrists, or languish-
ing in the state's prisons? They've installed a she-wolf under the
Capitol, a sick and depressed animal, not up to suckling Romu-
lus and Remus. The faces of the tourists look pasty in the light
of the Pantheon. Where is the baker that will knead them, where
is the oven that will give them a bit of color?
  Wrong, the music sounded wrong, it no longer moved him, it
was almost unpleasant to him, like hearing your own voice for
the first time, a recording coming out of a loudspeaker, and you

think, well, so that's me, that braying twit, that phony, that smoothie, and in particular it was the violins that were wrong, their sound was too lush; it wasn't the unearthly wind in the trees, it wasn't the child's conversation with the daemon at nightfall, that wasn't what fear of being sounded like, it wasn't so measured, so well-tempered, it should be more tormenting, more passionate, old panic fear of the green trees, of the expanse of the sky, of the drifting clouds—that was what Siegfried had meant to sing, and he had totally and utterly failed, and so now he felt weak and timid, he felt like crying, but Kürenberg had been reassuring and praised the symphony. Siegfried admired Kürenberg, the way he ruled with his baton, the plenipotentiary of the notes; but still there were times when Siegfried felt violated by him. Then Siegfried would get angry with himself for not putting up any fight. He couldn't; Kürenberg was so knowledgeable, and Siegfried was green and no match for him in musical theory. Kürenberg smoothed, accented, articulated Siegfried's score, and Siegfried's painful groping, his search for a sound, the memory of an Edenic garden before the dawn of mankind, an approximation to the truth of things, which was by definition unhuman— all that, under Kürenberg's conducting hand, had become humanistic and enlightened, music for a cultured audience; but to Siegfried it sounded unfamiliar and disappointing, the feeling now tamed and striving for harmony, and Siegfried was worried, but then again the artist in him enjoyed the precision, the clarity of the instruments, the care with which the celebrated hundred-strong orchestra were playing his composition.

In the concert hall there were laurel trees growing in green-painted tubs, or perhaps it was oleander; anyway the same thing that grew in crematoria, and even in high summer looked somehow wintry. "Variations on Death and the Color of Oleander" had been the title of Siegfried's first major composition, a septet that had remained unperformed. In the first draft he had had in mind his dead grandmother, the only member of his family to whom he had been at all close; perhaps because she had been such a strange and silent presence in the noisy and bustling house of his parents, forever echoing to the tramp of jackboots. And what a ghastly send-off they'd given her. His grandmother was the widow of a pastor, and had she been able to watch, she would have hated the technology and comfort, the hygiene and slickness, with which she had been turned to ashes, the deft and indifferent address, while the wreath, with the garish swastika ribbon that the SA Women's Section had contributed, was certainly repugnant to her, even if she would never have spoken out against it. But then, in the second version of his septet, Siegfried had tried to express something more universal and more suspect, a secret opposition, suppressed, brittle, romantic scraps of feelings, and in its posture of resistance his composition resembled a rose-garlanded marble torso, the torso of a young warrior or a hermaphrodite in the blaze of single combat: it represented Siegfried's rebellion against his surroundings, against the prisoner-of-war camp, against the barbed-wire fences, against his comrades with their boring conversations, against the war, for which he held his parents responsible, against his whole hellish and hellbent Fatherland. Siegfried wanted to pay them all back, and so, having read in an English newspaper that Kürenberg, who had been a rising conductor in Germany before the war, was now in Edinburgh, he had written to him, asking for some examples of twelve-tone music, a form of composition that was considered unacceptable in Siegfried's youth, and which now attracted him for that very reason, becuase it was frowned upon by those in power, his hated teachers at the military academy, his feared Uncle Judejahn, the mighty man whose glowering image in the vile uniform had hung over his despised father's desk, and Kürenberg had sent works by Schönberg and Webern to Siegfried in his camp, and sent a friendly note to accompany them. The scores were in the old Universal edition, published in Vienna before Siegfried's time and then banned after the Anschluss of Austria.* The music represented a new world for Siegfried, it opened a gate for him, not just in the barbed-wire prisoner-of-war compound, but in something still more constricting. And afterward he refused to crawl back under the yoke as he called it, the war was lost, and he at least had been freed, and no longer deferred to the views of the family to have been born into which had always seemed ghastly to him.

---

*Using massive military pressure, in February 1938 Hitler forced the Austrian government to accept participation of the Austrian NSDAP in the government. On March 12, German troops marched into Austria, cheered by large segments of the population and the new government. One day later, the "Reunification of Germany with Austria" was passed.

The greenery in the concert hall looked dusty. It probably was laurel after all, the leaves had the look of dried herbs swimming in soup, moistened but still brittle and unsoftened by cooking. They depressed Siegfried, who didn't want to be sad in Rome. The leaves reminded him of a succession of soups in his life: the Eintopf at the Party school that his father had sent him to on Uncle Judejahn's recommendation, the field-kitchens of the army, to which Siegfried had fled from school; the Party's Junker school had had green bay trees too, and there were oak leaves in the barracks, proliferating on decorations and on tombstones, and there had always been a picture of that twitchy and repressed type, the Führer, with his Charlie Chaplin mustache, looking benevolently down on his herd of sacrificial lambs, the boys in uniform now ready for the slaughter. Here, among the laurel and oleander of the concert hall, in this chilly indoor grove, there was an old portrait of the master, Palestrina, looking far from benevolent, no, surveying the orchestra's efforts sternly and reproachfully. The Council of Trent had accepted Palestrina's music. The congress in Rome would reject Siegfried's. That too depressed Siegfried, depressed him while still rehearsing, depressed him even though he'd come to Rome expecting to be rejected, telling himself he didn't care.

There is a trench going round the Pantheon that was once the street that led from the Temple of All the Gods to the Baths of Agrippa; the Roman imperium collapsed, debris filled up the trench, archaeologists laid it bare again, masonry stumps rise up mossy and ruined, and sitting on top of them are the cats. There are cats all over Rome, they are the city's oldest inhabitants, a proud race like the Orsinis and the Colonnas, they are really the last true Romans, but they have fallen on hard times. Imperial names they have! Othello, Caligula, Nero, Tiberius. Children swarm round them, calling to them, taunting them. The voices of the children are loud, shrill, voluble, so appealing to a foreign ear. They lie on their fronts on the wall that runs alongside the ditch. School ribbons transform the grimy faces into little Renoirs. The girls' pinafores have ridden up, the boys wear tiny shorts, their legs look like those of statues under a patina of dust and sun. That's the beauty of Italy. Suddenly laughter rings out. They're laughing at an old woman. Compassion always has a pathetic aspect. The old woman hobbles along with a stick, bringing the cats something to eat. Something wrapped in a foul, sodden newspaper. Fishheads. On a blood-smeared newspaper photograph the American secretary of state and the Russian foreign minister are shaking hands. Myopic the pair of them. Their glasses blink. Thin lips compressed in a smile. The cats growl and hiss at each other. The old woman tosses the paper into the trench. Severed heads of sea creatures, dull eyes, discolored gills, opalescent scales, tumble among the yowling moggy mob. Carrion, a sharp whiff of excrement, secretions and sex, and the sweet smell of decay and purulence rise into the air, mixed with the exhaust fumes on the street, and the fresh, tempting aroma of coffee from the espresso bar on the corner of the Piazza della Rotonda. The cats fight over the leftovers. It's a matter of life and death. Foolish creatures, why did they have to multiply! There are hundreds of them starving and homeless, randy, pregnant, cannibalistic; they are diseased and abandoned, and they have sunk about as far as cats can sink. One tom with a bullish skull, sulfur-yellow and bristle-haired, lords it over the weaker ones. He puts his paw down. He doles out. He takes for himself. His face bears the scars of past power struggles. He is missing part of an ear—a lost campaign. There is mange on his fur. The adoring children call him "Benito."

I was sitting at a zinc table, on a zinc chair, so light the wind might have carried me off. I was happy, I was telling myself, because I was in Rome, on the pavement terrace of an espresso bar on the corner of the Piazza della Rotonda in Rome, and I was drinking a brandy. The brandy also was light and flighty, light metal, like distilled zinc. It was grappa, and I was drinking it because I'd read in Hemingway that that's what you should drink in Italy. I wanted to be cheerful, but I didn't feel cheerful. Something was gnawing me. Perhaps the awful mob of cats were gnawing me. No one likes seeing poverty, and a few pennies weren't enough to absolve you here. I never know what to do. I avert my eye. A lot of people do, but it bothers me. Hemingway doesn't seem to know the first thing about brandy. The grappa tasted mouldy and synthetic. It tasted like German black-market brandy from the Reichsmark period. Once I got ten bottles of brandy like that in exchange for a Lenbach. The Lenbach was a sketch of Bismarck; I did the deal with a Puerto Rican in GI uniform. The brandy was distilled from fuel for the V2 rockets that were supposed to destroy London: you flew off in the air when you drank it, but that's all right, the Lenbach was faked as well. Now we had the "economic miracle" in Germany, and good brandy. The Italians probably had decent brandy too, but they didn't have an economic miracle. I surveyed the square. I saw the state being swindled. A young woman was selling American cigarettes from her dirty apron. I felt reminded of the cats. The woman was the human equivalent of those poor creatures, ragged and unkempt and covered with open sores. She was miserable and degraded; her kind too had multiplied too quickly, and they had been weakened by lust and hunger. Now she was hoping to get rich illegally. She was ready to worship the golden calf; but I wasn't sure whether it would answer her prayers. I had a feeling this woman might be murdered. I could see her strangled body, whereas she probably saw herself as a proper businesswoman, a dignified signora, enthroned in a legitimate kiosk. On the piazza, the golden calf condescended to nuzzle the woman. She seemed to be well known in the area. Like a buoy she stood in the flow of traffic, and the deft little Fiats swam boldly up to her. How the brakes squealed! The drivers, handsome men with curled, with waved, with pomaded hair, with buffed and scented scalps if they were bald, passed money out through the windows of their cars, took their packets on board, and their little Fiats would chase off to the next port of call, the next fraudulent little transaction. A young communist woman walked up. I could tell by the bright red kerchief over her blue anorak. A proud visage! I thought, Why are you so arrogant? You deny everything, you deny the old woman feeding the cats, you deny all compassion. A youth lurked in a doorway, greasy, as though dipped in oil. He was the cigarette-seller's boyfriend, her protégé or her protector; or maybe he was her boss, a serious businessman concerned about his volumes and his margins; whatever he was, I think he was the Devil with whom Fate had paired this woman. Every so often the two of them would meet on the piazza, as though by chance. She would slip him her takings, a bunch of dirty lira notes, and he would pass her fresh, shiny cellophane-wrapped packs. A *carabiniere* was standing there in his flashy uniform like his own monument, and was looking across at the Pantheon with a bored sneer. I thought, You and that little communist would make a fine pair, you'd nationalize the cats, the compassionate old woman would die in a state nursing home, the fishheads would be taken into public ownership, and everything would be organized out of existence. But for the moment there was still disorder and happening. Newspaper-sellers cried their wares with hoarse, pleading shouts. They've always had my admiration. They are the rhapsodies and panegyricists of crimes, of accidents, of scandals and national commotions. The European bastion in Indochina was about to fall. In those days, war and peace hung in the balance, only we didn't know. We didn't hear about the cataclysm that threatened us until much later, in newspapers that hadn't yet been printed. Whoever could, ate well. We sipped our coffee and our brandy; we worked hard to earn money, and if the circumstances were favorable, we slept with one another. Rome is a wonderful city for men. I was interested in music, and it looked as though a lot of other people in Rome were as well. They had come from many countries to attend the congress in the ancient capital. Asia? Asia was far off. Asia was ten hours' flight, and it was as big and remote as Hokusai's wave. The wave was coming. It lapped at the shores of Ostia, where a girl's body had been found washed up.* The poor corpse went around Rome like a ghost, and her pallid image terrified cabinet ministers; but they managed, as usual, to save their skins. The wave was approaching the cliffs at Antibes. *"Bonsoir, Monsieur Aga Khan!"* Dare I say that it's not my concern? I have no bank accounts, no money, no jewels, I weigh as nothing in the balance; I am free, I have no strings of race horses and no starlets to protect. My name is Siegfried Pfaffrath. An absurd name, I know. But then again, no more absurd than many others. Why do I despise it so? I never chose it. I like to talk shamelessly, but then I feel ashamed: I behave rudely, and I long to be able to show respect. I'm a composer of serious music. My profession matches my name for absurdity. Siegfried Pfaffrath, it says on concert programmes. Why don't I use a pseudonym? I have no idea. Is it the hated name clinging to me, or do I cling to it? Will my family not let go of me? And yet I believe that everything

---

*Koeppen weaves various contemporary aspects together. Katsushika Hokusai's picture cycle *The Great Wave* (1823–29) is here used metaphorically for the effect of France's colonial war against Vietnam (1947–54) on Europe. Yet "Asia is far," and the "Montesi scandal" deserves note. On April 9, 1953, 21-year-old Wilma Montesi was found dead. One year later, a journalist uncovered a connection with high-level Italian personalities after investigations had been stopped in 1953. Foreign Minister Attilio Piccioni eventually had to resign.

that's done, thought, dreamed or ruined, everything in the universe, even invisible and impalpable things, concern me and reach out to me.

A large automobile, gleaming black, noiseless engine, a lacquered coffin, the windows mirroring and impenetrable, had driven up to the Pantheon. It looked like a diplomatic conveyance—maybe the ambassador from Pluto was nestling on the plump upholstery, or a delegate from Hell—and Siegfried, drinking his brandy on the piazza and dreaming, aware of some activity but nothing out of the ordinary, looked at the licence plate and had an impression of Arab script. Who was it just drawing up, a prince from the Arabian Nights, an exiled king? A dusky-faced chauffeur in military livery leapt from his seat, tore open the passenger door, and stayed in bustling close attendance on a man in a well-fitting gray suit. The suit was English flannel, and it was the work of an expensive tailor, but on the squat body of the man—thick neck, broad shoulders, high ribcage, round elastic belly like a medicine ball, stocky thighs—the suit took on a rustic, Alpine aspect. The man had cropped bristly iron-gray hair, and he wore large dark glasses that were everything other than rustic, that suggested secrecy, cunning, foreign travel, diplomatic corps or wanted by Interpol. Was this Odysseus, on a visit to the gods? No, it was not Odysseus, not the wily king of Ithaca; this man was a butcher. He came from the Underworld, carrion smells wafted round him, he himself was Death, a brutal, mean, crude and unquestioning Death. Siegfried hadn't seen his Uncle Judejahn, who had terrorized him as a child, for thirteen years. Many times Siegfried had been punished for hiding from his uncle, and the boy had come to see his Uncle Gottlieb as the embodiment of everything he most feared and hated, the personification of duress, marching, the war. Even now he sometimes imagined he could hear the scolding, forever angry voice of the man with the bull neck, but he only dimly remembered the innumerable images of the mighty and universally feared tribune—on hoardings, on classroom walls, or as a paralyzing shade on cinema screens that showed the man in ostentatiously plain Party uniform and unpolished boots, with his head thrust avidly forward. Thus, Siegfried, since escaped into freedom, drinking grappa à la Hemingway, thinking about this square in Rome and about the music which was his personal adventure, failed to recognize Gottlieb Judejahn, it never even crossed his mind that this monster had come back from the dead and surfaced in Rome. Siegfried only observed casually, and with an involuntary shudder, a corpulent, presumably wealthy foreigner, someone of consequence and unpleasant, luring the cat Benito to him, grabbing him by the scruff, and taking him off—amid the shouts and cries of the children—to his magnificent car. The chauffeur stiffened to attention like a tin soldier, and shut the door respectfully after Judejahn and Benito. The large black automobile glided silently out of the square, and in the afternoon sun Siegfried caught a glimpse of Arab script on the licence plate, until abruptly a cloud passed in front of the sun, and the car vanished in a puff of haze and dust.

Asked along to the rehearsal by Kürenberg her husband, Ilse had been sitting, unnoticed by Siegfried, in the back row of the concert hall (which was darkened except for the lights over the orchestra pit) next to one of the green potted trees, listening to the symphony. She didn't like it. What she heard were discordant, inharmonious, mutually antagonistic sounds, a vague searching, a half-hearted experiment in which many paths were taken and none followed to its end, in which no idea asserted itself, where from the outset everything was brittle, full of doubt, doomed to despair. It seeemd to Ilse that the person who had written these notes didn't know what he wanted. Did he despair because he was lost or was he lost because whichever way he went, he spread the black night of his depression, and made it impassable for himself? Kürenberg had talked a lot about Siegfried, but Ilse had yet to meet him. Up until now, she had been merely indifferent. But now Siegfried's music disturbed her, and she didn't want to be disturbed. There was something in it, some tone that made her sad. But life had taught her that sorrow and pain were best avoided. She didn't want to suffer. Not any more. She had suffered long enough. She gave beggars unusually large sums, without asking what had forced them to beg. Kürenberg could have conducted elsewhere in the world for more money, in Sydney or New York; and Ilse hadn't advised him against putting on Siegfried's symphony for the congress in Rome, but now she was sorry that he was taking trouble over something inchoate and hopeless, an expression of naked and unworthy despair.

When the rehearsal was over, the Kürenbergs went out to eat. They liked to eat; they ate often, plentifully and well. Happily it didn't show. They did well on their good and abundant food; both were solid, not fat, well-nourished and sleek like healthy animals. As Ilse didn't say anything, Kürenberg knew that she'd disliked the symphony. It's difficult to argue with a silent opponent, and before long Kürenberg was hailing Siegfried as the most gifted composer of his generation. He had invited him back for that evening. Now he wasn't sure how Ilse would respond. He mentioned it in passing, and Ilse said, "You asked him to our hotel?" "Yes," said Kürenberg. Then Ilse knew that Kürenberg, who was a passionate cook, even on the road, and they were always on the road, was going to cook for him, and that was proof that he genuinely did admire Siegfried and was courting him, and once more she was silent. But why shouldn't she join him in inviting Siegfried? She didn't like to be left out. Nor did she want to quarrel with Kürenberg. They hardly ever quarreled. Their union was harmonious, they had been all over the world together, often traveling in grim and dangerous circumstances, without friction. Very well, Siegfried could visit them in their hotel, and they would give him dinner, that was fine by her. Kürenberg assured her Siegfried was a pleasant man, and perhaps he was; but his music, unless it were to change—and Ilse refused to believe that it could change, because these notes, however incoherent and disagreeable to her, were in their way a true reflection of a particular human destiny, and that made them unalterable— his music, however nice Siegfried might be, she would never get on with. Ilse looked at Kürenberg, walking along at her side, in his stout shoes and suit of coarse Scottish tweed, grizzled, balding, but with bright eyes in his good, solid face, a little heavy but with a firm stride and agile amid the bustle and confusion of the Roman streets. Kürenberg appeared taciturn, or, perhaps more accurately, firmly anchored in himself. Living on an intellectual plane, he was never impatient and never sentimental, and yet Ilse was convinced that his support for Siegfried was emotionally inspired; it had somehow moved him that in '44 a German prisoner-of-war in an English camp had turned to him, the voluntary émigré, and involuntary volunteer infantryman in World War I at Langemarck, and asked him for samples of the new music. For Kürenberg, Siegfried's prisoner-of-war letter had been a sign, a message from a Europe that had collapsed into barbarism, the dove that signaled that the floodwaters were receding.

They sat down in the sun, they enjoyed the sun, they sat down on the terrace of the wickedly expensive restaurant on the Piazza Navona, they enjoyed sitting there. They looked out into the calm harmonious oval of the one-time arena, they were glad that violent era was at an end, and they lunched. They lunched on little prawns crisply fried in butter, on tender grilled chicken, dry salad leaves dressed with oil and lemon juice, large sensuous red strawberries, and with their lunch they drank a dry lively Frascati. They enjoyed the wine. They enjoyed the food. They were serious and calm eaters. They were serious and blithe drinkers. They hardly spoke, but they were very much in love.

After lunch, they took the bus to the station district where they were staying. The bus was overcrowded as ever. They stood pressed against one another, and against other passengers. They stood in silence, calm and satisfied. At the station, they decided to pay a short visit to the National Museum in the ruins of the Baths of Diocletian. They loved antiquity. The loved the solid marble, the exalted forms made by man in his own image, the cool sarcophagi, the delicious rondure of the mixing-bowls. They saw the Eroses, fauns, gods and heroes. They studied the mythical monsters and gazed at the lovely body of the Cirenian Venus and the head of the Sleeping Fury. Then they stepped out into the cool, sleepy lane, shaded by high buildings, behind their hotel, nothing special but comfortable enough. They went into a butcher's shop, saw the bodies hanging on cruel hooks, bled, fresh, cool, and saw the heads of sheep and oxen, dumb, quiet sacrificial victims, and from the clean and beautiful diagonally hewn marble slab of the butcher, they ordered tender matured steaks, once Kürenberg had poked and prodded them with his fingers to test their hanging; they bought fruit and vegetables at open-air stands; they purchased oil and wine in old cellars; and, after looking for some time, and testing it with his teeth, Kürenberg found a type of rice that promised not to turn soggy when cooked. They carried their parcels home and took the lift up to their large bright room, the hotel's best suite. They were tired, and they enjoyed their tiredness. They saw the wide bed and they enjoyed the prospect of the cool clean linen. It was broad afternoon. They didn't draw the curtains. They undressed in the light, and lay down between the sheets. They thought of the beautiful Venus and the leaping fauns. They enjoyed their thoughts, they enjoyed the memory, then they enjoyed one another, and fell into a deep sleep, that condition of anticipated death that takes up a third of our lives; but Ilse dreamed she was the Eumenide, the sleeping Eumenide, appeasingly called the Kindly One, the Godess of Revenge.

It was time, he ought to go, he had said he would go, it was the agreed hour, they were waiting for him, and he felt unwilling, reluctant, afraid. He, Judejahn, was afraid, and what was his favorite saying? "I don't know the meaning of the word fear!" That saying had a lot to answer for, a lot of men had bitten the dust, always the others of course; he had issued the orders and they had fallen, on pointless assaults or holding doomed positions to satisfy an insane sense of honor, holding them to the last man, as Judejahn then reported to his Führer with swelled breast, and anyone who was chicken swung for it, dangled from trees and lampposts, swayed in the stiff breeze of the dead with his confession round his broken neck: "I was too cowardly to defend my Fatherland." But then whose Fatherland was it? Judejahn's? Judejahn's arm-twisting empire and marching club, hell take it. And there weren't just hangings, there were beheadings, torturings, shootings, deaths behind closed doors and up against walls. The enemy took aim, yes, of course the enemy was peppering away as well, but here it was your comrade who dispatched you with a bullet, you'll not find a better; it was your compatriot ranting, your greatly admired superior, and the young, condemned man didn't start thinking until it was too late about which was the enemy and which his comrade. Judejahn addressed them in fatherly fashion as "my lads" and Judejahn said crudely, latrine-style, "Kill the cunt," he always had the popular touch, always a hell of a guy, great sense of humor, old Landsberg assassin, in bloody charge of the Black Reichswehr camps on the estates of Mecklenburg, death's head on his steel helmet, but even they, the old gods, had turned their coats, Ehrhardt the captain dining with writers and other such shitheads, and Rossbach* with his troupe of pale-skinned boys, putting on mystery plays for the delectation of headmasters and clerics, but he, Judejahn, had taken the right road, unwavering and straight ahead, to Führer and Reich and full military honors.

---

* Judejahn invents stories about his time as a Freikorps fighter in the postwar period. Yet Koeppen, in contrast to Salomon, places emphasis on the violence and sees the development into an SS man as necessary.

He strode through his room, the carpets were thick, the walls were silk, silk screened the streetlights, on the damask bed lay Benito the mangy cat, looking blinkingly, sardonically up at Judejahn, as if to purr, "So you've survived," and then looking in disgust at the fried liver on a silver dish by the foot of the bed. Why had he brought that animal in here? Was it some kind of magic charm? Judejahn didn't believe in ghosts. He was just a sentimental bastard, he couldn't stand to see it, it had infuriated him, a kingly animal like that being tormented. Benito! Those snotnoses! Judejahn was staying on the Via Veneto, staying in an ambassador-class hotel, a billet for NATO generals, lodgings for presidents of US Steel, home from home for directors of chemicals companies, showcase for award-winning wide-screen epic bosoms, blackmailers and poules had their little coops here, all odd birds went to Rome, weird beards and wasp waists, fantastically expensive outfits, waists you could strangle the life out of with one hand, but it was better to grab the firm tits and ass, feel the arousing, palpitating flesh under the nylon skin, the wispy garter-belt stretched tautly over belly and thighs to the sheer-textured stockings—there were no cardinals staying here.

He had taken off his dark glasses. Runny eyes, watery blue. Was it foolish of him to stay here? He laughed. First, he was in the right, and had always been in the right, and secondly, well, the wind blew, didn't it? Forgiven and forgotten. It was a little joke of Judejahn's, and Judejahn liked his little jokes, like putting up at this particular hotel, albeit with a passport in which the name given was not his real name, and the country of birth was not his real country of birth, but apart from that the document was genuine enough, it was stamped with diplomatic visas, he was Someone, he had always been Someone, and he was now. He could afford to stay here, and enjoy the memory of his palmy days: he had resided under this roof once before, it was from here that he had sent messages to the Palazzo Venezia, it was in the hall of this building that he had ordered the hostages to be shot.

What was he to wear? He had a full wardrobe, he had suits of fine English cloth, tailored by nimble Arab fingers, he had become a cosmopolite, he put on perfume before going to the brothel for a relieving poke, the sheikhs had taught him that; but in whatever garb, he remained unmistakably the old Judejahn, an infantile type, a grim Boys' Own hero, unable to forget that his father, a primary schoolteacher, had beaten him for being bad at school. What about the dark suit? The reunion should be kept formal. But leave the perfume out. People didn't reek of musk where he was going. They kept the wild man out of sight. The Germans had recovered themselves. Were respectable people once more. Would they be able to tell where he had been? Once knee-deep in blood, and now, in the final frame, the desert sand?

There were jackals where he came from. Nights they howled. Unfamiliar stars pricked the sky. What did he care? They were orienteering aids. Otherwise he didn't need them. He couldn't hear the jackals, either. He slept. His sleep was tranquil, peaceful, dreamless. Every night he dropped into it like a stone into a deep well. No nightmares plagued him, no remorse, no skeletons. The sleeper woke when reveille sounded. That was welcome, familiar music. There was a storm blowing in the desert. The sound of the cornet wavered and died. The fellow was a slacker; he wanted bringing up to the mark. The sand clattered against the barrack walls. Judejahn rose from his narrow camp bed. He liked hard beds. He liked the whitewashed room with the metal wardrobe, the folding table, the washing unit, the rattle of rusty ewers and basins. He could have lived in a villa in the capital, highly paid, sought-after expert that he was, put in charge of reorganizing and training the king's army. But he preferred the barracks. It gave him confidence and a feeling of security. The barracks were home, comradeship, security and order. In fact it was words that held him together. Whose "comrade" was Judejahn really? He liked the view of the desert. It wasn't its endlessness that drew him, more its barrenness. For Judejahn the desert was a great exercise ground, a front, a continual challenge that kept him in trim. In the capital, tiptoeing servants would have hovered at his elbow, he would have fornicated with warm-bellied girls, wallowed between their thighs, he could have bathed in aromatic waters like a pasha. But in camp he soaped himself, scrubbed himself down with a stiff brush till his skin was raw, he shaved with the old German pocket razor that had accompanied him all the way from the Weidendamm Bridge to the desert. He felt good, like a scorched wild boar, he thought to himself. He heard man sounds: water splashing, buckets clanging, whistling, oaths, jokes, orders, boots scraping, doors banging. He smelled the barracks smell compounded from detention, service, leather polish, gun grease, strong soap, sweet pomade, sour sweat, coffee, heated aluminum dishes and piss. It was the smell of fear, only Judejahn didn't know it: after all, he didn't know what fear was. He told himself so in front of the mirror; naked, thick-bellied, he stood in front of the fly-blown glass. He did up his belt. He was old school in this. The belt held in his paunch and hitched up his buttocks. An old general's trick. Judejahn went out into the passage. Men flattened themselves against the walls, dutiful shadows. He ignored them. He was going outside. A blood-red sun floated on the sandstorm. Judejahn inspected the front. The wind tore at his khaki uniform. Sand cut into flesh like shards of glass, and rattled against tanks like hailstones. The sight amused Judejahn. See the sons of the desert on parade! He looked them over and saw dark, moist, treacherous almond eyes, brown skin, burned faces, blackamoor countenances, Semitic noses. His men! His men were dead. They lay buried under grass, under snow, under rock and sand, they lay near the Arctic Circle, in France, in Italy, in Crete, in the Caucasus, and a few of them lay in boxes under the prison yard. His men! Now that meant these here. Judejahn had little appreciation of the irony of fate. He did the old troop-inspector's strut and looked firmly and severely into the moist, treacherous and dreamy almond eyes. Judejahn saw no reproach in those eyes. He saw no accusation. Judejahn had taken the animal gentleness from these men. He had taken their pride, the natural dignity of these male harem children. He had broken them by making them obey. He had planed them down, by the book. Now they stood in front of him, upright and braced like tin soldiers, and their souls were gone out of them. They were soldiers. They were troops. They were ready for action and expendable. Judejahn hadn't wasted his time. He hadn't disappointed his employers. Wherever he went was Grossdeutschland, where he was in command it was Prussia's old glory. The desert sand was no different from the sand of Brandenburg. Judejahn had been forced out, but he hadn't been uprooted; he carried Germany around with him in his heart, Germany still one day the saviour of the world. The flagstaff soared in the storm, it soared up alone toward the sand-occluded sun, it soared alone and tall into a godless void. Orders were given. Shouts ran through the ranks of soldiers like electric shocks. They stood up even straighter and stiffer as the flag climbed once more! What a majestic symbol of meaninglessness! The red morning star glowed on a green ground. Here you could still flog used goods, nationalism, fealty and hatred for the

Israelis, those perennially useful people through whom Judejahn had once more come to money, position and respect.

The dark suit wasn't right, either. It made Judejahn look like a chubby confirmand and it enraged him as he remembered how his father, the primary schoolteacher, had forced him to dress up like that and walk up to the altar of the Lord. That was in 1915 and he had had enough of school, he wanted to fight, only they wouldn't take little Gottlieb. But when he had his revenge on them, they gave him his leaving certificate in 1917, and he got a place on the officer training course, not the battlefield, but later there were bullets aplenty whistling round the ears of Judejahn, the Freikorps, Annaberg battles, Spartacist uprising, Kapp Putsch, Ruhrmaquis, and finally the assassination squad in the woods. That was his seed-time, his bohème (Youth, sweet youth, said the song), and he never got another. In Hitler's service Judejahn became respectable, he made it, he put on weight, he got fancy-sounding titles, he married and acquired a brother-in-law: that opportunist Kapp comrade-in-arms, camp follower and carpetbagger, the Oberpresident and Oberbürgermeister, the Führer's money man, denazified and now once again top dog, the old mayor reelected by the people, by strictly democratic procedures. That was his way of doing things, that was his brother-in-law Friedrich Wilhelm Pfaffrath, who in his opinion was an asshole, and to whom, in a weak moment, he had written a letter: they weren't to shed any tears over him, he had landed on his feet. And then he had agreed to this idiotic reunion in Rome. His brother-in-law wrote that he'd fix everything. Fix what? His return, his decriminalization, his pardon, and then a little job at the end of it? The man was a windbag. Did Judejahn even want to go home? Did he require a certificate of acquittal, the freedom of a pardon? He was free anyway, here was his shopping list to prove it. He had weapons to buy, tanks, guns, aeroplanes: leftover gear that was no longer suitable for the next global dust-up, but pretty handy for a little desert fighting, for use against palace coup or popular uprising. Judejahn was accredited with banks, he had powers of attorney. He was meeting arms dealers from two hemispheres. There were old pals to try to recruit. He was in play. He enjoyed it. What did family matter against that? Shitty lot. You had to tough it out. Eva had been faithful to him, a faithful German woman, the type of womanhood one said one lived and fought for; and sometimes one even believed it. He was afraid. He was afraid of Eva, her unmade-up face and her hair-knot, the SA woman, the believer in Final Victory: she was all right, certainly, but nothing drew him to her. Besides, she was probably spent. And his son? That rat. What was going on behind that weird dumbshow? The letters he got hinted at changes. He couldn't fathom them. He spread out a map of Rome in front of him, like a general-staff map. He had to go up the Via Ludovisi, then down the Spanish Steps, from whose height he could control the city with a single cannon, yes, and then to the Via Condotti, to the middle-class hotel where they were all staying, waiting for him. They had supposed he would be staying there too, in the German auberge, as the guide books called it, with its cosy atmosphere of back home. And Friedrich Wilhelm Pfaffrath, the sensible advocate of sensible and realistic national policies, Pfaffrath who had made a comeback, and maybe even thought he was the cleverer of the two, because he was back at the tiller, and was in position for a new career in the new Germany, brother-in-law Pfaffrath, Oberbürgermeister and respected West German citizen, had wanted to take him under his wing, him, the supposed fugitive. That was probably how he'd sketched it out, he wanted to hold the vagabond in his arms, with all his past misdeeds and evasions forgiven him. But Judejahn would tell him where he could stick it, he'd been through too much for this idyll to charm him: dead or presumed dead, the bombed-out Berliner, the man who went missing in the cleaning-up operation, condemned at Nuremberg *in contumaciam*. But the High Court that passed judgments on fate, human destiny and the blind actions of history, was itself reeling about in a maze of its own, was not a Justice with blindfolded eyes, just a silly woman playing blind man's bluff, who, since she administered justice where there was no justice, had herself sunk in the morass of events that were without moral. The High Court had no evidence as to whether Judejahn was alive or dead, and so the High Judge had carefully donned the black cap and condemned to death Judejahn, accused before all the world as a monster, in absentia, with the result that the accused man avoided the rope, which was as well because people in those days were far too quick to reach for it, and for the Court, ultimately, the fact that Judejahn escaped hanging was just as well because the monster Judejahn had been earmarked for reemployment, war being a dirty business. The Oberbürgermeister had probably gone to

Rome in his own car, he could probably run to a Mercedes again by now, or maybe the city had provided him with the vehicle for the scenic ride, Italy, land of longing, land of Germans, and Pfaffrath the German had his leather-bound Goethe on his shelves, and tax-commentaries well-thumbed next to the man from Weimar, a dubious type, what good ever came out of Weimar, and it irritated Judejahn having to imagine his brother-in-law with his snout in the trough again—it was treason, the fellow had committed base treason and should have swung for it. But Judejahn had a car at his disposal also, it wasn't that he had to walk, no, but he wanted to, he wanted to make the pilgrimage to bourgeois life on foot, that was appropriate here, appropriate in this city and this situation, he wanted to gain time, and Rome, they said, Rome where the bishops had settled and the streets crawled with surplices, Rome, they said, was a beautiful city, and now Judejahn was going to see it for himself. He hadn't been able to hitherto, he'd been here on duty, given orders here, gone on the rampage here. Now he could stroll through Rome, could pick up what the town had to offer by way of balmy air, historical sites, sophisticated whores and rich food. Why stint himself? He'd been in the desert a long time, and Rome was still standing, not in ruins. The eternal city, they called it. That was professors' and priests' talk. Judejahn showed his murderer's face. He knew better than that. He'd seen plenty of cities go under.

She waited. She waited by herself. No one helped her to wait, no one shortened the time by talking to her, and she didn't want the time to be shortened anyway or for them to concern themselves with her, because she alone was in mourning, she alone was distressed, and not even her sister Anna understood that Eva Judejahn was not weeping for lost possessions, or rank or respect, still less was it grief over Judejahn, whom she had seen as a hero entering Valhalla, that paled her countenance; she was grieving for Grossdeutschland, she was shedding tears for the Führer, lamenting the fact that treachery and betrayal and unnatural pacts had brought down the Germanic idea of world-salvation, the millennial Third Reich. The sound of laughter came up from the lobby through staircases and corridors, in at her window from the courtyard came the smell of cooking and an American dance tune sung by an Italian kitchen boy; but she wasn't reached by the laughter or the lively new nigger song embellished by bel canto, she stood in her widow's weeds in the stone cage of her room, madness, incomprehension and fleeting time, she stood wolf-throated, pregnant with vengeance, in the delirium of a myth she'd helped to concoct, prey to her innermost fears, her graying straw-blond hair, sheaf of wheat left to stand when the frightened farm hands fled at the approach of a thunderstorm, her hair tied in a stern womanly knot over the pale face, long-skulled face, square-chinned face, sorrow face, terror face, ravened, burned out, a death's head like the insignia Judejahn wore on his peaked cap. She was like a ghost, not a Eumenide, but a northerly ghost, a foggy ghost that a madman had brought to Rome and locked into a hotel room.

She was in a small room, the smallest one in the hotel, that had been her desire, for brother-in-law Friedrich Wilhelm, who wouldn't understand that it was she who had to remove the blot from the name of Germany, Friedrich Wilhelm had undertaken the journey for her sake, so Anna said too, and Friedrich Wilhelm Pfaffrath patted Eva Judejahn gently on the shoulder and said, "There, there, Eva, we'll get our Gottlieb back, just you see," and she shuddered and bit her lip because he had said Gottlieb, he'd never dared to do that before, and it was treason to call the standard-bearer, SS-general and one of the highest figures in the godless Party Gottlieb, because Judejahn hated the name, priestly slime left on him by the schoolmaster his father, and he didn't want to love God. Family and friends called him Götz, while officially and in public he was G. Judejahn, Götz was an abbreviation of Gottlieb dating from his wild Freikorps days, but Friedrich Wilhelm, the pedant and owner of the leather-bound edition of Goethe, had found Götz unworthy, though it was pithy and Germanic, but it also summoned up the famous lines in his mind,* and it was a borrowed, occupied name, one should just carry whatever name one was baptized with, and so, daring and flush with confidence, he again said Gottlieb, although he too found the name ridiculous and unmanly. Black-clad she walked. Walked clad in black from the window overlooking the courtyard to the mirror over the wash-basin, stalked like a caged beast in a cell. She had kept her mourning all through the years, except in the detention camp, because she'd been arrested in her

---

* "Er Aber, sags ihm, er kann mich im Arsch lecken"—Goethe, *Götz von Berlich-ingen,* act 3.—Transl.

traveling-clothes, but once she was released, she borrowed a black dress from her sister, because her own clothes had disappeared, her wardrobes looted, and the houses Judejahn had owned had been taken away from her. And when her husband got in touch, to the perplexity of the family she did not put aside her mourning, because she hadn't been mourning her husband, the hero missing in action, and the fact that he was alive only added to the reason for mourning, he would ask after their son, she had been unable to safeguard him, and maybe Judejahn himself had gone to Canossa and was living like a prince; she didn't mind him sleeping with other women, he had always done that and told her about it, that was part of a warrior's life, and when he made babies, then they were warrior babies and good stock, recruits for the storm troopers and the Führer, but it disturbed her that he had hidden away in the Levant. She guessed that he too had perpetrated treason, blood-treason and racial betrayal in the soft enemy climate, in rose-scented harem darkness, in garlic-reeking caves with Negresses and Jewesses, who had been waiting for revenge, and were panting for German sperm. Eva would have liked to raise an army to fetch these children, Judejahn's bastards, home: to put them to the test, and have them live as Germans or die as half-castes. The kitchen boy in the yard was whistling again, it was another nigger song, brash and cheeky and scornful, and the laughter in the lobby rolled up the stairs and along the corridor to her, plump, complacent, and sometimes cackling.

Oberbürgermeister Friedrich Wilhelm Pfaffrath was sitting with Anna his wife and Dietrich his younger son in the lounge of the German hotel, and already they had made contact with visiting compatriots, with Germans of similar background and outlook, fortunate survivors but with short memories like themselves. VW-owners, drivers of Mercedes, redeemed by German efficiency and now once more valued bringers of foreign currency, they were conversing and drinking sweet vermouth, and on the table were street maps and guidebooks, because they were planning expeditions to Tivoli and to Frascati, but also to the rebuilt monastery of Monte Cassino; they meant to visit the battlefields, which held no terrors for these people, and one of their number would look and find and shout, "This was our battery position, we were spitting down from here, here is where we were dug in, here is where we held the line." And then he would show what a fine fellow he was, hats off, because he admired himself as an upright warrior, a sporting killer, so to say, he would talk about Tommy Atkins and GI Joe, and maybe even about Anders and his Polish army, but only maybe because Polacks were still Polacks. And in the military cemetery they would pay tribute to themselves and the dead with exalted feeling all round. The dead didn't laugh, they were dead; or they had no time and didn't care who among the living came to see them, they were changing phases, they climbed out of life dirty and guilty, perhaps not even personally guilty, into the wheel of births to a new repentance, a new guilt, a new pointless incarnation. Friedrich Wilhelm Pfaffrath thought it rude of Judejahn to be late. But perhaps he wasn't yet in Rome, perhaps he had experienced difficulties getting there, trouble with a passport maybe, his case was sensitive and required careful handling. Things shouldn't be rushed, but Pfaffrath was convinced that the time had come, seeing as his brother-in-law had succeeded in staying alive, to lose the file on Judejahn, carefully, discreetly, without fuss—one might still be compromised, some unpatriotic type might squeal—but the time of hanging was definitely over, for them at least, the Americans had come to their senses, they now had a truer measure of German circumstances and German usefulness, and vengeful judgments and hatred were no longer wise or appropriate. Roosevelt was dead and suspected of communist collaboration. And who was Morgenthau? A nebbish! Anyone who'd survived up until now would survive in future. And maybe Judejahn could be found a job in the Agricultural Union, just to begin with, and Eva would snap out of her craziness, because, no question, he, Friedrich Wilhelm Pfaffrath, was a nationalist, but mistakes had been made, you had to own up to them and make a fresh start. Hunger had made Prussia great! And wouldn't that apply to the rest of the country too? They'd come on a lot already. Not in terms of hunger—that was a figure of speech, a fortifying legend from past times of pride and shortages—because hunger was just the rumbling of empty bellies after wars that had been lost through deceit, best not to think about that, but in terms of prosperity, that was real and tangible and worth pursuing. And might the new standard of living not finally convince the sons, the lost sheep of the break-up of Germany, those driven away by a happily brief period of chaos, to come home to the ancestral way of their people? The Federal Republic had its democratic weaknesses, certainly, and for the moment it was hard to do anything about them, but overall there was order in the occupied land, and everything was ready for a tighter rein. Soon they would be able to see a little further, prospects weren't bad, and Pfaffrath had the right kind of track record; but as far as the sons were concerned, their lack of common sense, their neuroses, the way they followed their so-called consciences, that was just a sign of the times, a sickness of the times, and in time it would be cured like an overlong puberty. Friedrich Wilhelm Pfaffrath had in mind less his nephew Adolf Judejahn than Siegfried, the elder of his two sons, who had left him, while with Dietrich, the younger, he was content: he was now a Goth, had joined his father's fraternity, had learned corps regulations, acquired connections, was approaching his final exams, and was looking forward to the visit to the battlefield at Monte Cassino, as was only right for a young person. But Siegfried was somehow degenerate. All right, if he had to—let him be a kapellmeister: there were well-paid jobs in music too. Friedrich Wilhelm Pfaffrath was a well-informed man, and it had come to his ears that Siegfried was in Rome. That seemed to him like a good omen for a possible clearing of the air and reconciliation. It wouldn't be easy, because Siegfried still seemed to be wading in a swamp, figuratively speaking, and the programme of the musical congress was full of surrealism, cultural Bolshevism and negroid newfangledness. Was the boy blind? But perhaps that was the way you made your name nowadays, now that the Jews were back in business internationally, dishing out fame and prize-money once again. Pfaffrath had also read somewhere that Kürenberg would be conducting Siegfried's symphony, and it came back to him. "Do you remember that Kürenberg," he asked his wife, "who was our General Musical Director in '34, and was all set to go on to Berlin?" "He married that Aufhäuser woman," replied Anna. "Yes," said Pfaffrath, "that's why he couldn't go to Berlin, and we weren't able to keep him, either." And Pfaffrath had the impression that at that time, before the gauleiters had acquired all power for themselves, when he was Oberpresident of the province, he had supported Kürenberg, and that pleased him now, because it suggested that in choosing to conduct and promote the work of the son, Kürenberg was gratefully acknowledging the help of the father.

But up in the cage of her room, Eva listened out for the avenger's footfall. Spinning out of the revolving door, the porter's hand, white-gloved lackey's hand, hangman's hand, death's hand had given the carousel of ingress and egress momentum, most respectfully, your humble servant, always at your service, sir, a tip for death, sir. Spun by his hand out of the revolving door, Judejahn felt he'd been thrown out of the hotel, out of the security of money and rank, out of the safety of power that stood behind him, borrowed power to be sure, foreign power, the power of another race even, dusky Levantine power, but nevertheless state power with suzerainty and its own flag—all at once he felt powerless. It was the first time in a very long time that Judejahn had stepped out, a man among men, a civilian, without protection, without an escort, without a weapon, a stout elderly fellow in a dark suit. It threw him the way no one paid him any attention. Passersby touched him, brushed past him, knocked into him and muttered a quick desultory "Pardon." Pardon for Judejahn? He took a couple of strides. No one was keeping a respectful distance. Judejahn could have gone back inside the hotel, he could have rung the diplomatic mission of his employers, and he would have been sent the automobile with the Arab license plates. Or he could have merely waved to the hotel porter, and the white-gloved and serviceable fellow would have whistled up a taxicab with his shrill little flute. Back then—how stiffly they had stood, his guard of honor! Two lines of black uniforms. Twenty outriders, a car in front of him, another behind him. But he wanted to walk. He probably hadn't walked through a city for thirty years. When Berlin was a glowing inferno, when the whole world was on Judejahn's heels, he had walked a little, had crawled through debris, climbed over bodies, romped through ruins and then he'd been rescued. How? Brought low by chance, or, as his Führer would have said, by fate, doused with petrol, burned to ashes, and then not finished after all, the Phoenix resurrected itself, fate had rescued Judejahn and led him to the Promised Land, not the land of Israel, but that of some other dusky tribe. And there Judejahn hadn't been on foot either, only on the exercise ground, taking a few steps in the desert.

He got a grip on himself of course, old dreadnought, and if he fell, here was a railing to hand. Wrought-iron palings rose like spears into the sky—a palisade of power, wealth and rejection. A large automobile slid across the gravel drive. Judejahn remembered. He too had driven up here, more sweep, more gravel crunch, but he had once driven up here. A sign informed him that he was standing in front of the United States Embassy. Of course, Judejahn hadn't been to see the Americans; they hadn't invited him, they hadn't even been there at the time. But he had, definitely, so there must have been something Fascist in the building, some big production, and they had failed to exercise the necessary rigor. What was the Duce? A sentimental indulgence on the part of the Führer. Judejahn had a particular loathing for Southerners. He approached the cafés on the Via Veneto, and there they all were, not just the despised Southerners, the whole international clique was sitting there, sitting together as they had once done on the Kurfürstendamm, sitting there playing peace on earth, cooing in each other's ears, the deracinated ones, international, homeless golden jetsam, flying, restless and greedy, from one city to another, snooty vultures, escapees from German order and discipline. Judejahn detected mainly English spoken, the American version predominated, they were the ones who had benefited from the war, but he also heard Italian, French and other sounds, occasionally German—not so much here, for they were off on their own patch, making themselves pleasant to one another. Scum, rabble, Jews and Jew-slaves! The words frothed in his mouth like gall, and coated his teeth. He beheld no uniforms, no insignia on chest or shoulders, he looked out into a world without distinction or honor; there were only the epaulettes on the monkey jackets worn by employees of the gastronomic trade. But hello, what was this formation, scarlet-red, advancing against the street of the exploiters, against the plutocratic boulevard? Was the scarlet column a symbol of authority, an emblem of power? Was it the golden horde, the Young Guard, the Giovinezza, coming to clean up? Alas, it was a bitter deception that had been practiced on Judejahn; they were surplices, drifting about the gaunt forms of young priests, and, far from marching, the red horde was walking in a disorderly rout, and to Judejahn it even appeared as though they had a swaying and effeminate walk, because it had escaped his notice, while in power, the manly and determined way priests faced death under a dictatorship, and fortunately he did not guess that the scarlet-robed ones were alumni of the German Seminary in

Rome—that would have disturbed him even more. Money governed the Via Veneto. But didn't Judejahn have money? Could he not throw his weight around and buy as others bought? Some chairs stood outside a bar, extraordinarily flimsy-looking yellow chairs, they were ridiculous, chairs not built to be sat on, they looked like a flock of crazy canaries, you could almost hear them twittering. And Judejahn felt drawn to this bar, because, for some reason, it was empty at this hour. He didn't take a seat outside, he scorned the perilous chairs, went into the gaping interior and stood by the bar. He propped his elbow on it, he felt weary, it must be the climate that was sapping his strength, and he ordered a beer. An effeminate fellow in a purple tailcoat indicated to him that if he wanted to drink his beer standing at the bar, he would have to buy a coupon for it first, from the cashier. Behind the cash-desk sat the smiling Laura. Her lovely smile was famed up and down the street, and the owner of the bar would not let her go because of this smile that shone in his bar, which gave it a friendlier atmosphere and made the cash-desk a font of joy, even though Laura was stupid and couldn't add. What did it matter? No one cheated Laura, because even the homosexuals who made up the clientele of the bar late at night and on Sunday afternoons felt graced by Laura's steady smile. Judejahn was struck by it too. But inhumanity made him blind, and so he failed to realize that here was a child-like creature who was giving her best for no return. He thought, Nice-looking cunt. He saw hair black as lacquer, a doll's face lit up by the smile, he saw her red lips and red fingernails, he wanted to buy her, and in this moneyed street you had to buy or be bought. But again he stood there helpless and foolish and didn't know how to behave, how to address her, he wasn't in uniform now, the girl showed no fear, merely beckoning wouldn't do it. He was ready to shell out a lot of money for her, and in lira any sum seemed enormous. But how should he talk to her? In German? She wouldn't understand. Judejahn spoke no Italian. He had picked up a little English. So he asked her in English, not for a beer, but for a large Scotch. Smiling automatically, Laura gave him his token and directed him automatically to the fellow in the purple tails. "A large King George." "Ice?" "No." "Soda?" "No." The conversation didn't develop. Judejahn drank his whisky down. He was angry. He could only give orders. He couldn't even say a couple of friendly words to a whore. Maybe she was a Jewess? You couldn't spot them so eas-

ily in Italy. But he was little Gottlieb again, the son of the primary schoolteacher, who couldn't keep up with his class. He
stood there, as he had once stood in one of his father's hand-
me-down suits among his richer classmates in their sailor suits.
Should he have another whisky? Whisky was a man's drink.
Great lords drank their Scotch in silence, became drunks and lost
the war. Judejahn decided against another whisky, though he
wanted one; he was afraid the barman and the beautiful girl behind the cash desk would laugh at him for being tongue-tied. But
how many times had the taciturn customer seen the laughter
freeze on the faces of others? That was the question! Judejahn
made a note of the bar. He thought, I'll get you, see if I don't.
And Laura expended her sweet smile on his broad back. Nothing
told her he was a killer. She thought (if she thought anything at
all, because thinking was not in her nature; instead she went in
for a kind of vegetative musing), Family man, here on business,
straight, chance client, showing off with those dark glasses. He
was bored here, he won't be back. And if he did come back, he
would come back on her account, and she would realize that it
was on her account, and she would like him in spite of the dark
glasses, because the homosexuals who came here in the evening
bored Laura, they put their trust in any man who smelled of
man, even if she had nothing against homosexuals, who, after
all, provided her with a living.

Now Judejahn's thoughts returned to his in-laws, who were
waiting to welcome their hero back from the dead. He took a
look at the street map which he had folded up and taken with
him. He quickly got his bearings, as he had learned to do: in forest, swamp and desert, he was incapable of getting lost. Nor
would he get lost now in the jungle of the city. He walked down
the Via di Porta Pinciana, parallel to a high old wall, behind
which he guessed was a large, beautiful shady garden, perhaps
belonging to one of the wealthy aristocrats, the royalist clique
that had betrayed the Duce. It was warm and there was a smell
of rain in the air. A puff of wind whirled up the dust and made
his skin tingle. There were posters stuck on the garden wall. The
next year's intake was being called up for military service. That
could only be of benefit to the weaklings. Uncle Sam would provide the weapons. But where were the German trainers? Without
German trainers, every dollar was wasted. Had Uncle Sam for-

gotten how to count? A red CP poster burned like a beacon. Judejahn thought of the night of the Reichstag fire. That was the
uprising! They had answered the call! The beginning of an era!
An era without Goethe! What did the Russian-Roman commune
want? Judejahn couldn't read the text. Why should he read it?
They should be put against the wall: up against this very wall
here. In Lichterfelde they'd been put against the wall. Judejahn
took a hand in the shooting, just for the hell of it. Who said all
men were brothers? Those weaklings with their demands! What
if there'd been an agreement with Moscow? There were no
weaklings in Moscow. If the two big, strong brothers had come
to an understanding, a wider, more sweeping Stalin-Hitler pact?
Judejahn's head hurt. Missed opportunities, or had they really
been conclusively missed, and "The World Will Be Ours" belted
out into a bright dawn. On Sunday there was some race, Rome–
Naples, Naples–Rome. Gladiatorial bouts for weak nerves.
What were their names, the fighter with the net and trident, and
the other one with the sword? Germans pitted against wild animals in the circus. Germans were too good-natured, they were
outwitted. There was a Church decree printed on white paper
with a black cross. The Church always won out in the end.
Priests were cunning and stayed on the sidelines. Let everyone
else exhaust one another. After wars, they built up their own
strength. Grave-robbers. Jesuit jujitsu. Green paper. *Olio Sasso.*
To grease the wheels. War? Mobilization? Not yet. Not for a
while yet. No one dared. Little rehearsals in deserts, jungles and
remote territories. As once in Spain.* The coyote beckoned from
the ground floor of a swanky apartment house. A coyote was a
prairie wolf; Judejahn remembered his Karl May.† In this instance, the Coyote was an American bar. There was plenty of
polished brass on the door, and it looked exclusive and expensive. Judejahn had money, but he wouldn't venture into the bar.
Judejahn was thirsty, but he wouldn't venture into the Coyote.
Why not? Little Gottlieb was in the way, and he wouldn't do
anything out of uniform. Judejahn went on. He came upon a *fi-*

---

*From 1936 to 1939, Republican Spain fought in vain against the fascist Fran-
cisco y Bahamonte (1892–1975), who was supplied by the NSDAP with weapons and specialists.
†Karl May (1842–1912) is a popular writer of adventure stories and books for
young people that are partly set in the Wild West.

aschetteria. Straw-wrapped bottles lay in heaps, the floor was awash with wine. This was where the common people drank. There was no cause to fear the common people. You could control them. There was no reason to talk to the common people. The people were gunfodder. The Führer stood over the people. Judejahn called for a Chianti. He gulped it down. The wine did him good. He ordered another glass. He didn't taste the wine, but he felt reinvigorated. He strode out, to the famous square in front of the Trinità dei Monti church. The church had two pointed towers. Nuns from the Sacrè Coeur cloisters stood on the church steps. Judejahn was revolted by their long skirts, their cloaks, their coifs. Witches! Now he had the Spanish Steps at his feet, and Rome, and in the background the mighty dome of St. Peter's—the old enemy. He wasn't beaten. No one was beaten. The game had been drawn—thanks to treachery: the Führer had held all the trumps, gnomes stole them from him, orders hadn't been carried out—only Judejahn had carried out every order he had been given. He had left no mess. Had he cleaned up everywhere? Unfortunately not. In fact, as it happened, nowhere. The hydra had more than nine heads. It had millions. One Judejahn was not enough. He returned from the war, no conqueror, a beggar, a nobody. He had to support himself on the parapet. His fingers gripped the crumbling masonry. Pain welled up inside him. Rome swam before his eyes, a sea of dissolving stone, and the dome of St. Peter's was a bubble adrift on the wild sea. An old lady with blue-rinsed hair pointed with her umbrella at the great panorama of the Eternal City. She called out, "Isn't it wonderful!" The left tower of Trinità dei Monti rang out its benediction.

He went down. He went down the Spanish Steps, climbed down into picturesque Italy, into the idling population that was sitting on the steps, lying, reading, studying, chatting, quarreling or embracing one another. A boy offered Judejahn some maize, yellow roasted kernels of maize. He held out a paper cornet to the foreigner, to the barbarian from the north, said *"cento lire"* in a wheedling voice, and Judejahn knocked the bag out of his hand. The maize scattered over the steps, and Judejahn trod it underfoot. He hadn't meant it. It was clumsiness. He felt like giving the boy a thrashing.

He crossed the square and reached the Via Condotti, panting. The pavement was narrow. People squeezed together in the busy shopping street, squeezed in front of the shop windows, squeezed past each other. Judejahn jostled and was jostled back. He didn't understand. He was surprised that no one made way for him, that no one got out of his road. He was surprised to find himself being jostled.

He looked for the cross street, looked for it on the map—but was he really looking? His years on the fringe of the desert seemed to him like time spent under anaesthetic, he had felt no pain, but now he felt sick, he felt fever and pain, felt the cuts that had pruned his life to a stump, felt the cuts that severed this stump from the wide flourishing of his power. What was he? A shadow of his former self. Should he rise from the dead, or remain a spook in the desert, a ghost in the Fatherland's color magazines? Judejahn was not afraid to keep the world at bay. What did it want with him, anyway? Let it come, let it come in all its softness and venality, all its dirty, buzzard lusts, concealed under the mask of respectability. The world should be glad there were fellows like himself. Judejahn wasn't afraid of the rope. He was afraid of living. He feared the absence of commands in which he was expected to live. He had issued any number: the higher he'd been promoted, the more he'd issued, and the responsibility had never bothered him; he merely said, "That's on my say-so," or "I'm in command here," but that had been a phrase, an intoxicating phrase, because in reality he had only ever followed orders himself. Judejahn had been mighty. He had tasted power, but in order to enjoy it, he required it to be limited, he required the Führer as an embodiment and visible god of power, the commander who was his excuse before the Creator, man and the Devil: I only did what I was told, I only obeyed orders. Did he have a conscience then? No, he was just afraid. He was afraid it might be discovered that he was little Gottlieb going around in boots too big for him. Judejahn heard a voice, not the voice of God nor the voice of conscience, it was the thin, hungry, self-improving voice of his father, the primary schoolteacher, whispering to him: You're a fool, you didn't do your homework, you're a bad pupil, a zero, an inflated zero. And so it was as well that he had stayed in the shadow of a greater being, stayed a satellite, the shining satellite of the most powerful celestial body, and even now he didn't realize that this sun from whom he had borrowed light and the license to kill had himself been nothing

but a cheat, another bad pupil, another little Gottlieb who happened to be the Devil's chosen tool, a magical zero, a chimera of
the people, a bubble that ultimately burst.

Judejahn felt a sudden craving to fill his belly. Even in his
Freikorps days he had had bouts of gluttony, and shoveled ladles
of peas from the field-kitchen down his throat. Now, at the corner of the street he was looking for, he scented food. A cheap
eating-place had various dishes on display in its windows, and
Judejahn went inside and ordered fried liver, which he had seen
in the window under a little sign, FRITTO SCELTO. And so now
Judejahn ordered the liver by asking for *fritto scelto,* but that
means "fried food on request," and so, at a loss what to do, they
brought him a plate of sea-creatures fried in oil and batter. He
gulped them down; they tasted like fried earthworms to him, and
he felt nauseated. He felt his heavy body turning into worms, he
felt his guts squirming with putrescence, and in order to fight off
his disintegration, and in spite of his nausea, he polished off everything on the plate. Then he drank a quarter-liter of wine, this
too, standing up, and then he was able to go on no more than a
few paces, and there was the German hotel where his in-laws
were staying. Cars bearing "D" licence plates stood in tidy ranks
outside the hotel. Judejahn saw the emblems of German recovery, the sleek metal of the German economic miracle. He was impressed. He was attracted. Should he go inside, click his heels
together and rap out, "At your service!"? They would receive
him with open arms. Would they? But there was also something
that repelled him about these shiny cars. Recovery, life going on,
going on fatly and prosperously after total war, total battle and
total defeat, it was betrayal, betrayal of the Führer's plans and
his vision for the future, it was disgraceful collaboration with the
archenemy in the West, who needed German blood and German
troops to ward off its former Eastern allies and sharers in the stolen victory. What to do? Already the lights were going on in the
hotel. One window after another was lit up, and behind one of
them Eva would be sitting and waiting. Her letters, with their
obscure turns of phrase that spoke of the disappointment that
awaited him, the degeneracy and the shame, allowed him no
hope of finding Adolf his son here. Was it worth going home?
The desert was still open to him. The net of the German bourgeoisie had not yet been thrown over the old warrior. Hesitant,

uncertain, he strode in through the door, came into the wood-paneled lobby, and there he saw German men, his brother-in-law, Friedrich Wilhelm Pfaffrath, was among them, he had hardly changed at all, and the German men stood facing one another in the German fashion; they were holding glasses in their hands, not mugs of German barley brew, but glasses of Italian swill, but then he Judejahn drank swill like that himself and God knows what else besides, no blame attached to that away from home. And these men, they were strong and stout, he could hear that, they were singing "A Fortress Sure," and then he felt himself being observed, not by the singers, he felt himself being observed from the doorway, it was a serious, a seeking, an imploring, a desperate look that was leveled at him.

It didn't shock him, but it did abash Siegfried to see the broad unmade bed, which drew his eye though he tried in vain to avert it, the broad bed, the marriage bed standing four-square in the spacious room, it was shameless and undeniable, without sensuality and without shame, cold, clean linen laid bare, and it bore witness coldly and cleanly to functions that no one wanted to disavow, to embraces of which no one was ashamed, to deep and healthy sleep

and all at once I realized that the Kürenbergs were ahead of me, they were the people I wanted to be, they were without sin, they were at once old-fashioned and new, they were antique and avant-garde, pre–Christian and post–Christian, Graeco-Roman citizens and airline passengers crossing the oceans, they were locked up in bodies, but in bodies that were well-explored and maintained: they were excursionists who had made themselves at home in a possibly inhospitable planet, and who took pleasure in the world as they found it.

Kürenberg was attuned to nomadism. In shirt sleeves and white linen trousers with a rubber apron tied over them, he was bustling about at a pair of extra tables the hotel had put at his disposal, and I was made to ask myself what special arrangements he had come to with the management, because they must have had new wiring put in for him, he had adaptors with three and four plugs in the sockets, and electric leads ran like intertwining snakes to gleaming electrical gear, grills, ovens, infrared cookers, steamers, pressure-cookers; it was the most comprehensive of mobile kitchens, which delighted him and went everywhere with him, and he was preparing the dinner to which he had invited me, he was mixing, tasting, beating and spicing, his face was firm and manly, it had a massive calm that did me good to look at, while Frau Kürenberg, having given me her hand and spoken a few welcoming words, "How do you like Rome? Is this the first time you've been here?," twittering swallows of small talk, low swooping flights, was laying the table, bustled about, went to the bathroom, leaving the door ajar behind her, rinsed glasses, put flowers in a vase, and left the wine to chill under running water.

I didn't want to stand around idly. I asked Kürenberg what I could do to help, and he gave me a bowl, a cheese-grater and a piece of Parmesan, and told me to grate it. At first the cheese merely crumbled away into the bowl in hard lumps, and Kürenberg showed me how it should be done, and then he asked me whether I hadn't ever helped my mother in the kitchen at home. I said no. And I remembered the great cold kitchen in our house, the floor tiles always damp and just washed; the boots of the uniformed messengers and the friends of the domestics were forever making new marks on the wet, gleaming tiled surface to the irritation of the servants, who always seemed to be flying off the handle, hectically noisy and hectically nervous. "Where are you from originally?" asked Kürenberg. I told him the name of the place, and I was going to add that nothing tied me to it any longer, nothing but the accident of my birth, when I noticed Kürenberg looking at me in surprise. And then he cried, "Ilse comes from the same town," and she, wiping glasses, now turned to me, with a look that went right through me. And I thought, She can see the old avenue, the avenue with the cafés and the trees which have burned down now, but the cafés have probably been reopened, and people are sitting in them again, under parasols maybe because the trees burned down, or they've planted new trees, fast-growing poplars, she can see that just as I see it, objectively but with some emotion as well; or does she not know the trees burned down? I wanted to ask her, but she bustled out again into the bathroom, and Kürenberg was making a sauce using an egg-whisk, but I noticed his thoughts were elsewhere, he was upset, and then he said, having looked across to the bathroom as though to check she wasn't too close by, "I was once the conductor there. They had a good orchestra, good singers, a fine hall." "It's in ruins," I said. "They play in the castle now." He nodded. The sauce was finished. He said: "There was an Oberpresident Pfaffrath. Are you any relation?" I said: "He's my father, but he's the bürgermeister now." He peered into a steaming pot and called, "Ilse, quick, the colander." And she brought the colander from the bathroom, a sturdy mesh, sturdy like herself, and he shook the rice out into the colander, leapt with it full of steaming rice across to the tub, poured cold water over it, shook it dry again, and hung the colander and rice in the steam rising from the saucepan, and said to me: "It's a Javan recipe, the rice cooks and stays crunchy." They had got around a lot, he had conducted orchestras all over the world, and they had settled into this life, they had no house, no permanent residence, they owned suitcases, fine, large suitcases, and lived in hotel rooms like the one I was standing in. And then I realized that I'd known Kürenberg for far longer than I'd thought, I remembered, of course I wasn't aware of it at the time, I was a child, I didn't understand what was going on, but now I saw it as though it was before my very eyes: I saw my father showing Kürenberg out, I was playing in the hall, and the way Father shut the door behind Kürenberg I could tell by his reddened face that he was angry and he told me off for playing in the hall, and he went in to Mother, and I followed him, because I didn't know where in the big house I was supposed to go, and I was curious as well, even though I knew he was in a bad mood, as he generally was when people came to him for help, they didn't seem to understand him in our town, because they often came to him for help, and it never even crossed his mind to intervene in lost causes. Not out of hatred, no, he wasn't twisted (he didn't like them, that was probably true enough), but he was afraid of them since they had been declared lepers. And most of all, even at that time, he feared Uncle Judejahn. And as though it were yesterday, I could hear him saying to Mother: "Our General Musical Director"—he always expressed himself in long-winded ways, and titles never failed to impress him—"paid me a call, and asked me to try to obtain the release of old Aufhäuser, his father-in-law. I urged him to be mindful of his career and apply for a divorce—" And then Father caught sight of me, and sent me out in a rage, and today I know that old Aufhäuser had just been arrested for the first time; it was the day of the first little anti-Jewish boycott, and it wasn't till later, the *Kristallnacht,* that Aufhäuser's store was set on fire. I got the day off at the Junker school and I saw it burning, the first building I saw burned down. And Aufhäuser was back in protective custody, and my Father sat at the head of the table, ladling out soup, he liked to play the patriarch occasionally, and Göring and Goebbels were spitting venom on the wireless, and my mother said: "I must say it's a shame about all the beautiful things that were lost to the flames." And old Aufhäuser was once again in protective custody, and later on I came across his library; it lay in disorderly heaps in the attic of the *Hitlerjugendheim,* somebody must have carted it off there and then forgotten all about it. Aufhäuser was a bibliophile, and I found first editions of the classics and Romantics, precious old German and Latin volumes, first editions of the Naturalists, of the Mann brothers, of the works of Hofmannsthal, Rilke, George, bound volumes of periodicals like *Blätter für die Kunst* and *Neue Rundschau,* the literature of World War I, the Expressionists up to Kafka. I helped myself, and later whatever was left was burned, was blown up by bombs along with the rest of the *Hitlerjugendheim,* and Aufhäuser, the captive in protective custody was murdered—and this was his daughter. Could I bear to look at her? Where were my thoughts running off to? My thoughts rebelled. They said: She's in pretty good shape, she must be forty and hardly a wrinkle on her. And my thoughts went on: The Aufhäusers were wealthy, wonder if she got compensation? And then: He didn't marry her money, it was too late for that, he did it to oppose evil. And then: They love each other, they've stayed together, they're still in love. And we went to the table, we sat down, Kürenberg served the food, she poured the wine. It must have been a delicious meal, the chef deserved my compliments, but I couldn't bring myself to do it, nothing had a taste—or rather, it tasted of ashes, dead ashes blowing on the wind. And I thought: She didn't see her father's store on fire. And I thought: She didn't see our houses burning down, either. And I thought: It's over over over, nothing can be done about it, nothing nothing, it's finished finished finished finished. There was fresh spinach, sautéed in fine oil, and over it we sprinkled the cheese I'd grated myself, and my steak was two fingers thick, as soft as butter, and blood ran out of the heart of it, and the wine was as cold and dry as a fresh spring, I was able to taste that still in spite of all the ash coating my tongue, we didn't speak during the meal, the Kürenbergs leaned over their plates and took their nourishment seriously, and once I said, "This is wonderful," but maybe I didn't say it loud enough, no one replied, and then there was a raspberry soufflé, flambéed, almost tropical and yet with the aroma of German forests, and Kürenberg said, "We'll get coffee brought up; there's nothing like a real espresso." Ilse Kürenberg ordered coffee over the hotel telephone; a bottle of cognac appeared on the table and we talked about Rome.

They love old Rome, antique Roman Rome, they love the fora with their battered grandeur, they love looking at the ancient hills in the evenings, the views of cypresses and solitary pines, they love the now functionless pillars, the marble staircases leading nowhere, the sundered arches over the filled-in chasms commemorating victories whose names figure in schoolbooks, they love the House of Augustus and they quote from Horace and Virgil, they adore the Rotunda of the Vestal Virgins, and they pray at the Temple of Fortune. I listen to them, speaking knowledgeably of new finds, discussing archaeological digs and museum treasures; and I love them too, love the old gods, love beauty long buried in the ground now visible once more, I love the proportions and the smooth cold stone skin of the old statuary, but still more I love Rome as it is now, alive and manifest to me, I love its skies, Jupiter's fathomless sea, and I imagine we're drowned, we're Vineta, and up on top of the element that washes around us are ships never seen by us, sailing on dazzling seas, and Death casts his invisible net over the city, I love the streets, the corners, the stairways, the quiet courtyards with urns, ivy and lares, and the raucous squares with daredevil Lambretta riders, I love the people sitting on their doorsteps of an evening, their jokes, their expressive gestures, their gift for comedy, their conversation which is lost on me, I love the bubbling fountains with their sea gods, nymphs and tritons, I love the children sitting on the marble edge of the fountains, those tumbling, garlanded, cruel little Neros, I love the bustle, friction, barging, and shouting and laughter and looks on the Corso, and the obscenities that are whispered to ladies in passing, and I love the stiff, empty larvae of the ladies' countenances, which the dirt helps to form, and I love their replies, their humiliation and their pleasure in these indecent tributes, which they bury underneath their street-masks in their real faces, and carry home with them and into their women's dreams, I love the gleaming affluent shop-fronts, the displays of the jewelers and the bird hats of the milliners, I love the snooty little communist on the Piazza della Rotonda, I love the long, shiny espresso bar with the hissing, steam-belching machine and the men sitting there, drinking hot strong bitter-sweet coffee from little cups, I love hearing Verdi's music booming out in the passage in front of the Piazza Colonna from the loudspeakers of the television studios and echoing back from the fin de siècle stucco facades, I love the Via Veneto, the cafés of Vanity Fair, with their funny chairs and colorful awnings, I love the leggy, slim-hipped models, their dyed hair the color of flame, their pale faces, their great staring eyes, fire that I can't touch, I love the happy, stupid athletic gigolos in attendance, traded by the wealthy corseted ladies, I love the dignified American senators who get audiences with the Pope and can buy anything they want, I love the gentle, white-haired automobile kings, who spend their fortunes on supporting science, art and literature, I love the homosexual poets in their tight drainpipe jeans and pointy thinsoled shoes, living off awards and shaking their jangling silver bracelets coquettishly back from the over-long cuffs of their shirts, I love the old mouldering bathing-ship anchored in front of the Castle of the Angels on the turbid Tiber, and its naked red light-bulbs in the night, I love the small, secret, incense-steeped, art- and ornament-crammed churches, even though Kürenberg finds baroque Rome disappointing, I love the priests in their robes of black, red, violet and white, the Latin Mass, the seminarians with fear in their faces, the old prebendaries in stained soutanes and beautiful greasy Monsignore hats with funny red cords round their waists and fear in their faces, the old women kneeling at confessionals with fear in their faces, the poor cracked hands of the beggars in front of the carved and worked portals of the chapels and their fear trembling like the vein in their throats, I love the little shopkeeper in the Street of the Workers, cutting great slices of mortadella like leaves, I love the little markets, the fruit-sellers' stalls all green red orange, the tubs of the fishmongers full of obscure sea-creatures and all the cats of Rome prowling along the walls and the two of them, two firm silhouettes, had stepped up to the window, the tall French window, and they looked down into the illuminated pit of the street below, and they looked across at other hotels like their own in many-storied stone buildings by the station, full of travelers, electrical signs flashed their temptations, and Rome was ready as ever to be conquered, and Kürenberg was thinking about Siegfried's music, the flow of feeling he wanted to tighten and compress and cool for this city tomorrow, and Ilse stood beside him and looked at the roofs of automobiles creeping along the bottom of the street like an armored column of cockroaches, she saw the brief, harmless flash of lightning in the wires over the electric trolley-buses, she saw through the convention of pretending death didn't exist, the unanimous agreement to deny terror, the ownership of the buildings she saw was set out in the land register, and even the Romans, well acquainted with ruin and the devastation of former splendor, believed in the everlastingness of this particular arrangement of stones on the old earth, she saw the mystery plays of trade, these also based on the delusions of eternity, inheritance and certainty, she saw the blooming and withering miracles of advertisements, whose colors had played on her own childhood too, quicksilver lights or dragon candles, and how simple-minded of her father it had been to put up a wall of books, music and art between her girlish life and the store, a false bastion, mild lamplight extinguished for ever. She shivered and thought how cold everything felt. It's late, she thought. And she thought: This young man has come from my home town and he writes symphonies, and his grandfather may have played the harpsichord or the flute, but his father killed my father, who collected books and loved listening to the Brandenburg Concertos. She took Kürenberg's hand, forced her own cold and inert hand into the fist of the conductor, which felt warm, dry, firm and dependable.

Kürenberg was still looking down into the street, thinking: One could tell their future. He had met analysts, sociologists, economic planners, atom-splitters, international lawyers, politicians and PR men. They were a devilish breed. The devilish breed made up his audience. They went to his concerts. He shut the window and asked Siegfried, "Do you remember Augustine's saying about music, that it was what great men gave themselves over to when their day's work was done, to refashion their souls?" Siegfried didn't remember. He hadn't read Augustine. He was an ignoramus. There was so much that he didn't know. He blushed. Are they great, the men I know? Kürenberg asked himself. And if they aren't, where are the truly great men? And do they have souls that can be refashioned by music in the evening? Did Augustine know great men? And did those whom he thought to be great men think him one? So many questions! Kürenberg had a high opinion of Siegfried's work. He looked to him for surprise, for a wholly new language. It might sound horrible to the generality which lagged behind the times; but it would carry a new message. A new message for the few who were capable of hearing it. Were those the great men Augustine had in mind? Man wants to know, even if knowledge makes him unhappy. Kürenberg smiled. But he spoke seriously: "I don't know who you compose for. But I believe your music has a purpose in the world. Ignorant people may whistle when they hear it. Don't let that put you off. Never try to satisfy people's wishes. Disappoint the season-ticket holder. But disappoint him with humility, not with arrogance. I'm not advising you to climb the ivory tower. For heaven's sake, don't live for your art! Go out on the street. Listen. Remain alone. You're lucky to be lonely. When you're on the street, stay as lonely as you might be in the isolation of a lab. Experiment with everything, all the splendor and grime of our world, with humiliation and greatness—maybe you'll find a new sound!"

And Siegfried thought of voices, of the voices of the street, he thought of the voices of vulgarity, of fear, of torment, of greed, of love, goodness and prayer, he thought of the sound of evil, the whisper of unchastity and the shout of crime. And he thought: Tomorrow he will humble me, come to me with his laws of harmony and his schoolmasterly strictness, celebrated *chef d'orchestre* that he is, an exact reader of a score, a gardener with pruning shears, while I'm all weeds and wilderness. And Kürenberg said, as though he read Siegfried's mind: "I believe in our collaboration. There are contradictions in me and in you that don't contradict each other." And the life into which they had been pitched was contradictory, and they contradicted their kind.

Judejahn had felt himself under observation, and had withdrawn. He retreated, with his angular skull between his hunched shoulders—retreat or tactical withdrawal, the way a patrol between the lines in no man's land retreats or withdraws when they feel they've been spotted; no shots are fired, no flares light the night sky, fate hangs in the balance, but they withdraw, creep back through barbed wire and vegetation, back to their own position, and conclude for the moment that the enemy position is impregnable. And the murderer too, the hunted criminal, presses back into the shadows, the jungle, the city, when he senses the bloodhounds are near by, when he knows he's in the policeman's field of vision. Likewise the sinner flees the eye of the Lord. But what of the godless man who doesn't know himself to be a sinner, where does he turn? Straight past God, and into the desert! Judejahn didn't know who was watching him. He saw no spies. There was only a priest in the lobby—Rome was crawling with religious brethren—standing strangely transfixed and staring like Judejahn through the glazed double door at the animated company sitting at the table, drinking and talking. It was a German *Stammtisch,* a table established in the German way but transported provisionally to a southern latitude; and, objectively speaking, there was only the wood and glass of the double door to separate Judejahn and his brother-in-law, Friedrich Wilhelm Pfaffrath, but he had remained seated: whether he was holding forth here or in front of the town council at home, he had remained seated, whereas Judejahn had strode boldly on, boldly and blindly on with the watchword that God is dead. He had gone further than the burghers in the hall, but it was they who had made it possible for him to go so far. They had underwritten his wanderings with their lives. They had invoked blood, they had summoned him, exhorted him, the world will be won by the sword, they had made speeches, there was no death to compare with death in battle, they had given him his first uniform, and had cowered before the new uniform he had made for himself, they had praised his every action, they had held him up as an example to their children, they had summoned the "Reich" into being, and endured death and injury and the smoke from burning bodies all for the sake of Germany. But they themselves had remained seated at their table in the old German beer hall, German slogans on their garrulous tongues. Nietzsche clichés in their brains, and even the Führer's words and the Rosenberg myth* had only been exhilarating clichés for them, while for Judejahn they had been a call to arms: he had set out, little Gottlieb wanted to change the world, well well, so he was a revolutionary, and yet he detested revolutionaries and had them flogged and hanged. He was stupid, a dim little Gottlieb, worshipping punishment, little Gottlieb afraid of a beating and desiring to beat, powerless little Gottlieb, who had gone on a pilgrimage to power, and when he had reached it and had seen it face to face, what had he seen? Death. Power was Death. Death was the true Almighty. Judejahn had accepted it, he wasn't frightened, even little Gottlieb had guessed that there was only this one power, the power of death, and only one exercise of power, which was killing. There is no resurrection. Judejahn had served Death. He had fed plentiful Death. That set him apart from the burghers, the Italian holiday-makers, the battlefield tourists; they had nothing, they had nothing except that nothing, they sat fatly in the midst of nothing, they got ahead in nothing, until finally they perished in nothing and became part of it, as they always had been. But he, Judejahn, he had his Death and he clung to it, only the priest might try to steal it from him. But Judejahn wasn't about to be robbed. Priests might be murdered. Who was the fellow in the black frock? A pimply face, a haggard youth seething with lust under the womanish robes. The priest too was looking at the assembly in the lobby, and he too seemed to be repulsed by it. But he was no ally for Judejahn. Judejahn was equally revolted by the priest and the burghers. He recognized that the burghers' position was impregnable for today. But time was in Judejahn's favor, and so he would return to the desert, drill recruits for Death, and one day, when battlefields were more than tourist attractions, then Judejahn would be on the march again.

He fled the hotel. He fled the sight of the burghers, the priest, fled the eye of the unseen spy. It wasn't cowardice, it wasn't disgrace, it was a tactical withdrawal. If Judejahn had set foot in the lobby, if Judejahn had shown his face among them, the burghers would have leapt up, they would have clustered round him, but it would have been for an evening of hero-worship, and then they would have cast their bourgeois net over him. Eva might be lurking at one of the lit-up windows—a mother and a heroine,

---

*A reference to *The Myth of the 20th Century* (1930) by Alfred Rosenberg.

why hadn't she died that May of shame? But she was still alive; and Judejahn could imagine sitting with her in a German lounge, going to the job that Pfaffrath would fix up for him, coming home from the job that Pfaffrath had fixed up for him; they would eat roast goose and drink Rhine wine, presumably brother-in-law Pfaffrath's job would run to that, and on the Führer's birthday and on the ninth of November* Eva would wear the brooch on her dress—so long as it hadn't been stolen, the occupying forces were after souvenirs and valuables, Judejahn knew that—the golden swastika brooch, a present from the Führer, and she would stare at him when the news came on the radio, and Heuss spoke, and Adenauer spoke, when their neighbors played nigger songs, and she would stare and think: You're alive you're alive you're alive. And he would be alive and think of the desert, the desert from which he would reconquer Germany. He dropped into a cookshop somewhere on his way, which was now aimless, he entered a miasma of oil and batter and sea smells, he went up to the buffet, he could have wolfed the lot down, he was racked by an incredible hunger. There were some large white beans, a German dish, a dish from his schooldays and his childhood. He pointed to it, but the beans were not warm, they were not German, they were slick with oil, tart with vinegar, and they had a fishy taste as well, because what he had taken to be meat was blubbery fish; but he wolfed it all down, and then an order of pasta to follow, regular Italian-style noodles, the tomato sauce rimmed his mouth in a slobbery wet kiss, spaghetti dangled from his lips, they'd forgotten to bring him a knife, and he sucked them into his mouth like a cow eating long grass, and it took another half liter of Chianti to cleanse Judejahn and make him human again. Or so he thought.

The human reached the Piazza San Silvestro through a maze of alleys. He saw the electric sign announcing the telephone exchange. That suited his purpose. He went inside, saw the booths with telephones in them, didn't know how to use them, he wrote down the name of the Pfaffraths' hotel on a piece of paper, gave it to a girl at the counter, who looked up the number for him in a directory and sold him a telephone coupon, then he stood in one of the booths, dialed the number, he heard "Pronto," and

---

*A reference to Hitler's 1923 putsch.

he spoke German into the mouthpiece, said he wanted Pfaffrath, heard clicks and whirring and footsteps, and then Pfaffrath was there on the line, replying in the correct official style, aware of his rank. "Oberbürgermeister Pfaffrath here. Who's calling, please?" And Judejahn felt like shouting back, "Hello, you asshole!" Or should he rasp out his own titles, his military and party rank, or even the florid Arabian one he now held? Should he describe himself as Chief Eunuch or Harem Administrator or Desert Fox, or squeak out "Gottlieb here"? And he was such a shrunken little Gottlieb that he didn't reach up to the mouthpiece and he merely said "Judejahn," but he spoke the name with such emphasis that power, violence and death resonated down the line. Now it was Pfaffrath's turn to clear his throat, to change down from Oberbürgermeister to brother-in-law, presumably also getting over his terror on hearing the voice of the dear departed, pride and scourge of the family, whichever, whose resurrection he was awaiting; it probably took him a while to muster courage to confront Judejahn. And he said excitedly, "Where are you? We've been waiting for you." And Judejahn coolly replied that he had plenty to do and little time, and he summoned them to his own hotel for the following day, the splendid palace on the Via Veneto, there they would see Judejahn in all his glory, and he told him his assumed name, his cover name and passport name, ordered him, in the small booth—the Italian scribbles on whose walls were presumably smut as in any other booth, and Judejahn wondered whether the latrines at home had "Germany awaken" written in them again—ordered him to "repeat the name," and Oberbürgermeister Friedrich Wilhelm Pfaffrath duly repeated the false name, the official lie: he wouldn't appear before Judejahn as his benefactor any more, he would stand at attention, and Judejahn's creeping away from the German hotel had been no flight, his sneaking away had been a tactical masterstroke.

And once again the human being felt on top of things, in charge of his destiny. He left the telephone exchange in triumph. He was crossing the Piazza San Silvestro, on his way to conquer Rome, when there was a sound of breakage, a hullabaloo as of battle, a crashing and sundering, screams of terror and cries of death. It was a new building that had collapsed, its foundations had been miscalculated, twisted girders protruded from clouds of dust, people ran by in panic, and Judejahn commanded: "Seal

it off, keep back, seal it off." He wanted to bring a little discipline to the accident, but no one listened to his German voice, no
one understood him, and then came the sirens and bells, police,
ambulance and fire brigade, and from the church on the square
came a priest, they stuck their noses in everywhere, and Judejahn
saw that he was out of place here and in the way, useless at best,
and he stepped aside, barged his way through the crowd, and
then he remembered how at school, in his detested Gymnasium,
he had learned about the Roman belief in omens, and this here
was a bad portent. There were the wailing cries of a woman.
Had she lost loved ones in the ruins? The sacrifices that Judejahn
had offered to Death 'had never cried. It was odd, he had never
heard any of them cry.

So he drifted away down the Corso, a long intestine stuffed
with pedestrians and vehicles. Like microbes, like worms, like di-
gestion and metabolism, they proceeded down the intestinal
canal of the city. The weight of traffic was pushing Judejahn
toward the Piazza del Popolo, but he felt that was the wrong way
for him, and he turned back against the current, was jabbed and
barged, but when he turned round and looked, he saw it gleaming, white and gold and illuminated by spotlights, and now he
remembered, this was where he had driven up, the escort ahead,
motorcycle outriders to either side, and a long line of vehicles
behind him containing Germans and Italians, top officials, digni-
taries from the Party and the armed services. He pushed ahead,
backward, he had lost all sense of time and direction, the present
became the past, but he kept his goal firmly in sight, the marble
steps, the megalith, the white monument on the Piazza Venezia,
the national memorial to Victor Emmanuel II, which, through
some confusion or false information, Judejahn was convinced
was the Capitol and moreover that it was a building of Mussolini's, a monument erected by the Duce, in honor of history, to
crown the antique sites, and this was the white-and-gold-gleam-
ing annunciation of the resurrection of the imperium. This was
where he had driven up. Now he hurried toward it. Here on the
right was the Duce's palace. No sentries? No sentries. In the
shadow of night the walls were a grimy yellow. No one stood at
the gate. No window was lit up. This was where he had driven
up. A former visitor returning. Knock, knock on the door—the
master of the house is dead. The heirs don't know you—they are

among the bustling crowds on the Corso. Yes, he had crossed the square with the Duce, it had been Judejahn at his side, to lay the Führer's wreath at the Tomb of the Unknown Soldier. There were the sentries, feet apart, stiff and unflinching. Their posture was impeccable. But Judejahn felt nothing—no honor, no pride, no sorrow, no emotion. He was like a worshipper who feels nothing in church. He prays and God isn't there. He kneels down and thinks: The ground is cold and dirty. He sees the Virgin and he thinks: A piece of worm-eaten wood with paint on it. The people were not rejoicing. No singing, no huzzahs. Mopeds rattled past. No photographers appeared to bathe Judejahn in flashlights. A couple of tired carriage horses looked across at him from the cab-rank. Was he a ghost? He hurried up the marble steps. Behind him now were the columns of the magnificent temple which he wrongly attributed to Mussolini, and all that white splendor reminded him of something: it was a cake in the window of Süfke the baker, a cake that little Gottlieb had been fascinated by and never got to taste. And before him now was the black rump of the king's horse, Judejahn didn't know which iron-clad king it was, and he didn't care, he had never had any regard for the kings of Italy, from childhood up, influenced by the comic books of World War I, he had thought of them as wielding umbrellas rather than swords. But as he stood there, he or little Gottlieb, he had a sense of grandeur, he thought of the Duce who had built all this and had himself been desecrated, and he felt the grandeur of the history that had had such monuments built to it, behind which stood Death, the ultimate inspiration. Judejahn was bathed in light. Rome glowed. But it seemed to him a dead city, ready for the chop, the Duce had been desecrated, history had turned its back on Rome, and so had ennobling Death. Now people lived here, they dared simply to live here, they lived for business or for pleasure—what could be worse. Judejahn looked at the city. It seemed to him to be absolutely dead.

Late at night the Via del Lavatore is a dead street. The market stalls have been tidied away, and the shutters in front of the little eating-places, gray or green with age, blind the facades of the buildings the way gray or green cataracts blind the aged eye. In the little dead-end side-streets are the simple wine-shops of the people of the area, who live in small, high-ceilinged rooms in many-storeyed tenements. They sit on benches and stools at plain uncovered tables stained by leftovers and spilled wine, and order their half-liter of red or their half-liter of white, *dolce* or *secco,* and those who are hungry bring food with them wrapped in paper or in terra-cotta dishes, and spread it out before them on the tables, quite unabashed. Visitors are a rare sight in this part of town. Still, Siegfried is sitting outside one of these bars in the pallid artificial moon of a white lantern. A man is busying himself at his table, working an onion into a salad. Siegfried dislikes the taste of raw onions, but the man peels and chops with such gusto at the young green bulb, he anoints it with oil and vinegar and salt and pepper, he breaks his bread so reverently, that Siegfried is impelled to wish him *"Buon appetito."* This pleases the man, who promptly offers him his wine to try. Siegfried is appalled by the thought of the man's glass, and the oily and spirituous contact the man's oniony mouth has already made with it, but he overcomes his disgust and tastes it anyway. Then Siegfried offers the man some of his own wine. They drink and talk. Or rather, the man talks. He talks in long, intricate and ornate sentences whose meaning is lost on Siegfried, who has only mastered one or two expressions from phrase-books. But precisely because he doesn't understand the man, he is glad to spend time in his company. For a moment Siegfried is happy, and the two men sit together like old friends, one of whom has a lot to talk about, while the other listens to him or lets his attention stray, listening instead to some ghostly voice he doesn't understand either, but which, for the moment, he thinks he does. When the man has finished his onion, he sops up the last of the oil with his piece of bread. He gives the saturated bread to a cat which has been watching him imploringly for some time. The cat thanks him, and takes the bread under an arch; that's where her babies are. Siegfried bids *"Felice notte."* He bows. He wishes a happy night to the man, the bar, the cat and her young. Perhaps he wishes himself a happy night also. This late hour of the evening finds him content. Now he goes into the bar to buy himself a bottle for the night. Perhaps he won't be able to sleep. If you can't sleep, it's a good thing to have some wine in the house. It occurs to Siegfried to buy a second bottle of wine. He would give it to the man he was talking to just now. Siegfried thinks the man is poor. Maybe the present will please him. But Siegfried is afraid of insulting the man if he really is poor. He doesn't buy another bottle. As he goes out, he bows once more to his table-companion. Another *"Felice notte."* Did he do the right thing, though? Why did he feel awkward about his kind thought? He doesn't know. He's full of doubt again. It's difficult to do the right thing. His contentment has deserted him. He's no longer happy.

Siegfried's steps echo in the Via del Lavatore in the quiet of the night. His shadow runs ahead of him, his shadow merges with him, his shadow pursues him. Shortly, Siegfried is surprised by the noise and the gurgling of the Piazza di Trevi. Hordes of visitors are standing around the miraculous fountains and talking in a babel of different languages. Tour groups are industrious and offer night-classes in cultural history and ethnography. Photographers flash and click away: I was in Rome, you know. Haggard Roman youth leans over the edge of the fountain, and uses long poles to fish out the coins that the visitors threw in out of superstition, gullibility or just for fun. The tour guide says a person will return to Rome if he leaves money in the fountain. Does the visitor want to come again, does he want to return, is he afraid of dying in his own joyless country, does he want to be buried in Rome? Siegfried would like to return, he would like to stay. He won't stay, he throws no coins in the fountain. He doesn't want to die. He doesn't want to die at home. Would he like to be buried here? His hotel is close by the fountain. He can see its narrow, crooked facade reflected in the water. Siegfried goes inside. He walks through the porch. Alone

the old man behind the porch was cold. He shivered at his reception desk in the draughty entrance hall, in front of the board where the keys hang. He wore felt slippers on account of the stone floors, he had a coat thrown over his shoulders in the manner of an old veteran, he covered his small bald head with a black floppy hat in the manner of an old professor, he looked like an emigré, like an exiled liberal politician from liberal times, but he was only the manager of this little hotel. He was born an Austrian and would die an Italian, soon, in a few years, and it didn't matter to him whether he died as an Italian or an Austrian. Sometimes we would talk, and now, on my return, he greeted me with some agitation: "A priest is waiting for you!" "A priest?" I asked. And he said, "Yes, he's waiting up in your room." And I thought: There must be some mistake, and at this hour of the night. I climbed up the stairs, the stairs of the old hotel, little hollows had been worn in the stone steps, the walls were buckling, the floor on my storey was uneven. I made my way up an incline to the badly fitting door of my room. No light shone through the broad cracks in the weathered door, and I thought once more: A mistake. I opened the door, and there I saw him standing by the window in front of me, a tall, black silhouette, truly a priest, in the light of the spotlights that were still being beamed at the Trevi Fountain, its wild and fabulous creatures, its baroque, fleshy Olympus and its waters, roaring and lulling like the sea. He looked tall and gaunt. His face was pale, but perhaps that was just the spotlights. I turned on the light in the room, the naked bulb hanging over the broad bed, the *letto grande* of the hotel industry, the *letto matrimoniale,* the marriage bed that had been leased out to me, to me alone, for me to lie on, naked, bare, chaste or unchaste, alone, the bare naked light bulb over me, alone or with flies buzzing around it, and the rushing of the fountain and the babel of voices from all over the world, so they say, and he, the priest, now turned to me with a timid gesture of welcome, he raised and spread his arms, a movement which evoked the pulpit, and he was wearing a cassock, and then straight away he dropped his arms again, as though ashamed of the gesture, and his hands scuttled into the folds of his black garment like two shy reddish beasts. "Siegfried!" he called out. And then he spoke hurriedly, falling over himself. "I found out where you were staying, please excuse me. I don't mean to disturb you. I'm sure I'm disturbing you, and if I am I should leave right away."

Standing in front of me, tall and gaunt, confused and in clerical robes was Adolf, Adolf Judejahn, the son of my once so mighty and terrifying uncle, and I remembered the last time I had seen Adolf, in the Teutonic castle. He was small, younger than me, a poor little soldier in the Junker school uniform, in the long black army trousers with red stripes, little Adolf in the brown Party jacket, little Adolf under the black cap, worn at an angle over the regulation cropped and parted hair. I had run around like that myself, and I had loathed it, having to dress like a soldier or an official, and maybe he had hated the get-up as well, but I didn't know that, I never asked him whether he hated the

Castle, the service, the soldiers and officials; I thought of Uncle
Judejahn and I didn't trust Adolf, I kept out of his way, and I
even thought he was like my brother Dietrich, that he enjoyed
going around in uniform or took advantage of it and had his eye
on promotion, and for that reason I was amused to see him
dressed now in the garb of a priest, and I thought about the dis-
guises we liked to appear in, sad clowns in a mediocre farce. I
saw him standing there and I told him to sit down. I pushed the
rickety old hotel chair toward him, swept the books and newspapers and manuscripts aside on the marble-top dresser, I found
the corkscrew in the drawer, opened the bottle of wine I'd
brought with me and rinsed the tooth-mug in the wash-basin. I
thought: Judejahn has disappeared, Judejahn's copped it, Judejahn's dead. And I thought: Pity that Uncle Judejahn can't see his
son now; pity he can't see him sitting on my rickety chair; such
a pity, I think he would have had a fit, and that's something I'd
like to see even today. Was I exaggerating? Was I giving him
more significance than he really had? I poured the wine and said:
"You drink first. We'll have to share a glass. I've only got one."
And he said: "I don't drink." And I: "But as a priest, surely
you're allowed to drink a glass of wine. That's not a sin." And
he: "It's not a sin. But thanks, anyway. I don't want any." And
after a while he went on, "I'm not a priest yet. I'm still only a
deacon." I drank the wine, refilled the glass, and took it across
to the broad bed. I lay there on the broad bed, and it was like a
hint that my life was unchaste, which wasn't the case as far as
this room was concerned, and I don't know what unchastity is,
or rather I do, but I don't want to know, and I leaned back,
rested my head on the pillow, and I asked him: "What's the difference?" And he said: "I'm allowed to baptize." And then, as if
having given the question further thought: "I'm not allowed to
celebrate Mass yet. I have no power of absolution. I can't forgive
sins. Only when the bishop has ordained me am I allowed to forgive sins." "That'll keep you busy," I said, and then I was annoyed with myself for having said it. It was stupid and unfunny
and crude, and actually I like priests. I like priests I don't know.
I like priests from a safe distance. I like priests speaking Latin,
because then I don't understand them. I don't understand them,
but I like it when they speak in Latin, I like the sound of it. If I
could understand what they were saying, I wouldn't like listen-

ing to them so much. Maybe I do understand them, just a little. Or maybe I only think I understand them a little, and I like that, because in fact I don't understand them at all. Maybe I even misunderstand them, but misunderstanding them wouldn't matter, because if they're right and there is a God, then He will see to it that I take the right sense from their words, even if they are not the sense His servants mean to convey. If I could understand the words of priests as they were meant, I wouldn't like them. I'm sure priests can be just as stupid and obstinate and opinionated as the next man. They invoke God in order to rule. When Judejahn ruled, he invoked Hitler and Destiny. And Adolf? Whom did he invoke? I looked at him. He looked at me. We didn't speak. The tourists, no pilgrims, spoke in their babel. Time flowed with the water in the fountain. That was outside. There were flies buzzing inside. Buzz. Dirty flies.

There might be rats nesting in the cellar, but Judejahn felt drawn to it, he felt drawn down off the wide and monotonous Via Nazionale, down into this cellar, down the damp, dirty stone steps, gluttony drove him, thirst drove him, he was lured by a sign GERMAN COOKING, by a sign PILSNER BEER, German food for a German man, Pilsen was a German town, it had been cravenly surrendered, Pilsen was a Czech town, it had been lost through betrayal, the Skoda works were important for the war effort, beer was important for the war effort, gallows were important, conspiracy, subhumans, rats, foreign workers, danger spotted and averted by the Reich Security Office. Comrade Heydrich had taken action, Comrade Heydrich, who was like a twin to him, was dead—Judejahn survived. Always the same reproach. The voice reproaching him was Eva's. And he thought, Why is she alive, why did she survive? Thinking wasn't his business. Thinking was quicksand, dangerous, forbidden territory. Writers thought. Cultural Bolshevists thought. Jews thought. The pistol thought more rigorously. Judejahn had no weapon on his person. He felt unarmed. What was the matter with him? Why didn't he go out to a good restaurant, in good clothes, with a valid passport and plenty of money, and fill his belly, fill it the way the Jews were doing again, with *pâté de foie,* with mayonnaise, with tender plump capons, and then go on to a nightclub, well-dressed, moneyed, drink a skinful and pick up something

for the night? He could be well-dressed, well-accoutred, randy as
the Jews. He could compete, he could make demands. So why
didn't he? Guzzling, boozing and whoring, that was the Landsk-
nechts' way, that was the way their song went: he had sung it in
the Freikorps, they had sung it round the camp fire with Rossbach, in the Black Reichswehr camp they had bellowed it out, in
the killing grounds. Judejahn was a Landsknecht, he was the last
surviving Landsknecht, he whistled the tune in the desert, he
wanted to guzzle and booze and whore, that was what he felt
like doing, something was pinching his balls. Why didn't he take
what he wanted? Why the cookshops, the poky bars, why this
cellar? He was drawn to it. It was a fateful day. There was paralysis in the ancient air of the city, paralysis and catastrophe. It
was as though no one in this city could manage a fuck any more.
It was as though the priests had cut the balls off the city. He went
down, Pilsener beer, he descended into the Underworld, Czech
rats, barrels of Pilsener, he came upon a stone cellar, extensive
and vaulted, a few tables, a few chairs, a bar at the back, rusty
oxidizing beer-taps, beer-slops like vomit on the aluminum surface. There were two fellows sitting at a table, playing cards.
They looked at Judejahn. They grinned. It was an evil grin. They
greeted him: "You're not from this part of the world!" They
spoke German. He sat down. "Hummel Hummel,"* said one of
them. The waiter came. "A Pils," said Judejahn. The men
grinned. With the waiter they spoke Italian. The waiter grinned.
The men called Judejahn "Comrade." One referred to the other
as "My buddy." Judejahn felt at ease. He knew their sort: gallows birds, desperadoes. Their faces were like faces in a morgue,
ravaged by some horrible disease. The beer arrived. It tasted metallic. It tasted like fizzy lemonade mixed with poison, but at
least it was cold. The glasses were frosted. The men raised their
frosted glasses with the poisonous-tasting beer and drank to Judejahn. They were the right stuff. Under the table they kept their
knees and heels clenched together, and their buttocks. Judejahn
did too. He had always been the stuff. The waiter brought food.
The men must have ordered it. Fried onions sizzled on large meat
patties. They ate. They stuffed themselves. The men liked the onions. Judejahn liked the onions. They got acquainted. "It tastes

---

*A Hamburg greeting.—Transl.

just like home," one of them said. "Crap!" said the other. "It's
like Barras's. Barras was the only place I got decent grub."
"Where did you serve?" asked Judejahn. They grinned. "Take
off your glasses," they said, "you're no spring chicken youself."
Judejahn took off his glasses. He looked at the pair of them.
They were his true sons. He wanted to drill them. If he drilled
them, they'd be useful. He thought: Pair of hard bastards.
"Don't I know you?" asked one of them. "I'm sure I've seen you
somewhere. Well, never mind." What difference did it make?
They gave the name of a unit. Judejahn knew them well, a notorious outfit, trouble, heroes that went in where the Wehrmacht
feared to tread. They'd wasted a lot of people. They were under
Judejahn's general command. They had solved some of the Führer's population problems for him. They had committed geno-
cide. Judejahn asked after their commanding officer, a sharp
fellow, a real animal. They grinned at him. One of them traced a
noose in the air, and pulled it tight. "In Warsaw," said the other.
Hadn't Warsaw been taken, hadn't Paris been taken, wasn't
Rome occupied? "What are you doing now?" asked Judejahn.
"Oh, driving around," they said. "Since when?" "Long time."
"Where you from?" "Vienna." They were no Germans, they
were Eastern-mixed race, Austrian SS, they'd slipped through all
the controls. Judejahn eyed them the way a cobra eyes a toad,
and they thought he was just a big bullfrog. But he also looked
at them with the calculation and benevolence of a snake-breeder,
with the calculation and benevolence of a reptile-house keeper,
supplying reptiles to labs for poison and vivisection. Judejahn
sent men and boys to the bloody, stinking labs of history, he sent
them to the testing ground of Death. Should he tell them who he
was? Should he recruit them for the desert? He wasn't afraid of
giving them his name; but having eaten and drunk with them, his
rank forbade him to give himself away. The murderer-in-chief
doesn't sit at the same table as his henchmen: that wasn't the officers' mess ethos. They said, "We've got a car." They said they'd
"organized" one. They'd learned to organize. They were still
busy organizing. Judejahn paid the bill. It amused him because
they presumed he'd pay for everything. Judejahn never paid for
everything. He had various currencies in his wallet, and he
couldn't find his way around all the different crumpled bank-
notes, the inflated denominations of a war-ruined currency. The

war was Judejahn; and it was as though he'd helped to devalue money and inflate figures; it both satisfied and disgusted him. The men helped Judejahn to work out the exchange rate; they organized such money-changing transactions as well; and they could launder money, and pass off fake bills for real. Judejahn despised money and got through it. But he made sure he wasn't robbed. Little Gottlieb was impressed by the rich, and hated them. Judejahn liked their life-style, but not their lives. He had tried to do better. The rich were stupid. They had thought of Judejahn as a lackey who would do their work for them. But the lackey became a gaoler and locked them up. But in the end the prisoners managed to get away from Judejahn. The rich were rich once more. They were free. They were clever. Little Gottlieb once again stood in the corner eating his heart out. Once in a while there was a crumb from their tables for him. The constellations were not unfavorable to Judejahn. Wallenstein believed in the stars. Mars, Mercury and Clio living in rat holes. Exhausted, drained, quarrelsome, envious, covetous, selfish and forever greedy, they never stop their attentions. The press announced their abortions. Judejahn left the Pilsener cellar with the Eastern Germans, he left with the cadaver-faced, grinning men, left with the useful organizers, the Eastern Hummel-Hummel-callers, his soul-brothers and comrades-in-arms. Comrade rats. Rats climbed up to the street.

He was exhausted, and again I offered him some wine, and again he refused, and I wondered if he was this exhausted when he confessed to his superiors. I wasn't his confessor, and I couldn't give him absolution. I saw no sins. I saw only life, and life wasn't a sin. Nor could I give him any advice. Who can advise anyone? It meant nothing to me and it meant an awful lot when he exclaimed: "But she's my mother, and he's my father!" And so I learned that they were in Rome, my parents, my brother Dietrich, my aunt and Uncle Judejahn, he too, he was alive, and there was Adolf sitting in front of me, though not entirely, I thought, because his priestly cassock set him apart from us, he had freed himself, I didn't want to know at what cost, just as I too had freed myself and didn't want to know the cost. Where should I flee to now, seeing they were here, following me, because Adolf had followed them, her at least, his mother, whom he described in dismaying terms? So when he said to me, "He's my father, she's my mother," I didn't want to know. I'd had enough. I'd freed myself. I felt free. I really thought I was free, and wanted to remain free—and I wasn't a Christian. I don't mean I wasn't a Christian in the sense of Uncle Judejahn, I didn't hate Christians, but I didn't go to church, or rather I went to a lot of churches but not to hear Mass, or rather I went to hear Mass, but not the way they celebrated it. But if he was a Christian now and a priest, then surely there was the injunction that one had to leave father and mother—and hadn't he left them?

He buried his face in his hands. He'd told me about the end of the Teutonic academy, the end of the Nazi indoctrination fortress where they let us stew, where they were going to get their future leadership cadres from. There'd been handgrenades in our day, practice grenades that went off with a sharp crack and a sharp little flame on the playground, and then later they'd equipped the boys with real ones. But there weren't enough to go round, so they had to take some old and dodgy captured Greek-made grenades to make up numbers, and one boy had his belly ripped away by one because the pin had got caught up in his shoulder strap and worked loose, that's how the teachers accounted for the mishap. And then the teachers had given them guns, captured guns with rusty barrels from victorious days, and they were to go with the old men from the *Volkssturm* reserve, and defend the eyrie—the fastness of the defeated but still bloodthirsty gods—but luckily the gods started eating one another and losing their heads before they could all be killed, and the old Volkssturm men sloped off into the woods and hills, or they hid in hay barns and potato cellars, and the dashing instructors ran around like mice, because now they would be called to account for the bacon they'd filched, and now they were caught in the trap, they were sitting pretty in the nets they'd helped to knot themselves. And then it was announced that there was going to be one more train, and the instructors sent the children home on it, without guns, without hand grenades, just in their brown uniforms, and how could they get home, home was just a memory. The train didn't get far. It was attacked by fighter planes. Like furious hornets the fighters sent stinging volleys of shot through the splintering glass, metal and wood of the train compartments. Adolf was unhurt. But the train was finished, a crippled worm. The children continued on foot, along the tracks, on the gravel, stumbling over the ties. And then they ran into another train. It was a concentration camp that had been put on wheels and had also come to a halt. The children found themselves eyed by skeletons, by corpses. The children trembled in their Party school uniforms. But they didn't know why they should be afraid. They were German children, after all! They were the elect! Still, they found themselves whispering. "They're from the camps!" they whispered, "they're Jews!" And the children looked round and they whispered, "Where are our men, where is our armed escort?" But there were no guards left, and the train was standing between a wood and a meadow, it was a spring day, the first flowers were out, the first butterflies were flitting about, the children in brown jackets were confronted by the prisoners in blue-and-white convict clothes, and out of their sunken eye sockets the skeletons and the corpses looked right through the Party Junkers, who began to feel they had no bones, no skeletons, as if they were nothing but brown Party jackets, which some evil charm had suspended in the spring air. The children ran down from the tracks into the woods. They didn't stay together. They scattered. They went in all directions, without a word, without a salute or "Heil Hitler!" And Adolf sat down in the grass next to a bush, because he didn't know where to go. Now a wraith had concealed itself in the bush, and the wraith watched Adolf. The wraith was exactly Adolf's age, but it had only half Adolf's weight. Adolf was crying. He had always been told not to cry. "German boys don't cry," said his parents and instructors. But Adolf was crying. He didn't know why he was crying. Perhaps he was crying because for the first time he was alone, and there was no one there to tell him, "German boys don't cry." But when the wraith saw Adolf crying, it picked up the stick that was lying beside it, and emerged from the bushes, a tottering figure, an emaciated body, with beaten skin, shaved child's skull, a death mask, and the wraith in its blue-and-white-striped felon's jacket raised the stick, and its nose stuck out large and bony in its starved face, and Adolf Judejahn remembered the *Stürmer* picture and recognized his first live Jew, even though the Jew was barely alive, and the wraith, with the stick upraised in its trembling hands, screamed for bread. Adolf opened his pack, he had bread and wurst and margerine, they had been given rations for the journey, and strangely a pound of almonds as well, because almonds happened to be in supply, and Adolf handed over his rations to the wraith, which grabbed the rucksack and sat down a little way away from Adolf and tore off large pieces of bread and wurst and crammed them into itself. Adolf watched. He had no thoughts. No thoughts at all. There was an absolute void in his head, it was as though everything he had hitherto thought and learned had been cleared out, perhaps in order to make room for new ideas, new teaching, but that wasn't definite yet. For the time being his head was empty, an empty balloon dangling over the grass. And the wraith, seeing Adolf watching it, threw him some bread and wurst and called, "You eat, too. There's enough for both!" And Adolf ate, without appetite and without enjoyment, but also without disgust. When the other saw Adolf eating, he came nearer. He sat beside him. They ate the almonds together. The bag of almonds lay between them, and they both shyly helped themselves from it. "The Americans are coming," said the Jewish boy. "Where will you go?" he asked. "I don't know," said Adolf. "Are you a Nazi?" asked the Jewish boy. "My father," said Adolf. "My family are all dead," said the Jewish boy. And then Adolf thought that his own father might be dead, probably was, although nothing told him for certain. If he was crying, he was crying for himself, or maybe not even for himself, he didn't know why he was crying, perhaps he was crying for the whole world. But he wasn't crying for his father. And had he not loved his father? He wasn't sure. Had he hated him? He didn't think so. He could only see him as the official Party portrait on the wall—which left him cold. The Jewish boy was sick. He vomited back the sausage and the bread and the margerine. He vomited back the almonds as well. His teeth chattered, it was as though all the bones protruding through his paper-thin skin were rattling together. Adolf took off his brown Party jacket, and laid it over the boy's shoulders. He didn't know why he did it. Not out of pity. Not out of love. Not even out of guilt did he cover the boy. He just did it because he thought he was cold. Later they exchanged jackets. Adolf pulled on the blue-and-white-striped convict jacket with the Star of David. That touched him. His heart beat so hard, he could feel the pulse in his veins. The jacket burned. He felt it. Later they heard rumbling on the road. "Tanks," said Adolf. "The Americans," whispered the boy. His life was saved, but he lacked the strength to crawl toward the tanks. What about Adolf? Had he lost his life, did the armored column break it as it crashed and rumbled through the German countryside? The boys lay down in the leaves, and covered themselves with branches. They lay together and kept each other warm in the night. In the morning they went into the village. The young Jew went to look for the Americans. He said, "Come on." But Adolf didn't go with him. Adolf walked through the village. People stared at him, a boy in the black uniform trousers and red stripe, a military haircut and wearing a convict's jacket. He sat down in the village church. He sat in the village church, because its doors were open as no other doors were, and because he was tired, and because he had no place to go. And so the priest came upon him. He came upon him sleeping. Was it a vocation? Had God called him? On Sunday, the priest's text was: "Verily, verily, I say unto you, He that heareth my word, and believeth on him that sent me, hath everlasting life, and shall not come into condemnation; but is passed from death unto life. Verily, verily, I say unto you, The hour is coming, and now is, when the dead shall hear the voice of the Son of God: and they that hear shall live." Did Adolf want to live? Did he want to avoid condemnation? There were women and fugitives in the church, and men who had quickly slipped on civilian jackets to avoid imprisonment. There were American soldiers in the church as well, holding their helmets in their folded hands, and their short light rifles rested against the pews. They had survived. They said they were liberators. They had come from across the ocean. They were Crusaders. Adolf Judejahn had heard about the Crusades in the National Socialist academy, but his instructors had disapproved of them. The conquest of earth was their teaching, not heaven. And for them it wasn't worth it to conquer the Holy Sepulcher; and yet they had no fear of sepulchers. Adolf no longer believed his instructors. He no longer trusted human beings. He wanted to serve the Lord. God, Father, Son and Holy Ghost.

Death was at hand. He didn't want to die. He was scared. Judejahn had got into the car of his extraordinary subordinates, of the serviceable servicemen. It was a battered vehicle, almost a military vehicle, a jeep. They were in open terrain, on a reconnaissance mission, probing forward. Which way were they going? The direction didn't matter. The movement was all that mattered. Judejahn had ordered, "To the station." Why the station? He didn't know. But the station was an objective. It was a terrain. One could hide in it. One could find cover. One could go under, leave, disappear, fake one's death; Judejahn could become a legend like the Flying Dutchman, and Eva would be proud of him. The station, the objective, was near by. But Judejahn, sitting next to the driver—the other was sitting behind him, sitting on his tail—Judejahn sensed that they weren't going to the station at all, that their progress was rambling, they were driving around in circles, searching no doubt for dead ends and quiet alleyways, or alternatively for the roar and confusion of traffic where a gunshot might go unnoticed; they really thought he was going to pay, stupid bastards, they thought they had him in their sights, but Judejahn knew his way around, and that was the way you drove in the killing grounds: a blow from behind, a shot in the back, then the wallet plundered from the corpse and, in the lee of a wall, the car door opened and the body kicked out on to the rubble. He knew the ropes, and ultimately it was the Führer's orders to kill the commander who failed, the coward who surrendered, an order to anyone, but specifically an order issued to these Austrian SS, the Führer's praetorians. But Judejahn hadn't failed, he hadn't surrendered, and it was only in Rome that he was afraid, only in that damned priests' town, but he wasn't a coward and they couldn't do that to him. They planned on going to the brothel at his expense, but Judejahn wasn't about to get himself shot while attempting flight; he'd devised the method himself, and he wasn't going to be forced to flee. He was following tactical detours, on circuitous paths, on desert tracks, jackal strategy, but his goal remained Germany, Grossdeutschland was his fata morgana, nothing would deflect him, and he gave them an earful. The car stopped right away. The rotten metal quivered. It made Judejahn feel good, giving them an earful. They were his fellows, his bloodhounds, his lads. He chewed them out. They recognized their master's voice. They didn't talk back. They denied nothing. They would have licked his boots. He got out of the car. He commanded them, "About turn!" They turned. They roared off toward Valhalla. Judejahn would have liked to tell them to report to him. But where would he have had them come? Report in Hell? Judejahn didn't believe in Hell. He was a grown man. He was disabused. Hell didn't exist. It was something to frighten children with. The Devil was the priests' bogeyman. The only possibility was reporting to Death, to friend Death, it was Comrade Death they should report to, to Death, whom little Gottlieb feared, and Judejahn—following the school song of Andreas Hofer which little Gottlieb had learned—had sent Death into the valley many times, and not just into the valley.

Behind him was the tunnel. It lured Judejahn. He ran into it, it swallowed him up. Again, he went through a gate into the Underworld. It was the gate of Hades. The tunnel was long and lined with cool tiles, it was a sewer for traffic where buses roared and neon lights painted the Underworld in spectral colors. This was where they had meant to kill him. His instinct hadn't let him down; he'd leapt out of the jeep at the very last moment. He walked down the narrow pavement by the tunnel wall. It felt like walking through his grave. It was an elongated grave, a hygienic grave, it was a mixture of kitchen, refrigerator and pissoir. You got no earth to chew in the morgue. The victim of the killing grounds chewed earth. The victim had been young. Judejahn had been young at the time as well. The victim was a comrade. The field shovel quickly buried the victim. And others had swallowed earth, too. In Poland, in Russia, in the Ukraine, they had swallowed earth. They were made to dig a ditch. Then they undressed. They stood naked before the ditch. Photographs came into the possession of leadership circles, were handed round, scrutinized over breakfast; jokes were cracked, tit jokes, cock and cunt jokes. Procreation and death, union with death, the ancient myth. A professor of race and an anthropologist were dispatched to study their dying erections. The photographs appeared in the *Stürmer*. The *Stürmer* was opened out and pinned on school noticeboards, eight-year-olds read it. Eight-year-olds shot. Riddled corpses filled the ditch. Man was destroyed, man desecrated, man dishonored, and overhead was blue sky. The next up covered the first lot with earth. Over Judejahn was earth; the tunnel ran under the Quirinal Gardens. Popes wandered in the garden. Their prayers had not been heard; or what in heaven's name was it they had asked for from God? Two thousand years of Christian enlightenment and at the finish,

Judejahn! Why did they ever drive the old gods out? "Thou shalt not kill!" Was it that resounding off the tunnel walls? The Pontifex Maximus of old Rome had been unfamiliar with that commandment. He had sat and happily watched the gladiatorial contests. The Pontifex Maximus of the new Rome served the Decalogue, he had the Commandments taught, and ordered them to be obeyed. And had the killing stopped? Or had the Christian shepherd at least set his face against it, and said before all the world, "See, I am powerless, they kill in spite of me and my pastoral word?" "Justice for Judejahn" echoed off the tunnel walls. At school little Gottlieb had learned that even popes allied themselves with death, and there was a time, not so very long ago, when popes engaged the services of executioners, of people like Judejahn. And how many generals had paid homage to the popes, and how often had they received blessings for their victorious standards! Justice for Judejahn! And kings had walked in the Quirinal Gardens, enjoying the sunsets. But kings were less impressive than popes. Judejahn still saw them as the caricatures of World War I comics that little Gottlieb had just learned to read, the kings were short, sell-out was written all over their faces, and in their timid hands they held umbrellas. And hadn't Chamberlain carried an umbrella, Chamberlain, the bringer of peace, who had meant to deprive the Führer of his war, a laughable figure? Kings and their diplomats, what were they but pathetic umbrella-wielders under the massing clouds of disasters? Judejahn had no use for umbrellas. Little Gottlieb wanted to be a man; he wanted to defy God the Father and his own schoolteacher father. Men braved all weathers, they mocked at the raging heavens: men walked into the hail of bullets with heads held up, men walked through the fire-storm—that was how little Gottlieb saw it, and justice for Judejahn! The automobile headlights were like the eyes of great rodents in the tunnel. The rodents left Judejahn alone. They were off in pursuit of other booty. The hounds of hell didn't bite Judejahn. They hunted other prey. Judejahn came to the end of the tunnel. The Underworld unhanded him. He reached the end. The grave released him. Hades spat him out

he stood at the end of the Via del Lavatore, which was silent and deserted. It was a mild night. From the far end of the dead street came the sound of singing.

I wanted to shut the window, I wanted to close the sun-warped, wind-beaten wooden shutters in front of the windows, I wanted locks and bolts, because now babel was finished, they were no longer speaking Babel-fashion in the Piazza of the Trevi Fountain, one language had asserted itself over the others, and a choir of German women were standing in front of the pillared grotto, standing in front of the gods and demigods and mythic creatures in baroque costume, standing in front of the ancient myth cast in stone, standing in front of water flowing from Roman pipes, standing in the floodlight of tourism and the candelabra lights of the city, singing, "There stands a linden tree by the fountain at the gate," singing it in the middle of Rome, singing the song in the middle of the night, where was no rustling of lindens and no tree grew for miles. But down there by the fountain they kept the faith, kept faith with their faith, they had their linden tree, their fountain there at the gate, a sublime hour and they marked it in their song, they had saved their money and traveled far, and what could I do but shut the windows and the wooden shutters, but he came across to me by the open window, he brushed me with his cassock, and we leaned out, and he told me once more that he had seen my parents, my parents and my brother Dietrich, seen them through a glass door at the hotel, and he said to me: "Your parents are even more terrible than mine, their lives are completely lost." And I could see them sitting behind the glass door in their hotel, I hadn't been there but I could see them, I was too proud to go there to see them, and what could I do, I said "Keep your theology," but what could I do? Down there they were singing the linden tree song verse by verse, and an Italian who wanted to sleep shouted at them from his window, and a man who was with the women's choir, and was an admirer of the women's choir, yelled back, "Shut up, you wop!" yelled "Shut up, you wop!" to whichever window it was. What could I do? And a police car came and stopped by the fountain, and the policemen watched the singing women in silent astonishment, and then the police slowly drove off, disappeared down a side street. What could they do? And a man emerged from the Via del Lavatore and joined the women and the man who had yelled, "Shut up, you wop!" and he was glad to find them, glad to have bumped into them. He was glad. Judejahn had followed the song, the German song, and the once-mighty man listened in reverence to the song of the German women. Their singing was Germany, was the motherland, it was "By the Fountain at the Gate," it was the German linden tree, it was everything one lived and fought and died for. Not murdered for. Judejahn had never murdered. He was just an old warrior, and this was balm to his old warrior's soul, this was music to renew the soul at night. When they finished, Judejahn called out "Bravo," and he went up to them, and introduced himself, albeit under his assumed name, and since they were standing in line like a company for inspection, he followed his instinct and addressed them briefly. He spoke of lofty singing in historic hour, of German women and a stirring encounter on Italian soil, greetings from home in the regrettably faithless land of German longings. And they understood him, they took his meaning, and the man who had called out "Shut up, you wop!" shook Judejahn by the hand and thanked him for his pithy words, and both felt the tears well up in their eyes, and both manfully held them back, for German men don't cry being full of German hardness but they are soft-souled when they think home thoughts abroad, thoughts of the fountain at the gate, of the linden tree evoked by the voice of German women

I thought:

I don't believe you, it's not your vocation, and you know that God didn't call you; you were free, for one single night you were free, one night in the woods, and that was all you could stand, you were like a dog who's lost his master, you had to find yourself a new master; then the priest found you, and you told yourself it was God calling you.

But I didn't tell him what I was thinking. He bothered me. He bothered me with his news of the family. What could I do? I didn't want to hear his news. I didn't want to hear anything about them. I wanted my life, just my own little life, no life everlasting, I wasn't greedy, no life of sin. What was sin, anyway? I just wanted to live my selfish life, I wanted to be there just for myself alone and to get on with my own life, and he wanted to talk me into going with him, I was to go with him, he was scared on his own, and call on our family, and how I hate that word, and how I use it purposely to express my loathing—the family, the prison they wanted to lock me up in for life, but I'd escaped, I'd been sprung, I'd set myself free, I was truly free, I never wanted to go back there! Why was Adolf looking for them? And why didn't he go to them, once he'd found them, why did he come to me? Did he want to convert them? Did he want to convert me? He said: "He's my father." And I said: "He's my father, but I don't want to see him." And he said: "She's my mother." And I said: "She's my mother, but I don't want to see her. And I wanted nothing to do with my brother Dietrich. And Judejahn was dead, so I'd hoped, and if the Devil had let him go, then that was the Devil's own business. I wanted to stay out of the way of Uncle Judejahn, the mighty Party general, lord over life and death, terror of my childhood, black bogeyman to the brown adolescent.

But he said: "We have to do something. We have to help them." He didn't say, "I must save them." He lacked faith for that, and he didn't dare say it to my face, either. And I said no. And I looked at him. Gaunt, uncertain, wretched he looked in his clerical robes, the lanky deacon, not even ordained yet. And I teased him: "How do you want to help your father Judejahn? What about baptizing him, since you're not able to forgive sins? That's what you told me, that you can't forgive sins yet."

He trembled. I went on looking at him. He was powerless. I felt sorry for him. He thought he had God on his side, and he was powerless.

There were manuscripts on the marble top of the washstand, there were sheets of music, and Kürenberg was expecting me to come up with music that important men would listen to to renew their souls. Flies were dancing round the bare lightbulb. Under the lightbulb, the broad hotel bed lay exposed, chaste and unchaste, the *letto matrimoniale,* the bed of marriage and concubinage. I imagined a man and a woman copulating, and I was disgusted, because their union might produce life. I was powerless as well; and I didn't even want power. A fly had drowned in the remains of the wine in the tooth-mug. It had drowned in an almighty binge, in a sea of intoxication; and what did air matter to us, earth and sea and sky! Had God guided the fly? No sparrow falls from a roof. I asked: "Where will you sleep?" And I thought: Shall I offer to share my bed with him? And I thought:

I mustn't offer him my bed. He had lodgings in the dormitory for priests. He made to leave and I saw him going toward the door, and I felt sorry for him again, and I thought: He is trying to get free of them. And I asked him what his plans were for tomorrow, and he seemed not to know, he was loath to reply, maybe he didn't want to give me a reply, and then he said he was going to St. Peter's and I offered to meet him at the Angels' Bridge, by the Angels' Castle, I didn't want to see him again, but I said a time, and he said he'd be there. Now it was becoming quiet in Rome. The women's choir had gone, the tourists had left, and a man somewhere had turned a stopcock and the water in the Trevi Fountain no longer bubbled up over the baroque Olympus of gods and demigods and fabulous beings. The bubbling of the fountain stopped; it was history. The silence was audible. In it I now heard his footfall, going down the stone steps, he, the priest, the deacon, climbed down through time as through a tunnel. I looked out of the window, I saw him leave the building, I followed his progress. Like a lean black dog, he loped across the silent, dead square and turned into the passage that leads to the Piazza Colonna. I took the glass with the rest of the wine and the dead fly in it, and I tipped wine and fly down the drain. He was powerless

they were both walking down the passage, one already at the exit to the Corso, the other still near the churches in the Via Santa Maria in Via, and workmen were cleaning the mosaic floor of the passage, they sprinkled sawdust over the dirt people had brought in with their shoes, and with large brooms they swept up the mixture of dirt and sawdust. Other workmen spread ready-mixed plaster on the swept stones, then with a sander smoothed it into the cracks and gaps in the mosaic. It made a sound like the whetting of long knives. The sleeping city was a provocation to Judejahn. The city mocked him. It wasn't the sleepers that annoyed Judejahn, let them lie in their stinking beds, in the arms of their lustful wives, let them be sapped and lose the battle of their lives, no, he was indignant at the totality of the sleeping city, each closed window, each bolted door, each lowered blind incensed him; he was furious that the city was sleeping without his say-so; there should be steel-helmeted patrols going through the streets, with MP insignia on their chests and submachine guns in their hands, and the patrols would see to it that Judejahn's command to sleep was kept; but Rome was sleeping without his dispensation, it dreamed, it lulled itself to security. Rome sleeping was sabotage, it sabotaged a war that was far from over, or that hadn't properly begun yet, Judejahn's war. If he could, Judejahn would have roused the city; he would have used the trumpets of Jericho to rouse the city, those trumpets that made walls collapse, the last trump, which had first impressed little Gottlieb, and which he learned to laugh at in heathen scorn. Judejahn was out of power. He was dismayed. He couldn't stand it. In the desert he had lived in a dream. The barracks in the desert were under his command; the barracks had left him the illusion of power. A wall was stuck with fresh posters; they were still wet, and smelled of printer's ink and of paste. Again there was a commandment from the Church next to a communistic summons; the summons red and aggressive, the Church's edict white and dignified. One was the work of an old power, the other of a new, but both lacked a straightforward brutality, a final disavowal of thought and persuasion, there was no clenched fist, no absolute belief in force and command, and Judejahn wondered whether he shouldn't throw in his lot with the Reds, he would teach them discipline, but little Gottlieb was against that, he hated the unpatriotic lot, he believed in Germany, and he believed in private ownership too, albeit with a reallocation of property to Judejahn's advantage and into exclusively German hands, and because of little Gottlieb's unwillingness, Judejahn couldn't join the communists; he had once intended their elimination, only a feeble and corrupt world had got in the way. In the Piazza Colonna he took a taxi back to the Via Veneto, back to the big hotel, back to the fortress that had been his headquarters, the headquarters of the great and powerful Judejahn.

And Adolf, who didn't hear the knife grinding, and didn't see the posters on the wall, Adolf found the sleeping city quiet and giving peace to the restless soul. His way home was like a walk through a great graveyard, with imposing tombs, ivy-grown crosses and old chapels, and Adolf was glad to find the city as quiet as the grave, perhaps he too was dead, that made him glad, perhaps he was a dead man walking through the dead city, a dead man looking for the lane with the hostel for visiting clergymen, they also dead, lying dead in their dead beds in the dead hostel—it couldn't be far. And there was its light, the light everlasting. And Judejahn had the taxi stop early, and got out

the homosexuals were gone. No need for Judejahn to hear their twittering. The pretty waiters in their cute purple tails were putting the chairs on the tables, they patted the red chair cushions with their hands, and perfumed dust swirled up, lavender, cologne and spicy aftershaves, and the beautiful, smiling Laura was counting up the money in the till and the coupons of the waiters, and once more the totals didn't match, but Laura smiled her beatific smile, the serene and mindless miracle of her smile, and the heterosexual owner of the homosexual bar accepted Laura's smile and the discrepant totals with pleasure and a good grace, business was good and he was a kind person, and Judejahn, unseen by Laura, the owner, the waiters, was stalking the terrain, he hadn't forgotten how to hunt, he peered through a crack in the shuttered door, the way a thief peers or a killer, and he saw Laura, saw her smile, it touched even him, did its magic on him, but the smile tortured him as well. Laura's eyelids were nightblue, her face powdered white and her lips were hardly painted, she seemed very pale, seemed delicate and timid, spun from the night and shrinking back into it, and Judejahn turned the door handle, it moved, his great heavy hand lay on the handle, a frail handle of silver bronze; but then Judejahn withdrew his hand again, a man can't be sure, she's a Jewess, a Jewish chick, in Poland anyone consorting with Jewesses swung for it, and again he pressed the handle, and again he left it, Jewish cunt. Was he frightened? The night porter of the hotel saluted him, touched his gloved hand to the peak of his cap, saluted Commander Judejahn, the man giving orders here, albeit under an assumed name. The silky stuff shone on the walls, it was like a room in a brothel, little Gottlieb could have imagined nothing finer. Why hadn't he picked up the girl? Why didn't he take her? He would have screwed her and slung her out. Screwing her would have done him good, and it would have done him good to sling her out afterward. On the damask bedspread lay the mangy tom, Benito. He stretched, arched his back and blinked his eyes. Judejahn ran his fingers through his thin fur. The beast stank. He stank to high heaven. The tom looked at him sardonically: You've outlived

yourself, you're out of power. Could Judejahn tell the porter he
wanted a girl? Once he could have done. He could have got a
hundred. He could have embraced them and sentenced them.
Should he call Eva? They would be petrified in her middle-class
hotel. They got scared there at night. They were scared of death.
Why shouldn't Judejahn scare the middle-class hotel? Perhaps he
could have spoken with Eva in the night. He could have cleared
the air. It was good to speak on the phone. Orders to suicide
squads were phoned or wired. You never gave them in person.
Eva was a German woman, a National Socialist, she would understand him, she would appreciate that Judejahn hadn't yet
died, that he was walking along the edge of life. Eva was a German woman like the German women by the fountain singing the
beautiful German song, but she was more than those women, she
came from the elite, she was his wife—she would understand
him. It had been stupid of Judejahn to be apprehensive of meeting Eva. What was there to tempt him about that Italian—maybe
even Jewish—woman in the purple bar? That girl wasn't his
type. She wasn't German. But there was something about her
that made him want her. She was a whore. Or she was a Jewess.
A hot skinny Jewish harlot. That was miscegenation. He had no
need to fear the girl. He could hate her. That was it, he needed a
woman to hate, his hands, his body, needed another body, another life to have and to destroy, only when you killed were you
alive—and who other than a bar girl was still attainable for Judejahn's hatred? He was deposed. He was powerless

and Eva slept, slept stretched out, slept in her narrow cot in the
small hotel room, slept tensely. Only the knot of her hair was
loosened, yellowed corn left to stand, straw not harvested and
put in a barn, whitened and grizzled. But she slept deeply, dream-
lessly, with mouth foolishly agape, gurgling slightly, smelling
faintly of the skin on boiled milk, the irate, sleeping Norn of nocturnal oblivion

given over to nocturnal oblivion, moved only by the commotion
of his snoring, Dietrich Pfaffrath slept on one of the hotel's softer
beds. The wine he had drunk in the hall with his parents and the
other German guests of similar views had not made him sleepy,
and his suitcase was open at the foot of his bed, for Dietrich was

hard-working and ambitious, and even on a family visit to beautiful Italy he was preparing for his law exams, and he was confident of passing them, and so he had been reading in the law books he had packed in his suitcase. And Dietrich's fraternity cap had also accompanied him on his journey, because one might meet members of other fraternities in sufficient numbers to take over a bar. The cap with the colored ribbons lay beside the law books, and Dietrich was sure that both his fraternity and the law would stand him in good stead. Then there were the road maps in the open suitcase, because Dietrich enjoyed taking the wheel for his old man, the Oberbürgermeister, and he had carefully marked the places to visit on the map, and written their names down on a separate sheet of paper, with the sites of battles in red ink, and the dates on which they had been fought. But beside the suitcase, tossed out of bed after the lights had been turned out, poorly aimed and missing the suitcase, there lay a magazine, an illustrated journal he had bought at a kiosk when he thought no one was watching, in Rome where he didn't know a soul and no one knew him, and on the cover of the magazine was a girl standing there with legs spread, standing there in full fleshy color, with her blouse open to the waist, and in wide-meshed net-stockings over the full-color fleshy thighs—on that evening she had taken the place of his beer for Dietrich, and he had exhausted himself between those thighs. He was powerless against the habit, but he was powerfully driven to the powerful whom he wanted to serve, he wanted to sit in the house of power, and share in power and become powerful himself

Friedrich Wilhelm Pfaffrath slept contentedly with his wife Anna, united in one bed for the holiday, though not united in any embrace, at home they had separate beds. Why should he be dissatisfied? His life appeared without blemish, and life on the whole rewarded those who were without blemish. Nationalist thoughts and feelings were once again resurgent in Germany, albeit in a Germany of two separate halves, and personal popularity, reputation, continuity and the democratic process had made Friedrich Wilhelm Pfaffrath the head of his city once more, absolutely legitimately, not by deception, electoral fraud or bribery, still less by the favor of the occupying forces; the people had freely elected him to be their Oberbürgermeister, and even though he had once been Oberpresident and the administrator of great Party sums, he was content, he was without blemish. And yet unfairly a nightmare came to haunt his blameless sleep: brother-in-law Judejahn rode up to his bedside on a snorting steed and in his black uniform, and a choir sang "Lützow's Wild and Daring Chase," and brother-in-law Judejahn pulled Pfaffrath up on to his snorting steed, and into Lützow's wild and daring chase. And they galloped up to heaven, where Judejahn unfurled a large, luminous swastika flag, and then he dropped Pfaffrath, pushed him away, and Pfaffrath fell fell fell. And against that dream the mighty Oberbügermeister Friedrich Wilhelm Pfaffrath was powerless

I'm powerless. I wash. I wash in cold tap water from the sink, and I think of the water flowing through the old Roman pipes, flowing to me from the sad blue hills, across the ruined masonry of old acqueducts as Piranesi drew them, into this basin—I enjoy washing in this water. I walk barefooted across the old stone floor. I feel the firm cool stones underfoot. It's pleasant to feel the stones. I lie down naked on the broad bed. It's good to lie down naked on the broad bed. I don't cover myself. It's good to lie alone. My nakedness lies bare. Naked and bare, I stare up at the naked and bare lightbulb. The flies buzz. Naked. Bare. Music paper lies white on the marble. Or maybe it's not white any more; the flies have smirched the paper. I hear no music. There is no note in me. There is no refreshment. Nothing to refresh the thirsting soul. There is no source. Augustine went into the desert. But in those days the source was in the desert. Rome sleeps. I hear the noise of great battles. It's distant, but it's a terrible tumult. The battle is still far off. It's far off, but it's terrible. It's far off, but coming ever nearer. Soon the dawn will break. I will hear the steps of workers in the streets. The battle will be nearer, and the workers will move toward it. They won't know they're moving into battle. If asked, they will say: "We don't want to go to battle." But they will go to battle. The workers are always there, marching into battle. The little communist girl will be there, too. All proud people will go to battle. I'm not proud, or rather I am proud, but not in that way. I am naked. I am bare. I am powerless. Naked bare powerless.

Translated by Michael Hoffman

ARNO SCHMIDT

Scenes from the Life of a Faun

1

(February 1939)

Thou shalt not point thy finger at the stars; nor write in the snow; but when it thunders touch the earth: so I sent a tapering hand upward, with beknitted finger drew the slivered ‹K› in the silver scurf beside me, (no thunderstorm in progress at the moment, otherwise I'd have come up with something!) (In my briefcase the wax paper rustles).

The moon's bald Mongol skull shoved closer to me. (The sole value of discussions is: that good ideas occur to you afterward).

The main road (to the station) coated with silver strips; shoulders cemented high with coarse snow, diamonddiamond (macadamized; – was Cooper's brother-in-law by the by). The trees stood there, giants at august attention, and my look-alive steps stirred beneath me. (Just ahead the woods will retreat to the left and fields advance). And the moon must have still been bustling at my back, since sometimes sharp rays flitted strangely through the needled blackness. Far ahead a small car bored its bulging eyes into the matutinal night, wiggled them slowly looking about, and then clumsily turned the red glow of its monkey's butt toward me: glad it's driving off!

My life?!: is not a continuum! (not simply fractured into white and black pieces by day and night! For even by day they are all someone else, the fellow who walks to the train; sits in the office; bookworms; stalks through groves; copulates; small-talks; writes; man of a thousand thoughts; of fragmenting categories; who runs; smokes; defecates; listens to the radio; says "Commissioner, sir": that's me!): a tray full of glistening snapshots.

Not a continuum, not a continuum!: that's how my life runs, how my memories run (like a spasm-shaken man watching a thunderstorm in the night):

Flash: a naked house in the development bares its teeth amid poison-green shrubbery: night.

Flash: white visages are gaping, tongues tatting, fingers teething: night.

Flash: tree limbs are standing, boys play pubescing; women are stewing; girls are scamping open-bloused: night!

Flame: me: woe: night!!

But I cannot experience my life as a majestically unrolling ribbon; not I! (Proof).

Drift ice in the sky: chunks; a floe. Chunks; a floe. Black crevices in which stars crept (sea stars). A pale white fish belly (moonfish). Then:

Cordingen Station: the snow prickled softly on the walls; a black switch-wire quivered and husked hawaiian; (at my side the she-wolf appeared, covered with silver grains. Climb aboard for starters).

The great white she-wolf: growled the greeting, took a savage seat and tugged out her textbook by one corner; then from her pen she extracted many jagged inky threads, ducked low, and gazed with her round eyes into an invisible hole. The red swarm of my thoughts circled a bit about her, snarling, with round eyes, yellow-rimmed. (But then here came another, a black one, and I whetted my mouth and stared disapprovingly at the dirty slatted benches: sparkling thickskulled brass screws, roundheads, beaded through us: how can you escape stuff like that?! The she-wolf scratched in the frost on the window, for her girlfriend to get on: ergo: Walsrode).

"Heil, Herr Düring!": "Morning, Peters."; and he brought out the joke: ‹Flowers for the gentleman?!:—: No thanks. The lady's my wife!›. Hahaheehee. (Outside a silver claw hacked through the clouds, ripped open a thin one, pulled back again): hahaheehee. His glances philandered among the schoolgirls, the curve of blousey silk; the thigh-filled skirts.

Lovely browed: schoolgirls with smooth facial secrets, serious immobile eyes; heads of bobbed sandy hair turned on slender necks, while the porcelain hand wrote minced English, in the blue notebook. (And add a little morning sun!: And there it was now, on time, red between yellow slits of cloud; hoo-whee-called the train, as if from the universe's gullet, disinterested and extragalactic).

Stopped in the station: (Somebody close that door!. "Batten the hatch!").

Sunrise: and scarlet lances. (But at the back it was all still stiff and ice-blue, no matter how high He held up those salmon-red vacant tapestries).

Through the compartment window: the woodlands quite petrified! (And beyond, pastel pink and blue); so still that No One could get through (he would have to balance his way on tiptoe, eyes open wide and arms at an angle; (and maybe take root like that! An insane urge seized me, to be that Some One: to pull the emergency brake, leave my briefcase, tapered balancing arms, crystal eyes, flint & crown)).

Fallingbostel: "Heil!": "Good-bye!": "Good-bye:–": "Heil-ittler!"

Commissioner's Office (= Prometheus' rock). Colleagues: Peters; Schönert; (Runge was still on Party detail); Fräulein Krämer, Fräulein Knoop (typists); Otte, male trainee; Grimm, female trainee.

Fräulein Krämer: small and of reptilian grace. She stood at the file cabinet, glanced slyly our way, and then rubbed her pelvis adeptly against the table edge; pulled back her green cardigan into the central-heated air, projecting her subtle apple-sized breasts, and gazed ever so dreamily at her thin smooth finger-sprigs as they snapped among the index cards.

"I'd sure like to get under your skin, Fräulein Krämer!" (Schönert, sighing uneasily. Once again): "I'd sure like to get under your skin." She stared at him mistrustfully out of the far corners of her eyes (has troubles enough I suppose).—"Yes indeed," he protested piously, "if only this much:—" demonstrated: about 8 inches.—Her mouth, at first pleated nonplussed, relaxed, in eddies and dimples, then she puffed syrupy (even I bestowed an appreciative and managerial smirk: Schönert, the bastard. Sure, he wasn't married!), and went over to her girlfriend, whispered two sentences to her, demonstrated—: (distance of about 12 inches), and she too

burst into bright and nervous laughter (but all through the propositioning kept up her businesslike dog-earing. Then: her glance slithered cautiously through the furniture over to him, Schönert).

Ora et labora, et labora, et labora: "What a flumper." Peters (the Silesian) grumbled testily over his documents, gnawed at his pencil, thrust his teeth over his lower lip and pondered. (Now that was interesting! I had often listened in on his primal tones: the unintelligible ones were either botched Slavic or French, from the years of Napoleonic occupation of Silesia, 1808–13. So that on principle he would say: "Agreed, savey" = not "savvy," but "c'est fait"; "Damn 'ansumbul" = not "and some bull," but "ensemble." And now he had just called the so-and-so a "flumper".—Found it later in my Sachs-Villatte: "flambart = lively fellow, jolly chap," so more or less comparable to our "live wire" or "card").

Morning coffee break (immediately after which we are open to the public): films, soccer, the Führer, jokes, "From the lad who takes himself in hand will grow a man who takes his stand" (Peters), Party Convention, office intrigues, leaf through magazines, chew and rustle: "Well, Schönert?"—

Most peculiar!: Schönert, well-steeped in the classics, too, had read *The Odyssey* 23, 190ff., and disputed the possibility: it would rot much to quickly! Why even a pile driven into the ground would last a lot longer (since otherwise the capillaries of the stump would still be intact and go right on osmosing: any farmer knew that). "Not a chance that it could last for 10 or 20 years!" Ergo: Homer the Ignoramus?! Right?.

At the window: white-maned horses stood before long wagons; peeped from stalls; were led at the hands of boys; joggled a hoof against the pavement; greenish figs fell out of them; they pondered and snorted. (Prisoners in leather. And colorful carters appeared and shouted in humanese. All in winter).

And of clients sleek and broad of brow a host (well it only lasts from 10 to 12. And was quiet today). Stamp papers. Two permits. "Yes, and then you've gotta go to—Room 14. One floor up.—OK?"

A young girl wanted to get married (red skirt, yellow sweater, broad and happily fecund), and I patiently explained that she was still missing diverse "papers," "required by the latest regulation," birth certificate of the maternal grandfather; a signature was missing here on the wedding license (Oh, she had one child already, which explained the chassis, Grand Canyon: should you tell her: better not to get married?!)

There is simply no communication between generations! My children are strangers; just as my parents always were. Which is why in biographies relatives are consistently less important than lovers and friends. We stand around like a group of waiters. (Children only break up a marriage that much faster. In our circles).

Stamp one more: "Go ahead and close up, Fräulein Krämer!"

Lunch break: means munching sandwiches. Then get a bit of exercise.

I don't know (in front of stores); I don't know: for me "department store" is always congruent with "indoor family pool"; erotic fluorescent waves in both, artificial and overexposed.

A bevy of girls invaded with tongues flapping merrily. (Peters also wants to buy a piano in his old age. And learn to play. Ah well).

SA, SS, military, HY andsoforth: humans are never more trying than when playing soldier. (Surfaces periodically among them about every score of years, something like malaria, of late the pace is quicker). In the end it's always the worst ones who end up on top, to wit: bosses, executives, directors, presidents, generals, ministers, chancellors. A decent person is ashamed of being a boss!

The dark red bus purred softly my way from behind, slowly pushed along past me, and for a second I gazed into the faces, some ten of them, bisected by chrome bars thick as your thumb, dully splotched by moistured panes, indifferent and large-eyed. (And then, the mill on the Böhme, and the Quintus Icilius monument).

"Watch out, Dr. D's coming!" Peters hissed as he entered and dug deeper into his passports; Fräulein Krämer's thin lesbian fingertips itched faster at her dark Underwood, and trainee Otte lifted the heavy index box to his chin with a demonstrative gasp, the eye of the Lord maketh cattle to wax fat, behold: he came:

Commissioner Dr. von der Decken: tall, gray and fat; sovereign placidity among the great folds of his foggy face; the eyes swept heavily across the desktops and us other objects. He gazed long at my right hand (constantly twirling its pencil while the mail was rapidly scanned: make you feel pervous, Serenisime?, next page: turn it over. There he still stood, presidential, monumental, potentatial, iguanodontial, ohgod, how we despised each other, like the Emperor of Aromata, next page: turn). "How late is it, Herr Peters?" "Uh—3:30, Commissioner, sir, thirty-four." "Thank you" (grumbled out all deep and Hindenburgish), "Thank you". Then departed. And I read and turned pages; Krämer daintily picked her nose; and trainee Otte removed the box from his sternum. ("Did he ever made a face", Peters eagerly: "like a monkey chewin' putty!"; and we wheezed with laughter at the heroic metaphor: but it's definitely another one of his silesianisms!)

Early dusk today. (Schönert had heard the weather report and prophesied overcase and rainy). The desklamp dyed the green formulas an even deeper Marbusian hue (I seen him serve the Queen / in a suit of rifle-green), and Otte brought me the folder with 500 signatures; yet once more; he had finished stamping them (some ordinance for all localities; for public posting), and he helped me, wordless and already a Stakhanovite. "Düring." "Düring." Five hundred times. (And to think people envy us our retirement benefits! For cryin' out loud!)

God knows: drizzling already; but the train pulled in through the spritz on time. (Peters wanted to go to the movies).

The haggard newspaper distributor: I had strayed into the car for "Passengers with Extra Baggage," and watched how, as we moved by, he opened the window and shot-putted the packages to the lonely signalmen's huts (so they could then divvy them up in the villages). "Well, Herr Singer, how's the tournament going?"; and he gave me reticent, Hadleyburgian information. (Was, you see, an impassioned chess player, polygonal and penurious, ‹Walsrode Germania Club›, and so charmingly fanatic that he didn't smoke when "in training"). "Heilittler, Herr Singer."

Stillest moor air: a farmer took shape ten paces ahead; at first just gray, as if puffed from smoke; (then he seemed to wear blue trousers; his stooped back stayed unhued); hands vapored slowly around beneath him; then he pulled himself up

to full breadth, cracked his whip making the air moan with
pain, hollow: and the shadow-patched horse at his side disappeared, nor did he reappear to me again later. (Had tubered
off, I suppose, sown away; somehow).
Lights of the village, and sadness, as the mist resembles the rain.
Late hot lunch: a sailor's fate. Fried potatoes and elastic black-
red slicelets of sausage. "Got your Hitler photo yet?" the Eg-
erland March inquired, only to declare at once: "No, no,
don't have it yet / but we'll buy one, you bet!". (Like a photo-
flash came Christmas memory: candles shimmered, deft and
bemused, little soft faces of molten gold above white slender
necks, bowing, dissembling and sanctimonious. Ever so cozy
the stench from the mulled wine adulterated with cinnamon
and cloves, red in its Sunday glasses; and I too had folded hypocritical hands across my belly, drawing on one of my three
fat Brazils. But hadn't been able to endure it after all, and
reached for the quaint old 1850 atlas I had picked up for a
few pfennigs in Verden. Shutter closed).
(Long ago I kept trying with books. As gifts for wife and children. But for years now it'd been nothing but electric pots,
linens and meat grinders; primum vivere roundaboutum.
With savage joy my son examined the extralong Hitler Youth
dagger, what is headed for a fall should be given a shove; the
new dress draped on my daughter at the mirror, candy-sweet
face: my daughter. Shutter closed).
Turning the dial (looking for news): "Kadum Soap beautifies
your body. / —Kadum Soap is summa cum laude!" And so
sincerely spoken, in a plum-yellow D'youloveme voice; must
be Saarbrücken; keep dialing. (They think they're some kind
of scenic cultural overview!).
"Pope Pius the Somethingth: gravely ill", and I just raised my
eyebrows in disapprobation and kept turning: who still travels by zeppelin these days?! (When I consider that of our six
great classical authors not a one was Catholic . . . . . When I
further consider that half of them—oh, and much the better
half: Lessing, Wieland, Goethe (in chronological order!)—
were opposed to every revealed religion . . . . : why then,
I know what I know!)
"Tired: goodnight". (Have my own room on the ground floor all
to myself; with the years and children my wife has forgotten

me; permits it only with greatest reluctance). Across the way
at Evers's and Hohgrefe's lights still on.

In the john again: black and odorless cold. (I really am tired;
well, tomorrow's Saturday). (Ashes drifted over the concrete
moon, ceaseless, flushed away by the pallid wind, lured away,
carted away, poured away). (Then, hours later, it had edged a
bit further along. In my shirt at the window).

Four degrees above freezing, drizzle, windless, for now. (The
sheets ice-cold).

I flipped open the pliant, blue Kröner edition, and read the letter
that Friedrich Nietzsche sent to Jakob Burckhardt from the
Isle of Skye in the Hebrides in 1891: ". . . . . On the beach
among planks and other driftwood warped by storms, while
a whole skyful of starfish slowly swarms about me as I write:
we are building our ‹dragons› with no roof for the timid; the
sail, bordered in red, is already billowing on the foremast.—
Two of the boats will set out first, as scouting party, as ravens,
as Templar knights. I, leader of the main division, will follow
a few days later with the six remaining ships: my next laughing epistle [sic!], will already be sent to you, my friend, from
Helluland, just as soon as we have selected the sites for our
shanties . . . . ." (but here the text fuddled and I turned the
page, and strayed among fragments and glosses until I
awoke.—Happens to me often, leafing through books that
way. Though it's funny, since I usually can't stomach N!).

Kitchen solitaire: tiled cold and empty. Children asleep; wife
asleep; I: awake!—The silly red thermos bottle with its clayey
coffings; two cold-cut sandwiches, two with cheese: lovely
gray-golden slabs of "harzer" (not the stinky and runny kind:
that I don't like! Certainly a fine thing for a man to have ‹his
ways›. With a sneer).

Wind snapped in the garden and followed up with slurping watery footfalls.

The branches rattled in the night. (My coat billowed now with
brief braggadocio). Some rain whispered with the asphalt
road. (Like black wet woolen stockings, it meandered a long
while down through my thinkways. Or like a hearse, having
lost its way in great forests, groans, with black white-edged
curtains fluttering behind). Haggard bushes, too, clattered
skeletoned sarabands; the pavement glistened up at the lonely

streetlamp; stray notions were stirring like lemures up in the attic; my guts twanged out a puff: cozily warm up my back— *c'est la guerre!*

(*I'm no longer of mountain regions:* nor of the pasty hash dialect their inhabitants speak, nor of the countless vaultings of earth, tellurian baroque. My landscape must be level, flat, mile-wide, heathered, woods, meadow, fog, taciturn).

(*Not just geologically:* but intellectually and morally as well, the age is aptly called Alluvial: washed up. Lake dwellers and cavemen; minds full of the lumber of pile work or grottoes; Saxon Switzerland of the intellect. Lovely name: "Bell-Beaker Peoples"! Neither brachy- nor dolicho-: coeliocephalic! From forever standing at stiff attention, all things grow prognathous: 'ssir, Herr Neanderthal!)

There will be a delay!: all trains are late, ETA uncertain (and with brusque, official pride his fiery-red cap deplored this irregularity so fraught with responsibility). So we mutely took the couple of steps and shoved one after the other

into the tiny waiting room: at once dark circles began to take shape around each of us, unthinking, pocket-handed; only after some time had elapsed did murmurs arise (that would last for a good ten minutes; then they would grow furious, etc. etc., the well-known routine. I took care always to keep my she-wolf in view).

Which she noticed, and pulled snot up her nose, saucy and inviting, above her girlfriends. (The homework seemed still to be much the same: discussions of curves, Galsworthy, Wien's heat law, and "Didja read the fourth act?".—) The wind grew louder; crouching, it leapt here and there, stretched, breathed cavernously, and rummaged sportively in the slush; then it came to my window, reeled off three sentences in Gaelic, snorted away (for laughter, 'cause o' my mug), and was gone. The dark stains beneath us grew larger; the fellow in red picked up the telephone again; it hummed in his thin cord, and he made cautious and peeved inquiries.

So my thoughts went, and my meanwhile body stood at one corner of the station like an empty bus deserted by its driver.

Finally everything was shivering: from the back of the black iron-serpent it invaded coat collars. Puddles slurped in girls' flats (while the fat dragon sputtered flaccid steam that babbled and wobbled indecisively over the leaden gravel).

Smoking section: they inhaled and dreamed; and pro forma I too extracted a chic Attika.

The she-wolf: she ripped her breakfast sandwich into two handy pieces, slowly and with bemused fingers, so that a thick amber pearldrop of cheese rolled down into the glacial crevices of the wax paper (kindred souls, right?!). Then an apple. Then Schmeil-Norrenberg ‹Biology›.

"Lord, it's Runge!" (shamming): "Well?!" (Peters, Schönert, la Krämer, all of them, surrounding). And he told them, the proud and short of it.

About Bergen-Belsen: (as an SS man he had been assigned to duty on the camp staff, the fat bastard). "Oh, they all work nice and hard there!", with a pinched and lordly smile: "the Jews." Pause. He nudged the index card closer to his big blue eyes; but he just had to let it out: "And if they refuse—they string 'em up."—?!!?—: "On a special gallows."

Nothing! I know nothing. I don't meddle in any of it! (But this I do know: All politicians, all generals, all those who in any way rule or command are scoundrels! No exceptions! All of them! I still have a very good recollection of the big pogroms; I haven't forgotten how the SA hacked at Dr. Fränkel's typewriter with an ax, how they tipped the screaming piano out the window, till he committed suicide!: But lo the day shall dawn, you fine sons of bitches. And woe to him who then decides to give you fellows ‹another chance›!)

"Christ?: castrated himself!"; this was Schönert again, who read Matthew 19 verse 12 aloud with emphasis, the parallel passages, referred to the Skoptsy, and then went on spinning out his mangrove ideas. (But not all that far off the track, is he? Ventilate the matter a bit more sometime).

A small dark client, i.e. beltenebros, with a quite disproportionately high-set bust, was keeping Peters more than busy, who engaged her in long and excessively official conversation, while performing numerous carnal acts upon her with his fish eyes. (No harm in it: just sad! "She'd make a helluva triangle on the floor". Luther was the same way: he "could not look at a woman without coveting her" either!).

Then the typists' Saturday plans: "Has the commissioner issued any instructions about this noon?—Well then: ladies!", and I grumpily reached again for my folders, with a cold textile grip.

An Iron Cross of Motherhood!: It was old hunchback, drunken Benecke, him with the 14 kids; all of them right out of the funnies, red-haired, cross-eyed, teeth like Mah-Jongg tiles, a set of trolls: paddle his rear!

And so one cross for Mother: and she proudly spread her hands across that fat maternal tummy. (As long as the state goes on paying premiums for tupping, then we needn't wonder when our space keeps getting smaller.—But then: what am I a civil servant for?!)

When the well-known decree went out from Caesar Augustus, the world's population came to about 50 million. (Schönert confirmed this). Now the productive portion of the earth's surface is pretty much a constant. This agreed to as well. At the moment we have 2.5 billion people, i.e., fifty times as many; and every day they increase by 100,000: and so?! And now the opinions started bouncing off one another. (I'm all for sterilization of men—that's not castration—and for legalized abortion. There simply ought not to be more than 1 billion!)

Argumenum ad hominem: "Okay, then go get yourself sterilized, Herr Düring!" (Challenge and triumph: well?!): "Why right away, Herr Runge! Sooner today than tomorrow!". And Schönert, too, nodded in voluptuary amazement: "A free ride. And the pleasure's the same!", and bent deeper still over Fräulein Krämer's chair. (Then technical details: how it's done: bayonet in, foot down, and out. Or with a p'tatapeeler.)

"Left!:—Left!: - - A song!" (Labor Service), and the uniform marionettes jerked past legs adrumming, obediently laid back those Teutonic heads and burbled enthusiastically: "Oh say-crud land of loyalltee . . ." (and meantime millions were perishing in their concentration camps!) And the dashing gravediggers went on bawling, to be distinguished from a like number of mutton only in rough outline, my face delved deeper wrinkles, I sensed more ruins, more limbed corpses ("And like the eagle's winged flight / our spi-hirits so-hoar on high: fly on!"); No sardonic nod from me; no bitter smile; not me! Only a damn shame that I, seeing this, will have to play blindman's buff with the rest. (Well, maybe you can just stand off to one side. We'll see). (Elephantiasis of the idea of the state).

Nails chewed at the edges, indifferently dressed, broad face surrounding dull eyes: "A passport, please." (In very subdued clear High German: now that's worth something!). And I questioned a biography out of him myself. (Wanted a visa for England: i.e., to emigrate. Sly devils, these writers. They all had no ‹dependents›, and were freely mobile. While folks like us). "Distinguishing features?": "—: Perhaps: wears glasses?—" he suggested; nods and this and this. (But then it was too much for me after all, and I handed it to Master Otte to fill out in his splendid Sütterlin hand).*

‹*Communal Reception, 12 noon*›: and it was another Reichstag session, with Hurrah and Heil and glee club and lusty bellowing; for closers: "passed unanimously". (Plus: "A song!" And were so proud: in England there's always that disgusting pro and con in parliament: but we're united, from top to bottom!). And throughout the populace the serene, happy conviction: the Führer will take care of it! God, are the Germans stupid! 95 percent! (I.e., the others are no better either: just let the Americans elect themselves a Hindenburg sometime!)

People were carrying on like flags; their lips fluttered, their hands flapped, many of them ran swirling before the others. At the open windows the radios simmered and seethed their snappy music, into which gray wind now blended. Rain-light reappeared between the buildings, and soon thereafter liquid pins were skidding across asphalt seas.

Insensitive to the fate of my countrymen?: Whatever engages in brown carryings-on, brays marches, and does wild commerce with a groat's worth of words, is no countryman of mine! He's Adolf Hitler's countryman! (A half million perhaps are different, i.e. better; but then we ought to give ourselves a different name, emigrate, to Saskatchewan,—oh, it's all a sadness and un, and I stamped my skinny legs farther down the pavement. Or to the Falklands for all I care).

Rain scratched the panes (of the compartment); it grew dark again in our iron tube.

---

*The notes follow Dieter Kuhn's *Kommentierendes Handbuch zu Arno Schmidts Roman "Aus dem Leben eines Fauns"* (Handbook commentary to Arno Schmidt's *Scenes from the Life of a Faun,* Munich: Verlag text und Kritik, 1986. Sütterlin hand: A cursive writing developed by graphic artist Ludwig Sütterlin (1865–1917) that was obligatory in the Third Reich.

Brawl of wind: the hail prattled energetically. (Walsrode).

Woods: the entrance had been hurriedly hung with disorderly fog, whose lower hems still dragged loosely back and forth over the grass; and so, one corner raised, and a look inside:—(Dropped it. Damp in there. Shrubberish. Me).

"Walk on over to Trempenau's. Get some cold-cuts". And I walked along, stooped beneath the shallow sky hatched with rain, full of domestic bitterness and resigned.

The great white she-wolf: she laughed through cunning teeth, and bought rich red meat, and flabby pale sausages. Then she swung long-legged into the bicycle frame, setting her sucklers aquiver, and slid away, alert and cloudless. Between rain and sullen trees.

My favorite cat: even with my mere modicum of knowledge of the universe (tee-hee: what does one star feel when another gets "too close"?), I'm sure she'll soon transport her young to the open field, far off, so that she won't be completely neglected herself. (I've seen her do it out of jealousy once before!)—Exactly the same with people: once there are children, the man is neglected. (For years now my wife, sullen and with sly sincere excuses, has avoided gratifying me! There will be consequences!).

"Well, Miss Femininity?" (my daughter): came up bright-voiced and wanted a mark for notebooks. "You're sure you're not underage for this movie?" I warned reproachfully, and she gave me a ladylike slap(!) and laughed.

"Water—'s—ready!"; in wooden clogs and bathrobe with bundled towel, I stalked into the scullery, to the tub of gray.

Naked (and scalded red); but it's almost too cold! I lathered my chilled rear and appurtenances; resolutely arose and terry-clothed everything dry.

Rap at the pane: "Hàlloo!" Käthe Evers (the she-wolf): she probed with squint-eyes, recognized me, took a good look at it all, including chest and legs, and laughed aloud. No doubt of it: her laugh exploded, and she ran around the corner of the house. M. (Cosmotheoros: doesn't that mean "peek-at-the-world"?).

Clean underwear; and then I strode once more among the endless and dreadful, black-red tapestries of life, wailing, menacing, lingering in sleep.

Sitting in the armchair: the clock obediently twitched its little numbers at me. (Sometimes the big one inside would let out a haughty and squeezed laugh: "Ah!"; "Oh!"; then the hum of the courtier chorus returned). The cats pulsed inside their fur; breathing. Pulse means life. Maybe we are born between two breaths of the sun (ice-age; inter-ice-age). Presumably the conception of "time" is also dependent on the size of the living being in question; I have another conception than does a 4,000-year-old sequoia, or an infursorium with a second of life, or a δ-cepheid star, or the Leviathan, or the stranger nearest me, or my neighbor . . .

In the shed: the latest thing is for bicycles to get taillights and license numbers: as if they were at fault for the accidents! I have a better idea: no vehicle would be allowed to have a motor that could propel it faster than 25 mph: that would quiet things down at once. (But more than likely some manufacturer of electric lamps, or the friend of one, was sitting in the Reichstag; probably the simplest explanation).

The sun burned out at the lower edge of the sky (down to cloud cinders); out of the woods a gray moor-ghost arose; grass and withered things dripped much and snored (next to my high shoes, my trousers). I adjusted my head on its leg-stand to horizontal and measured about me: five lights, 200 degrees of woods, then marshland and muddled field (and no radio, no newspaper, no Volk, no Führer!). Wind accommodatingly coiffed my hair (which I'm not fond of at all!), and whish-purred washily and figarosy: cut it out!

Across the road, to where the she-wolf was oiling the garden gate. (And I walked in the grayvity of the air, as if through great winter coats, my hands closed tight and ear stilled). Cold. Gray ice-mush lay thin before every step; the woods cast desolate rings around the ashpit world; we gawked into each other's spotted souls (while coagulating gases eddied from our mouths. Hairy meaty troughs, that's us. And locked in the cold carton of slush). A mute return to our respective houses. (Later I saw her again at the window, tugging the curtain to one side. Soon I shall be a white-haired old man, with stump teeth and veined finger-tubing, leaky hearted, with tough grisly notions, cluck cluck.)

At the very last: bloody cloud torsos piled in the west, the light's mass grave, drenched in gore, in smokiness. (The woods lay

like a blue wreath mourning in silence around my horizon).
The lunar wake light burned out quite rapidly too; the squar-
ish houses in the development cast faint furtive glances from
yellow nooks, velvet yellow in parlors, very soft images.
(While out there clouds were dying!). Wire rattled once along
the fence. *Sotto voce*. All this happening above sheet 3023,
ordnance map.

"And spring: comes: tothevalley": there's just no end to it! (And
wife and kids hummed contentedly along, and even clapped
too!). "But in Spain 'tis one thousand and three": dead, that
is, at least; well, the civil war is finally drawing to its close
(though with yet another guard tyrant!).

Wind grumbled in the evacuated night; clouds still moved about,
whole wagonloads, gray; but it was cold again; the tiny feverish stars were already twitching.

Without sleep and the makis of thought crept quick as cats out of
every shrubbery: documents claused with honor; schoolkids
collared-sailor; pimply military bullied; punk lecheries
stroked almond-milkily about my leg; summer trips of old
slunk tigered light closer, in the green willow-basket of
woods; the she-wolf sauntered past several times in search of
seed; (and therefore not a continuum: a heap of bright illustrated tiles; a museum of flash-shots. I burrowed onto my
other side, groaning and) cascades of immature headscarves
scrutinized me; numbers painted white obligingly milestoned
by (if I stray into algebra, then that's it for the night); and ever
more dealings in old curios, neck or naught, until, in fact, I
heard the one-o'clock train whistle to me from Jarlingen.

Cloud isles with melting shorelines, a trim bright red skiff drifted
there for a long time. (In the tidelands of my morning
thoughts, wheels trundled now and again, a neighbor's lethar-
gic curse. Get up, hop out of my pajamas).

:Me?: Young?! (At the mirror: Ugh!). There is indeed a wide-
spread misconception among the afflicted that they are twice
as interesting at age 50 as at 25: if I tucked in my little round
belly, I was tall and slim (sure, and if I had lots of money I'd
be a wealthy man). Hair moderately mildewed; behind the
glasses goggly eyes:—No sir!! I stoutly turned my back on the
fixture (then into my trousers and shaving, shaving, o thou delight of swains: that's the most disgusting part!).

A bush, which in lieu of leaves had titmice wearing chic black berets: bent forward with a defiant show of canary-green bosoms, and scolded for food.—"'ve we still got a piece of bacon rind, Berta!"; but my wife was apparently still sweeping up, and yelled back in annoyance: "Don't bother me now.—: Later." I closed the door again: bueno; gave the titmice the word, and read for a few minutes (no "Morning Benediction", not to worry! Still prefer my "Écumoire").*

"Holy Gohod we praihaise thy name:" (from Evers's wide-open radio across the way, while the old lady mugged pork chops and swept out her dress; and then the real gospelization started up). Even on long-wave there was solemn chewing on Cheesus Kraist, organs droning with bovine warmth, and there was no saving oneself from all those dairies of pious kindness. Wait: Radio Moscow, pfweewitt: and some ‹Character Sketch› or other tumbled out of the loudspeaker: I don't understand a thing about music, I admit, but that sure was too crude for me! Marches, doodle waltzes, oom-pah music: no need for that either!

Rearranging furniture: is my wife's passion; every three months I come home to a strange house.—At first I was upset as usual; then indifferent: go ahead and do what you want! And I helped carry and shove, whistling the while: fine with me! (Besides which, she was happy that I was so cooperative: voilà, both sides served!)

Cock-a-doodle-doo: cackcackcockle; and they whetted their feet on the ground, plucked, beaked machines, in the bark, (one flapped several feet into the air, gabbling), and were dreadfully stupid. "All leghorns", oldman Weber explained proudly (convinced that came from the German "legen", much the same as Saanen goats from "Sahne". How awfully ignorant "the people" are and thus so easily deceived!: when I hear a Führer-speech, I automatically compare it to Agamemnon, Pericles, Alexander, Cicero, Caesar, and on to Cromwell, Napoleon, Wars of Liberation, "Parties no longer exist for me"—and what an ass he was!—and can only laugh at the resounding charlatanry. While "the people" think there was

---

*Clode-Prosper Jolyot Crébillon's (1707–77) work *L'Écumoire au Tanzai et Néadarné* (1732 or 1734).

nothing like it anywhere ever, and don't see the consequences: instead of taking their cue from the dupes of millennia past, and thrashing the rear ends of such mountebanks!—But ultimately ignorance is its own fault, and no cause for pity, and Weber wouldn't have believed me anyway, because "legen" seems so right, and "horn" sounds so Siegfriedian: therefore I slyly pronounced it just as fecundly as he, and we understood one another, too. And how).

"Foxes snatch chickens. Hawks snatch chickens." (People snatch chickens!—: Wars snatch people; plagues snatch people, death snatches everyone!—But that's going almost too far; I won't think about that any more!)

And speaking of Weber the cobbler!: One of those fellows who can go on for hours telling how they "served under three Kaisers," and with pride no less. He had even spoken with one of them: they had been standing guard in front of the royal palace in Berlin; the coach pulled up: Present arms!—!!(—At this point he invariably added "'nd did we evah!"). "From Pomerania, my lad, right?" his majesty had remarked affably, and then "Fine, fine" or "Stout fellow" or some other such unforgettable phrase: what a thrill, right?! Weber swung his spoonchisel like a misericord and kept stroking away at his (long since shaved-off) mustache.

Daddy's little girl's pastime: "Just imagine, dad: Käthe Evers from across the street's a ‹sexion leader› now!" (That was the great she-wolf, and I lent an ear: "Mm-hm."—Well, in my day, youth movements had flourished too; back then ‹Pluckfiddle Jack› and ‹maidens' hostels› were all the rage: youth presumably comes only in packs. But that was respectable at least, compared to this ‹National Youth›!)

Actually I was always a loner—always!

She was singing at the window across the way: a very simple folk song, the medieval Lochheim school, and with such sweet intensity that I was immediately suspicious: wasn't it you who almost bored a hole in my scullery window yesterday?! (And right off Gerda sent up a military salute).

A child wearing gloves, incessantly declaiming the word ‹palikánda›, recitativo secco, presumably a name it had coined itself to designate some Spicy Islands or other. (But in time the interminable singsong proved too much for me, and I made an attempt to silence it by mental telepathy; in vain again, of course; and so resigned myself to having to put up with it).

A deer-, a dear-, a wandering deer-vish: at Weber's door, exchanged the password, and came converting; to the New Apostolic Church, and got fresh in that pious-familiar way common to all members of his tribe: "I possess the Book of Books," he insisted with nauseating sanctimony. *"The Encyclopaedia Britannica?!"* I cried with feigned envy: "I'll be damned!," and we stared in contempt at each other, for a bit, holy Holbach, is there no end to such idiots!—"We are here below but a brief span of time: you must regard all you possess as merely lent to you: house, money, clothes– –" (his really looked as if they had been). "Our Lord Jesus: called only the simplest folk to him as apostles to proclaim his word: who could neither read nor write!" (absurdly triumphant!) "Just keep holding fast to your precepts", I said in disgust, letting the fellow babble on his way, and Weber met his kismet.

I am a servant of the heath, a worshiper of leaves, a devotee of wind! (And I exchanged heated words with myself for having responded to the monkey in the first place.)

"Field drill!"—" and my wife pointed in distress at Paul Düring, age 16. "Let him do some knee-bends and shake the crap loose"; and my zebraic son, Feirefies, was enthusiastic. ("The expressions you use, Heinrich!"; my wife).

Let me see your school notebooks"; and he handed them to me haughtily, as if to a lunatic. Leafing through: English satisfactory, French satisfactory, German satisfactory minus. (You have to take a look once in a while. Though my father, in all seriousness, would almost go crazy if I brought home a mere ‹good› instead of a ‹very good›; made dire prophecies, threatened to "yank me out", and played the regular fool). So, I put pedagogical wrinkles on my brow, but said nothing: was satisfactory after all, and that was that. (Above all, avoid lending support to teachers' grandiose fantasies that school is the world's navel or good for life or whatever). Then I weighed the notebooks in my hand, and gave it a try: "Tellmepaul—: you ever studied up on communism?". He tumbled off his cloud and climbed right back up: "What the—" he began, and shook his head in merry derision; scornful: "Not worth the

trouble! The Third Reich put all that behind it long ago."
"Meaning you know nothing about it, and let other people do
your thinking for you?" I challenged him coldly, "Have you
compared it to National Socialism?: You'd probably get quite
a surprise.". "No comparison," he said coolly and with infinite superiority: "what we have is a weltanschauung"; and departed, a man once again sure of himself. (No point in saying
anything to anyone!)

"What exactly does immunity mean, dad?" (intended as the
hand of reconciliation I suppose), and I explained it to him.
"But why Reichstag members exactly?" "Probably because
they'd all be arrested first thing," I said nastily, and we could
at least laugh a bit together. (Then I gave them each two
marks: since human ingenuity has yet to devise a way for us
to take our goods with us into the next world, from time to
time one must teach children a disdain for money, cautious
wastrels: "And spend it: saving is nonsense!" I added. Even if
it makes every hair stand on end: I had to endure enough of
the damned piggy bank complex as a child!)

Another hour till mealtime: so some easy-chair reading.– –
Hold it.

Ants in the parlor!: Behind the bookcase, they streamed out from
under the baseboard by the hundreds. Gerda swept them up
onto the broad gray dustpan, and I sprayed a fine mist of
DDT. (What a shame. They're bright fellows. Many murders
and catastrophes: how they would rail against the Leviathan—i.e., me!; menacing and desperate, shaking their antennae, stamping defiance and heroic courage with all six feet.
And my slit muzzle relentlessly blew poison and death. Hast-
ings and fleeings, innumerably jointed, limberly escapist).

We humans, too, ought to be beheaded: very quickly, before old
age and sickliness torment us, quite businesslike, with no
transition. In your sleep. Or at woods' edge as you walk to
the station, attacked by four hooded figures, dragged beneath
the scaffold: plop!!

At the bookcase: The big Spanish edition of *Quixote* by Diego
Clemencin, six volumes quarto. Madrid 1833–39: like to have
that!

Swift, Cooper, Brehm: of the thirteen volumes, I've always been
most interested in the "Fishes". And then the "Lower Ani-

mals". (The most repulsive was always "Insects"). Whoever
wants to write a book has to have a lot to say: usually more
than he has.—Middle High German perhaps?: often in cas-
tles: Soltane and Canvoleis, Belripar and Montsalvaz, Cardigan and Grahars, and all those other ancient magical names
that leave you sitting there moaning at knuckles. Or medieval
tales: Herzog Ernst (the journey through the hollow mountain, that especially. And the Agrippinas); Fortunatus and his
sons. Great man, Ludwig Tieck (And in contrast how stiff-
legged and precocious Goethe's prose seems, so "respectable"
and Privy-Councillorish: it never once dawned on him that
prose could be an art form; you can only laugh, e.g., at the
pompous bungling of his "Novella"!)

Every writer should grab hold of the nettle of reality; and then
show us all of it: the black filthy roots; the poison-green viper
stalk; the gaudy flower(y pot). And as for the critics, those intellectual street-porters and volunteer firemen, they ought to
stop tatting lace nets to snare poets and produce something
"refined" themselves for once: that would make the world sit
up and take roaring notice! Of course, as with every other
grand and beautiful thing, poetry is hedged in by its comple-
ment of geldings; but: the genuine blackamoors are the ones
who rejoice in the sun's black spots! (All of this for the re-
viewers' albums).

Tierra del Fuego: Young Darwin travels to the Fireland.—Must
be lovely: wide dense cold rain forests. Savage light from endless cloudworks. Sea and hard mountain heads. No men and
no snakes: lovely! (I'd loathe tropical jungles. I'm for cold forests, endlessly spare. I'd love to see the ones in northern Can-
ada. And, as noted, those of Fireland.—"Din-ner's-read-dy!")

One still on the loose, a loner, between shelved abysses: give him
the shoe! (That's how I'd like to die too: running darkly
among tree torsos, inspecting herbs, puppy-tracking berries:
and then hit with a half-ton meteor!: Jagged flame, compacted
head. Sela (probably Hebrew for ‹that's it›)).

Roast with sauerkraut ("Music to Dine By: from German Broad-
casting"; and once again the ever-popular favorites, a tilting
at melody, opus 0.5).—Cats have a passion for sautéed
mushrooms, with onions, pepper, salt, caraway.—"Lie down
a bit."

I waited patiently for the dishes to be done.
Last try: I cupped my wife's right breast in my hand, and coaxed: "C'mon". (Swallow). "Let's, what do you say!"– –. "But you've still got such a nasty cold", she sidestepped with hypocritical concern (as if I were a daddy of 70!), and, when I didn't let go of her mammary flesh at once, added "Ouch," with martyrific composure.—: OK, the end.—
OK, the end!!: once-and-for-all the end! I went to my room, M., and stretched out for a while. (At my age you simply can't think anymore after a good meal. At best maybe a little work.—What I trust most are the beauties of nature. Then books; then roast with sauerkraut. All else changes, legerdemains).
"I'm going for a little walk.—?— Toward Benefeld.". Shuffling wind waded insolently through the blue and gray puddles, blew rings on them, almost splattering.
‹*Cordingen Lumber*› on the sign above legs directly ringed white and blue; (apparently had been yellow and black at one time).
At a village window: the typical knotted curtains of the central Lüneburg Heath, and behind them the vase of asters: cold white, colder wobbling violet. And the wind was running again in great gray groups. The world, a new unplastered construction, drafty, and at best a charcoal stove inside (to dry it out; desolate and echoing, like a deserted ballroom).
"Come: let's play Winter Relief Fund": She shakes her little box, and He sticks something in; I gave my ten pfennigs and got back a gray fish with button-eye as proof I'd payed my taxes; and they were standing on every corner, collecting, farmers and townsfolk of Brandenburg stock, costumed in brown and belted with shiny leather, caps like French gendarmes, frozen a pretty red, and I smiled, and kept pointing at my fish (my, he's a hard-working fellow: I'll hold on to him, with his blue eye!).
The large munitions factory, ‹Eibia›, with its railroad tracks, streets, giant bunkers (overgrown on top with camouflage forests), and thousands of workers. While down on the Warnau lay the whole little New Town of a hundred bright houses, and very prettily done.—But elderly light gnashed on high and wallowed and weltered, grew gray and severe, the black slowly pushing my way. Bald bushes were already rapping witches' knuckles.

Skat jargon (had had a beer): have they ever actually been collected, from "pants down" for open nullo, to "the man with the long club"? Would make a doctoral dissertation for a "folklorist", they shrink from nothing. (But what else should I think about?! Death? God?: ah, good god! Even the most beautiful evening sky above the Oster Moor passes away: why should an old stink-sack like me want to be eternal?! Swellheaded Christian bunch!—So head back).

Piece of country road. Moon. Me: We stared at each other, until old stony-face up there had had enough and with help from the wind sleight-of-handed himself a shade of blue, two against one, smeared the road with pasty white light (and ogled me for a long time from behind gauze, veils, cloths, trays, bales).

The ‹Coaster Express› at the Cordingen station: a lopsided giant carousel with varying circles of light and whetting samba music: ". . . and from the top—: / it's no go! It's no go!". (Followed at once by "Maria from Bahia", and on the nimbly flowing conveyor belt, the she-wolf with wide calves and cartwheeling coat. And Paul was watching eagerly, too).

Encore une fois: the spongy moon in curdled cloudworks. Left: houses gray and soapy; black ajarred doors leading in; roofs wrinkled clear to the top. On the right: along the sallow rag of meadow, wool and silk, and populated by the shades of enslaved, half-starved trees.

Genealogical research: my son quizzed me greedily (and as usual treated as a sport: who can trace back the furthest). Thankgod it quickly came to an end with my illegitimate father, and disappointed, he jotted it down. Nor in the other lines were there any great men to be hunted down—officers, politicians, artists: had all been very simple honest folks!

"Turn on the news.": weather; results from the latest charity drive; soccer; even now the after-throes of the ‹Day of the Assumption of Power›. Crisis in rump Czechoslovakia (they definitely want to occupy that too: well, I'm curious how long they'll get away with it).

In bed: the days passed, regularly, like tearing pages from a calendar. At once the grave countenance of "my" commissioner appeared to me, and I got the frenzied notion to tattoo something on that broad forehead of his, with indelible ink: so he'd have to run around forever like that! I wavered for a long time between "Bon voyage!" and "Vote Communist!" (and his wife gets it big on her belly, just above where the hair starts,– –: "Come in!"? Nah.– –"Encore"? Nah. No good. But then it hit me: "Welcome Stranger!," in Bodoni Antiqua, so painstakingly I engraved it; and avenged, giggled off to sleep).

Radium numbers: only three. To the john, number one; and then to the window: boulders of air with polished edges; across the way, fields and roads done in angular woodcuts by the moonlight, until barely recognizable.

Idea: if we had gospels by women, by Mathilda Margo Lucy and Johanna, you can rest assured that the redeemer would have been of female gender as well. (The death mask of the moon was still hanging in the stonegray sky).

The gaunt silver-mailed face (behind the house): the Don Quixote of the stars. (And the earth is his fat Sancho Panza with pork-chop heart and big baloney imagination: why just yesterday, didn't "Your Hit Parade" start off with "When Huba plays the tuba down in Cuba"?? What kind of insensitive automata could ever
(a) lyricize & musicize
(b) sing it and cut a public record
(c) even buy it
(d) broadcast it
(e) sit there and peacefully (or excitedly for that matter) listen to it!
(:Who does all that?!: your famous ‹Aryan German›! An employee of Western Christian Civilization, Inc.!)

Achillean fellow, the moon: dragged a stiff cloud corpse behind him around our earthenware Troy (blustery).

Her girlfriend (in the train): She wore a pair of dark snow-goggles, by the aid of which every modern teen thinks she's donned a spell of wide-eyed mystery (if only they could keep their mouths shut then!). This one had Sarah-Leandering eyes and mutely opened her book, its cover coarse-fleshed, emphatically made for the Volk:—?—: Hans Friedrich Blunck! (That too!).

What wretched trash! (Besides which, she held it so that the gilt edge kept flashing in my eyes! That too!).

And the poor she-wolf!: a black fountain pen (with golden belt) rotated in its yellow grove of fingers, slowly and sadly gleaming; josephine baker, cul de Paris; her brow mutinied, her mouth lipped reluctantly on lycéean word-grids; her worn-down shoes stood with toes turned wearily in. (Afterward, came something fervid about "medieval German painting", as she gruffly told her friend, and asked her for a few makeshift syllables.—Pretty sight, the way the young savages brewed away angrily at the spectral stuff: just keep right on rebelling!)

"Sure, Herr Peters!". Outside, white cloud balls rose up from the horizon; the elastic wind bounced by, and then again, like a high-jumper. "Didja hear Goebbels yesterday?" (And the way he speaks, Quick & Slow, vaulted words, round as eggs, and all of it crap, invalid and outrageous): "Sure, I heard him." (Wasn't true at all! I've got more serious things to do with my time!). "Now that's a real conviver!" (Peters on Goebbels. = Shrewd character. From ‹Qui vive› of course).

Take a look around the platform: in the impoverished, red-frozen sky the solid saucy moon, grin silence. A tractor hammered, jeered stench, popped impertinent; ‹Pfeiffer Coal Company›.

On past the book store: it still seems remarkable enough: when I was just a schoolboy, my father gave me an English dictionary one Christmas, and apparently expected storms of enthusiasm. Today I stand nodding reverently before the great Grieb-Schröer and would like to have it.

Scandal, scandal: Otte's cousin (the one from Berlin) had used the occasion of his visit to give himself a promotion to squad leader in the SA, and was now to be excommunicated.: Just like the "Führers" up top, who are forever thinking up new titles for each other, new ranks and Arabian-Nights' uniforms. The whole nation is in the grip of a mania for medals and badges, enthusiastically weaving away on the legend of its own grandeur!: The sort of thing that truly fits the Germans to a T!

In which case, I'd prefer Schönert's snappy smut; "Yes?", and you really did have to laugh: he gave me a clandestine peek at Fräulein Knoop's coat-of-arms—the busy and fat one, pinky-white and frosty—a naked girl with a candle in her hand, and the motto "nosce te ipso"—. A well-honed mind, Schönert's (though not a polished one); but he's "against" them too, as far as it goes, and mutual nausea is enough to create a kind of

working sympathy; and, after all, most people are ignorant to
the same degree they are clever.

That's the musical instrument I hate the most: the people's ac-
cordion! With its bloated, wishy-washy, knobby tones.

HeilittlerSomethingIcandoforyou?" (and play the citizen, fine,
and keep the nation going; let not thy right hand know. So I
raised it lightly in German greeting, while balling my free left
fist: will divide my life that way: an open half, supportive of
the state. And the balled left).

(I reserve for myself any action against the state!: that's necessary for my personal security! For the state can forcibly con-
strain me to participate in anything its responsible-
irresponsible leaders may feel like thinking up: whereas in an
emergency I do not have the power to force the state to pru-
dence or justice or fulfillment of its duties. Therefore I must
constantly resist the arbitrary power of the state—not forgetting that most fundamental right: being allowed to leave said
state unendangered and with all my property intact. And
don't anyone come along with the lofty objection: that as a
petty civil servant I simply lack a broad overview of things!!
And may your generals and politicians roar as brazenly as
they like about the Golden Age that has just burst upon us: in
ten years you'll have totally demolished Germany! And then
we'll see who was right: little Düring, or all the big shots and
95 percent of the German people! But I am completely outraged by the notion of joining in the dance, of being forced to
join against my better judgment; and I will shape my actions
accordingly!)

A telephone call: "Herr Commissioner? – –. – –.": "11:30, yes
sir.— Yes sir." Bang hang up.—"Meeting of all department
heads in the boss's office," I explained to Peters, "another
major housecleaning for sure: bewailing of infirmities."

In the Commissioner's office and silence. Naturally he kept us
waiting to impress us; eight men and the lady caseworker with
the Queen Luise badge on her blue linen Valkyrie breast. All
right by me: all gets deducted from our work-time! (Unfortunately from our life-time as well). Hissing of the radiators.

Above him on the wall: von Seeckt, the "Founder of the New
German Army", Heil, with persuasive monocle: a tradition of
upper-echelon officers that can be traced to Wodan (cf. Ru-

dolf Herzog's report concerning the Götterdämmerung:
". . . his one lone eye flashed and glinted").
"No, you may go, Frau Woltermann."; leaning back (he looked
as if he were thinking very incisively about nothing). "Which
of you has—uh—" skillful pause; once more he casually
picked up the document (although he knew every detail of the
contents; to be followed at once by the customary dressing-
down)—"had some higher education?", he said it with lofty
commiseration: "—matriculated perhaps." ("Or whatever"
would have been even better. Whereas his diss for his PhD had
been on "The economic history of cabinet-making in the prin-
cipality of Leiningen, its contemporary importance and its
prospects for the future"!) "The other gentlemen may return
to their work—", like being at the court of Prince Irenäus.
And now he looked at us three more closely. "You're only
twenty-six, Herr Schönert?—twenty-seven?—Hmm.—Yes,
well, that won't do, thank you." He looked intensely at the
window and gave himself a long pinch under his white chin:
God, how difficult it was to make oneself understood with
mere-high-school graduates! "Do you still know any foreign
languages?—Latin or English or French?—" (Very hesitantly,
as if it were hopeless; and avoid the "and" at all cost; and I
smiled to myself, arrogant and forbearing, malicious and pa-
tronizing: oh god, how we despised one another!!). "I sure
don't 'nymore, Commissioner, sir," Nevers declined, believa-
bly aghast, and so he too left us, alone. "Well then: you do
speak English?" he asked in English, indulgently and with a
genial smile; and we exchanged a few ragged idioms, copro-
lithic phrases, while I labored to imitate his botched pronunci-
ation. Yez. (Yes). "Fine," he said, more soberly and
businesslike: "by the way—where did you learn to speak English so—uh—tolerably well?" "In the first world war, Herr
Commissioner. Served in France; and then as an English prisoner-of-war. Was camp interpreter; I still read it fairly often,
too." "Ah, you were a soldier!" he feigned surprise: "—uh—
your rank?". "Just an enlisted man, Commissioner, sir", jauntily (i.e. the last three months as a noncom, but I wasn't about
to tell him that: with people like him it's best to set boundaries
and keep as much distance as possible!)
"Ah yes: And you're already—uh—?". "Fifty-one, Herr Commissioner". He nodded, lips pressed tight: "That does nicely!"

he said with emphasis; then: "Do you have any particular leanings, active member in a church or that sort of thing?". "As a civil servant, sir, I know only church-es", I declared as prescribed by regulation: "I do not care if I write ‹catholic› or ‹turk› or ‹agnostic› in someone's passport." He weakly smiled his approval: "Not religious then," he summarized, nodded, came to a decision: "Really is high time such nonsense came to an end." Directed to the clock, more lively now: "Fine, then, Herr Düring!—What we are concerned with is the following: recently we received orders to set up a kind of archive here in the office, dealing with the history of the district—we'll clear out a room or two in the cellar for it—uh—and we'll have to gather materials, documents and such from the various towns and villages, sift through and file them. Possibly local parish records as well; and—should there be time—perhaps from those of private individuals as well. On the whole a massive task—and of course carries a great deal of responsibility with it" he dutifully interjected, "and then, too, it presupposes—a certain—knowledge of foreign languages. Latin, French, English principally, I'd say—uh—you would have to inspect most items, I presume, out in the field—in" he interrupted himself, and looked over to the large district map on the wall—"—in—uh: Ahlden and Rethem, for instance: mountains of material there I'm sure; Walsrode, too, perhaps; possibly Stellichte, at Herr von Baer's—" he waved this aside testily, as if I had made some irksome request: "—well, I know him personally, so I could—if need be—arrange for your – – being admitted.—" he raised his head in affable candor: "Quite interesting work, wouldn't you say?!—You're an intelligent fellow:—?" (What an impudent bastard; but I at once gave tit for tat: I smiled such a blissfully stupid smile and gave such a silly obsequious nod that he noticed, and grew deadly serious; he gnawed slowly on his gray sausage lips. Pause). "I should be most hesitant to assign this to one of our highschool teachers," he continued dispassionately, "since those gentlemen make difficulties and demands enough as it is.—Would you want to take it on?" and with eyes ever so bright and clear, like Nietzsche's mountains in the forenoon. I briefly knit my brow; then (by way of clarification) I inquired as to the duration of the special mission. "Yes, of course," he said with a nod, "I would propose that you devote three days a week to it—and I'll add another, older trainee to your department.—Who could stand in for you those three days every week? Whom would you suggest? Peters, Schönert,: which is the more dependable?" (Typical rotten trick, passing the question on to me!). "The more dependable is Peters: the more intelligent Schönert—" I said critically, feigning concern. "Which means?" he demanded (secretly smiling and curious; but I did not betray myself). "If I may make a suggestion," I hesitated manfully, and then ethically: "Herr Peters!". "Fine," he nodded to me with satisfaction, "There are, however, some—further incidental instructions you'll need, and—I also want to satisfy myself fully as to your qualifications—: could you come by my place for an hour or so this evening?" (‹Place›, how modest: it was that twelve-room villa on Walsrode Road!) "Shall we say then—: 6 P.M.—: is that agreeable?!" (How silly, considering he's the ‹master› and I'm the lackey!); to close the deal, forced a cheese-smile, and nodded into the void with a look of torment and overwork.

"Well?!" (curious), and I told them in brief. (And Peters was proud to be my stand-in; and Schönert wasn't offended or anything: nooo: relieved!: Spirit of my spirit! That's precisely why I did it that way. Would've been a catastrophe the other way around).—Wind springs up outside and clouds.

David Copperfield: Schönert suggested that the name of the supporting hero, Steerforth, be transcribed phonetically into German as ‹Stierfortz› (= bull fart) (not all that wrongheaded; he's always coming up with something new). Then lunch; sandwiches and a stroll.

Clouderama (like the Judgment of Paris): a slender nimble one in most clinging white; a proper fatty with baronially rounded butt, and majestic bosom of fat, as if built by the Romans. (Later, then, the breezy skinny one with red piratical hair and the narrow bluish back of a busy whore: so She's the winner!)

In front of a movie poster: the she-wolf with schoolbag. She was comparing legs, breasts and blonde giggles with her own (and didn't lose; though her face was blunt and gamy): "Might I ask a favor of you, Fräulein Evers:—". She merely turned her massive head (was not to be surprised). "Käthe" she said laconically through her teeth, and I laughed awkwardly:

"—OK, fine—: Fräulein Käthe—". "Käthe" she said more menacingly "—what is it?!—". Confused and giddy, I swallowed hard: "Please, Käthe", I said (and our eyebrows whipped blissfully: She's the winner!): "Could you stop on your way home and tell my wife: I'll be taking the late train this evening. And so on." "And so on." she repeated imperturbably, nodded that she was agreeable, and then coolly reimmersed herself in studying the line of the calf: placed her foot forward (and seemed satisfied).

Blue silk sky and embroidered with white (but a pattern, some homey proverb, was not to be made out), and I stalked on through streets frozen dry, and inspected the ancient shop windows: a man really ought to own a Visolett magnifying glass like that. Six inches in diameter, for maps and such; but they were scandalously expensive too, guaranteed twenty marks, and I then went on to muster the hollow spectacle frames in their perfect rows.

Pooh!: Bedouin dust pelted an ashen path down the blustery street, cloaks of sand spooked about, setting the wind horses to snorting outright.

A very cool résumé of Hanoverian history: how it all sort of coagulated peu à peu: the principalities of Bremen and Verden; Lüneburg and Celle; the earldoms of Hoya and Diepholz; right in the middle along the Weser, bounded in quince-yellow, the merry little enclave of Thedinghausen. The connections with the Court of St. James; the French and Prussian occupation. (Sure: learned in school).

Memories (school memories): Max Hannemann and Kurt Braunschweig: those two had great literary talent; essays of humorous social criticism. (All vanished!).—A cloud carefully watered the clearing across the way (but left me in peace), and then drifted off on its mission.

Light in the office: the desk lamps, bent like bobbed-haired women, mutely diligent; the angular printed forms turned an unbearable forest green and gave sweet pain; empty posters of light askew on the walls and overlapping like expressionist paintings. "Not taking the train tonight, Herr Düring?". "I still have to go see the commissioner. At his place." Lower lips shoved forward in admiration; with Peters it was respectful envy. And rompings of coulds, black and red behind spears of pine.

October pibroch (and here it was February): and a whole clan of gray clouds, ladies from hell, marched my way; the fields began to mutiny hoarsely; skeletal bushes grasped (clutched) one another in despair. At her shop window, a sporty salesgirl appeared and wrestled down the iron grating. (Then another girl, superfluous, who helped her: fewer people!) More fans of bare trees, brown lace fans, giant tracery; more books and square feet per capita: therefore fewer people!)

The curt moon sat on the rim of the steeple; the one black bell, in the belfry opening, growled dully to those below.

The lilliputian whinnies of the doorbell: hauntings in the house. First, distant and meaningful slam, then the taking of many more stairs than could belong to the gloomy flight, a cavernous clang and murmurings, it dragoned its way to just behind the door and lay there in keyed-up ambush:

The maid: a wagtail aflutter and proper and affected as a fancy doll ("What a pair of lung lobes!" Schönert would have marveled). "Yes, the Herr Commissioner is in." "I know," I said pointedly, "and he knows too. Please tell him that Düring is here. Dü-rrink." (Well, go on: yellow stairwell, vaulted; silly pretenses).

From the little mirror in the guest toilet came abrasive shrill light (pictures of Schandau and Königstein, curlicued soil, as if designed by some Balthasar Pöppelmann or other: hate thy neighbor as thyself!).

The elegant chairs leaned back with an easy superiority; the table's broad stump was missing mossy roots (and fungal gelatin of floral yellow on the side).—I entered, so artfully clumsy that I almost tripped over the brown tendrils in the carpet: my my, that did please the boss qua boss (and in general).

Smiling, he approached the round table: he acknowledged me, o joy! The table lamp (its shade pasted with delicate grasses: looked quite nice!); first guidelines & recommendations, available resources, "—my library is, of course, at your disposal—", Dictionary of German Biography (: know it all better than you! And we turned our bespectacled faces to one another, benevolently—he—and maliciously—I).

"The records will only date back to the Thirty Years War at best". "In any case do keep me informed about the more interesting findings." And I jotted it all down on my pad with

zealous nods, thrilled, probably wrote ‹Mooncalf Moses› between the lines too, smiled submissively, and dotted the i on ‹compoop›.

"You have a bicycle, don't you?": "Yes sir, Commissioner.", and gazed at him with earnest schoolboy eyes, the beloved instructor of the Working Classes: which means I'm to pedal all over your district?!. "You live in—uh:—", "Colony Hünzingen, Herr Commissioner." "Ah—I see": "Yes, sir. Just off the new road Benefeld-Ebbingen—". "Ah, the one they've improved on account of the powder bakery!" he nodded, drawing cross brows (was, you see, a big government thing, top secret, and absolutely not under his jurisdiction, the Eibia!): "Well then, obviously you have your monthly rail-pass for Fallingbostel,—" (I tucked a bow like a railroad switch) "and hold other expenses down as much as possible. Of course we'll cover any necessary items; but: within limits, understood?" Ductile and tranquil: "But of course, Herr Commissioner." (but mix in a dollop of petit-bourgeois pique): "but of course!" "Good."

He leaned back (therefore, end of the official segment; and now yellow Sir Lion wants to amuse himself somewhat with the Mouse; and I gazed at him as intensely as if I were about to paint his portrait—:—?—?—:)

She hit the switch with an energetic graceful slap (his daughter) and the funnel of light took its position in the room around us. I was cut asunder between glare and shadow, and I sensed bodily discomfort.

A white face: very pretty, arrogant, barred by two red lip-bolts; eyes cold and chemical, her young hair made one swift motion (18 years old; therefore in the girls' high school, therefore in Käthe's class. And it was too cold upstairs to study).

('Yes, Sir Lion?"): "Tell me—Düring—" (the pause was wonderful!) "—hmm; have you ever dabbled with philosophy? = Kant, Schopenhauer." (jauntily): "and so on?"

(Are you in for a surprise!): "Yes, in the past, Herr Commissioner; I read a lot of that sort of thing; as a young man."

He smiled, supercilious and academically blessed; very much amused with formica sapiens: "Why only in the past, Herr Düring?" (most snidely): "Have you outgrown it?!". (And his daughter, behind us in an armchair, her silken legs tucked high, let her book fall very slowly).

I drank down the cognac (unsanctioned; the plebs has no manners); in the junkyard corner of my brain I searched for something appropriate for this nandu; and lo, a rusty cerebral
spiral lay right at hand:

"At one time I had" (and now the first hammerblow!): "a wise
boss" (and not a word was true!), "who explained the following to me: let us presuppose beings with a two-dimensional
sense of space—who live here on a single plane—" (I passed
my hand in the air, just above the table) "—and if I were now
to penetrate their living space with the fingers of my hand—"
(I let them dangle like the tentacles of a jellyfish) "—what our
two-dimensional beings would perceive now would be—": "5
circles", he said, furrowing his brow (so he's been able to follow thus far). "Yes. Five separate beings;" I said darkly, "individuals. But without ever guessing or being able to determine
that, farther up, in three-dimensional space, they are subordi-
nated to another unit—my hand.". "Or: I thrust my thumb
down into the plane of their world—" (which I did:) "—and
then pull it out again—i.e. it disappears for the guys down-
under; and then a little later stick my index finger in at another spot in their world. For them that means: two distinct
beings, widely separated by time and space; but nevertheless
they are bound together in the higher unity of my three-dimensional hand." (He frowned and thought it over; somewhat disconcerted; but I went right ahead, icily: Tu l'as voulu,
George Dandin!)

"Then the gentleman," ('twas I myself: the gentleman! Victory!)
"supporting his argument with sufficient proofs, suggested
that our three-dimensional world, too, is likewise overshad-
owed by a four-dimensional one. And that one apparently by
a five-dimensional one; for a description of electron movements, the best choice is a six-dimensional space, etc.—I suppose I could reconstruct the argument even now" (I
threatened obsequiously; and then added casually): "I then
worked my way through Hilbert's ‹Non–Euclidian Geome-
try›, etc.—: So here we are, equipped with a completely inadequate intellect, (one of the Demiurge's dirty tricks!), splashing
about in a sea of imponderables: ever since I've given up the
pursuit of metaphysics. Fits of speculation come very seldom.
These days I stand here and keep track of what those ridicu-

lous old ladies (the Parcae) may have in store for me and the rest of the world."

He protruded the tip of his tongue (that's not all that ladylike either) and thought for a long long time (surely not an appropriate ‹Weltanschauung› for a Prussian civil servant; but when it came to natural sciences, he seemed to have the usual not-the-vaguest of most ‹academics›, of the ‹classically educated›; easily confused and impressed: so there: I, too, can be antiseptic!: "Vote communist," and I gaped all the more 'umbly).

The daughter (very pretty face—but I mentioned that already?!), with her thighs spread wide and visible a long way up, slowly turned a ring on her little finger, and gazed at me through impenetrable lashes. (Just like in the picture).

Another topic (a Parthian shaft): "You read a lot, Herr Düring?" (Just like in the army, when the general sometimes inquires: Children? Six? Good man; good man: keep it up!!—So then, keep distance!): "Now and again. Sundays. Herr Commissioner."

"What sort of things do you read?" (‹sort of stuff› would have been even better). "Prose mainly, Herr Commissioner". (confidentially): "Things like: epics, lyric poetry, ballads: they're not for me".—"—And what sort of stuff is?" (finally ‹stuff›! Now coldly): "Wieland, a lot of Wieland, Herr Commissioner; Cooper, Holberg, Moritz, Schnabel, Tieck, Swift; Scott too." (I didn't mention ‹Expressionists›: not to you;): "and Romantics—" I added, mollifying with sweetness and light (because these fellows don't know the Romantics anyway: not their grand pioneering in artistic form, nor their concerto grosso of words, don't know Wezel, nor Fouqué, nor Cramer, you goldbrickers!). He nodded slowly and solemnly at each name (hadn't the vaguest, and I gave him a farewell jab):

"In Germany, you know, we have a very simply method for recognizing an intelligent person."—":?—". "He loves Wieland." —But he had some strength after all; he replied with dignity: "I don't know him." "Oh: but the Commissioner knows so many other things," I said quickly, making use of the lofty third person, and so insincerely, giving him an inane and wicked smile and left him to draw his own conclusions (amusing, how we despised one another; and nevertheless wanted to impress each other, both of us. Maybe we are two

tentacles of the same four-dimensional jellyfish, slowly swaying, full of bright stinging vesicles, thalassic; and we can't perceive good and evil either: if I were to thrust my hand through
that two-dimensional world in order to rescue a kitty meow-
ing down there, a hundred thinking transparent triangles
might very well perish while I'm at it! One universe is always
emanating out of the other: we emanate the world of technological forms. Bense). Then a bow to the daughter of the
house: long legs!

The night had a round red taillight of a moon. (Only thing missing was the license plate; otherwise all according to regulations).

Railroad switches bowed and scraped: respectfully: Düring!; sig-
nals jerked supplicating scrawny arms (with fingerless sauc-
ered hands); squiddy eyes stared red and green out of tin-
boxed lids; below, sinewy iron braced right and left against
itself: small station.

Strangely restive in the forest today: ⟨The mists lie low. The game
it has no scent, nor clearer view⟩. Or: ⟨Among the branches,
rustlings. The snow it roils and swirls; no breeze, no draught⟩.
Or: ⟨Howling in the woods⟩. (And so on past, ever deeper.
With howling.)

The crow described a grating black line in the echoless air. Moon
appeared and examined me icily from clouded lids of yellow-
silver. The emaciated shrubs huddled closer together in the
terrible pallor. So I stood for a long time, imprisoned in the
gaunt garment of the garden. The moon grew sharper, bright,
like an orator before a starry mob. Wind honed my face; and
after a time solitary flakes shot in from the east (then once
again shallow cold). As I entered the house, my steps danced
a muffled bumpkin dance around me, the frozen curving path
thumping me up to the stiff front door.

"Late aren't you? Everything's cold." (my wife), and she
scolded, the words balling in her mouth, scoffed and ran out
of breath (my wife). Eventually I managed to calm her down:
the honor: at the commissioner's home!

Beating of war drums along the Memel (ten o'clock news): how
long can they get away with it?

One thing emanates the others: the n-dimensional emanates the
(n-1)-dimensional; and it the (n-2)-dimensional:: but who is
N??!!

(1) *All that exists* refers either to the Invisible or the Divine Pleroma, including what has occurred both within and without the Pleroma, or to those things belonging to the visible world.

(2) The Divine Pleroma contains 30 Aeons, of which 15 are male and 15 female.

(3) The head, root and source of all these Aeons is the one, invisible, eternal, unbegotten and unknowable God, (N!), who by virtue of these his attributes is called Proarchon, Propater and Bythos, which is to say: the First Principle, the First Father and the Deep Abyss.

(4) This God of the inscrutable deep has taken as his spouse a principle which is named Ennoia or Innermost Thought, Sige or Silence, and Charis or Grace.

(5) And upon being impregnated by Bythos, this spouse bore to him Nous or Understanding; the Only-Begotten Son, the Father, and the principle or root of all other things.

(6) Together with Understanding was also born Aletheia or Truth. And this first Tetrad or foursome is the root and source of all things.

(7) Out of this Tetrad arose yet a second Tetrad, consisting of Logos or the Word, Zoë or Life, Anthropos or Man, and Ekklesia or the Church.

(8) These two Tetrads form an Ogdoad, that is: an eightfold principle, which is likewise the root and source of all things.

(9) Logos moreover has brought forth out of himself a new Dekad, that is a tenfold principle. These ten are named: Bythius or the Deeps, Mixis or Fusion, Ageratos or That-Which-Never-Dies or Never-Ages, Henosis or Union, Autophyes or the Self-Begotten, Hedone or Lust, Akinetus or Immobility, Synkrasis or Moderation, Monogenes or the Only-Begotten One, and Makaria or the Blessed One.

(10) Anthropos sired with Ekklesia a Dodekad or twelvefold number of Aeons; the names of these are: Parakletos or the Comforter, Pistis or Faith, Patrikos or Paternality, Elpis or Hope, Metrikos or Maternality, Agape or Love, Aeonous or Eternal Reason, Synesis or Intelligence, Ek-

klesiastikos or the Son of the Church, Makariote or Blessedness, Theletos or That-Which-Is-Desired-of-It-self, and Sophia or Wisdom.

(11) The whole Host of Aeons consists of this Ogdoad, Dekad and Dodekad, the parents of the first being Bythos and Sige, of the second Logos and Zoë, of the third, however, it is Homo and Ekklesia who are the parents.

(12) Not all Aeons are of the selfsame nature, and among them it is Nous alone who exists in perfect and eternal communion with Bythos or the inscrutable God.

(13) From this arises a longing of Aeons to find union with Bythos, which longing so heated the last of the Aeons, Sophia, in particular, that in her rutting she would have been virtually swallowed up by the universal omnipleromic creature, had she not been held back by Horos or the Limit, that is, he who is the force which holds all things to their nature, to their bounds and character and which determines and encloses all things that come within his circle and so prevents them from being swallowed up by Infinity; and thus he brought her to herself once again and returned her to her nature, to her circle and limits.

(14) Nevertheless Sophia, overheated by her ruttings, conceived, but the very violence of these motions caused her to miscarry, and she brought a deformed child into the world, bringing upon it all manner of fears, distress, terrors and afflictions.

(15) It came to pass, however, that Sophia was once again cleansed by Horos and returned to her position among the Aeons within the Pleroma; her bastard child, however, Enthymesis or Desire, and its companion Passio or Passion, were banished from the Pleroma and ejected by force.

(16) Enthymesis, who was also called Achamoth because she had been untimely born of Sophia, was from thenceforth in darkness, in the void, having no form, no figure and light; for this reason Christos on high took pity upon her and impressed upon her something of his nature, but then pulled back from her, and left her half perfect and half imperfect.

(17) And since through him Achamoth had now received a soul, she had a still greater longing for that light which she lacked; but when she pressed her way toward it, Horos held her back, and she was overcome with grief, fear, care and sadness and tormented by repulsive thoughts. And this is the origin of matter, all liquids come from her tears, all light things from her laughter, all heavy things or corporeal elements from her sadness and dismay . . . . (and so on, to 40.); gets to be too much).

The black steed of night: with the broad silver blaze, tears, laughter and dismay, kept snorting at my window.

(All that is incomprehensible: to resolve it into more comprehensible parts).

2

(May–August 1939)

The bright village: awakening it blinked and opened all shiny windows; every house crowed like a cock, and curtains flapped pastel wings to the tune. (One pair had fat red polka dots; pretty, against puffed-up pale yellow).

Bushes in scaly sea-green capes appeared along all paths and waved me, trembling and yearning ever deeper down the road; stood as spectators at meadow's edge; did trim gymnastics; whispered wantonly with chlorophyll tongues, or suddenly whistled loud trills; the bushes.

The maid in her violet smock tipped the bucket and glittering yellow waste water, setting her black flies murmuring below. Blue-scarred cabbage and flabby onion spikes. The nimble door gave another whack: and sealed the silence. Good. (Silence: good!)

Snouts of wind grubbed all through the grass, and snored a bit, blue yearling boars breath by breath. A dog burst on all fours out of his planked gable and bayed back and forth, making his chain rattle-snake and yawping: "Mornin', Herr Vehnke!" (In Rethem).

"I can go right on down now?": I can go right on down now.

In the basement archives: whitewashed walls, and mice in all boxes: black mannikins, did inquisitive acrobatics along the walls, leapt arches, dwelt in Rethemic labyrinths, (bring bread crumbs along tomorrow).

With a good cellophane ruler (graduation finely etched along the base) you can actually make reliable estimates to a tenth of a millimeter: wonderful! And I shoved and aligned the crystal-clear two-dimensional tool back and forth: wonderful!

Plus the magnifying glass: and below it the map, scale 100,000:1: the thin hill hatchings indicated high points; fire lines scored through forests; every tiny blacktangle was a house, where cows grunted, windowpanes sparkled, around the house the fence had been painted green; and I knotted my fingers for yearning, and pummeled my chin in energetic exasperation: I have to see every one of these houses; every shingle on the roof wants describing; so come on!

And away we went with the year 1760, with "consequential advancements" and "the noble Austrian conquests": meaning an official report. Meaning keep it– –meaning the ‹Politica› file. (Had folded close to a hundred blue file-covers and divided up all the topics. History on the ‹grand› scale is nothing: cold, impersonal, unconvincing, sketchy (false besides): I want nothing but ‹Private Antiquities›; there's the life and mystery.

I reconstructed all the old villages for myself with their pastors and bustling administrators: names from parish registers, records, statute-books, newspapers, from gravestones. (This evening still got to make the box for the slips of paper, Din A 8, i.e., about $3\frac{1}{8} \times 2\frac{1}{16}$ inches. Bearing names, forenames, birth and death dates if ascertainable; plus a thumbnail sketch of the matter: where found etc.) Read, turn the page; Read, turn the page. Read.—Turn the page—

The carton "French Period," and I hesitated before slitting through the thick dirty twine:

first a quick review of the history of the district of Fallingbostel in those years:

    (1) From 1796 on, the Army of the Armistice, until the Peace of Lunéville, Feb. 9, 1801.

    (2) On April 4, 1801, the Prussian General Kleist moves in with 24,000 men; remains until the end of October.

(3) Brief interregnum.

(4) On May 26, 1803, occupation by the French under Marshal Mortier (after June 19, however, Bernadotte is in command).—June 3, 1803, the Convention of Suhlingen (down near Hoya), absurd, but probably the only proper thing to do, where the Hanoverian Army surrenders.

(5) In September 1805, the French occupation troops (with the exception of the 3,000 men left at Fort Hameln—: quite right: where Chamisso was later stationed!) march off to Austria;—meanwhile the area is ‹liberated› by Russians, Swedes, and the German-English Legion.

(6) Dec. 15, 1805, Haugwitz's Vienna Tractate, by which Hanover is ceded to Prussia (in exchange for Berg, Ansbach and Neufchâtel).—After Jan. 27, 1806, then, Prussian troops under Graf Schulenburg occupy the territory.

(7) Following Jena-Auerstädt (Oct. 14, 1806), Hanover is first occupied by the French, "under personal disposition", and heavily taxed.

(8) On Jan. 14, 1810, our district is added to the new Kingdom of Westphalia of Everyday's-a-Holiday Jérôme. As part of the Département Aller.

(9) On Dec. 13, 1810, it is annexed to the French Empire by virtue of a ‹senatus-consulte organique› (nice term that, isn't it?!)

(10) Then in the fall of 1813, "liberated" yet again, and until its dissolution in 1866 part of the Kingdom of Hanover; since then part of Prussia. Aha . . . . . :—

Ahhhh!!!! – –

The grand old map!!

There ran the curly lines of brooks round the black dots of houses; through a charming hill number, the 6 and the 2; melted into tiny millponds; the country roads crossed cleverly over them: many, for my heart too many, brooks (and I followed each breathlessly: to its source on a slope; or to where it cautiously seeped and trickled together out of brackish moor). Angular village markings; circles crossed themselves ecclesiastically; while the post horn proclaimed a relay station. At this spot.

And the forests!: hardwoods encircled silence; conifer forest spiny and silent. Hunters prowled in fir, pulled red hands out of somber carcasses; deer hurtled (with a *T*) in a crouch; cows stood submissive in pastures; wind hummed to itself; grass whisked; the bird of my soul vanished in the undergrowth (of the forest of 1812).

Must one follow through on good intentions, or is it sufficient just to formulate them?!

I took hold of the map by one corner: the splendid cartouche ‹Le Secrétaire général de la Préfecture de Halem, et le Ingénieur ordinaire des Ponts des Chaussées Lasius›. I folded it at one corner again, with clutching covetous eyes. Then I put it into my blue folder (into mine; the unmarked one).

Fingers drumming: how should that folder be labeled?—‹Come with me›?; or ‹Düring: Private›?– – Finally I came up with ‹Background Material›, and I squinted an eye and regarded that first-class term:—

That belongs to me! (Cold as can be!) Me!: I am the true owner, for whom these things have been lying in wait for a hundred years! For No One but me do these gentle hues of demarcation gather round and enfold me. No One but me sees here at this house-dot: the two young gooseberry bushes: whispered declarations of love, stretched slender green arms, together, in their hunk of night (beneath star scrapments).

And so: into ‹Background Material›: cold as can be!

The heavy woof of warm air enveloped me at once, and smelled of cabbage and heavy good soups, and tasted salty to smirk of cheeks, and chapped the thigh-sized cudgel arms of the confident farmer's wife.—"Noo, thanks! Really, I can't eat another bite!"

(A ‹Powder Mill› was in fact already there in 1812, where the Eibia stands now. Before that even, surely).

A. C. Wedekind? Wedekindwedekind—: ah, he was the editor of the almanac / born 1763, just up the road in Visselhövede (and next to Pape, "the" son of the town). Interesting man all the same: was subprefect of the arrondissement of Lüneburg, where he died in '45; and a historian not to be snorted at either: aha: Wedekind!—

Lord: Wedekind!!: could that possibly have been the famous youthful sweetheart of the poet Pape?! Frederike W. was her name, died in November 1794.—And I quickly made a note to myself to check it in Visselhövede.—

What's that supposed to mean, the MERDE written in all the margins? –,–,–,: oh that. (And continue with precision worthy of a Balthasar Denner.)

Rural outhouse: and the larvae swarmed like rats' tails in the brown papered crap. (Those'll make for some real pied perky flies!: Only just imagine!)

At any rate the axis of the commissioner's swivel chair is not that of the earth.– – How often my handwriting has changed: from stiff childish gothic, to the roman hand encouraged by foreign languages, then a peculiar blend of the two. With Greek δ for d. These days I'm back to scribbling a messy German hand: and then signing my name roman style!

O my: statute books!: 35 quartos, the whole series (and for the third time now; first in Schwarmstedt; then in Buchholz; I already had a complete set in the district archives). Well.— Undecided.—

(Then I'll simply take the whole series with me: as background material, before it's destroyed! If only for the names that keep appearing. Which means making a big parcel; part can go by bike, and the rest by mail: and will I ever lie in wait for them!)

It is certainly only to the good if all these items are available at two different locations: in Fallingbostel; *and* at my place! Right?—"Heil, Herr Vehnke!"

On my bike along the Aller (rode by way of Ahlden): there it was: a blue bright stripe, in which poplars stood; bending closer here to brush and smack with the meadow grasses; on the other side a plowman came to hatch out shallow slanting lines of brown.

Contest question: did Cooper use "Felsenburg Island"* in writing "Mark's Reef" or not? (And/or Öhlenschläger's "Öyene i Sydhavet", which amounts to the same thing).—At first I was sure I knew: yes! Then again later: No. And I still don't know for certain even now!

Hodenhagen: Düshorn, Walsrode, the turnoff:

Bright blue: the puddles fluttered and pulsed beneath the spring wind; quiver clouds swished about; you walked, pushed the bike, and rode through the green springy cage of twigs. (And

---

*Johann Gottfried Schnabel's *Die Insel Felsenburg* (in four volumes, 1731–43).

farmers rattled past with dung-water. Children spun like tops around houses, hogs gnashed, cars hummed. And the clear cold wind bound us all).

Dark red and wind-flexed: the skirt. Her long legs lifted and lowered the staid pedals; and there ahead of me was my she-wolf, riding no-handed and equable beneath the apple boughs, setting the sky swirling even more than before.

"Vogelsang, Castle of the Order": my son Paul; yearning fanatic dimwitted: "Better do your homework!"

Reread: Spittler, Havemann, Kobbe, Wiedemann, Pratje, Hüne, Mannecke, Pfannkuche, Reden, Ringklib, Guthe; plus Thimme, of course Thimme above all. And Jansen. (keep calm: in 3,000 years it'll read like Homer's catalog of ships!).

And so now for the file box: and I crouched contentedly in the backyard, and cut the fine boards with jig and panel saws, and rubbed the edges with sandpaper, and glued, and hammered in the fine wire nails: lovely pensive work; in the pale yellow evening! (Great trade: carpenter!)

Raspberry bushes, red-eyed and silent: in Evers's garden; and out back the she-wolf was binding boughs to blackish lattices. Her plaid skirt knelt at the edge of the bed; the wide yellow calf lurked in the greensward, boa constrictor, shapely (till her father came, and with oldster faces askew we squabbled about something—always think of "pigeons" whenever I say or do that—this time it was postal regulations, parcel sizes and such. Weight limits. Because he, though actually a railroad man, had one of the books).

Wait!: I might as well nail those two broken laths to the fence while I'm at it!—(The clouds were still stretching long pointed red reptile tongues toward the sun).– – –

"Morning, Herr Peters." "Heil, Herr Düring!: You're sure looking good!" (envious; now it was my turn to pretend misery and be careful): "Well, just come on down with me to the cellar and have a look at those stacks of files down there!" (more testily): "and ‹looking good›?!: dried up, yes; like parchment: I've lost seventeen pounds already!" and: "just you ride a bike fifteen miles to Rethem every morning: *and* back again the same evening: that'll soon make an old man of you! Believe you me!"

"Sure: tanned, sure! You get a tan whether you want to or not!"

"Seifert was in again.". "Which one?: Walrus-Seifert or Seyffert-with-a-y?" The fat old man then; and had managed to pro-duce another illegitimate child, his fifth, with his new milk-maid, and had been proud as a brontosaurus and so drunk that he had even invited Peters to the baptism, and had had to be ejected: "Crazy buzzards!".

Brow furrowings: his thought in fat solemn procession, gave a sly nod, and showed disapproval of the blue-splotched restive morning light: "Yesyes: I've been down to look at your opera-tion," (‹operation›!): "You've made up a separate file for each locality, and then for events of general interest – –". I coughed, cold and respectful: "'ssir, Herr Commissioner". "Find anything special?:—". Concise, but not too prepack-aged: "This week—nothing, sir. At the moment most of it's from the days of the Napoleonic occupation, 1810." "aahy-ess," he said slowly and historico-philosophically, "we did in-deed belong to France once—my my—". (Only ‹How time flies› was lacking). "Uhh–not Fallingbostel itself, Herr Com-missioner," I reported with fussy delight (just what bosses love, for the lower echelon to be so very typically "lower eche-lon", body and soul: then they can smile indulgently: so, smile, my Bajazzo! I'm doing you the favor. And going on simply aburst with zeal, Mr. Dutiful, sharpener of pencils): "only the northwest half of the district as far as the Böhme: this was ‹Kingdom of Westphalia›:?" and gazed at him expec-tantly, blue-eyed, top-studently: are you ever stupid! (And sure enough: he gave an imperceptibly perceptible shrug, deri-sively licked his upper lip, his glance wandered off with him: off: to where no one from the lower echelon could ever reach him: "Yes sir, Herr Commissioner!")

"Well then, Heil!": "Heil 'ittler, Herr Düring!".—"And: Fräu-lein Krämer: button your blouse a little higher: think of the havoc you wreak among our male trainees!".—"Noo: not outright scandalous; but let Herr Schönert explain the biolog-ical effects to you."—And once again: "Until Monday, then. And those lists have to get to the army registration office!" "'ll see to that, Herr Düring."

But outside: sky of porcelain: white bellynesses, blue dust cloth; and here below a draft moved through the spindly bushes as if doors stood open all round (making my shirt flutter at my breast and setting my gray hair enthusiastically on end). Even though this was most decidedly still Land of Bureaucrats: telephone poles escorted all streets, turning stiffly at every curve, each one in its dark brown uniform and straight-edged: they will not rest until every square yard is stretched full of wire overhead and fitted out with pipes below!

The birch antennae brushed against my windjacketed flank; a very yellow leaf arrested me in my tracks; my eyes made sweet haste: mirrors for cobblestones and girls' skirts, houses and trim nylons, nimble cars, deftly dodging, and flickered glances from farmhouse windows. "Hello, Herr Vehnke.—Yes; today is probably the last time.—Yes, I'm on my way down right now", and the stairs ran their striped way before me, a little bit into the center of the earth. (But only a little bit).

The chest let fly with wood rot: boggy, roachy, disgusting—;—and I armed myself with much patience and tweezers (scissors—pencils—pad—magnifying glass—Langenscheidt—avanti!). Insect larvae and cobwebs.

And all higgledy-piggledy: The great cholera epidemic of 1831 (right: Hegel, Gneisenau, etc. died during that one).—For the fun of it, I went over a couple of tax forms from 1824, checking off items: just let Someone rack his brains someday over what the marginal note "Approved: Düring" may mean. (But by such antics I now knew by heart all the species of vanished coins, thalers, guldens, friedrichsdors, etcetera, even Bremen groats!).

Pretty, pretty: a study by the famous architect, Johann Christian Findorf (d. 1792), colonizer of moors and founder of villages . . . : Aha!: had actually planned the same sort of project for the Ostenholzer Moor; with map-sketch and cost estimate. Interesting item. (‹Background Material›??).

And here: a sixteen-page register with appraisals "of those effects remaining in Ahlten Castle, having fallen into French hands upon said castle's being taken on July 25, 1803"; and it was superb: they had listed every piece of junk: "one teapot with a horn handle" along with "cash monies and valuables"; "genuine porcelain"; "kitchen utensils"; "nine pieces of bleumourant livery cloth, together with a remnant of yellow fabric, two yards: 162 talers"; "one petit point settee"; and believe it or not "six chamber commodes with divers upholstery: 24 talers".

Then: muskets, horses, harness, fodder, "firewood": "One plea-
sure-garden with more than 200 exemplars of orange, lemon
and laurel trees, likewise those of 100 rose and pink stocks";
"one cabinet of books, historical, amusing and gallant"
(Probably, then, erotica, "posizioni" and the like).

And the cellar: "one aam of Tokay wine from Thomagnini. two
kegs of Hungarian wine from Rebersdorff. one aam of 1704
Rhenish", and on it went.—: "three hogsheads Pontacq"?
Qu'est ce que c'est que ça?!– –: Oh sure: red wine from Pau.

Summa Summarum: 178,278 talers 18 groschens! And that was
1803!: Leaves your trap gaping!—I mean, that had been—in
today's money—approximately—in Reichsmarks: well?—:
about two million marks!: now that's something for the commissioner! (And naturally I'll make a copy for myself, so I can
learn all the old details and particulars!)—And moving on
with unflagging diligence, turning page on page; skimming
each, reading some: three boxes always beside me: "Important," "Dubious," "Trash." The last one is filled and emptied
three times a day. For pulping).

11 o'clock: means another good hour.

French period again: at that time Hünzingen was administra-
tively (deep in my bones, isn't it?!) part of—at that time—:
(a) the Département of the Mouths of the Weser, "Bouches du
Weser", (Prefect, Graf Carl von Arberg; General-secretary,
von Halem: ah, the fellow who had helped project that grand
map I found recently!);
(b) the Arrondissement of Nienburg (Subprefect, Salomon);
(c) Canton of Walsrode, and finally
(d) Mairie of Walsrode

And had a total of 98 inhabitants. Walsrode 1441. Stellichte
311.

An Appeal to the Populace: to capture runaway French soldiers.
Signed: Tourtelot, Lieutenant of the 34th Legion of the Gen-
darmerie in Nienburg. Reward: fifteen talers a head. Had 25
mounted gendarmes and five on foot "under him" ("Nico-
demes non triumphat / qui subegit Caesarem"; five men always made one ‹brigade›).—About 40 names on the list of
deserters; with description of appearance, age, height, unit
and full arrest warrant details.

Here again: reports by the village mayors of Bommelsen, Kroge;
Forester Ruschenbusch of Stellichte.

Here again: break-ins at isolated farmsteads, thefts of foodstuffs, interrogations and evidence, hams and hard sausage (with signatures ‹Paul Wolters, for me and my brother›). And I looked at the district map: was right in my neighborhood, Ebbingen, Jarlingen, Ahrsen. Apparently always the same fellow, "short and scrawny."

Here again: a farm girl had been approached on the moor one autumn evening by an unknown man and asked in fractured German: if he couldn't. And afterward he had also relieved her of half a sack of potatoes. (That's really the only reason she'd reported it!—And once again he had been "short and scrawny"; she hadn't made out his face more precisely in the dusk, "he didn't take off his hat", but an older man: and I pondered lasciviously how she might have determined that. But then I grew serious once more, and took out the list of names again: short and scrawny. Short. And scrawny).

And older: that leaves really only two men who could possibly be considered: Thierry, of the 21st Chasseurs à cheval; and Cattere, of the 16th Regulars. Thierry and Cattere.

A werewolf: two farmers had seen its shadow: hanging close behind their wagon. And it had constantly "jangled": "like with chains"! So the brothers had laid the whip to their horses, and with quaking voice cried out the appropriate charms, à la "Phol ende Uodan",* and just before the farmyard there arose a great and untoward swish in the "upper air"; signed Witte and Lüderitz of Kettenburg, together with that of the village mayor and his clump of red seal.

And so things continued with letters back and forth, for several years. But then I stopped to consider: the lonely fugitive in the moor! And I puckered my brows and gazed at my windjacket's horsedung-colored sleeve: had simply deserted! In a single bound left rank and file and leapt onto the open moor (and had apparently lived there in hiding for years on end, ‹and paying thee no notice›:† even in the white desolate winter: so you can do that sort of thing!).—For starters then I gathered up all the records (I mean, ‹personnel› is part of my department too, isn't it?!).

---

*Two Germanic deities. Quote from the *Second Merseburg Incantation* from the tenth century.

†From *Prometheus* (ca. 1775) by Johann Wolfgang Goethe (1749–1832).

"Eat yondah at Stegmeiah's t'day: he knows 'bout it!"

A distant red tile roof in the flimmering muddled meadows; a moth, dazed by the heat, stumbled after its shadow; wind stretched its hot long limbs, rolled over contentedly once more, and fell asleep.

Still a relatively new house; and the hot glow drew me around the corner, brightly stuccoed, sun-drenched, to the broad servant girl at her whooshing carpet beater: "Yeah: the mastah's home", and the handle flexed again beneath the veined wrestler's arm: the hand that guides the broom on Saturdays– –

An old farmer with toothless stinking voice: "Nope, none a that at ouah place. Nope, don't know nothin' 'bout it. Nevah done nothin' like that."; and he gazed expectantly at me from round puddled eyes. (But soon the son arrived, and grumbled things right.)

The old man was eighty-six, and grew more lively as he ate, and told tales about how the hated Prussians had marched in, 1866: he was only thirteen, and when he called his sheepdog ‹Bismarck›, they asked him if all the dogs in Hanover were called that; and he had answered: "Nope, jist the sons o' bitches!" And how they had thrashed him there in the field, and then that evening the local boys had surrounded them and given them a terrible beating: broke the rifles over their backs!, warming & growing young in his lies; and we were delighted with him and his tall tales: "Thanks so much!—Be seeing you.": "Was our pleasuh."

And now for the rest (but then that's it; I'm quitting today at 4; in this heat I'm going swimming).

Baron de la Castine?: Where have I heard that name before? Where have I . . . . . (look it up at home).—Two books: Karl Gottlob Cramer "Hasper a Spada" (Lovely items; missing in my own collection, too!).

(Then went ahead and leafed through the deserter story again: curiouser and curiouser!).

The mis'rable bastards!: were they busy chopping down another whole section of woods again? The robots?! And growling with anger, helpless with rage, I pushed my bike along the soft narrow path, crack, another old trunk came crunching down, causing the terrified bushes to dive to both sides, leaves atremble: these damned farmers!

These farmers!!: these bunglers!!: Look, here, I'll prove it: in our village there are twenty-five farmsteads, each with about 120 acres (counting it all, wood, meadow, field): Each of them has his own threshing machine; every other one his own tractor. That threshing machine is used 10 days a year, no more, then it stands in the shed: so that two of them would suffice for the whole village!! And one of the things costs 2,000 marks: so twenty-three times 2,000 are spent to no purpose! What an insane waste of national wealth! What extravagance at the cost of the consumer! If all these farms were merged, making giant-sized Canadian farms (or, if you like, Russian kolkhozy!): and then the farmers were put to work as well-paid eight-hour-a-day workers (they're forever wailing to you about how much they have to drudge, and all for nothing they say: every factory worker lives better: so let's do it!): a hundred-weight of potatoes would sell for one mark! (And that's just one example; I'd like to meet the fellow who would dare tell me straight to my face that this is "efficient!").

And what unsanitary pigs they are for the most part: nothing but filth and fat!—The whole thing needs to be rationalized; business on a grand scale. (Or then again: reduce the population. That way the old system might possibly be retained).

It's the same with trades!: pure antediluvian methods! How would humanity get along without shoe factories?: one half would go barefoot, and a pair of shoes would cost 200 marks, and every fifth shop would be a shoemaker's. Trades were the medieval attempt to meet the material needs of a very sparse population, while using what were still childish technologies; only students of German literature and guild masters attribute profound metaphysical value to the system: they live off it!—But I'm all for Salamander shoes (or Bata; it's all the same!).

And so I rode through the pieces of my life: swaying atop a bicycle. (Haven't the least desire to be a god: much too boring, to begin with. A demigod, now that I'd like!).

A swim, a long one (in Bottomless Lake): lying on my back, and moving only a little, a kind of coziness about it. Swaying sky with tired white patches (if only that silly paddler weren't here!).

The exotic beach (white narrow sand, with find black sludge patterns): girls in green and dark-red swimsuits; brown lads, colorfully bisected by their trunks, with clear melancholy adolescent eyes. And the hard grass, ruffled white-green around the blue-green whorl of pines.

Sunset: the setting sun is itself not beautiful!: red, fat, repulsive, bloody, blind.—But later then the sky; and the static streaks of the clouds!

In front of the house: the wind gave a Mongol snort from its corner and rolled yellow dust into fibrous rope-ends; sucked the shirt off my chest, and amorously lifted the bell-skirt from the she-wolf (to the waistband, making her toothy face gape with laughter; and she kept her hands on the washline, till it sank back on its own; raspberry lips called motherwards and she made thorny fingers).

Clean and oil the bike (forced to wear an old apron): "They figure one husband's worth about three children, Herr Weber," my wife declared, suggestive and honey-sweet. (And He even laughed! take off the rearview mirror and replace the worn-out nut. Remounting the saddle tool-bag is the worst part; they're constructed so that on principle you always have one wrench left over!).

Wind fondled the sable of the night, till they whispered and murmured; an owl screeched at us and laughed lewdly. (Or was it Käthe across the way?).

Syrupiev Chocolatovich: my son!: "You're going to turn into pure sugar, Paul!"; for he was shoveling down the pudding literally by the bowl (and I bet him that on Sunday he could eat a basinful: I'll bring the ten extra packages you'll need from Fallingbostel, ‹Almond›, agreed? And he say's it's a deal!). Before that, Sunday morning, they have ‹Premilitary Training›, with camping in tents, trooping the colors, and all the apparently inevitable and terribly interesting operatic ceremonial. At seventeen he can volunteer for the army: become an officer: "Can I, dad?!—Or maybe the gruppenführer can speak to you about it sometime." (An out-and-out cool and deliberate threat, unmistakable); and my wife made honored eyes: "If he becomes an officer! With his secondary schooling: just think how jealous the Alsfleths would be!". "That settles it of course," I said bitterly, and: "whatever you like!".—"His birthday's coming up in August—: whatever you like!—" (Rather than let him set the party hacks on me!: if a man has

such an urge to stand at attention, then don't get in his way:
God, what a different sort I was at his age! Had had a solid
democratic education! And whenever people showed up in
troops, always turned my back!—And is my wife a fool!)

"*What sort of station have you got there?!*" "Weather prognosis"; "agency dispatches"; "termination of broadcast at 2400
hours": German, would you please speak German!– – (Ah,
that's it: the Babeling Swiss, with confederated specialties:
"Keep dialing!". But then in fact a lovely choir: "Vieux
Léman / toujours le même").—And the constant hassling of
Poland!—

"*Heil, Herr Peters!*" (that's the only difference: he wears the
yoke patiently and even proudly: I pull a face whenever I slip
in and out of it!): "They have to show those Poles a thing or
two!"; and his tongue deftly whipped up a cock-and-bull
story in the dish of his big mouth, about mutilated German
settlers, German loyalty, and lots of raped women: "No sir!:
they need their toes stepped on!"

The train window rebelled with a clatter in its frame; the sun fes-
tered by the woods; a blue farmhand plowed into the slimy
earth; a harrow harped (acoustical nonsense of course!): "Do
you realize, Herr Peters, that ultimately that might mean
war?". But he hadn't taken part in the World War, obstinately
scratched the back of his thick head,: "The Führer doesn't
want war!", and sat there silently sulking away. (Just as if
someone would punch me in the face, snatch my money away,
and then scream: "I detest acts of violence!" Charming. And
that's what goes down with the SA!)

"*Who's the man-in-green there?!*" (softly to Schönert, and point
with my ear, while he entered a promotion into the fellow's
papers: "Gröpel.: The Forester of Walsrode." "Aha".) And I
sociably introduced myself to his red leery-little foxface: they
always know the old milestones, hidden paths, and so on:
"Good! I'll drop by sometime, Herr Gröpel!—Yes, of
course", and a deceptive imitation of a laugh. (Proverbs:
"Show me a liar . . .": that one was made up by a mad civil
servant, personnel department. "Barking dogs . . .": a forester.
"The public good . . .": a grand tyrant.—Here are another
two nice ones: "Takes more than a new pair of shoes to
dance": for authors. And "not everyone with a long knife is a
cook": when iron generals go in for politics!)

"*May I have Saturday* for a trip to Hamburg, Herr Commissioner?"—"?"—: "It's for official business—uh: semiofficial.—I'd like to find some reference aids for my project; and look up some things in the State Archives.– –I have an acquaintance there, a Dr. Teufel!" I lied, impatient and impertinent, and he nodded, convinced and cagey.—: "Reference aids?" "Yes sir: a few volumes of the Gotha Almanac.* And a small technical dictionary.—Naturally at my own expense", ambitious and supportive of the state: "but I am interested in the task assigned me, and I'd like to do it well. Herr Commissioner." (Peters couldn't have said it better: well done!).— "Well, all right.– –Where are you prior to that, on Thursday / Friday?". "Parsonage at Kirchboitzen, and in the village. Herr Doktor" (a little variety in the title for once; and then came his dry little pestled laugh: "Well all right").

And once again: the morning sun was already melting to gray clouds; heard wind leap, leap and fall asleep, deep. My two feet dolted the bike along for me; so I could watch other things and take note: the field of cabbage, the rows of potatoes, the bands of wheat; barley ponds waved green; the dust rolled solemnly about my front wheel (and the bottle in the baggage gurgled).

Woods are beautiful only when you can leave the path at any time and cut, wade, duck right through them (yet another argument against mountains). I give my vote: flatlands! (Ah, condemned to be a paperpusher: if only I had a mere 10,000 marks, to knock together a log house, solitary somewhere in the moor and woods! I turned a piece of fallen brushwood in my fingers, bark, crack, turning, turning, tosshighintheair: another glance across the countryside: far off two farmers were drawing deep lines in their potatoes; then give a lurch: to the parsonage gate.—Was only eight thirty).

Church noises: which means bells, singing, congregational mutterings: I made a wide circle (around the congregation).

With nice puffed-up cheeks and a large, gentle hooknose: the pastor's daughter (and a pretty, dainty garden behind her: the weeping birches lay back in the wind with foliage combed in

---

*Genealogies of the German nobility, which were published from 1763 on in Perthes-Verlag.

a sweep, and it shoved them right respectably, hastily blowing their hair from behind up over their heads and sending skirts to the fore, too: just like my big pastor's daughter's here: "Yes. Just a moment please. Herr– –". "Düring. From the District Commissioner's Office." "Ah yes!".

Children (counting out): Eee–ny–mee–ny–mai–ny–med;: / Fall–inthe–river:–and–you–are–dead!!"; and with shrill voices, they shoved the lonely dead man, thirsting for revenge, from their midst. (And for me the sun is either two fingers wide, or a belching golem of fire: depending on what use I have for it!).

Green-patterned air, brown soil, gold herringboned. ("In these Christian lands certain small loaves or cakes are displayed, of which the priests say that they are gods; and what is more wonderful still, the bakers themselves swear that these gods created the entire world, though they themselves have prepared them from flour, the remains of which they will show to you").

"Why of course, Herr—uh": "Düring, Herr Pastor". "Yes, goes without saying!"; but first he let me present all my credentials, proof that I was worthy of processing ecclesiastical files; then, however, he grew quite pliable, brought piles of documents, parish registers, gossiping and cursing in clericalese. I was also permitted to admire his library; praised his Ammianus Marcellinus (who is generally underrated! Tells many remarkable tales!). And he was pleased; his specialty, moreover, was Alexander: "But Herr Pastor! All we have there are very late and undependable sources! And even those based exclusively on the accounts of his followers: a third of the truth!: but the other side has to be presented as well!". "No, no, Herr Pastor!: why just imagine if we had a history of our times, the sole basis of which were the diaries of Goebbels and Göring: what then?!"; and the comparison delighted him no end.

"No, I'll be eating at the inn, Herr Pastor.—Has already been ordered."—"Oh.—: but you will come by later to join us in the garden, won't you?!". "Would love to, Herr Pastor".

And now at last to business: were a couple of huge piles, and two more ancient mustified crates (ancient: that is, 1800; but gave off an immoderate stench!). First a general survey. And I ill-humoredly bit my lip, not wanting to begin, when what did I pick up first but the papers from the years of occupation: steady. Steady!

Interesting (what a bulwark of a word!): the famous Continental
System: What All was forbidden, a very modern sense of the
economics of war in fact:
(a) no exports of ores and metals, whether processed or not;
weapons and ammunition, as to be expected; leather and
textile fibers, wood; foodstuffs of all kinds; even fertil-
izers.
(b) no imports of finished textiles (naturally, all of this directed against England!); but even English buttons, playing cards, horses, tobacco, sugar, soap, rum, etc. etc.
All described in detail; and I decided to take the old public notice
back to my commissioner. Amazing: you could go out and
paste it up on any street corner! (And the establishment of
these ‹départements hansésatiques› was certainly not attribut-
able to "wicked games the Corsican played with German
thrones and dominions", as our frock-coated historian types
and teutonizing Shatterhands are fond of expressing it: but
quite simply to the bitter necessity of effectively blockading
the entire coast against wholesale British smuggling and infil-
tration by troops of partisans; the Germans were sabotaging
Napoleon in any case, wherever they could!: no sir: was very
much the right thing to do!)
"One stoup of wine" was what he had drunk?: how much is
that? (Ah yes: does vary a lot, but at least between three and
three and one-half quarts: holycow! And I tucked in the corners of my mouth, respectful and envious: He could polish off
that, without singing a duet?!)
Wait!!: waitwaitwait. (Two more reports: that had really been an
out-and-out cause célèbre, hadn't it?!)
Söder?: that's the large farm directly behind us; the fattener of
swine! And Meyer?: I leaned back and put my pointed tongue
to my lips: Meyer, Meyer: why sure!: the big-time farmer close
by Heins's Inn in Ebbingen! And Ahrens, the fellow who lives
further up the main road, toward Visselhövede.
Had chased him twice: once driving him into Griemer Woods:
where he had disappeared in the direction of Söder. The other
time from Jahrlinger Road off to the west; short and scrawny.
And I took out my map and measured and compared: judging
by that, you could locate his lair—only approximately– –and
I pursed my brows and rubbed my teeth against my lips—
approximately– – –

(To be sure: a cursory glance at the other items too: ordinances signed by Graf Kielmannsegg, Minister; laws about cutting peat; stipulations concerning carriage service, national mourning: but then back to my deserter, Thierry or Cattere.)

Thierry or Cattere: Thierry, born July 16, 1771, in Bressuire, Poitou; single; occupation—yes, how to translate that: well today we would probably say something like ‹skilled mechanic› five-foot-six-inches tall and slender; distinguishing marks: saber scars on forehead and shoulders; speaks broken German (that certainly would have helped him! Cf. that farm girl recently!).– –And Cattere: born July 18, 1773, in Lisieux—that's in—Normandyaha—; married, 3 children (well, simply one more reason: I thought of my own family and brushed my hand over them); occupation, baker; five-foot tall and slender; no distinguishing marks, but known to be irascible and headstrong: had stabbed a corporal! (That would of course provide the basis for constructing a plausible story: argument with superiors.—But that seemed too simple for me: because to desert like that, and above all to remain in a strange country, for years: there's nothing simple about that. That takes a very special mentality!)

And then of course there's another stumbling block!: We northern Germans are generally right tall and sturdy: would they still call a man only five-foot tall "short"?: Nooo: that would be more like a "dwarf." Wouldn't it?—But then I had my doubts again: and so things stood as they were: Thierry or Cattere. (But an extremely interesting case: the reports were now more than two years apart: he really must have had some sort of permanent base of operations! And presumably very near to where I live). (And not in the woods: because any forester would have found that at once!!—Which leaves, then, nothing but marsh and moor; and I pulled my map over to me again).

In the chaise in the pastor's garden: tanglements of foam, and against blue background (while the lawn and I sailed along below, warm pastoral: old books are valuable not because they tell: of tanglements of blood and mucus, of fingers hooked and teeth straddled! But because such clouds and cragged lights are captured in them, clever and filthy remarks.—"Why, goes without saying, Herr Pastor: with pleasure!").

A new scale: wind-force six: topples chessmen. (Thankgod that's what we had; so a sociable gathering.)

The Herr Pastor had read Virgil's Georgics until he didn't know how to differentiate anymore between oats and rye. But for all that it was a quaint sheltered life (that I must say! I must!): he and his daughter had even given names to individual fruit trees: "Our Anselm is bearing well this year!" (but that's perfectly in order, what with their being large individuals; every dog has his: haven't they introduced that among the sequoias in California?: so there!)—"But just think of the widow of Tekoah, Herr Düring!". (now was the time to make a joke, though I knew my books of Samuel): "Of Tekoah": I said tentatively and as if surprised: Is that a noble family by letters-patent? Or somewhere in the Gotha?," and he laughed most edifyingly. "You will excuse me for a half hour or so, Herr—uh," he wafted his broad and black way inside to some confirmands or other, and I was left alone with his lovely puffed-up daughter.

A depraved creature by the by!, and we cautiously lechered ourselves awake with all kinds of double entendres; naturally she knew the she-wolf and was even in the same class with her. And the wind haggled lewdly behind our backs, and tosseled with gentle innuendos; screaming, larks snared themselves in the silver loops of the clouds; the plaintive bass of a team of oxen dwindled past the hedge; the red cliffs of evening, almaden alto, towered above the box tree.

Picking plums: I gallantly climbed the ladder, and tossed them into her lovely wide willow basket; bees, bumblebees and wasps hummed about our flushed faces; and I gazed not undeeply

(a) into her piebald décolleté

(b) into the overfilled sky: with foliage, cloudwork, stripes and colors: it was too much, above and below; and the knife of the moon was already wedged in a branch. (So what: for most of your life you have to park your conscience anyhow!).

Merry ride home (and I thought often of the red and yellow pastor's daughter): in front of the delicate bracket of the moon was a big fat decimal: all written in silver pen between mellow black clouds and silent tree limbs. (Like some mathematical jargon perhaps: cloud times, bracket, linden ribs).

"Yes, I've got to go to Hamburg in the morning" (professional shrug): "on office business". (conciliatory): "You got something special you want me to bring?" And it was darning yarn of rare hues, that couldn't be had in Walsrode; "Oh, and listen: square mother-of-pearl buttons, too: like these! I'd best give you a stocking to take along." (And wash the sweaty soles; and between the toes a zooish stench rose: so quick, rub the soap over it!)

Spend the night outdoors sometime, really ought to!: the brief shower drubbed me daintily. (And across the way, Käthe still had a light on); now and again a leaf ran over; wind snuffled; a hunted star appeared; a branch coughed; now and again. Affirmation of water. Leaves scratched my nape, moist and loden-jacketed, until I laughed and stalked on (still have to see the carpenter: want to have him make a sturdy plywood chest for me, with a lock, compartments and a tray; for the expropriated documents in my collection; stuff of dreams). (The shiny curve of the moon's plowshare dug ever deeper into the sallow dripping lawn of clouds, and I too discovered my invisible path more elegantly into the meadows).—

Window with no curtains (mine!): I can live only in right-angled brightness (and on my desk a bookcase with firm and fluid contents). Rain smutted lazily and warm down the pane, watery and possibly fecund: and so quickly pack for tomorrow; I can shave early in the morning, and that will surely hold me till I get back.—

And ready, step outside!: the sky was just turning pale yellow and keen blue, and the gaudy air was like hovering water: good omen for me! In my tuliped red mouth. On my veined hands.

Good omen for me!!: across the way Käthe was washing in catch-as-catch-can style: she balled water in foamy fists and brushed it over her belly skin; jumped wildly about, clapped and crabbed across her back with strong arms; took hold again of her shimmering hips, her great-eyed breasts, and then let herself be wrestled dry by a most enviable terry towel; dressed only in panties, came to the window, tugged the elastic at the front and peeked inside. Then she saw me standing there, and vanished (yet without haste; and started singing grandly: ". . . the clohouds / echo-my sohong / far over the sea . . .", alto, then whistled another snatch, and flashed and slammed the door: was certainly no more than meet and just I'd say: she had watched me that day in the scullery hadn't she.—And with wistful wide eyes I thought of my prudish wife, who had not let me see her nude fourteen years now: well she can keep her filth to herself!).

It's really cheap!: one hundred twenty-seven miles round-trip (including the Sunday discount for the return) comes to five marks sixty, I slipped the small official brown cardboard tab into my trouser watchpocket, and picked up Wieland, "Clelia and Sinibald". (: But forever on the move, like a reporter, that wouldn't be for me either: a small wild tract of woods: that's me!).

Change trains in Visselhövede (the first time); and as I walked, I gazed over at the old steeple, where Samuel Christian Pape (1774–1817), the genial poet, had spent his heath(en) youth: another poor devil who fretted too much over the reviews of his poems (instead of telling the caboodle to go to hell, with the sovereign insouciance of Walter Scott or Schmidt; don't read the stuff on principle!—I had read the lovely little biography Fouqué had written for his 1821 edition of Pape's poems, and had also run across many living relatives in my archive work. Naturally I also know the supplement to them in Gubitz's "Gesellschafter": if you're gonna do it, do it right!).

Wieland: among us Germans, no one has reflected more profoundly about prose forms, no one has experimented more boldly, no one has supplied such thought-provoking patterns, as Christoph Martin Wieland: but then that was perfectly natural; for only such forms could incorporate both the great store of figures he drew from imagination and life and his extensive knowledge of history, literature, etc.—The stiff-jointed, didactic "Agathon" is still very much of the old school; but almost immediately afterward, the great adventures in form begin; even "Don Sylvio" and "Danishmend" are chock-full of the most exhilarating artistic devices, from whose charming tempi all moderns could learn. Suddenly everything shatters into anecdotal discourse: the imperishable "Abderites" swirl across the agora, and Sheikh Gebal counters the poetry of the "Golden Mirror" with truth of his own. There is still much undue length and brittleness; he still had not succeeded fully in unleashing his godlike voice; but the very next step brings with it considered, logical, important progress: dialogue. It is after all grammatically self-evident that the living present tense has a much more compelling psychological effect on the reader than the seemingly restrained pluperfect, which is only the twaddling of old maids. (This is likewise the source of the enchantment of lyric poetry, or even optically convincing drama; both, however, commensurate with the lightning-like brevity of their effects, are incapable of absorbing broad-ranging, weighty intellectual matters: only prose can do that!) And so Wieland here tried out the first of the techniques for employing the present tense: Apollonius of Tyana tells his tale in a Cretan grotto; and "Peregrinus Proteus", still far too lightly regarded, sits down with Lucian among Elysian shades. And as an old man he tries yet a second innovation: the epistolary novel. And with all its faults, the inimitable grand mosaic of "Aristippus" is a success (along with the finger exercises "Menander" and "Crates"); for the reader receives each letter in a constantly renewed present; he is addressed from all the cities and provinces of Greater Greece; the most beautiful humane moments appear woven into significant historical events; and the truly invaluable discussion of the "Anabasis" and the "Symposium" are likewise organic parts of the whole—they're boring only to victims of jazz: "Aristippus" still remains the only historical novel we Germans have, i.e., that gives us life and knowledge; aurum potabile. Wieland is my greatest experience of form, apart from August Stramm!—(And what all could be said about his verse narratives, tolle lege; but that would mean intoning a new hymn: take and learn!)—He is the example of how a great writer of prose labored with diligence and profound thought all his life to perfect one of his two modes of expression.—(And by way of contrast: for Geothe, prose is not an art form but a junk bin—aside from *Werther*; and "Truth and Poetry," where, however, there is no problem giving form to the material to begin with—: divergent fragments glued together by force; novellas crudely knotted along the main threads; collections of aphorisms; commonplaces of all sorts—dead sure to be put in the mouth of the least likely person: think of the avuncular, worldly-wise "maxims" he has

little Ottilie write in her diary!—The most flagrant example is
Wilhelm Meister, especially "Meister's Travels": what he gets
away with there, e.g., in chapter transitions, is often so primitive it would shame any well-bred, self-respecting high-school
senior. A brazen formal shambles; and I pledge to produce the
evidence any time at all (if I didn't have to put my capacities
to more serious uses: Goethe, stick to your lyric poetry! And
your plays!).—

In front of the main station (was only 7:52): a car tallyhonked;
in the distance fire engines tooheetoohawed merrily; the air
delicately layered itself from white to blue; and the red-yellow
subway stormed around the curve with lowered head. (The
secondhand bookstores are over on Königstrasse, or on Neuer
Wall; Hauswedell is too expensive, no point in that. Maybe
step into Woolworth's first).

Buttons and darning wool: well, let's hope it's right.—Harsh
lights and subdued noisiness. (How did that go?: ribbons bubble, belts loop adders, jaws gape barrels, eyeballs
rummage– –?– –. Can't remember!).

Or wait! That was it: ‹In the Department Store›
: Fourth floor: Hands are yapping bright-dyed fabrics jaws
gape barrels eyeballs rummage distance buzzes may-I-help-
you's boxes slumber armchairs settle clothing jungles coated
forests ribbons bubble elbows jostle buttons ogle stockings
shelter digits finger D-mark pieces thighs are reaching down
from bottoms.

Instant love is undertaken for a raven Titus head, and while
kerchiefs loiter round other necks, she slyly rends the rustling
fabric, so that her average-sized breasts come bobbing up, the
triangle of her face grins out above the crevice, and while
the aged lady floorwalker does her watching, I wait, among
the nylon rushes of massive female legs.

Third floor. Scanty praises pointing lifting saucers circle vases
taper fatties snarl behind their cheekpads lanterns cable iron-
ing-boardly mirrors marvel belts loop adders yarn-balls cower
motley helots mouths start stumbling word prostheses calves
are reveling hips look privy cashiers clamor butt-end eyeballs
teeth agaping snapping grating noses farting brain bits out.

Skirt hems slink about girlfriends (high-school seniors); car-
pet-stretches, mutely bedded roundabout by housely wives

(oilcloth souls, bodies like shopping bags); records gently playing for us folk wired for sound, black-smocked girl trainees drag around cardboard boulders, escalator solemnly trimmed with statues, and right next to them signs blockade atop scratchly cocomats: Only one fifty! Hey you! Customer! And more bovine leather, batteries, smoking gadgettes; chamoisly the world is off to rack and ruin.

Second and ground floors: Rifles barrel bamboo vipers glasses twitter dunes of coffee lips gone crooked buckled clucking words out trotting rippling toddling hot dogs bronzed with dots of mustard scales with taloned pointers subtle yellow tiny show-offs thick potboilers brash trash photos rigid jackets upright stairways ramble rosy gristled earfuls napes of buffet-worthy matriarchs with earnest censure luggage boxing doorways flailing as you leave.— (It's by Schiller, I think: ". . . Children wailing mothers straying dumb beasts moaning under rubble all are running bolting fleeing . . .").

And hard horse-sausage!: I can't help myself: I love to eat it! Near us, in Neuenkirchen, there's another doughty artist in the craft: "Give me a string of ten, please: or better: you can package them and send them to my home, can't you?—: "Yes!: add the wrapping and shipping charges to the bill!" (They're easy to keep fresh in summer, too; hang them in a dry, airy place where the flies can't get at them: they just keep getting better and harder!). "And give me another two to take along with me."

At the secondhand bookstore: "Yes please:—this way!", and he led me to the long low row of the Gotha: soft linden green "Letters of Patent"; chalk blue "Ancient Houses"; dark violet "Barons"; dark green "Counts" (I don't need the court annuals). "The price depends primarily on the date: up to 1918, two marks fifty; after that, three marks fifty", and discreetly stepped back his vigilant yards: "I'll find what I need, all right?!"

Eight volumes in all (and sorted by the familiar even and odd numbers): 20 marks. "I can look around some more—?". "Yes, of course!". And right at home, I strode to the bookcases, leafed through Droysen's historical atlas ("A bargain: only 30 marks!"; nah, too expensive). Read once more page upon page of Galiani's "Dialogues sur le commerce des blés", one of the most brilliant books from that period in France; the "Thessalian Nights" of Madame de Lussan. Then went ahead and bought the complete German edition of Scott, 1852 ff. Stuttgart, with its countless charming brownish foxings (and He even apologized for the fact, the nincompoop!): twenty-five volumes for fifteen marks: "Pack them with the others", and I gave him my address for the C.O.D. package: "No!: sixty-four!—number 64." (And paid 20 marks of it on account: "And then enter just the fifteen marks on the C.O.D. slip!": because of my wife!).

(Swift: "Gulliver's Travels": very simple structure:

First Book: the genius tormented by the termites; and I recalled that unutterable description, oh how often, teeth gnashing, I had wept and laughed over it: the way the wretches swarm on through the triumphal arch of his wide-spread legs, every last bit of Lilliput, generals and politicians at the head: and look up as they pass, grinning at the tattered seat of the giant's pants!—

Second Book: the disgust at things organic: where the pores of the skin grow big as the mouths of teacups; he rides astride the oak-barked nipple of his colossal patroness: the smell almost kills him! And the calf-sized hymenoptera rev their motors, circling his life—Gong!:

Third Book: against philologists and technocrats, against "pure" and "applied" sciences: only the magicians know much of anything; but you're terrified and it would be better otherwise! The masses?: drudge and drivel; and if they don't obey, their sun is taken away (even though the island of "Laputa"—the ruling "upper class"—can never be sent crashing down as threatened: they'd end up blowing themselves kaputa! The hope is that those down below won't figure that out some day and emancipate themselves from those "on top": oh, is it ever witty!)—

Fourth Book: the grand final loathing of all Yahoos, not excluding Swift: and I put down my reichsmark on the Yahoo's counter, and pocketed the wee thing, for my own travels into several remote nations of the world.)

Lunch at the fish galley: and I bit into the golden-brown filet, and forked the cool greenish potato salad, and wolfed down a second helping, and gulped half an icy liter of beer: lat me heer dwelle al my lyf! (Like Herr Walther in Tyskland).*

Fine and now?!: the train leaves at 2:50, and how should I spend the hour and a half till then?—Decided: off to the art museum: nothing cheaper than that. I checked briefcase and hat down below, and first climbed to the top, part of my strategy: while I'm still running at full steam: only need to walk downhill later on!

Homely and slick: the smearings of the Third Reich hanging down every wall: grainy landscapes with incredibly broad-hipped sheaves offered palpable support for the suspicion of intellectual crop failure; men of character sent populist gazes out into an invisible Greater Germany; maidens stuck in their folk costumes as if in urns: the dauber had wrapped the squat rustic heads in such anacondas of blond braids that it made you want to offer the poor things an aspirin. Sculptors had done stark nakeds, with strict party-line physiques and eternally proud profiles, all with a striking family resemblance; nor had they omitted the irresistibly folksy *Horse Breaker,* curbing his stallion single-handed (but I've served in the horse-drawn artillery and know how it's really done!)—and it all was so oppressively monotonous, and standardized expressionless, and forgettable a hundred thousand times over, and executed with such hopelessly obvious technique; and the contentment of the master race sprawled like a fat sfinx in every room.

Oh God!: another *Kneeling Girl* peeking around the corner! And I walked wickedly right on in and gaped despairingly at her painfully to-scale rear cheeks; and the *Meditating Girl* adjacent looked so exactly like her that you could have switched signs and been done with it! (Me unhappy?: Me?!: I can still think whatever I like!!: Have my house, a tolerably stultifying job, and a vocabulary larger than that of all party members put together; moreover, two separate sides to my head, while the brownshirts have only one. Unhappy?!: Noo!!).

But wait: look at that! (and I had to offer small congrats to the clever management downstairs!): way at the back and quite

---

* "Tyskland" is Norwegian, Swedish, and Danish for Germany. The reference is to Walther von der Vogelweide (ca. 1200).

casually things grew more angular and less soporifically Aryan, people looked out from under their brutally low brows into uncanny things emanating from them; a hand was once again something white-spidery, and a back courtyard could make you shudder, and Otto Müller set everything to rights again:

"Otto Müller: Girls in the Park": and the two naked teenagers peered somberly from under their hair at the spectator, stuck out their still skinny legs among grass and wild flat plants, turned aside unvirginally and went on lying in wait for cautious dark-green life: and I smiled wild and triumphant: 'nd they say he's still livin' on Lammer-Lammer Street: 'nd doin' what he pleases: long live our grand and holy Expressionism!!

Color blindness is rare; art blindness the rule (but should I therefore consider myself perverse or in error?!). There is even a Sanskrit proverb that says, most people give off sparks only when you land a fist in their eye!: and so, painter, paint! poet, write! with your fist! (For they have to be awakened somehow, the semipeople behind the boundary line: so simply let yourselves be cursed as "ruffians" by the faint-hearted; as "arsonists" by the firefighters; as "breakers-and-enterers" by the sleepers: they should thank their appropriate gods that somebody has finally awakened them!).

Schnorr von Carolsfeld Wedding at Cana: nice colors; but otherwise skim milk.

And I sat and looked and dovetailed my fingers, and missed my train and the next one: Meister Franke *Group of Women from a Crucifixion* (right at the bottom, on the left where you come in, second room).

*The Lady in Green:** sat there, and glanced over her narrow shoulder only now and then: she had been waiting 500 years for me! She spread her cloak more cleverly, raised her white powdered nose and laid her intelligent forehead farther back: her slender fingers engaged in a sly and amazed game, branched decamerously (especially the small-stalked ones), and the pointed tongue of grass licked its way lesbically deeper under her robe:

---

*Mary Magdalene, who can be seen in Meister Franke's *Group of Women at Crucifixion* (ca. 1425).

Lord: that hairdo!!: the long yellow tresses against the linden-green velvet cloak and the white kerchief: that was no kerchief anymore: that was a cache-nez! Most decidedly! (And how chic her halo was perched!: the others wore theirs in good bourgeois Aryan style, like kerosene lamps.—She could stand up and without further ado walk across Broadway: the guys and dudes would wrench their necks to get a look!)

A reconstruction of this St. Thomas Altar *on the wall:* now wait!– –Can that be right!– –:

First: the treatment of the foreground: in his other panels it's only a meandering mud wall; the background a massive ticking-red tapestry of stars. But here: daintiest herbs (as in Leonardo's *Virgin of the Rocks!)*, dandelion (ah, when it's painted like that, you simply have to use the magic word ‹Taraxacum›!), and the beaded kidney-shaped leaves of incognita Franckii, leek and buckhorn. (Which then means: immense progress compared to his other—presumably earlier!—style).

Second (the different format: that too); and the poses of the figures—to be sure, it's a matter of extrapolating from clues; but it can hardly be otherwise!—: when the official assumption here is that this fragment is from the lower left of a four-paneled square? Impossible!! From both the way the heads are held and the most primitive sense of symmetry, you have to conclude that it's from the lower left of a nine-paneled square! And doesn't belong in the same series with the others at all: why can't he have painted several crucifixions?! (After all, the holy masquerade was the only possibility an artist had back then!)

I appeared at the barred, white-gray window; the guard plodded by glancelessly; my heart flickered and swallowed. Below, an endless red freight train whistled its way out of the station into the dusty summer time: 3:50 (and they close here at 4:00!). And so I doggedly returned to stand before that overly graceful crouching girl and despoiled her sweetly with my semi-senescing eyes– –no: out of here; very inconspicuously; maybe I can still catch the interurban to Rotenburg. But a photograph of her; and the two girls in the park: four marks, there!)

Last rakish strokes of sun along Glockengiesserwall, and the warm air suddenly pivoted, sylph of straw, and laid her soft arm-sheaves about me. Next to the flowing streetcars and trotting workers. Right out on the street.

In the briquette-colored iron of the main station: my furrowed face beside the raging horned locomotive; behind girlish hips on green stilts. And the thundering steam bagged us bumpily, me groper-in-fog, and her plump gold-trimmed suitcase (and beside it, the delicate brown-meshed calf).

"Your attention please! the interurban for Bremen is now departing from platform five: All aboard and please close the doors behind you!"

The pickax of the moon was toiling in the inert cloud gravel: Rotenburg.

I don't want to go home!: so I stayed the night in Visselhövede: would have been one o'clock anyway before I got home. The giant inn-keeper, erstwhile masseuse: "Wasn't a man who didn't squirm beneath my hand"; fried potatoes and farm sausage (plus the bed, only two marks fifty!).

The perennial hotel room: from next door came giggling like traveling salesman and maid; and then the dull rhythmics: you, you, you. . . .

Breaking loose in installments (Piecemeal, breaking loose halfway). (And overhead the indefatigable dance music: I've never danced in my life. And even now I hearkened with no envy to the misshapen tumult: workers in bib and tucker, factory girls and farm wenches, sweated up in dancehall and garden. Then the little music got insistent again; then the tomfools rotated in their well-pressed fabric shucks: yes, if you could run alone with her across a wide meadow, dashing at one another hand in hand, with the she-wolf, howling, and apart-yet-near race back through the bushes: more like that; yes). (Finally something like ersatz sleep).

Outside once: wild cloud waters buzzed like angry insects about my ears, drenched my pajama collar, moist at the elastic banded belly.—

Drink some water: I'm all for water! At home I drink it by the quart. (And then again some 100-proof; for variety; but seldom. Simply a matter of opposites: civil servant; and—yes, and what?—. All right, today a little 100-proof!).

Smoky morning, warm; (and the five miles are a mere morning constitutional: no: more like sultry! And smoky as the day when Bedloe strayed into the Ragged Mountains: so most anything may happen to me today!)

The dry heath: I walked across it, a cocksure forester, and my long straight walking stick swung smartly and daringly at my side. The juniper berries were already turning black, though lots of gray-green ones still hung there as well: big handsome fellows, the bushes; five feet taller than I—: more than that; so they're at least four hundred years old: the days of Luther. (Oh screw Luther!).

Long live whatever struts the earth adorned and clad in green (to wit: the fields and the forests. But I also greeted forester Gröpel: out of respect for the opening of Tieck's ‹Runenberg›:—yes, I greeted the forester, and his stiff chamois-tuft disappeared, twenty-one twenty-two, into the new growth alongside his dandy muzzle: gone for good?—?—Yes sir: so let's march on!).

The brown paths with their water welts. Men out in the peat, somber and slow with shovels, and those big fibrous bricks (bosh: everyone knows what it looks like!). Distant dots of farmers toiled tending watery potatoes: may they taste bitter in your mouths (do that in any case!). Wind gave a single crack in the firry frameworks, sailplaning grandly across the moor, come and gone, come and gone: stopped: very quiet again. (And smoky; two sheep stand in the background).

Between tracts 123 and -24; then the path down along the edge of the woods: the wild fern; yellow the old, green the idle young, the strapping lads. Ever more casual and lonesome, my path wound its way, and probably would finally have come to an end, when I called a halt: Say!: this was the area where Thierry and Cattere had kept on disappearing! (That is to say: Thierry *or* Cattere.—So I slipped my briefcase behind a bush at its stem, and investigated the terrain:—.—.—do a thing or two, before the jaws of darkness devour me; defy him a little life: him, Mister Death!).

And they came fuming up! 10,000 poisonous soft gray beings, with beady red eyes, and gobbled me up, so I broke into a moaning gallop, and bellowed like a panicky cow, and slapped my palms, already occupied by horseflies, against my neck and at my precious face, and still on the run, scampered round a tree, stormed up its ladder of boughs:

Yow, yow, yow!—: they were still down there fidgeting above the path and muttering truculently, and I kept batting at the dot-shaped pain, wherever it appeared, and panted and blinked: horseflies!—Whoo!—But they don't come up this high!

Thirty-five feet up (can I ever climb when I have to!): so then, thirty-five feet, and heaving a sigh I looked around:

The reedy surface: really quite large, maybe 400 × 500 yds (and my tall tree surely equally as old): the long assegai blades, tempered yellow, stood motionless and dense, ten-feet high, a botanical army. (Was the lowest point in the area, trysting place for evening fog and brown water-slings.—Over on my far right, discernible only by its vaporous roof: the Söder farm).

And my gaze went stiff and spurred:

Almost directly below me, so that I hadn't even noticed it till now, a gray steadfast thing: smarter duck of the head, peering deeper still::

A gray clapboard hut!– –: I took the daring step, one tree further; wrapped myself atop the new branch, grabbed wildly at wooden struts, let myself hang from the brown tree, banged the edges of my shoes to find bark stairs, took a buxom pine lass in my arms (she pricked me, the savage virgin, the second sex, and trembled as I ruthlessly mounted her), fished for bottom and stood.

Right, and where was it now?!: looking wildly about me. I picked up the long scrawny bough (wet underneath, ugh!), and I used it, but cautiously, to part the grass sarrisae to my left, Winkelried II: nothing. To my right. A little more: Aha! I waded a couple steps in that direction (was quite dry, by the way, the ground), nudged sharply with my tool arm:—!

An old thing: small; two yards long, two wide. Or two and a half at most. I lingered long before I uncorked the wooden bar, and the plank door sank, slowly and solemnly, into my arms.

The Haunted Palace: silent!– –. (A small window, long and wide as your forearm. My head turned above me back and forth).

The thick posts still solid, massive oak, and couldn't get both hands around them; the wooden walls silken gray and lightly warped.

I squinted harder, and balanced over to the corner: a piece of faded uniform on a black rusty nail. A hundred years of dust

stirred beneath my finger; rot ripped, weary and relieved; with
a very puckered gentle mouth I blew the dust from the shoulders: and into the small hollow of my hand rolled a hard
roundness, and I rubbed the button shiny on my sleeve. Gilt
brass, beaded rim and of finely grained convexity; I turned the
inscription back and forth beneath my bespectacled eyes:
twenty-one (large). And in a circle around it "Chasseurs à
Cheval": Jacques Thierry it was!! (And gold-plated for sure; I
rubbed it again, silly and eager: my heirloom!).

In the far corner a stubby earthenware bottle, bound with straw:
blackish desiccated contents, lemuric and opiate: must have
lived like a faun, skittish and all pricked ears. (In a certain
sense a precedent for me, is it not?!—Value of the historical
example: you can do this sort of thing!—The civil servant always needs his precedent!)

Outside (leaning against the doorpost): the world invisible; or
just the smoky sky. And now and then the slashing cry of a
sylvan bird.

Calmly and mechanically I picked up my briefcase (now unchal-
lenged by horseflies) and took the nearest path.

"Well now" (the nodded greeting). "Just now getting home, are
you?". "Yes, that's right," (most peevishly): "even had to
spend the night!" (But the darning yarn covered as alibi).

On the ordnance map 1:25,000: the hut is not marked! Judging
by that, No One knows about it!! (But by way of precaution
I'll have a look at one of the 1:5,000 plats in the land regis-
trar's office in Fallingbostel.—I was almost tempted to write
the flying school in Luthe and have them take an aerial photograph of the area for me; and dragged the wanton notion
around with me for several days, imp of the perverse: noo,
better not.—But I can write to Bressuire and ask for documents; and I did it at once in my quaint French (high-school
and occasional reading); but certainly quite comprehensible!
Oh, so what!).

*Hans Fritsche:** "They act as if they're sent from heav'n / and
coo in English when they lie!";† and then went ahead and ap-

---

*Hans Fritzsche (1900–1953) was, next to Goebbels, primarily responsible for
German Radio from 1933.
†Quote from Goethe's *Faust I*, V. 1141. See The German Library, vol. 18, *Faust,
Parts 1 and 2.*

plied it to Great Britain: even then, Goethe himself had seen through them!—: What an ignoramus!! And he's Goebbels's right-hand man! (like master, like . . .). Instead of realizing that at the time, circa 1800, German ‹englisch› was used as the adjective for ‹Engel›, (= ‹angel›); E. T. A. Hoffmann uses "englisches Fräulein" a good ten times, and he's not talking about any old Miss! But it's typical of these quarter-educated rulers of ours; and "the people", themselves a shade duller still, believe it all of course: no sir!: out of my sight, you leg-horns!—But seriously: that's no longer a matter of spade-work: those are preparations. Against England!

The dahlias swung and swayed in the gray-green Sunday twi-light; the pinks indignantly shook their finely fringed heads (probably because my stinky feet in their greasy leather husks were standing beside them!): "I'm going for a little walk, Berta." "Don't be too long, though; thunderstorm's coming up."

As tall as I (Käthe; within woods' edge; black skirt, white blouse); the moon a flame behind her ear, the single gust of wind as a warm comb for her hair: she bit into her lip and waited for me: "Yes."

The drowsy cloud: once again it opened its reddish slant eyes and purred; warm and still. (Which means "sheet lightning"). The gray dry grass was full of our hands and breathings.

There: she daintily showed one of her little gold-plated claws and purred longer this time (the thunder cat). I quickened my pace, encompassed by white hoops. Once a whole host of air waftlets came through the shrubbery and obligingly fanned and cooled my back.—"You're being careful, right." she mur-mured past me (and at the proper moment I pushed myself away, as disciplined as a man on his silver anniversary).

Wrinkled brow: "No need for the washboard face" she advised softly, lazily, and observant. (Then one more time).

She combed her hair and scraped the harrow through it so roughly that her face opened up with pain, but in her savagery did not stop for all that: beautiful! (Spirit of my spirit!).

The black wind leapt up, like the bass giants in the overture to Iphigenia; water appeared all through the air, and within sec-onds we were pasted in our clothes, from the neck down to our firm thighs.

Parting in front of the house: the she-wolf howled something into the abandoned night, and I, spectacled owl, laughed as if part of the Wild Hunt: tooth of shark and eye of skate, be eternal subjugate!

"My God, look at you!" (accent on "look": my wife.—And diarrhea later on; had been a little much for me: thrice the she-wolf!).

Aug. 23, 1939: pact with Soviet Russia:?!—: it's only a matter of days now! And I gave it some thought: what had been good as gold during the last war?: coffee, tea, cocoa; tobacco. And so I brought them with me from Fallingbostel, and the airtight tin of navy-cut. Cigarettes in tropic-proof packages. Rum and hard liquor.

Still 2,400 in the savings account: I withdrew two-thirds of it, and went on buying (a vote of no confidence in the state: Jawohl, mein Führer!!): leather for shoe soles and Conti-rubber heels. Hardware items; plus a new axhead and two blades for my bow saw. Shoelaces, matches: "I'm speaking to Herr Pfeiffer himself, am I not?: Could you still get four tons of coal to me today? And two of briquettes?—That's correct: four and two.– –No, number 64: I'll drop by during my lunch hour and pay for it.—Fine, fine!"

Oil, sugar; envelopes, paper; laundry soap.—Wait: bicycle tires. Flashlight batteries (but they don't last, damn it all!). Light bulbs: always need to keep the radio in good repair, so a couple of tubes in reserve!– –Revolver?: and I wavered for some time; but then it did seem overly romantic, and I stuck with my heavy bowie knife. Then a massive leather belt with brass buckle, nice and wide (good as a corset for the older gentleman, wouldn't you say?!).

Wait. a pair of rubber boots (the heavy-duty sort!).—: "Was able to buy our winter coal at a bargain price, Berta: special sale: twenty marks a ton," I tossed a lie her way to cover up my purchases; for she was already getting nervous, "and tomorrow there's a case of wine coming, too: it's always better to have something in the house—" (laying it on thick): "for when your brothers come!"—Then back to the office:

"Well, Peters?!": "I mean those Poles are getting awfully big for their britches, Herr Düring!", and Schönert too (well, he was still too young). The most lustfully outraged were the women, Krämer especially. And the August sun burned.

When I was walking down the street (: Hurrah, the cotton down!) / a charming girl I chanced to meet: Hurrah the cotton down!—: "Käthe!!". She came up, bumped the wind casually to the side with her hips, and gave her rear a slap with the back of her hand:?

"Käthe: a tip!:," and I hastily explained the whys and wherefores. She wrinkled her face up at once, giving it brief, menacing thought—: "So what?" she growled; and: "I haven't got any money.". I crumpled a 50-mark bill into her hand, advising: "At least buy yourself some good toilet soap, skin cream, and the item a woman needs most: make it several cartons." "No problem: put it in your briefcase, that way your parents won't notice; and lock it up in your wardrobe at home.—And tell me if it's not enough." She still had the money in her hand and was concentrating with a pout;—"Well, all right," she said hesitantly at last: "Soap, you say? It'll be scarce?". "Everything, everything, everything," I shouted nervously: "Shoes, Kotex, toothpaste: depend on it: in fourteen days you'll only get it all with ration books!". "Oh, you don't know how it was, Käthe!" (impatient): "don't be stupid—" (she lifted just one eyebrow, and I apologized at once: all right. It's settled). "Fine," she resolved, nodding thoughtfully: "I'll do it. Write it down for me, everything you think I'll need". "Sure, bon."

And back again: "Try to convince your parents in a roundabout way: that they should buy food and coal; the more the better!". "Mhm.". licking her lips she gave a decisive turn of her head, eyes searching for the nearest shop: "Mhm." Menacingly soft: "But listen, if this turns out to be nonsense . . . . . !"

The Böhme was already moving uneasily in its meadow wash, fields steamed gold, gray soft horseflies bit in notorious fashion; loden coats were still roving about young lads, the sedge had not yet died out.—Wait: back to the hardware store again: "A pair of hinges, please.—.—. No, no: for a very simple door to a shed; but good strong ones." "And the screws to go with them too, please" (two in reserve).

Kites stand atilt above Colony Hünzingen, high up: I gave my wife two hundred marks: "Buy new shoes and warm underwear for yourself and the kids in Walsrode.—And when the delivery van comes from Trempenau's, first have him give you the bill and check it!". "Yes, but," she was quite annoyed! "Don't go spending all our money, you hear!" and her eyes were little nest eggs. "Here, here's the bank book—" I said grandly (she really doesn't need to know a thing about my other money!): "there's still 800 marks in the account: if you're smart you'll spend it today: all of it!"—"You're really crazy, you and your war," she said calmly and suddenly very resolute (having rescued now this precious member o' the spirit world from evil): "Only 800 left!!", and she jumped up and paced back and forth, the wailing wife: "Stop carrying on so wild about it all: Weber's already been asking what's up over here!". And I followed her out into the kitchen: "Berta," I approached her, (dutiful and delighted): "You know what you have to do!". "Sure, sure", she said over her shoulder, haughty and disdainful. (So there it is: my conscience is clear!)

Aug. 25, 1939: permanent pact of mutual assistance between England and Poland; and the malheur was rolling up into a nice little ball: "Well, Berta?!". "Oh, you've got a screw loose!", angry and defensive. (Now it's only a matter of hours!).

Actually I ought to go over to Kirchboitzen again today; but I would rather put my museum in order: that's my job, too!: have an urgent need to augment my knowledge for my tasks! And whistling, I gazed at the lovely "collected" maps and beyellowed documents, and arranged them in the compartments of my chest, carefully laying the button, wrapped in tissue paper, with the rest. (Then once again with furrowed brow out to the shed: nail the board to the back wall; the readiness is all!).

‹*Wandering Willie's Tale*› from ‹Redgauntlet›: that is a splendid story, and much too good for it not to be commented upon these days; these days, when they're all Kolbenheyering and Thoraxing (or, more precisely: mediocring!).

Inviolable sanctuaries ought to be created!* and while I nailed I composed my letter addressed to the League of Nations: "Gentlemen:" (or better: Excellencies!: otherwise they won't lift a finger!).

"Your excellencies:

In light of the tremendous destruction which all wars in all times—and none more than the most recent—have caused to

---

*Schmidt outlined this in his *Gelehrtenrepublik (Republica Intelligentsia)*, 1957.

mankind's collections of art and literature; and in light of the far greater dangers to which these will be exposed in the next inevitable armed conflict and in those yet to follow, I—although a German–hereby take the liberty of submitting the following proposal to your worthy assembly.

(§1)The erection of inviolable cultural sanctuaries at several sites on the globe—with a minimum of at least three—, each to be constructed, maintained and administered cooperatively by all nations. For this purpose, I suggest small and otherwise useless islands located as far as possible from all areas of political and economic conflict—e.g., Tristan da Cunha, South Georgia, St. Helena, Easter Island—, where, upon erection of appropriate facilities, would be collected the largest possible stocks of mankind's books, together with the most valuable of its irreplaceable works of art.—The employment of any weapon whatsoever within a radius of . . . miles would be forbidden.

(§2)In order to render impossible any misuse of these sanctuaries and to avoid providing any power with a pretext for intervention, neither the products nor the prototypes of engineering or of any other applied science will be accepted.

(§3)One copy of every book published in the future is to be sent by its publisher to each of the "Culture Islands"; likewise the originals of paintings and sculptures or a copy, if possible executed by the artist himself, of equal merit.

(§4)Provision is to be made for the greatest living artists and scholars to find security of person and the opportunity for unhampered work at one such site whenever they may wish it (or upon retirement or in case of war).—The decision concerning an individual's worthiness could be left to a League of World Artists, though this too must first be created (but not to the Nobel Committee; one need only think of Rilke, Däubler, or Alfred Döblin—while a turd like Sienkiewicz becomes a prize-winning turd!)—In the future all important men could, moreover, be buried here together, creating world shrines.

(§5)Hopeful young talents, who have shown proof of ability, could be encouraged by granting them permission to live worry-free on these islands for a period of time, during which they would at last have the easy access, so necessary for artists and thinkers, to mankind's cultural achievements.

(§6)Other intellectuals would also be rewarded with admission for a few days: not, however, physicists, chemists, technicians (for the same reasons already noted); furthermore, entry is forever denied to all politicians, professional military, film stars, boxing champions of all weight classes, publishers, rich gawkers, etc., or to persons merely wishing to find asylum in times of war.—Permission for such special visits is to be extended by each island's administrators.– –
Considering the magnitude of the preparations necessary, (establishment of a commission, selection and purchase of the islands, construction of the physical plants, selection of personnel, transport of items of culture value, provisioning with supplies, etc), all of which, even at a modest estimate, may require years to complete, the project must be begun at once.—I am confident that none of your worthy delegations would wish to veto such an undertaking: mankind will one day tender you its reverent thanks for the preservation of its most sacred possessions!—
With the deepest respect, I remain your: Heinrich Düring.
P.S.: With reference to (§4). I hereby take the liberty of applying at once for a visa granting lifelong asylum: the mere mention of my epoch-making research concerning the district of Fallingbostel should obviate any further substantiation. I am in my early 50s, six-feet-one-inch tall, of no religious persuasion, free of infectious disease, and at no time have I ever been a member of the NSDAP or any of its affiliated organizations."
*(Except for the GLF:** but everyone had to join the Labor Front.—Well, I'll append it anyway by way of precaution. "P.S. 2: Except for the GLF.".—There.: My conscience is clear!: yet once more!).
The sun?!: a madman careering about up there with his howling molten rivers! (And we respectable folk still call them "stars" and genteelly celebrate the misty luster of the spawn of hell!). I spat right in the sun's blotched face, trod the earth with hasty, hacking steps, and ripped open the buttonholes at my

*German Labor Front (in German DAF: Deutsche Arbeits Front). The NSDAP-workers' organization after the destruction of the trade unions in May 1933.

chest, revealing the sweat and sparse hair below me. I hacked at a fork in a branch with the edge of my hand: that damned duffer up there: Supposed to see everything, hear and smell everything—my heartfelt sympathy by the way!—and allows a war to break out again!: ergo he's included it in his ostensible plans for the world?!)

"Staar-light: Staar-bright! / First staar we see tonight!"*: Children with their brightly flickering paper lanterns, they too want to free themselves of this workaday life: with lights, with words. In the dusk. Not a dumb idea!).

"What's up, Berta?": she came hastily toward me: "A call from the Herr Commissioner himself: you're to report to the office tomorrow without fail! Absolutely no fieldwork". After a pause, from the kitchen: "What's going on?". "Maybe somebody's sick—?" (wily, phlegmatic and shrugging). "Oh, that's it" (plausible and relieved: they don't want to know!)

In the night her hand on my shoulder: "What now?"; for my wife was standing in her nightshirt beside my bed, and a very bitter and crude joke tickled on my tongue.—: "Just listen, Heinrich: motorcycles!"

Indeed!!: indeed: there the throbbing machines stood, gaping cyclopsically, over by Hogrefe's fence; then to Alsfleth's. Then— "Go on down there, Heinrich: there're lights on in every house!".—And so slip on a jacket.—

"What's up, Herr Heitmann!" (From the army registration office, in Falling), and at once I recognized the stack of brown cards: "Call-up orders, huh?!—On our way; just like '14/'18." And he proudly: "Well, this time it won't last as long as it did in your day, Herr Düring!"; and I raised interested eyebrows:?.—"I mean, this time we've got the Führer", indulgent and disdainful of my advanced senility. ⟨You idiot⟩ I immediately thought, but translated it in citizenese: "Yesyes, of course" (and made to go him one better): "all be over in four weeks!" (don't you notice nothin'?!). But: "At the outside!" he confirmed emphatically, and remounted the saddle: "Well then: Heil!!" (Would I ever love to be that brown!).

Nothing more grisly and pitiful: than two nations going for each other's nation-antheming throats. (Man, the "animal that bawls hurrah"; as a definition).

"What is it, Heinrich?!": and with my head I mutely motioned toward the Spreckelsens' next door, where the young wife,

tears streaming down, was tying up her pale husband's bundle; at three in the morning: she ran into open wardrobes and ripped apart their piles of underwear (and on the occasion of his changing his underpants they did it one more time; without worrying about the open window).
Nessun dorma!!

3
(August–September 1944)

In a dream: back in Hamburg again, with Käthe (in railroad uniform, with lantern and hoo-whee whistle). And we filed through the window bars, inside we wrapped the paintings in blankets, tilted, whispered, knotted; left behind our briefcase with ID papers (bogus, of course!) as if by accident. "Windowpanes for the boss", we said, as we grumpily showed our passes (from Käthe's father!) at the main station. She had martially draped the conductor's coat over her mighty shoulders, the black bill of a cap set in her hair, her no-small-talk mouth underscored her sturdy mocking eyes. Alone through lamplorn trains, in the rumbling third-class night, travelers with large lightweight burdens, ‹On to victory the wheels must roll›, mostly mute, and my wide condor-lady propped her tubular legs under the seat opposite, oh, timeworn greenish white toothpaste ads around her (and mounted photographs of ‹Wasserburg› and the ‹Hainleite›); the iron rushed round us on its way; we slew straying Polish husbands and wives; towered up out of semi-doors; lugged up stairways; crept through chessboard landscapes: black-forest, white-meadow; I bit a red pencil in two, pelted arc lamps, battled in shoes, Käthe encamped in armchairs and me on a breast-hunt, in the vertically striped carpet of a blouse, flying houses and migrating birds above Ernst-August-Platz.

(The paintings had to be stashed then behind dressers and bookcases with double backs. I coolly ordered the measured boards from the carpenter. On Sundays we would drag them up out of hiding and silently inspect them; in one newspaper was an article concerning unidentified thieves and coal-filching).

Warm and foggy (at 5:30 in the morning); this evening then: off to Chateau Thierry! (Quite superfluously—and purely to round off my knowledge—, I'm going to study known cases of lycanthropy: actually, actually you can only giggle over such gloomy goings-on!).

Nowadays all you can do is escape halfway. Given the density of population! (Or, rather: you must divide yourself; live a double life; but burn out more quickly. Far from any sort of Christian paradise).

Joachim von Wick: had been postmaster in Walsrode; and I affectionately gazed at the letter from my collection (b. Aug. 26, 1756, d. Walsrode 23 May 1827.—I've got into the habit of browsing through my ‹Background Materials› every morning!).

Main road: you walked among these hot days as if among tall columns. (Golden, green-flecked. To the train).

Brief diversion: I imagined that I was a famous corpse and Berta the Widow was guiding people through the ‹Düring Museum› in Fallingbostel: there in the display cases, under glass, lay my manuscripts (e.g., my request of Finteln to finally put his thumbprint on his ID—"his last letter. Yes."—next to it the grand but still unpublished biography of Fouqué). On the wall a portrait of me by Oskar Kokoschka, with only one ear and highly unchristian flesh tones. A re-chording, ‹Celeste Aïda›, warbled by me;: "Here the carpenter's pencil that he always made it a point to sign his name with—" (this was often stolen by admirers, but was always lying there again, one mark thirty a dozen from the Westfalia Tool Company). And out in front of the building with tower (= the church), I stood tall in my metal tux, a hand lifted in polite disgust toward the District Commissioner's Office . . . . "The boots he died in . . .".—"Uhwhat were his last words, ma'am?" (the ‹Spiegel› reporter with his red morocco writing pad);—: "Uh—‹Long live art—uh—: Long live the fatherland!›. Uh: Germany, that is". "Ger . . . many . . . : Ah;—: Thank you!". (Whereas I had merely gasped ‹shit› ten times!). The grand finale, the niche illuminated a sulfurous blue where stood the slender urn with my ashes (because I definitely want to be cremated; it's much more hygienic!); the unpretentious marble plaque:—come on, quick?—‹Here lies . . .› (aw bull: not lying at all!)—okay ‹'inder me not›! (without the ‹h›; that makes it especially vulgar). Or better still: ‹Don't get 'indered!›. (Which fitted my case at the moment very nicely, having to catch the train!).

The larks twittered your ear deaf; (and I had to stand again too; since now, during the war, there's one car less: there are too many people!!).

What would I do with 10,000 marks?!: buy eight acres of wood and moor in the district of Fallingbostel; and a heavy barbwire fence around it, i.e., seven acres (because fences like that cost money!). which makes about 110 × 185 yds, better than nothing!—Or finance a new edition of Albert Ehrenstein.—Or a pilgrimage to Cooperstown; and immediately I pictured it to myself: up the Hudson as far as Albany; from there cross-country via Saratoga Springs, then on to Otsego County. And naturally the first thing you have to do is—"Heilittler, Herr Düring": "Sagosago, Paleface!"—climb Mount Vision for the classic view of the town. The sun arched through the dirty compartment window, and I was still standing there, hat in hand. (Before his grave).

(If only I could get hold of the ‹Autobiography of a Pocket-Handkerchief›; the travelogues and his historical works on the navy. And the ‹Rural Hours› by his daughter: I still know far too little!).

Schönert was a prisoner in Africa, Peters in Normandy, Runge had been killed in the east in '43: no great loss there! (But little Otte, not even eighteen, now lay by Monte Cassino!).

Wooden buskins with a pair of diagonal straps (there haven't been any leather shoes for ages now!); but they looked chic on long legs, and Krämer had even painted a sepia stripe up her brown calf: and it actually looked like a very elegant seam on a pair of silk stockings! How grand, Mother Nature, the glory of thy invention!: "Just how far up does that stripe go, Fräulein Krämer?". "And who gets to draw it on all the time!" She fixed a dove's pious green eyes on Steinmetz, our part-time drooling dotard: "My little sister does, every evening", she breathed, hushed as a church ("yet He who speaks of ‹evening› speaks of much". This was followed by further remarks about ‹Pandora's Box› and ‹that ball Columbus showed Isabel›; Schönert's spirit was still manifestly among us).

Faithfully following new regulations to use the smallest possible phormat for every letter (looks cute with a "ph", doesn't it?), I wrote practically nothing but postcards, or used 4 × 6 index cards for frasing in-house memos (the "f" in exchange for the above; for pedants).: All is lost already in the east, and the Germans are retreating through France, and I cheered to myself: a man whose prison is finally bursting open!! And even should I have to live for five years on water and bread: if these bastards, Nazis and officers, are swept away, then my world is gold-plated! So I elaborately rubbed my hands, and was so amused that Krämer gave me an astonished smile (any man is a delicacy these days, and in an emergency you'd even settle for me, right?).

An absurdly fat woman as executive secretary: ‹E pur si muove!› She needs dehydrating too.

Breakfast break (forty minutes today, Saturday. And then it goes straight through till 3 o'clock).

Saccharin tablets in the coffee: and even they had long since grown scarce, only to be had by swapping ‹under the counter›. The cardboard buttons broke when you sewed them onto the shirt; and oldman Steinmetz had actually offered Krämer four textile points (= one pair of stockings) for a roll in the hay. I had done my shopping well beforehand, and given my modicum of vanity, was completely independent as far as clothing etcetera went; so that I could use my points exclusively for: new lenses in my glasses, soles for my shoes, a handful of nails without an iron ration coupon, and a roll of film once when Käthe was on leave. (Over sixteen months ago now; had been in early May. Late ice age).

An outraged Fräulein Knoop: ‹mussel salad› the menu had read, no coupon needed, and they had started to eat it, when Kardel had found the snail feelers: yech! (Transition to frog's legs, oysters, beche-de-mer, and all other possible exotic abominations, rotten eggs and shark fins). Steinmetz, too, came by, smiling extra elegantly, stroking his imaginary moustache, and told us at length, like the Red Book of Hergest, all about Paris in the old days: "M'syour" they had all sworn: "It tastes like coconut". Spicy, spicy. "Oh," said Knoop, incredulous. "I swear by the pillow of the Seven Sleepers!". (Well, in that case).

"*Over by Bergen,* they're setting up an officers' training school," Fräulein Krämer informed us; excitedly aware of her serviceability as high-class whore. (If only we could get back to the medieval notion that every soldier is more or less ‹disreputable›,—rightly so: the "foe" never did him any real harm!— about on a par with the hangman, and to be avoided by every decent citizen!).—Still time for a quick walk.

*Summer sun: shadows: Peter Schlemihl!:** Nowadays he'd join a circus and make millions! If only a ‹man in gray› like that would appear to me, and offer me something for mine, something useful in these times: a tobacco pipe that never burned out; a car that didn't use any gas, a horse-sausage that never got smaller.

Chewing in front of a bookstore: German-silver rhymes scrambled at anchor, bloatings: Blunck, Heribert, Menzel, Kolbenheyer, ‹Choric Verse›, ‹Quex, a Lad for Hitler›, and all the other balladmongers of the Third Reich. A magazine, "German Faith" was an SS-wedding: a squad-leader masquerading as a priest of Odin blessed the couple beside an anvil with a sledgehammer *that* big: magic fertility rites. (Plus "The Blind Goalie"; probably some more of your ballads. Or a soccer novel. Who gives a damn Nowadays).

Eduard Vehse's 48-volume work, *History of the German Courts, the German Nobility and German Diplomacy since the Reformation* is going to need a supplement that goes on up till 1950!: what charming items could be added: the courts of the Wilhelms, of the Eberts, of the Hindenburgs, of the Hitlers, together with their accomplices and successors!

Or: "Correspondence between Two Notorious Personalities: (to wit: God and Satan); and then simply the dates: Hell, April 20 . . . . . : Heaven, April 22 . . . . . (And the notation: "The aforesaid individual who goes by the name of Shakespeare has even now arrived . . . .". Etc.).†

A cat approached, looked at me doubtfully, gave an embarrassed laugh, and I cut one of my three slices of coldcuts into little

---

*Refers to *Die wunderbare Geschichte des Peter Schlemihl* (*Peter Schlemihl's Remarkable Story,* 1814) by Adalbert von Chamisso (1781–1838). See The German Library, vol. 35, *German Romantic Stories.*

†A play on ideas by Düring: April 20, 1889, is Hitler's birthday; Shakespeare was baptized on April 23, 1564.

pieces for her and laid it on a sheet of wax paper:–.–An old woman, perched on a bike, precariousing among school-children.

A children's choirlet recited dutifully: "Fold my hands. Bow my head: / The Führer's commands / Give daily bread! / And free me from all dread!"; and I simply could not help myself, I had to walk over to the hedge and have a look at these five-year-old beings, in big and tucker, sitting there on the narrow wooden benches. The nurse (who had led them in reciting these vile verses), placed a small piece of glassy candy into the little tin cup each held by its handle, and they all stirred at it with their spoons, ‹cooking› it vigorously: what sort of regime is it that can dream up this sort of thing?! (But immediately I recalled that I, too, had learned as my first little song: "The Kaiser is a very nice man (sic!) / : and he lives in Burrlin"; and so it seems to be the universal, inevitable method of providing ‹civics› lessons! Oh, the bastards, the lot of them!! To pump such verbal swill into defenseless, fragile, unknowing beings! Or the equally senseless harangues about the "Blood of Christ"!: children ought to grow up in total intellectual neutrality until they're 17/18, and then be put through a couple of rigorous courses! They could then be presented alternately with the fabulous fibs about the "Holy Trinity" and the Nice Men in Berlin, and, by way of comparison, philosophy and natural sciences: and then you shysters would have to keep a sharp lookout!).

Then the nurse gave a shriek, and a whack to one of the urchins, and I moved behind me. (Still have to get ten—marks to the parish office; for two schoolkids who copied the death register for me: grinning: money's not worth much anymore!).

"We want to serve you faith-full-lee: / faithful uhunto death. (Yes, death!)": But why, for heaven's sake?!

Dust-girded recruits: mindlessly flapping their feet, twitched and tossed their brown-sweated heads, and hurled the heroic words from them: "We want to pledge our lihives to you . . .": Yes, but why, for heaven's sake?!!

With me you're totally wasting your measured syllables!! Before you decide you want to die for the fatherland, you'd best take a closer look! (And "My Life for the Führer"?!: for a politician I wouldn't grab hold of my ass!!).—

A *letter from Schönert* (just arrived; and la Krämer read it aloud in triumph): well, this time at least they weren't exposed to the hideous trench warfare we had in the first World War. (But then aerial warfare in those days was a silly idyll compared to now! And outside the next detachment was already bellowing a song of Lora and Dora, and of Trudy and Sophy. And I thought of my tall girl, my distant girl. Of Lena and Irena: of Anne-Marie.—"Hand me those coal-ration cards, Fräulein Krämer, so I can stamp them", and she reluctantly pulled herself away from the window; her face had pouted itself out of joint—).

Past noon and still another 3 hours!

Hot in the office, and reverie came to pat our faces with soft, empty hands. Eyes yawned (it is simply too long without a break!); hands loitered at official business; under the chairs oblique legs stretched; Krämer slowly pulled some zipper or other through the silence, and then typed away at her metronome, distant droplets, on dainty hooves, in a forest of dust. ("Pan sleeps"; that was coined by some office worker, somewhere around three in the afternoon).

"You're decking yourself out like a bride!"; for she was clandestinely doing her nails, Fräulein Knoop, and her black mourning (for the second fiancé already) looked attractive enough set against her white over-stuffed face; she made heavy chestnut eyes, rolled her anklets down further, and taking a breath, tugged at her skirt; then dipped and pumped her fountain pen and counted, listlessly and softly, bookkeeping noses. The new trainee gazed timidly at where the strap of her bra cut visibly through her fat back; turned his red head away and projected the image onto the far wall. The old man was sleeping now, quite unabashedly, but behind his green glasses, unconvictable (was just an old office fox, and still quite useful!)

After half an hour one of them whispered the question: "Do you think there'll be a thunderstorm today?—Can we still go swimming later on, do you suppose?—" A quarter hour later I answered in an elderly, envious voice: "Both, Fräulein Krämer". A door slammed resolutely; the old man awoke with self-control, and loftily entered a name in his book; Robin the Red had moaning visions of Krämer, first with, then very much without her swimsuit; Fräulein Knoop went to get new ink; and I rapidly stamped my way through another eighty clothing-ration coupons.

"Boss's in a bad mood today!": and sure enough: he had written numerous nasty remarks on every petition, sort of in the style of Frederick the (thankgod) One and Only, and then at the bottom a steady stream of "refused"; "reject"; "no"; "impossible!"; "how dare he?!". Once he had even added: "not to be processed in the future": all the better for us! And now for the last folder . . . . . . : "The boss wants to see you right away, Herr Düring!"

Two or three gusts of wind, and clouds of evil portent. (Through the corridor windows; in passing).

"At one time you told me about that—deserter, the one from 1813—?" (gravelly coughs): "Just imagine, Düring: they say there's another one now. In the same area. Been there for years! I've been following the matter for some time"; he shoved the forester's report into my hand, and watched me, with lurking amusement.

Breached bulwark: my face. (No doubt of it: Gröpel, the son of a bitch, had apparently been spotting me mornings!). And his was an ample gray rag. (Plus four additional reports by farmers: remember those names). The rag ripped open in one place; he sneered new words together, and alertly I countered them: for all I care he can turn my stomach till the next ice age! (Has had a more proper education maybe; but not the man to dare the deed).

"Yes, looks like we'll have to make a raid on our new ‹faun›," he proposed merrily, daring me. He gazed at me intently: "They say he's about fifty-to-sixty-years old. Gray hair; tall and scrawny"; and he brazenly took my measure; and I stared at him, unshaken and cunning: something different about you today, too?!—?—Ah, well look at that!!: all at once he was no longer wearing his party badge! (Just like old Häusermann and the rest of the sewer rats: lookie there!). I ‹took the floor›: I said coldly: "May I please ask a personal favor—Herr Doktor—?" (and he leaned forward more snugly): "—You are a Party member, are you not: could you give me the address of the District Party Leader: a petition on behalf of my daughter: you are a friend of his—" (And how: for Christmas he had given him a carpet paid for out of our funds!).—He sat there

ever so stiffly; he said politely and flatly: "Kirchplatz 3".
Looked at his calendar: "The raid will be next week then. September 8." "Yes sir, Herr Commissioner."

All right, then, that's the end!! and I whistled a dry and bitter
tune: over!: the end! All right!. (So, clear the place out and set
fire to it, tonight!—And I'll give the forester a kick in the
pants yet. Or two. All his files and cards and ration books just
might get lost sometime. it'd take him a good six months just
to fill out new forms!– –But it's over, over, over!—Oh, Käthe!)

"Well look at that:—it's already started to rain, Fräulein
Krämer!" And "Heil!" "Right. Heil!: have a good weekend!"

"Thirteen convoy ships sunk!"; the loudspeaker sang and
thumped in the human paddock; words met, strict and gray;
and the limp watery dead drifted pathetically through our
crowd. Rain befingered me. The apparatus bellowed bake-
litely and triumphed on: "For we're sail! ing! 'gainst Engel-
lannd!: Engelland!"; Herms Niels and Herm. Löns, the
German Hit-Tune Company! (But the other side's got Vansit-
tart & Wells). I waded mutely through the slush of muttering
and teeth; many heads had eyes in trumps; laughter, too, appeared, and two women sizzled "Super!" And still they sailed
from every window, spare and manly; No one was sobbing or
walking stiffly with cobwebbed eyes; but it was raining
harder, silver-gray drops splattered up from the pavement,
hand-high, around my walking shoes.

A dog leaped, with head turned in the thicket of legs. The dead
hovered up ahead with limp bluish arms, hung garlands of
eyes about me where I stood, one ate with me, uneasily, from
my teaspoon. (And it was lovely out on the main road: you
were all alone: no one drives a car anymore! At most there
are the funny wood-gas buggies that Hitler claims will win his
war!—Old grass threw itself excitedly from one side to the
other; but now once again, the scudding smoky blue).

The music surged and burst in fragments (here too): oldman
Weber stepped out under his sign: "They'ah keep'n' it up—
hah: sunk ump'ty tons ag'in t'day!" And proud. I nodded as
piously as I could, and first made to walk by; but then I added:
"Shame about all those supplies: why one freighter like that:
we wouldn't have to do a stitch of work the rest of our lives!"
"Hmmm," and it went on hudibrasing behind me. (Then a

shaky bass barreled something about the Rhi-hi-hine: oh happy days were here again, 1944!).

"*Well, Berta!*" (still in deepest mourning): our son had been killed on the Murmansk front fourteen months earlier; as an off. cand., doing his required eight-weeks frontline training. First home on proud leave from the school, as admired sergeant and cornet: "Well, dad?"; as if he had it made now! When the worst was yet to come! And I screwed up my face to smile, inspecting the peacock, till he turned away, offended. Explained to him why, too, certainly; but he had heard too much about battle as the ‹tempering of a man›. "When not on duty, I'd rather not mingle with the rank and file!" he had informed me with astonishment when I once suggested that, whenever possible, he go among them from time to time: to hear some good common sense! OK, bon!—Sure, and then when the local Branch Leader showed up, my wife came back hard to earth, threw a bowl of potatoes at the Führer's picture, and went into sobbing spasms. (Me: I felt nothing! You don't really dare tell anyone that; but I felt more distant from Paul than from some stranger; for Cooper I can still weep, even now. But I recognized ‹my boy's› shallowness and dreadful mediocrity: his mother's!: actually I should have said to her: you bear a generous portion of blame in this, you pompous woman! If only you had helped me preach reason to him, instead of whooping over the silver cord wound about his bird-brain!!).

(*Then the epitaph:* "What should we put in the newspaper, Heinrich?!" implored the Prostrate Lady in Black. "‹Paul fell›" I said sternly, "‹one of many deluded children›!": I would have done it too!!—Oh!: she didn't want to go that far; particularly since her mite of a conscience did not, perhaps, quite absolve her: for, oh, how disdainfully she had looked down her nose at the poor corporal-drudges from next door. How she had puckered her mouth to a penny, and gone out for a strut on the arm of her son! How her sassy tongue had let fly when I termed ‹the officer› the most dispicable of all beings: "Jealous of your own son, huh?!"; and had gone off laughing to the pantry, to slip him the last of our supplies!—Yes, and so she decided in favor of something original, "Fallen for Greater Germany"—well, if that's what you want?!—But she didn't let Gerda volunteer for antiaircraft duty anymore!).

And so: "*Well, Berta?*" (as a greeting). Yes, yes. And she had tickets for the six o'clock movie, too: "Come along for once!". (And I groaned inwardly: I usually never go; for the same money I can buy an ordnance map!—Well; once is not a habit; and maybe she would sleep better, and I could disappear more easily tonight).—"Feddersen wants you to stop by, too"; and I furrowed my brow deeper still.

"*Heil, Herr Feddersen*". "'fternoon, Herr Düring". And he, craftsman-dictator, rummaged unhurriedly among his fabrics and scissors. (Had ordered myself a canvas coverall, as camouflage in the woods; was quite superfluous now. Or, then again, not: since I would probably always want to walk among trees; so coolly try it on!). And with his heavy gray hands he smoothed the fabric over my limbs. (Did I want stirrups fitted on the trousers?—Well, I'd think about that); but my heart cursed and flickered within me, and he promised delivery in four weeks. "Three", he added, after we had complained some about the weather, and I had let him dig deep several times in my large ‹House of Neuerburg› tin. "And don't forget the green peaked cap" (for my prim pate): "and remember the double seat, too, please, sir!: the main thing's the durability!". "Sure; the buttons covered with fabric, of course.—Good-bye!"

Facing books (back home again; another hour yet till the movies). Balzac, Balzac: not a poet; no rapport with nature (the most important criterion!). Only every twenty pages is there anything really good, a precise formulation, an allusive image, a sudden spark of imagination. How ridiculous, for example, his deadly descriptions, all of them two ungainly printed pages long, of the boudoirs of the haute volée!: can anyone fit together the fragments of such inane puzzles? And keeps repeating the same figures, motifs, situations, as only a prolix proser can. He never gets his men right; nothing but incroyables, curmudgeons, journalists, poison-concocting doorkeepers (how soothing, in contrast, even Cooper and Scott). His women: courtesans and wallflowers. Psychology??: Oh my!!: for the one and only ‹Anton Reiser›* I wouldn't take all of Balzac and Zola put together!

---

*Cf. Anton Reiser, *Ein psychologischer Roman* (*Anton Reiser: A Psychological Novel*, 1785–90) by Karl Philipp Moritz (1756–93). See The German Library, vol. 10, *Eighteenth Century German Prose*.

And then there are the new scribblers in Blood and Soil: compared to them B. is no less than a god! For example, these panegyrics here on the jacket:
"the captivating charm of unpretentiousness" (when there is no way to hide the total imbecility of it all!),
"a manly and open book" (when the author, with much painstaking embarrassment, manages a weak thrust of his abdomen!),
"that finally fills a gap of long standing" (if by chance the fable doesn't for once date back to Homer, but merely to Hesiod!);
and I lovingly caressed my old Pauly's *Encyclopedia of Classical Antiquities.*

As for new poets: it is indeed a great rarity for someone to make the fine distinction between whether that's an office window glimmering there on the horizon or a large heavenly body about to rise. (And when it's finally circling overhead, they lie there in their close-curtained alcoves, breathing raspily, and dreaming of chubby secretarial hocks; or of how they never passed their high-school comps): for whom do poets write really? For the one in a hundred thousand just like themselves? (Because the one in ten thousand who might be a potential reader never discovers the contemporary poet at all; and at best has gotten as far as Stifter).—No sir!: I would not want to be a writer! (And ‹nationalist kitsch› is the same thing as moldy mildew: nationalist means kitsch!).

Still need to calculate: when, where, and in what phase the moon will rise tonight. (Yes: it's clear;—for the most part. And blessed be K. Schoch's table of the planets; even the dumbest Düring can manage with it. And it's absolutely precise).

(Long ago, as a boy, I was always drawing stylized maps on large sheets of graph paper, with right-angled islands and infinitely intricate bays and canals: most probably the ‹labyrinth-complex› of primitives with their edifices, tombs, mines. Now it's in woods; and on a map scaled · 25,000:1. Relaxed, so to speak. More natural. More nimble).

And tonight I've got to set fire to my hut!!

"Hein-rich!".—: "JustimagineHeinrich: Fräulein Evers is home! On leave!—Over there!" (No doubt of it! In the name of him who will one day be my boss! "Is that so," and show con-

trolled surprise. Words, yes.—Back upstairs: and to the window!—:).

"Ah—Fräulein Evers!": innocent, jaunty (and shaking terribly); the hand across the fence said ‹Käthe!›. My breath was violent and mechanical (the way wind mingles with foliage); my eyes whispered (as if vegetal); my heart battered at my jacket (: and tonight I've got to set fire to our hut!!). "You coming along to the movies?" choked out hastily (so she'll know where I am). "Oh. Not tonight," and she gave a dry, collusive laugh: "got to clean up first; after the trip. And lie down for a while." (Meaning she might be free to talk later on!) "Goodnight": "Goodnight, Herr Düring". (And so a good night! good!).

The movies: first *News of the Week:* glorious victorious torpedo boats rocking at sea (with the appropriate goading musical accompaniment), and beaming ‹Boys in Blue›: "If only we could die just a little for Greater Germany!". Tank cavalcades and artillery (the French used to be the world's best artillerists!: they invented it all, hollow charges, trajectory charts; and I thought of the old descriptions of chain-shot and case-shot in the memoirs of General von Brixen, at one time Rüchel's adjutant, an original edition of which adorned my Background Materials. As early as 1795, the French were directing their battles from the air! For example, at Fleurus!).

Then the ‹Documentary›: the Alps, naturally (also with obligatory heroic instrumentation; the clouds sailed rapturously to a variation of the overture to ‹Der Freischütz›); lakes and ah, such snowy peaks. Patinaed cliffs: stony bijous fifty-feet high, in rusty bushranger outfits, ferny feathers on their hats, sassy tottering bouldered skulls. A milk-white team of oxen forded the river (brass began to swell hymnically, as an accompanying mighty stream). And everywhere in that landscape swept so obligingly clean, were ‹German Men and Women›, patented, heads so full of character and trust in the Final Victory. ("Yes, Berta, it's charming!").

Stupid and saccharine: the feature. Decorative waltzings about ("Aren't the costumes simply dar-ling, Heinrich!"; Willi babbled with Lilian; and Hans Moser, the sweet little rascal: ah boys and girls, if only there weren't such nasty penalties for 2nd-degree murder!

Inflammatory banquets, with someone blowing smoke right out of the screen, and people drinking beer and smacking their lips (1944!—Although I don't doubt that a person with a sufficient dose of punch in his belly can manage just about anything!).

The Kaiser, the Kaiser, His ‹darling Majesty›, actually danced in very person with her: and getting a good grip on her furbelowed skirt, with her curtsying hands, she glided in nearer: giant close-up (Oh Swift in Brobdingnag!), soundlessly unbolted that hangar of a mouth: dental slabs the size of dictionaries occupied her jaw bow, beneath nasal pilasters; her eyelashes bristled like carpenter's nails. From the cavern came an alluring waltz (and the soulless gawkers began to rock imperceptibly to the prescribed tempo, as the Lestrygonian head up there swayed back and forth).

Yes, and so then the Kaiser danced with her, clumsily to an aPaulLinck tune, and it was such a high honor (maybe she'd already done service ‹under› 3 kaisers); but the ‹class difference› proved just a teensy too big after all, and so she accepted the Honved musketeer, dashing and debonair, as erotic surrogate: and it was All so stinking false and absurd, so gushy and German: no sir! I happily shut my eyes: at least then all I smelled was the sweat around me, and I heard the little thing beside me sob convulsively (probably as the Kaiser strode back to the Hofburg—lonely and tragic as only the Viennese can be).—She deployed herself decoratively on a regal bed, and necked a bit with Morpheus; until her penis in Honved uniform came to rescue her: thankgod! (And straight for the exit!– –"Ah, it was all just so lovely, Heinrich!": my wife. "Wonderful, Berta"; and we middle-classed homeward. Eight o'clock and sunset).

It's the maddest thing in the world, (and you really ought to hear my pencil rustle as I write!), that you can hold five hundred years of painting in one hand: Francke's green Magdalene and Mueller's girls in their green park (seems then that ‹green› is the tertium comparationis!). And I went over to the map of the Département of Weser from 1812: lithographic green was the border around the Arrondissement of Nienburg: where I lived. (Beneath broad leaves; fenced-in by sulky pine needles. Käthe's stockings had been green just now, ah, just a tiny bit of ankle; greenish too the insectile moon in the pink of evening; greenish cow dung and envelopes, pencils and backs of many a book).

Keep your shoes on!
Cloud tongue-lashings above backyard gardeners: we ripped up
scrawny pea vines and ravaged ranks of plants (and the globes
of our butts, mine behind me included, jutted out foolishly,
how disgusting). Beyond, a cutlet of moon was swimming
above the night; a breeze came up and called out Ho! and Evening!; a tardy child leaped and bounced steadily along over
the ground, right up to us, beside the black pendulum of its
shopping bag. Wind-tears appeared in Weber's eyes (and he
let a fat gob slither out of his bearded muzzle, and then carefully rubbed the rest of it around his jaw with the back of his
hand: don't waste none of it!).
It is a horror beyond all measure to be me!!
"Uh—*Herr Evers!?*—would you perhaps still have a piece of
fuse left?—From when you blew up that boulder out at the
back of your field recently?– –Oh; just a short piece: about
so—!" and I showed him: 12 inches (I sure would like to get
it under the commissioner's skin!).—The yellow chitinous
body of the moon crept up black branches. A planet, Venus
let us hope, fixed in amber).
Wrestle down the blackout shades (and inconspicuously get
ready for the hut: to hell with the rascal with the tattooed
brow!—For the last time!). I gingerly picked up Thierry's button and rubbed it on my sleeve: wicked its sparkle, and fraternal. (And I waxed sullen, stony, like a great thunderstorm: for
the last time??!!—Rubbing-)
"*Come to me from out the air,:* / Arise from ocean deep,: /
Though fast asleep in darkened lair,: / Or up from the fire
leap—: DÜRING is your Lord this night! / Obey him, every
shade and sprite!"
Well?!———(Listen:———?
———Nothing: Fff).
I twitched my left, more nervous eyebrow and walked by
stiffly.—"Heinrich!". "Don't forget: the current's awfully low
again: bring the lamp while you're at it!" and I fetched and
bore the good old kerosene glowworm: good thing I bought
that reserve canister back then! (Wise old Düring, right?!).
The news (but it, too, very murky and low): all fighters
had returned to their air bases; but neither did they forget
their customary and time-worn ‹straightening the frontlines›

("Trustworthy as a bulletin from General Headquarters" is
how they used to brag!). The Pope was suffering once again
from acute apparitions of Mary (cf. Scheffel's *Castle Toblino,*
p. 398); and enemy bomber formations were approaching as
per usual (meaning, presumably, Berlin again).

The hierarchy of the three Christian denominations (and of the
countless minor ones as well) goes on feeding obtusely off the
same inadequate arguments that were just barely reasonable
to intellectual middlebrows of 2,000 years ago. Since which
time, as understanding has grown with each century and in
each individual, there has been increasing exasperation with
the disastrous gulf between the generally recognized necessity
for charity toward one's fellows and their unswervingly sha-
manistic arguments for it: a third of the blame for our present
desperate intellectual situation can be laid to this contradic-
tion, which still disquiets most people, and has even driven
generous men, in the anguish of their rage, to malign love itself. It really is high time to relegate Christian mythology—
and all its gods, demigods, seers, heavens and hells (and, of
course, all the earthly set decorations, stage equipment and
costumed extras as well!)—to where it historically and de-
servedly belongs, namely, right alongside those of Greece and
Rome, etc.: that would settle things down considerably both
within and around us.—

The kerosene lamp in my hand took a bound with me, and shook
off its frosted bonnet. The cupboard gave me a push, that I
parried only with difficulty, and its doors thrashed away at me
too. My wife tottered behind the lattice of her apron and held
a table in her hands! The panes snarled clear and savage in
their frames; a cup leaped up and landed at my widespread
feet; the air jumped (just a good thing that the windows were
all standing open for summer!); I lurched through doors with
head on the slant, danced about on the staggering staircase,
and fell at the front gate into people.

"They're bombing the Eibia plant!!" oldman Evers clangored
and shook like a black coat, I grabbed for something Käthean
and we were already galloping, technical emergency corps,
behind the wind in the same lurid direction, with pattering
soles, vaulting fences; two crows hurtled by; one turned
around and screamed at me: cad! caadd!

Another jerk and throb, and afar the houses laughed, bright and demented, out of windows clinking to shatters. The she-night clapped with thundering paws, Explosia, and countless crashes played tag around the horizon. (Lightning bolts hacked tonight from bottom to top; and each one thundered amply jovian as it vanished into its horrified cloud!).

The long road wrenched. A tree pointed finger masts at us, lurched some more, and closed the branching cage behind us. We scrambled over the red-checked earth, through flame-gorged ruins, our jaws chewed the smoky jellied air, we shoved the brawl of lights aside with the plates of our hands, and our feet doddered along before us, in shoes with criss-cross laces, hugging together. The flailing light battered our brows beyond recognition; the thunder crushed pores and glands underfoot, and filled our open mouths with gagging avalanches: then ponderous sabers were scarving at us again.

All trees dressed as flames (on Sandy Hill): a housefront stumbled forward menacingly, with silky red foam at the corner of its maw and windowed eyes ablaze. House-high boulders of iron rolled tumults about us, blackish, the very sound of which was lethal! I threw myself on Käthe, wrapped her with wiry arms, and tugged at her greatness: one half of the night was ripped away, and we fell to earth slain by thunder (but clambered up again, defiant still, and gasped helplessly into all volcanoes).

Two railroad tracks had torn loose and were angling off like crab claws; the pincers turned about and in a resounding arc passed lovingly over us (and we ran and ducked beneath the languid iron lash). From below came a defiant pounding at our bones; the gaping muzzle of a pipe appeared and lazily spewed acid.

Every maid wore red stockings; each with cinnabar in her pail: a tall silo of powder scalped himself, and let his flowery brain truffle over: while below he performed hara-kiri, and repeatedly rocked his monumental body above the bleeding gash before discarding his torso. White hands gesticulated busily in the everywhere; many had ten unjointed fingers *and* one that was nothing but red nodes (and beneath us the grand dance of wooden clogs stomped in rhythm!). Hitler Youth slunk about werewolfily. Fire brigades wandered lost and nimble. Hundreds of arms spurted up from the sod and distributed stony handbills, "Death" inscribed on each, large as a table.

Concrete vultures with glowing iron talons flew by over us screaming dissonantly, in great flocks (until they spotted a victim over in the development and pounced on him). A yellow-toothed cathedral stood bellowing in the violet-fringed night: so its fat steeple exploded into the air! Clusters of ruttish red flares lilted above Bommelsen, and we had diachromatic faces: the right side green, the left a cloudy brown; the ground danced out from under us; we threw our long legs in time to it; a rope of light looped in berserk curves across the sky: to the right a bonbon translucence, to the left a deep frenzy of violet.

The sky took on the shape of a saw, the earth a red lively pond.

With black human fish flopping about: a girl, naked from the waist up, burst toward us barking impudently, and the skin dangled at her shriveled breasts like curly lace; her arms fluttered back from her shoulders like two white linen ribbons. The red dishcloths in the sky blustered and scrubbed blood. A long flatbed truck full of baked and boiled humans glided by soundlessly on rubber tires. Ever and again airy giant hands grabbed hold of us, lifted us up and tossed us. Invisibilities jostled us against one another, till we were quivering with sweat and exhaustion (my beautiful sweaty stinky girl: let's get out of here!).

A buried tank of alcohol shook itself loose, rolled out like bindweed on a hot hand, and dissolved in a Halemaumau (out of which fiery brooks flowed: a dismayed policeman commanded the one on his right to halt and was vaporized in the line of duty). A fat-lady cloud stood up above the warehouse, puffed out her balled belly and belched a pastry head high, laughed throatily: so what!, and knotted her trundling arms and legs, turned toward us steatopygically and farted whole sheaves of hot iron tubing, endlessly, the virtuosa, till the shrubs beside us curtsied low and babbled.

An incandescent corpse swooned and fell to its knees before me, offering its smoldering serenade; one arm was still flickering and broiling petulantly: it had come out of thin air, "From heav'n above", the apparition of Mary. (The world was altogether full of them: whenever another roof rolled up, they

shot out from the cornices like divers, helmeted or in their
naked hair, flew a little distance, and burst like paper bags on
the earth below. In God's own scalawag hand!).

The ruby-glass pulsings of a fire anemone in Döblinesque groves;
benignly it waved with a hundred hawser arms (on each of
them nettledown surged), then cautiously dived deeper into
the sea of night, and skirmished on, but furtively. A three-
story bunker began to stir: it grumbled drowsily and rippled
its shoulder bladings; then it discarded roof and walls with a
gurgle and the vertical dawn suddenly made for us gowns of
flame-colored taffeta and many faces of fierce roses (until the
black thud pulled the earth out from under us like a rescue
net: a car with firefighters plummeted whirling from the heavens, buckled a few times, and with a nod perished in the
gravel, the corpses propped together in jumbled animation).

(*For a while* broad silent flakes of fire fell about us, *come di neve
in Alpe senza vento:* with hand and cap I batted them away
from Käthe's graven image, interceding all about her: she
brushed one from my gray smoldering hair, and went on
watching the keelhauling of hissing shadows).

A rigid man appeared in the sky, a blast-furnace in each hand:
he prophesied some death and death, so that I pushed against
my hand, and saw the bones dark within the fiery flesh. Two
long thighs of light tapdanced down those walls there; the
road blanched at the sight and melted partly away. Lots of
greasy black bags were being carried past us on stretchers: the
workers from the third shift, their chief conductor explained,
and with fluttering tongue stepped back into mute vanguard.
Meteors Klaxoned through the upper air; farmhouses shook
with laughter, sending their shingles flying down; fire fountains were frolicking godforsaken everywhere and sparks
geysered in jets.

In the weeping clutch at road's edge, a woman went mad: she
tugged her skirts with fat hands, up to her belly, unjammed
her mouth, wooden wedged, and tumbled down before her
coarse yellow hair into the jiving rubble; all at once the
ground before us began to glow: a thick vein swelled up,
forked brighter still, throbbed and blubbed soupily, and rup-
tured with a sigh (so that the white air almost throttled us,
and retching we groped into rearward gloom. A pine caught

fire and screamed, skirt and hair and all; but that was nothing compared to the orders troated in bass from vats of light and to the gnashings of fence-high flaming teeth).

And now: the fat woman from a while ago rode a hunk of horse through the air just above us, smoldered and ignited desperate for her mamma! From behind, a steady wind harried us between the legs, dragging wheezes and condoling dust with it, and when it took the notion, made wavering tents of sparks. A penis of light, tall as a chimney, twitched and thrust into the smutty tangle of night (but then broke off too soon; but was already replaced on the right by a red-bearded pillar of flame whooping up a clog dance, till the grit beneath us groused and burped).

A *whistling voice* ran toward us, preceding someone who had gone and caught fire; his forehead got pasted to a tree stump and he wriggled there for a long time. The jagged boomings flailed at us like morning stars; the caustic light gnawed the skin around our eyes; beside us shadows buckled at the knee. Bunker B1107 bellowed like an ox before tossing its matted concrete skull high: then its gut was torn open and the red blaze punched the breath out of us. (I pasted more wet handkerchiefs over Käthe's gaping mouth and big trembling nose).

The black-yellow tatters of night flew! (Once the harlequin lass wore nothing but red scarves!): four men ran in pursuit of a giant snake that leapt over the railroad embankment, up front hissing and slobbering; they dug their heels in and roared it seemed (but only the faces gaped wide; and the ridiculous helmets of the brave idiots). Posters of light sprang up so quickly around us that you couldn't even read all the rumblings (eyes were simply pasted shut by the toxic colors, and slit open again only in pain and reflex: "Come on! Käthe!". Flaming whores smacking their lips, all in red, with sharp face and rakish makeup, made a hot excursion our way, distended their smooth bellies, crackled laughter, and came closer still into the bawdy strumpet light: "Come on, Käthe!").

The night licked its chops again with many blank lips and tongues, and showed us a couple of alluring stripteases, sending bright tassels drizzling down around us: then endless rattling applause set in (and foot-stampings to make your head ring). Trucks full of gesticulating SA drove in a little too close:

the lads jumped down, hissing like lighted matches, and vanished (while their vehicles likewise skipped and melted away).
A whining boy came toward us bearing his arms askew: like
a towel his hide shagged vertically from him; he displayed
coppery teeth, and whimpered in time to the detonations,
whenever the gorilla pounded his chest.

In the earth's interior sound rolled like nonstop subway trains:
those were the grenade cellars!: Good!: Better than if they got
lobbed at the innocent-guilty! All flashing flames slashed at
uniformed German Maidens. And they were still breathing as
we carted them off across lawns by their sturdy legs.

"Käthe!!"

"Get down!!!"

Because right next to us the bunker began to crow, and raised its
red comb so stiff that we did fall a great fall and shared our
tremblings, as, with buffeting of walls, it flew away over us.
In its place here first appeared

a morel of fire (and 30 men could not have got their arms
around it),

then the Giralda,

then many apocalyptics (and glistening brushwood mountains).

And only then did the sound send us in a seamless tumble onto
the grass, causing houses over in the developments to toss fry-
ing-pan caps into the huzzahing air: "Käthe!!"

"Kää-tää!!!

I bounded my hand up her legs, scaled her panting belly, en-
clasped her shoulders: "Käthe!!"; her head wailed from stupe-
faction; horrified, I ironed away at her face: "Ow!"

A crude block, big as a sideboard, bit the back of my hand:
"Käthe!!".—She threw her legs up and grappled like an
adder.: "Hair!" she roared with no restraint. And frantic, I
felt her all over, her brow, her hollow ears, the furred back
of her head. And tore at her shoulders as she screamed: "My
hair!!!"; and still she made no move up!

Her mane: fumed in the hot stony maw!—I threw myself to one
side, and ripped out my pocketknife, splitting a nail, and
turned savage to hack away at her, till she gave a shriek and
pummeled me: "Now?!!!"—"No: not yet, not yet!!".

"Now?!?":—"Ow—I," she tore off the medusan head, scratching me in pain as I lifted. Red brushes sprouted from the earth

and stained the screeching clouds somewhat purple; several times the sky collapsed (and the red-black fragments fell below the horizon). Käthe barked and wagged her calves; with a howl we bit at each other's invisible faces, and crept between the heaps of stars around to our left, till we found ourselves once again inside bags of noise, inside the grove of swords, till it grew dark again; till I

"There: that way!: follow the tracks!"

Along the railroad: we dodged a locomotive hissing down on us, bellied along runners growing ever darker: "Come on, down Rain Strasse", and then the other track, Bomlitz-Cordingen—: now I knew exactly where I was, and led the way swiftly and smoothly: "Can you run, Käthe?!" "Yes. I'll manage. I seem to be all right otherwise!".

In the Warnau: "Hooooooo—": "Lovely." "Water!" We wiped ourselves with sand and grass, and helped each other when our arms would stretch and bend back no further. "Damn, I can't get my shoe on!".– –"No, wait. I can just do it." (But she limped away more heavily in my arms).

"Oh!–:–": an army of crazies brandished daggers of light above the woods; the blades cracked and yowled (and afterwards, of course, much crimson blood flowed down cloud wadis). The meadows bounced beneath our callous hoofs (cased in leather); blackness prickled round our callous skin; to the world I looked: tame to the touch, middle-class hero, a stiff-nosed office worker: won't you all be surprised!

Little beech brigades, oak athletes, pine archers: they are our bodyguards, as once upon a time in Sherwood Forest: "Such outlaws as he and his Kate"; and with that we pushed deeper into the woods: I knew the disposition of every blade of grass; was that piece of bark lying there like that last time?: here a fox had scrambled across the ground, there a human, now two humans. Grasped junipers, toed moss and cold mushroom caps, mushroom snacks, the ant making menacing pincers at my Conti-rubbered heel; in my trouser leg the sting of keen foils of grass.

We ran easily and glided in pursuit of our own limbs, across disks of wind-stilled meadow, until I landed in the pliant prickly arms of a broad-hipped young fir (her boughed legs spread wide, lusty pelvic trunk, my hand detected moist mossy wrinkles; and the palpitating breastplate whooped: "Käthe—?-"."Yes. Right here." (at my sleeve.))

The moon fumbled a few seconds beside us in the brush of the westerwood, distorted, red with rage. Around the corner: there it took its stand, small and ominous, above pine bludgeons, highwayman in rags of cloud, right there in front of us: scram, you!

"Ah, now I know.—But: this foot, damnation!"."Wait. Just a second!".—

Kerosene lamp: the flame was the size of a cedar nut; just above it yellow and blue hair of fire, sulfurously agile.: "C'mon in. Careful with that door!". (Noiseless, the well-oiled hinges.: "Fine!").

"Hm: Fine!": she stood there looking about her contentedly (the shutters sealed felt-tight), then sat down on the old familiar blanket, and groaned a bit at her foot. "Wait, I'll help you." Unlace it wide;—gently maneuver the heel out: "All right?"; and she threw back her head against the plank wall and gnashed on a ‹Yes›.

Her big red foot!: 2 toes were already broken and swollen big as sausages ("Wait, I'll heat some water"; and the tin can, a ferrous brown brimful, crackled atop the folding solid-spirit stove: "Takes 5 minutes, at the most!").

"Ohboyohboyohboyohboy!"; to take her mind off it she looked around: my furnishings: "Just like before." Soap and half a towel; nails in the wall, here and there. Food supplies, two blankets, matches, machete and compass. "Have you got adhesive and a bandage?—Great!". The little telescope, magnification of fifteen, and very collapsible: "Has come in very handy? Right?", and I told her the story of how I had used it to spot the commissioner's car coming down the main road over there; and she examined it, pulled it out full length, turning it over.

Two books: Ludwig Tieck "Journey into the Blue; and Scarecrow". Fouqué "Magic Ring".

Two paintings: Otto Müller: "Hmm—" a repeated show of approval. Franke "Group of Women". "This was the one here, right?" she asked, and pointed a finger at the Green Courtesan (Heavenly and Earthly Love. No ‹Christus› or bloody whatever!).—(Get the utensils from under the floorboards).

"Come here, I'll wash you.—": Full bath out of a tin can. (First pedicure; and she delightedly moved her ankle in its secure bandage: "Great!"; praise and confidence). Rub cream on the burns on hips and ribs; and she gleefully braced her downy moist belly against my face. (Then she examined me as well, pricked open three blisters, and checked buttocks and testicles. And we fell ever more deeply into each other).

The cavantinas of the wind.

I found myself everywhere in the lattices of her great fingers, in the yoke of her long arms, the broad sash of her legs. Heavy. (She would say perhaps: I bore him like half a suit of armor; his body hacked at mine; everywhere he found breasts to tweak).

(With these pale yellow bodies of ours, we are badly camouflaged! Wonder if Indian war paint—apart from the shock effect—might not have had the simultaneous effect of optically resolving man's obtrusive body into more natural images with dark and bright patterns and stripes? For the prowl through umbrage and underbrush? Brown from earth ochers; green from plant juices; and fungi yield dyes too; berries. Like our modern tarpaulin: it's exactly the same thing!– – –: "Yes; I sowed a broader band of reeds around outside: a good ten yards at least! And planted forty pines: almost all of them have taken root!– –Well, it doesn't matter now: Later." Then RIP-soap, rest in peace, for me: all out of a pea can).

The Ladie's Supper: and she gloried in digging the liverwurst out with my pocketknife: "Manohman!" "I haven't eaten this good in years!"; filled up. (And for tea, a bag hanging daintily from its thread: even Americans use one twice. The English four times. Germans eight.: "Sweetener?". "Noo!: Anything but that! Barbarian!".– –"You really live quite the life here!". "Only for today, Käthe." And she, touched and satisfied: "mmm").—How late??: well—: past eleven for sure: 11:43 P.M. to be precise. We were, however, a long way from being able to sleep, took the blanket and sat down before the door, half naked as we were: "That'll burn for days yet!" (The Eibia rumpus): "The fire'll eat its way along the endless conduits—as far as the Lohheide; maybe over to the thieves' den in Munster—just keep moving down all the shafts: ab-so-lute-ly hopeless!"

We watched, with plain eyes and upended faces, reed and wood, as beyond them, distant, constant, the red sea seethed and jostled. I was weary of all words: washed-out words, slurped away by billions of tongues, Dietrich-Ekartish words, worn ragged in billions of baggy mouths, Fritsche-Goebbelsish words, run down at the heel on all airways, broadly bruised by all lips, nasaled, expectorated, stark-baked, shit through brooms: mother tongue! (Oh, what a charming, ingenious term, is it not?!).

But when that tongue is burning in your mouth: in Mine! When thickets are houses to you: to Me! When the wind whisks your arms and legs: Ours, ours, ours! (Encompassed by skin, swished by hair, foot tappings, back rustlings: and now they were driving me out of my paradise, by means of commissioners and foresters? Really?!—She rubbed my forearm soothingly: it really is absurd).

"I have one more bottle of beer inside, Käthe.": "Hand it over.". She drank languidly and endlessly; then concentrated her nose, and gave a discreet burp, my charming toad. I quickly kissed her on her cold beer

"I have one more bottle of beer inside, Käthe": "Hand it over." She drank from it languidly, endlessly; puckered up her nose then and gave a discreet and charmingly droll burp. I quickly kissed her on her cold beery lips; and put my ear to her body, listening for new burblings there– –but this time her chest just grew fuller and broader.

"Let's hope all the houses have been destroyed!". She eyed me critically, but then nodded: compris. Then shook her head: "Doubt it".

"Where do you have to report to next?". "To Nancy" (lazily). I calculated briefly with eyebrows and lips; shook my scorched head: "Noo, Käthe: you won't need to show up there!– –In—: two weeks! They'll be at the Rhine". Shrugs: "Then I'll just have to report to Karlsruhe". Another wince. The most delicate fog floated our way from the reeds: where is its source? (Lovely image: a mossy foundling, soundless fog bubbles up out of it. Absurd of course. Gone!).

"What do you news gatherers actually do?" "Hffff" (through her nose): "Telephone operator, lots of that. And the orderly

room". And I gave a bitter nod: knew already what was coming. (She; coldly): "They won't leave a woman in peace till she's given in. What riffraff those officers are. And those creeps at the paymaster's too. But you know the bastards. You were a soldier long enough". "Yes. Unfortunately".— "Enough of this".

The fog licked our toes: the ground only needed to disappear now, and then you'd just float off, hands in your pockets, an ecstatic head laid back, Käthe beside you. (But those were just words again: away with fables of infinity! Better just to sit right here!).

"Another six months. Nine, at the outside!" (the war): "and then hunger is really going to stalk about. We'll all trim down ever so nice and slender!—Have you still got good soap and such, Käthe?". "Huh-uh" and shook her head; but she gripped my knee a bit tighter with her hand, and I knew that it meant 'thanks for the tip that day'. "As soon as you're back here, I'll see you get a couple of boxes." She turned a bit of her profile toward me, and asked hardnosed: "Has your wife still got some? Or Gerda?". A warm dry current of air had wiped the fog away; our feet were once again propped at an angle to the ground: "No."

"Just don't get married, Käthe!: No old man, no disabled veteran, no churchgoer, no conceited ass with big expectations.—Find someone who's good in bed and who won't bore you."

"In the end"—I patted myself with the flat of my hand, the proof: "all that's left are: works of art; the beauty of nature; pure sciences. In a holy trinity.—And keeping in shape." (Stop it, for heaven's sake. Your mouth—my mouth—just trots off, driveling away: cut it!).

But now I simply had to let out a savage laugh: "And that is that! Käthe!: Burn it down! No other way!—Tomorrow morning we set fire to the place"; and when she tried to talk me out of it: "They'll come with police dogs, and pick up the scent. And fingerprints: they'd nab us soon enough". Shaking my head, in protest: "No sir." (that everyone doesn't do some time in the course of his life is ultimately just a matter of luck. Not that you have to be a cutthroat or such!).

"Fine."; and I wrapped her up in the blanket: her bright arms knelt beside her sunflower face. "Shall I throw another log on the fire?". "Show it to me first"; and she held the humble piece of wood in her hand for a long time; simplicity, ephemerality, obscurity, rigidity; and handed it back without a word. (It then cast light onto the flickering ceiling, and muttered to itself. Just as with Thierry. For the last time). (Then profoundest exhaustion).

(Piece of a dream: an image 'Remembrance': old man on a park bench. Hedges form individual compartments, little summerhouses, too. He can see himself at various stages in life: as a child. Alone in a swimming pool amidst many halves of girls. Walking, bent over books, a distant country home. In the middle of the park a large marble statue of Käthe. No dots).

The night in a black formal coat (with only one button, sewn on slipshod); day came first in a red and yellow dressing gown, then in a sloppy smock of clouds. (Me among the reeds: stinking things up).

I stuffed empty bottles, tin cans, everything that would not burn, into the tiny metal stove, pulled off the pipe, the size of my arm, and walked out with it. "?". "Ditching it all in the pond out back" (callous). Whatever'll burn, spread over the floor. (The rest in a rucksack).

We looked all around us, but not at each other.

So then: the match to the fuse! It was five minutes long (and ended in the clump of solid-spirit placed beneath what was left of the firewood.—Wait: throw that shutter on it too; and those loose boards).

I helped Lame Kate up the ladder of branches, down the steps; the secret path ran noncommitally through fern and the dry little of needles (and we didn't look back even when—far behind us now—it started to crackle and sizzle: most likely sparks from the fire last night were what ignited it!).

Hazy and dry now (autumn near): and the sight of the woods for a dowry.: In 4 weeks I'll already be walking among black wet tree trunks. Over a bloodied parquet floor. Alone. In my new canvas suit).

At the edge of the thicket, and we walked more cautiously (hesitantly). The pull of the woods was so strong that our hair pointed back behind us (where now there was only a thin rope

of smoke still dangling from the clouds). A covey of birds eddied slowly across the sky—"Come on now."

Something, anything else! (And the sun rode on high in the
dry smoky haze): Look at: her whittled head: "Käthe: if you
were the sun, what would you do?". She understood; her
laugh emerged slowly from beneath stony mourning eyes:
"We-l-l-l . . . .:":

"Sometimes I'd rumble across the sky like a four-engine job".
(And disconcerted we raised our faces:?—: No. Looking. Lips.
Smile some more).

"Sometimes I'd come up black. And square.—*And* with a bang."

"For poor people I'd cook soup at no charge. And for artists."

"Sometimes I'd reverse course at noon, my cloud skirts billowing." ("When you had already seen enough."). "Sometimes
I'd belt my waist very tight and appear as a Golden Eight."

"The astronomers would constantly have to issue updated reports as to my whereabouts: ‹Reliable witnesses report having
seen the sun in Hamburg, lying in a vegetable cart, blinking
among the oranges›!"—

"Sometimes I'd throw a veil over me and chase the moon": a
complimentary curtsy! "Aha!" (resigned).—"Sometimes I'd
stop at the window during the day and watch you and that
skinny Krämer woman!" (Sfinx eyes).

"Your old gray pants—I'd scorch those!!"– –"Are they really
that abominable?!" I inquired in surprise and arched my
lower lip: in that case, away with them!

A drowsy cow made a childlike bound to the left, and the old
farmer gave a loud slap of the reins and cooed the appropriate
word of command. To his brindled bass-baritone.

((Käthe sings something like:

"Trees in red and yellow jackets / standing round a
farmyard; / and they nudge each other whispering, / once I've
walked by.

Along green tracks my heart is shunted / (Leaves are ruffling;
let them fall); / eight thousand lads in lincoln green / (Leaves
more leaves, let them fall).

The moon's light afloat. Berries berry. / The farmer mumbles
curses / ahead of evening's horse with November's face, / enigmatic whimpers the wheel.

Your hand reigns in the flaxen / rigging of my hair; in the / white columned jumble of legs; in the / dusky coilings of my corners.")).

"How long do you have here exactly?". "Ten days.", and our faces achieved a glorious ease: Nowadays who thinks ten days ahead?!

Translated by John E. Woods

GREGOR VON REZZORI
Löwinger's Rooming House

In 1957, for reasons and under circumstances I won't go into now, I stayed for a few days at a place called Spitzingsee, in upper Bavaria. As I had to spend the greater part of my time there waiting, I often went for walks. On one such excursion, I discovered a place to hire boats at the lakeside.

I am not a dedicated oarsman; on the contrary, a traumatic experience in early adolescence put me off rowing forever, and I still tend to regard it as a vulgar and in no way exhilarating pastime.

The instigator of this aversion was a relative of mine, my senior by many years, a man who was recommended to me as a paragon in every sense. He was what one calls a *Feschak* in Vienna: an Uhlan squadron leader who had returned from the Great War safely and in one piece, he had adapted to civilian life easily and become a successful businessman, was handsome, elegant, a sports- and ladies' man. He used to spend his Sundays at a rowing club on the Danube, and since it was hoped that his company and the fresh air would influence my frail character and wan state of health beneficially, I was often encouraged to accompany him there. I transferred all my carefully nurtured hatred from him to the club he frequented.

It was rigorously exclusive; already at that date, 1927, one of the conditions for admission into the aquatic society was watertight proof of Aryan birth. The comradeship of its members was generally regarded as exemplary. These venerable gentlemen— one and all of an optimistic disposition—would climb into the single sculls, double, foursome, and eights, and heave up the river moving like metronomes all morning, then turn and shoot back down on the crest of the current in little more than a quarter hour. Under the showers, where they then sluiced away the sweat of their labors, I was to hear the remark that became the basis for my lifelong animosity against rowing.

I was scarcely thirteen and very shy. I hated the studied nonchalance with which these muscular men dropped their shirts and shorts and stepped naked into the showers. There they would stand, spitting and spluttering, their hair plastered over their faces, and, without the slightest abashment, mix yellow jets of urine into the clear white of the water, send farts reverberating around the tiled walls, and discuss "women."

A prominent subject was Josephine Baker, who was appearing at a Viennese theater at the time. Needless to say, I was head over heels in love with her, and I suffered torments as I listened to the detached professionalism with which her charms were discussed as though she were some favored racehorse. "Class," my dashing relative said, turning his face in a screwed-up grimace to the nozzle, soap suds oozing from his armpits and pubic hair, "that's what she's got, class, even though she's black. Better than a Jewess, though, all the same. I tell you, if I weren't in training . . ." And like an echo coming from the tiled walls a voice answered him: "Well, let us know if you succeed—it's only fair among friends and members of the same club."

Thirty years later, then, on the banks of the Spitzingsee, I felt not the slightest desire to hire a rowboat. Out of sheer boredom I exchanged a few words concerning the weather and the business prospects of the morrow, a Sunday, with the proprietress. The woman's odd accent arrested my attention.

"You're not a Bavarian," I said.

She shook her head.

"Yugoslav?" I ventured.

"No," she said, "you'll never guess."

Nevertheless I tried; the gulash of nationalities and accents in Central Europe is indeed quite confusing, but an attentive ear can generally localize them, and to my trained one it was clear that she came from some neck of my own woods.

"I'm from Bucharest," she finally admitted, and I delightedly addressed her in Rumanian. "But I'm not Rumanian," she added.

"What, then?"

She was Ukrainian.

Her evasiveness aroused my curiosity. "What did you do in Bucharest?" I wanted to know.

"I was an artiste," she replied with a coy mixture of demureness and twinkling eyes that put me on the scent of some nocturnally practiced art.

"A dancer?"

No, a singer, not of the operatic or *Lieder* kind, simply a singer in a Russian chorus.

I felt a thrill. "In a garden restaurant behind the Biserică Albă?"

She gazed at me in astonishment. "How did you know?"

Yes, that indeed was the question. By the grace of God alone, apparently, and it confused me even more than it did her, for I had never set foot in this restaurant, wasn't even sure on which street or passage behind the Biserică Albă it was situated. But I had heard the chorus, every night, a whole summer long.

It was a summer that according to my memory consisted solely of lavender-blue skies and unfulfilled longings; only a few isolated events and disjointed situations still hover in my mind; the one thing I remember distinctly is that it was insufferably hot; no dog showed its nose on the streets until sundown. I spent most of my days, certainly most of my evenings, under a canopy on the terrace of my tiny apartment, which was perched on the flat roof (today one might grandly refer to it as a penthouse) of one of the high-rise buildings that even at that early date and especially in the quarter around the Biserică Albă had shot up all over Bucharest. At that time my passion for horseracing had taken me by the scruff of the neck in the truest sense of the word: I'd been thrown, had dislocated three joints in my spine, and was obliged to wear a plaster cast around my neck and shoulders, like the unforgettable Erich von Stroheim in *La Grande Illusion.*

With this mishap my own illusions, which had also been sweeping, evaporated into the lavender-blue heavens: my intention, for instance, to transport steeplechase horses to Abyssinia, making a fortune with them in the flourishing colony of the Italian Empire, and then returning home to convince a certain young lady that her refusal to unite her life with mine had been a mistake.

I felt no need of company. I stayed at home, cooked my own meals; a half-crazed jockey who had lost his license ran my errands. I lay on a deck chair in the shade of my canopy and read, and when it got too dark, I laid my book aside and drifted back into the dreams which the paling void above my head had absorbed so effortlessly. And night after night, on the stroke of nine, the strains of abrasive-sweet young girls' voices singing *"Hayda troika,"* the prelude to an ensuing nonstop revue of banal Russian folk music, rose from one of the alleys below me.

More than once I crossed to the balustrade and looked over in the hope that in the deepening dusk the glow of light that certainly marked the spot would rise to me, too, for it was audibly clear that the singing was being done in the open air, and my knowledge of the gardens and bars amidst the towering walls of the stark *modernaki* buildings told me there would be garlands of colored light bulbs dangling over the tables between potted lemon trees; the orchestra dais too would be framed in a blaze of light, and a multicolored neon sign with the name of the place in Russian letters and a double-headed Imperial Eagle would decorate the entrance. In my mind I saw the chorus girls clearly before me: the stiff, puffed bells of their skirts, the sturdiness of their legs in red saffian boots sticking out beneath, their embroidered blouses and blank doll-like faces with lurid circles of carmine dabbed on their cheeks, their streaky hair beneath the gold-edged triangular bonnets that always reminded me of the all-seeing eye of God as depicted on icons—all these details remained imprinted in my memory because they had been merely imagined, images evoked by the melancholy of the songs. This dragging melancholy came not so much from the *shirokaya natura,* the weighty Russian soul, as from the robotlike monotony of the girls' singing; wafting aimlessly through the lofty echo chamber of those nights, the melodies became tokens of the emptiness of my days. Although I often thought of going down to find out whether everything was as I pictured it, this intention was also to remain unfulfilled. I was irresolute that summer, apathetic, not, I reassured myself, in the Oblomov sense, more in the nature of Dürer's *Melancholia* or the medieval drawing of Walther von der Vogelweide, sitting on a stone mulling over a finished chapter of life while vainly seeking the key to the next. Apart from which I knew I'd have to change lodgings in a few weeks' time.

This tiresome necessity was due to my own neglect; I knew from experience and acquaintances' repeated warnings that for some reason the Bucharesters were given to changing their dwelling places with astonishing regularity and that the dates of transmigration were fixed as irrevocably as the advent of spring or fall: in May, on St. George's Day, and in October, on St. Demetrius's. On those two days not a single van was to be had in the whole city; the streets were choked with carts and wagons precariously loaded with everything including the kitchen sink. I'd heard it said that neighbors on the same floor would rather swap flats than face another half year in the old one; those who did not have the foresight to get extension clauses in their leases past these dates were liable to be evicted without ceremony. It happened to me. With the dawn of St. Demetrius's Day, the new tenants stood puffing at my door, and I had no choice but to gather my few belongings and descend to the street. By luck I soon found lodgings at a place called Löwinger's Rooming House.

This establishment was run by a family consisting of Mr. and Mrs. Löwinger, his mother-in-law, and his sister-in-law. My Löwinger, who looked like a prematurely aged rabbinic student, was a peace-loving gentleman pampered in every conceivable way by his womenfolk. By way of profession he sold lacquered pens—cheap, brightly colored wooden pens used mostly by schoolchildren; the colored lacquers on the shafts had a pleasant marbleized look but the disadvantage—or advantage, for Mr. Löwinger—of chipping and flaking easily, so that the pens frequently had to be renewed. Nevertheless, Mr. Löwinger's profit was slim enough. He also ran a line in carved imitation-ivory pens in whose holders lenses showed the Castel Sant'Angelo in Rome or the Eiffel Tower in Paris, tiny, but in minute detail, as though viewed through the wrong end of a telescope. But these more expensive items had nothing like the turnover of the wooden ones.

Mr. Löwinger augmented his income by gambling, playing games that demand intelligence rather than those that depend on Fortuna's smile. At chess, dominoes, and all advanced card games he was more than a match for most of the players who sat waiting to try their luck in the cafés, although, by his own admission, he was a dilettante compared to his father, who had lived on his source of income alone, never done a stroke of work in his life. One advantage he had had, Mr. Löwinger said ruefully, was that the cafés were full of suckers in those days.

Mr. Löwinger Junior was a mite of a man, a fact he himself never ceased to marvel at, since his father had stood at six feet four and weighed nigh on three hundred pounds. Minute again in comparison to her husband was Mrs. Löwinger, whereas her mother and sister were positively Amazonian; the old lady with iron-gray hair reminded one of a fairground crystal-ball gazer; the sister, Iolanthe, was similar in type, with Oriental features and pronounced physical charms. When I moved in, Mrs. Löwinger was four months pregnant. The long-term lodgers informed me that this was regularly the case with Mrs. Löwinger at intervals of five to six months, and that the next miscarriage was surely imminent. Only once had one of her pregnancies gone the distance, but the resulting infant had been so small and feeble that the lodgers had laid bets on its chances to survive. One coarse gentleman remarked that the only one to make a killing had been the infant itself; it had died within the hour.

This initial conversation characterized the general tone of Löwinger's Rooming House. With one exception, a lady of whom I shall relate in due course, the boarders were exclusively male: traveling salesmen, students living in Bucharest for the term, a starving Russian sculptor, a man with radical political views who'd started professional life as the rear end of a horse in a circus, a journalist down on his luck. Regularly and for months on end the house was peopled by the members of a wrestling troupe, the glorious gladiators of what they themselves called "Luptele Greco-Romane."

Largely on their account the meals served at Löwinger's were gargantuan. The Löwingers were Hungarian Jews who came from the region of Temeshvar, where Hungarian, Rumanian, Austrian, and Jewish culinary arts mingled in happy harmony. Both the mother-in-law and Iolanthe cooked exquisitely. The whole community ate at a single *table d'hôte,* all except the Russian sculptor, that is; he was too poor to participate and preferred to starve in his garret alone. When the wrestlers were present, extra portions of noodles and other pasta were added to the already sumptuous dishes, since with men like Haarmin Vichtonen, the Finnish world champion, and Costa Popowitsch, his Bulgarian counterpart, or the Nameless One with the Black Mask, who always mysteriously and decisively made his appearance toward the end of the tournaments, it was not merely a matter of keeping up the muscle tone but of keeping up their weight as well; the very walls quaked when they entered the room. Outside the ring they were mild as lambs, at times quite timorous. Duday Ferencz—whose task it was as Hungarian world champion to play the savage Philistine in Rumania with no regard for fair play and so incense the Rumanian spectators to outbursts of scorn and hatred (in Hungary this lot fell to Radu Protopopescu, a Rumanian)—Duday Ferencz once complained that the public had stormed the box office and made off with the night's take. In answer to our question as to why they, the mightiest men in the world, hadn't intervened, they looked at one another wide-eyed and said simply, "But that might have led to violence."

The wrestlers traveled a lot between their sojourns at Löwinger's Rooming House and had a tale or two to tell; the mealtimes grew longer by the day. The students, whose families apparently feared their offspring would come to grief on their meager allowances in the big city, were bombarded with packages from home, from the contents of which the boys readily distributed what they were incapable of eating themselves. Rumania was a rich land in those days; sausage and ham, pastries and pies, flowed into the house in vast quantities. When the point came where the mere mention of food turned our stomachs, someone would invariably have the brainstorm: "Cherkunof's starving!" meaning the poverty-stricken Russian sculptor upstairs.

Cherkunof was a rather unpleasant man who hardly ever deigned to show himself: some maintained this was because he had no shirt to his name, and indeed, if one did happen to run into him on the landing, he would clutch his threadbare jacket over his naked breast and mutter something that might as well have been an apology as a request to go to hell; even the Löwingers, who hadn't received a penny in rent from him for years and allowed him to stay on out of sheer brotherly love, did everything they could to avoid him. Iolanthe had made attempts to draw him into the family circle but had been sent packing, although one vitriolic tongue at the dining-room table implied that Cherkunof's reaction had been prompted not so much by the victuals she'd offered him as by the libidinous favors she'd expected in return: poor Iolanthe was no spring chicken, and she badly wanted a man. Be that as it may; after weeks of solitary confinement, during which he might well have died and been well into the process of decomposition for all the other Löwinger inhabitants could have cared, Cherkunof would suddenly find himself confronted with a string of well-wishers bearing whole salamis, liverwursts, apple strudel, and chocolate cake. Again, and perhaps understandably, his response was anything but thankful. With livid, hate-filled eyes he would stare first at the untimely offerings, then at their bearers, among whom, to top it all off, the rear end of the horse was prancing—a man whom Cherkunof as a White Russian loathed with all his being because of the man's Bolshevik convictions.

"You vont to poison me?" he shouted. "Vell? You vont to poison me! See vat I think of your offers! So to your offers!" He spat, and went on spitting on the slabs of bacon and poppy-seed buns until the foiled benefactors beat a hasty retreat, laughing their heads off.

It was my first experience of such a milieu, which only served to heighten my enjoyment of it. After the splendid isolation of my "penthouse" near the Biserică Albă and the Russian restaurant I never saw, I delighted in adapting myself to a community, however motley. Not that I felt so out of place; with my plaster-of-paris collar, my bizarre professional ambitions and brief past among jockeys, trainers, stableboys, and frisky fillies, I fitted in quite naturally to this freak sideshow and did my best to blend in.

As is often the case when men of none too delicate upbringing congregate, the level of conversation at Löwinger's Rooming House was earthy to say the least. No respect whatever was shown for the Löwinger ladies, very likely for the simple reason that Jewesses were not considered ladies. They themselves had long since become accustomed to the fact that everything pertaining to the human body, particularly its sexual aspects, was openly discussed in basic terms at Löwinger's. The wrestlers were an exception, it's true, and not out of celibate necessity as sportsmen but out of genuine purity of spirit. Only Costa Popowitsch, who couldn't deny a hearty female following, would reply vaguely and in a general way when approached on the subject, but he never quoted personal experience. The Greco-Romans' reticence was more than made up for by the salesmen, however, who delighted in giving detailed descriptions of their latest conquests. The rear end of the horse—his name was Dreher, I remember—gave lectures on sexual repression and emancipation; the students were content to listen, risking only occasional contributions; whereas the uncrowned king in this respect was undoubtedly Pepi Olschansky, the luckless journalist. It was his boast that he'd never left a well-filled petticoat unexplored.

Sometimes things got out of hand and Mr. Löwinger gently reminded his guests of his mother-in-law's advanced years—a dangerous admonition that usually evoked only catcalls and the Ruthenian adage "Never try and shock Grandma with a flash of your cock; she's had bigger in her day," and the rejoinder that people living in glass houses shouldn't throw stones, as Mrs. Löwinger's constant state of pregnancy was tangible proof of her husband's voracious appetite and he shouldn't make life more difficult than it was already.

This last was a reference to a very real problem with regard to receiving visitors at the establishment. The Löwingers had a small dog, a brown pinscher with cropped ears and tail and the habit of kicking up a tremendous racket whenever strangers appeared at the house, making it hard for the inmates to receive even the most innocent visitor unnoticed. Pepi Olschansky insisted on the right to cohabit regularly, once a day minimum, and his lady friends were understandably daunted by the glaring attention the dog's hullabaloo drew to their furtive flights over the back stairs. Pepi threatened to slit the pooch's throat one day if he didn't shut up, which the dog somehow seemed to understand, for he henceforth bared his fangs and howled at the very sight of Pepi. If Olschansky made even the slightest motion to shoo him away, the yowling beast made straight for his beloved protector, the starveling Cherkunof.

The odd thing was that sexual assuagement was to be had right there on the premises, but no one availed himself of it. It was an open secret that Iolanthe would be only too eager to oblige a friend in need; she was in her mid-thirties and eminently ready for plucking. Nevertheless, for some enigmatic reason, she found no takers, again perhaps simply because she was Jewish; one couldn't "stoop that low" was the prevailing attitude; even Cherkunof had declined.

As was her optimistic habit with each newcomer, she'd welcomed me with open arms, immediately suggested that I take my siesta in her room, as mine overlooked the busy street. But I refused this and all other offers as well, knowing that nothing would remain a secret at Löwinger's for long: it didn't need the dog to pinpoint one's movements on the ancient landings; twenty pairs of cocked ears noted every creak. So although I would have liked to sample Iolanthe's ample charms, my fear of appearing ridiculous in my fellow boarders' eyes and thus jeopardizing my integration into the community was stronger. I was savoring the questionable comfort of conformity for the first time in my young life, little knowing that I was soon to be confronted with it as an apotheosis.

Apart from which there was another female present, the servant girl Marioară, a Rumanian country maid of most extraordinary beauty. She was tall, with a sumptuous figure, wonderful shoulders and breasts; erotic promise emanated from her like a golden aura. As was the custom with girls of her station, she wore traditional peasant dresses; the wide belt that separated the bounty of her wraparound skirt from the thrust of her low-cut blouse was pulled so tight that the tips of a man's ten fingers met with ease around it; inimitable, the grind of her behind when she walked.

It was said that she went to bed with every Tom, Dick, and Harry at the drop of a hat. And with the same vehemence that the male connoisseurs at Löwinger's considered it slumming to steal into Iolanthe's room, they proclaimed it a must to have spent at least one night's dalliance in Marioară's.

Needless to say, I did everything to give proof of my qualities as a seducer. But, to my disappointment, Marioară's only response was the taunting gleam of her smile, as if it came through veils of lust. The fact that I always found her door locked seemed ample evidence to me that she preferred the others' company to mine.

Nevertheless, I was quite popular in Löwinger's Rooming House. I enjoyed the reputation of being gregarious and witty. The days when a wanton masculine assessment of Josephine Baker's charms would make me furious were long past; now, when conversation turned to the fair sex, its various physical and inherent attributes and shortcomings, its needs and foibles, I could chip in with an observation or two, these based not so much on wide experience as on a kind of expedient philosophy.

Thanks to my checkered academic career, I had come by a rich repertoire in bawdy jokes and verses and could usually crown each specific erotic circumstance under discussion with a pertinent quotation and thus ascend from the earthy detail to the sublime realms of porn poetry. This facility earned me much applause. The melancholy of my recent past was soon forgotten.

It would be wrong to suppose that an era of vigorous activity now dawned for me: I simply took life as it came. The plaster cast around my neck was no great hindrance—except when tying my shoelaces—and was therefore not a good reason for staying away from some form of study or other useful occupation, but I used the accident as a welcome excuse for a long period of recuperation. Money was no problem; I had saved a little to finance my aborted Abyssinian enterprise, and life in Bucharest at that time, especially under Löwinger's roof, was cheap. I did nothing in particular and a lot in general. To pass the time of day and still my curiosity, I often went with Mr. Löwinger on his gambling sorties to the cafés; the experience I gained there in respect of types of humanity and their behavior was not to be found in any handbook. Sometimes he took me along on his trips to outlying villages, where he replenished local stock in marbled pens, and I still carry with me the vivid memory of dusty country roads, of oxen sauntering home along them by the orange glow of evening as though paddling through shallows of burnished gold, of the resinous smell of fresh-cut logs, piled high in blocks before black forests above which the grass-green domes of the Carpathian outriders loomed like a child's cutout pattern; or, in the midst of this magic, a shepherd boy swathed in sheepskins sitting cross-legged on a tree stump whittling his stick but not looking up; or the dirge of boys' unbroken voices through the open windows of a Jewish school, their pale egg-shaped faces framed by long earlocks; or the stamping of dancers at a peasant wedding, the sweat flying from the fiddler's brow, the girls' plaits streaming out from under their slipping head scarves; of meadows couching the silver of a stream, storks stalking through its marshes, accelerating and then rhythmically pulling themselves up to an azure sky; sparkling drops of water shooting in streaks from green flax whipped by girls hidden by the willows—these and many other priceless memories. . . .

My supple tongue had won me the friendship of Pepi Olschansky, the luckless journalist. I could never quite decide whether I liked or loathed him. He was a small, wiry fellow, red-dish blond, with devilishly vivacious brown eyes, a pointed nose, a pointed chin, and a thin-lipped mouth that could twist itself into the most perfidious smile I've ever seen. As a German from the Bukovina, he'd served in the former Imperial Austrian Army, and quite famously, apparently; talk had it that he'd been awarded the Silver Cross of Valor. Some rays of this glorious past were still around him; although I had never seen him in any-thing but rather shabby civilian clothes—hatless, even in those days; no stick, let alone gloves—I envisaged a first lieutenant's star glistening on his collar when I thought of him, but that may well have been because certain aspects of his glamor aroused un-pleasant memories of my rowing relative in Vienna. Olschansky was not so militantly brash as the other blade, though, and was light years ahead in intelligence and education. His literary taste was impeccable. He even composed verses himself, a talent that had led to his dismissal as editor from a German-language news-paper in Bucharest.

A romantic story. A privately printed edition of his poems had found its way into the hands of the Queen Mother, Maria, who was something of a poetess herself. Pepi was summoned to Con-troceni Palace and received graciously, indeed on an equal foot-ing; thereafter her resplendent majesty commanded Pepi's undying devotion. When in the course of a political intrigue a certain statesman persuaded the publisher of Pepi's newspaper to launch a slanderous campaign against Queen Maria, and the publisher in turn commissioned Pepi to write the articles, Pepi adamantly refused. It came to a flaming row, news of which leaked out and caused a public scandal: the statesman resigned, the newspaper temporarily ceased publication and came under public fire when eventually it returned to press; Pepi was sacked, branded a traitor by the Germans in Bucharest, and snubbed by them thereafter. This gave him a rather dubious aura, which he sensed not without guilt and which he tried to make up for with insolence. At the same time, there was something of a martyr about him: after all, if a man is a true outcast, then he isn't much helped by the reputation of being the gentleman who never be-trays a lady—especially since the queen could not compromise herself and therefore could not express her gratitude. Which was why she never again received him at the palace. All of this made him intensely interesting for me, of course.

Since he had just as little to do as I, we took to going for long walks together, and I learned a lot from him. He knew his Bucharest, a city I had till then regarded as a sloppy conglomeration of Balkan disorder and faceless modernity, but under Pepi's tutelage, hearing his expert account of its history, I came to see it in a different light, began to apprehend it, as one does a new language. Its jumble of junk came to life and started to speak, told a story of boyars and Phanariots,* monks, pashas, and long-haired revolutionaries who had descended from the mountains. I was given the code to the Rumanian arabesque and found much that complemented my own character, by birthright, which till then had been blurred by the stamp of my Austrian education.

Löwinger's Rooming House stood near a park that bears the sweet-sounding name "Cismigiù." I was used to rising early since childhood, and my equestrian period had strengthened this habit. While the Löwinger rafters were still ringing to the snort of snores, I stole away to walk in that park. It was fall. Nowhere in the world have I seen colors to match those of Rumania in this season. It may well have been the fact that Pepi Olschansky came with me on these matinal marches that finally endeared him to me. He was a bad sleeper since the Great War, when a howitzer shell had exploded right beside him and buried him; although the shrapnel had not struck him, the blast had peppered his back full of particles of earth which now, after so many years, still kept festering their way out.

Not that this heroic misfortune alone made his company welcome, but it did prompt me to be civil, and his apparent liking for me did the rest. With the same indulgence I imagined he'd shown with his cadets in the good old days of the Imperial Army, First Lieutenant Olschansky did me the honor of allowing me to pay for his umpteen *tzuikas* in the bars on our way along the Calea Victoriei, winding up with his *marghiloman* at the Café Corso, then returned the compliment by accompanying me to the racetrack, where I nostalgically stuck my nose into the stables, chatted with the jockeys and trainers, and gave Pepi hot tips on how best and quickest to lose my money at the betting windows.

---

*The boyars were a Russian dynasty of princes before falling from the Tsar's grace in the eighteenth century. Phanariots are Greeks from Constantinople (Istanbul), who, for the most part, left the city in fear when it fell to the Turks in 1923.

These visits helped me close a chapter of my life; I realized that my career as an amateur jockey was at an end, not so much on account of my fractured spine, not even because the few weeks' participation at Löwinger's *table d'hote* had sent my weight rocketing to a level I knew I would hardly even have the energy to reduce. Even if I had—to ride for three hours at the crack of dawn, drink six cups of hot tea, don a rubber vest, shirt, one lightweight and one heavyweight sweater, a leather jacket, and pound the pedals of a bicycle for an hour, then collapse into a steam bath and eat nothing but potatoes with a sprig of parsley for the rest of the week—I knew that it would be impossible to pick up again where I'd left off. And since turning points have always fascinated me—a change of time's quality, so to say, when a mere change of atmosphere can alter the course of one's own life or that of a whole epoch—this change from the open-air solitude on my roof above the Biserică Albă to the lusty carni-valesque existence at Löwinger's Rooming House became a part of my biography that has recurred in my thoughts ever since. As I'm unable to put my finger on any one circumstance that would logi-cally explain the tangent, I am inclined to think that a new chapter began with the day that I was released from my plaster collar.

Löwinger's was agog with excitement that day, and it was only with the greatest difficulty that I kept the whole company of long-term lodgers from going with me to the clinic. Still, my escort was large enough: all four Löwingers; Pepi Olschansky, of course; the rear end of the horse, named Dreher; and a salesman who had a car.

"I had no idea you'd such a large family," said the assistant doctor I'd made friends with over the months.

"Yes, a colorful bunch, aren't they?"

"At a guess I'd say that with the exception of the blond one with the pointed nose and the fellow with the gray forelock, they're all from Galicia?"

"No, from Temeshvar."

"Watch out that the doctor doesn't see them. He eats Jews on toast for breakfast, bones and all."

"He can hardly make more of a botch of my neck."

"True, but he can add a couple of digits to your bill."

I can still feel the coldness of the big scissors blade as it slipped underneath my cast. "Please be careful," I requested. "Remember I put a sweater on underneath to keep the cast from hurting. I wouldn't want it ruined."

He applied pressure and began cutting. It went much easier than I'd imagined; there was a dull grating sound and the cast fell apart. The sweater was nowhere to be seen.

"You've absorbed it," the assistant said. "Must have been good wool, pure lanolin. It's protected your skin, all right."

I felt oddly naked and chilly. "Will my head fall off if I nod?" I asked.

"Give it a try."

I did. My head stayed put. I gingerly turned it first to the left, then to the right.

"Keep doing that carefully," he said, "come back tomorrow for a massage, and we'll show you a couple of exercises which will help as well. The doctor will want to see you too, so come without the Semitic caravan, if possible."

Outside in the corridor my Semitic caravan welcomed me with unrestrained joy; all three Löwinger ladies had tears in their eyes, and Iolanthe threatened with a kiss.

"Be careful, for the love of God!" Mrs. Löwinger cried. Her mother took me by the hand and led me to a chair. "Slowly does it now, boy, take it easy, one step at a time."

I felt like a peeled agg: "Like the baby in Philipp Otto Runge's *Morning,*" I said to Pepi Olschansky.

He smiled his perfidious smile. "Iolanthe will be only too glad to change your diapers," he answered.

The rear end of the horse shook his wild gray revolutionary's mane. "I trust for your sake that you regard the occasion as one of rebirth. With that shell of plaster, shake off the shackles of the useless and asocial life you've led till now, and apply your energy to a more worthy cause!"

This was not the immediate case. That night, after an evening of revelry and mirth at Löwinger's table—the Greco-Romans showed me all manner of tricks and exercises to strengthen my atrophied muscles—I sat up with Pepi. "I feel weary and very content," I said. "Why on earth shouldn't I complete the pleasure and allow Iolanthe to rock me to sleep? She's really eminently beddable and would certainly show her gratitude."

Pepi reached across and selected a cigarette from my case. "The same thought has often crossed my mind," he replied. "Generally speaking, I've nothing at all against Jewesses, but with Iolanthe it would somehow seem like a betrayal of one's race and creed. I don't understand why it should be so, but everyone here feels the same, even Cherkunof."

"I think I know what you mean," I said, in a flash of inspiration. "Committing a sin, like sleeping with one's mother."

He looked up in surprise, then laughed aloud. "You're dead right, that's it exactly. A strange thought, the taboo in a nutshell. Have you ever thought of writing?"

The thought was alien to me and I somewhat asininely asked, "Writing what?"

"Stories," he said, "perhaps a novel, who knows? You're extraordinarily observant."

I laughed and right away dismissed it from my mind.

I was more preoccupied with another incident. One evening the conversation had—once again—turned to Mr. Löwinger's amazing knack for any kind of game. Olschansky had expressed his doubts. I murmured to him, "Be careful! I've watched him winning money from sly old foxes in various coffeehouses."

"Yes," jeered Olschansky, "at dominoes, or tarot, or poker! But not at games of real skill."

I myself had once tried to hold my own against Mr. Löwinger in morris, which had been a forte of mine in my boyhood. But here too I had lost miserably. Olschansky waved me off with a sneer. He insisted on challenging Mr. Löwinger to a game of chess.

"Now *you* watch out," he muttered back at me. "At the military academy, I used to beat people who wound up on the general staff." Nevertheless, he lost the match after a dozen moves. "One game doesn't mean anything!" he cried, running his hand nervously through his hair. "Would you like to see who wins two out of three?"

"Gladly!" said Mr. Löwinger timidly, peering up at his women, who sat around him with immobile fences. We all formed a thick ring around the two opponents: they had long since stopped being players; a duel was being fought.

It was soon decided. Olschansky lost the second game within a bare quarter hour; insisted on playing the third one and lost it so fast that he leaped up, furiously knocking over the chess board, and stormed out of the room, slamming the door behind him.

"Not that I'm normally a poor loser," he later told me. "But I couldn't stand that nasty lurking and finally that triumph in the faces of those Jewish harpies. Did you see the way they sat there, to the left and the right of that little Yid? That unkempt crone, that lecherous Iolanthe, that screechy anemic bitch with that eternal bun in her oven, those witches, all three of them so greedy to see me humiliated that I couldn't even think about any moves. I had to keep fighting the puke rising in me."

"That's known as psychological warfare, isn't it?" I asked, a bit maliciously. "Didn't they prepare you for that at military school?"

Olschansky ignored my baiting. "You know, I really believe they're capable of certain kinds of witchcraft," he said. "Being lucky in a game isn't sheer chance. A man is lucky if he has a certain rapport with the world, the time, the place he's playing in—"

"Yes, but not in chess," I broke in. "A chess player, as the popular adage so nicely puts it, has the law of action in his hand!"

"What do you really have in your hand?" he said, passionately earnest. "You get to recognize that in war. During the first few years in Galicia, I saw a whole lot of Jews. You can experience all kinds of things with them."

"What?" I asked. "Don't keep me in suspense! Do they really slaughter Christian children to enrich their Passover matzos with protein?"

"No, but they believe in one God!" he blurted out, downright fanatically.

"So do my aunts," I said. "One of them goes to Mass every morning."

"It's different, it's different!" He was working himself up. "They've got their God in their blood. They can't get rid of him. . . ." He suddenly threw up his hand as though to shoo a fly away from his nose. "But what nonsense I'm talking, don't you think? Tell me about betting on horses. You say I can bet on win, place, and draw?"

I'm no longer sure whether this conversation took place before or after the Löwingers took in the new female lodger. It caused quite a stir when it was announced one evening that a young lady had moved into room number eight and would be joining us for meals. Mr. Löwinger, who in spite of his scrawniness had undeniable authority—"the dignity of a microbe" was Pepi's defini-

tion—appealed to the male assembly in a few well-chosen words
to exercise restraint in the lady's presence, at least for the first
few days: she was not only a pure country maid but a schoolteacher to boot.

The suspense that built up as we awaited her entrance became
so great that even Cleopatra would have had her work cut out
for her, and Miss Bianca Alvaro was no Queen of the Nile. She
wasn't exactly nondescript, not unsympathetic, but decidedly
not winning either; neither pretty nor downright ugly, more on
the small side than on the large, more blond than brunette. Neither her name nor her physiognomy gave any clue as to where
she came from. She might have been Jewish, but then again perhaps not. At a rough guess she was in her mid-twenties. She had
been studying German language and literature at the University
of Jena, and was preparing for a state examination in order to
teach German at the local *Gymnasium.* "The only thing one can
say about her with any certainty," Pepi remarked, "is that she has
luscious tits. She can try and flatten them as much as she pleases,
but a connoisseur will spot them a mile off. They're high-slung
with a prominent sideways jut; the nipples probably tickle her
armpits, a sure sign of quality. There's not much more than a
good handful apiece, but they're as firm and juicy as young mel-
ons. One will be better able to judge in summer when she wears
lighter dresses."

Mr. Löwinger's appeal proved unnecessary, as things turned
out. Miss Alvaro's mere presence sufficed to quell all appetite for
discussing sex. The change in the tenor of our talk was so
marked that one day when she excused herself and left the table
earlier than usual, everyone else, including the three Löwinger
ladies, remained seated as if by secret arrangement and simultaneously launched into a heated discussion. The first attempt to
explain the phenomenon was offered by Iolanthe, and coming
from her, in the form of a mournful sigh, it sounded overwhelming: "That's the difference when you're a lady," she moaned,
looked across to her mother for confirmation, realized what
she'd said, and lowered her eyes in panic.

"Bullshit!" Pepi Olschansky spluttered, "lady . . . lady . . .
she's nothing but a bum-beater, that's all. I've never seen anyone
better equipped to become a schoolteacher. She has a way of
looking at a man that's more sobering than castration. I'm al-

ways expecting her to chide us about our dirty fingernails or the way we hold our forks. If Duday Ferencz were to go up to her and say in his beguiling Hungarian way, 'Miz Alvaro, eet would geeve me great pleasure to screw the ass of you,' she'd simply look up and answer, 'Dear Mr. Duday, you surely mean you'd like to screw the ass *off* me, at least I hope you do; you're mixing up your prepositions and adverbs again, and in so doing you completely alter the meaning of the phrase and express a desire to perform an act of sodomy on my person which is generally confined to pederastic relationships. So if, as I trust, the heterosexual method is more to your taste, I suggest that until such time as you have grasped the finer points of our language you'd do better to avoid risking embarrassing misunderstandings and stick to straightforward, basic phrases such as "*Miss*"—not *Miz*—"*Miss* Alvaro, how about a fuck?" ' " We all burst out laughing, and the matter was settled for the time being.

A few days later Miss Alvaro was to cross my path directly. Pepi and I passed through Cismigiù park on the way back from our walk one morning and stopped by the chestnut tree in front of our temporary home; its fruit was thumping to the ground. I stooped and picked one up, peeled off the knobby skin; the nut was shiny and immaculate—"Rather like me when they took off my cast," I remarked to Pepi.

"It doesn't stay that way, unfortunately."

The Löwinger house, which dated from the mid–nineteenth century, was distinctly rural in style, one-storied with a tin roof. It stood facing the road, a narrow courtyard alongside.

Just as Pepi and I entered the yard, Miss Alvaro emerged from the front door and the little brown dog scampered out between her legs, spotted us, and shot forward, yapping furiously, recognized Pepi, gave a howl, and shot back again. For fun I threw the chestnut at him. I hadn't actually intended to hit him, had thrown the nut high, but the dog must have seen the movement of my arm, for he accelerated wildly and ran straight into the missile's trajectory, taking the blow squarely in his exposed rectum. He was even more surprised than we were and let out a scream as though Lucifer himself had raped him. Pepi and I roared with laughter.

Miss Alvaro marched up and planted herself in front of us, glared at me with her big brown eyes, shook her head slowly and incredulously, and said, "*You?* How could you do such a thing? I would not have thought it of you."

I was very embarrassed. Olschansky came to the rescue: "That's his hunter's blood coming out," he said maliciously. "Didn't you recognize it from the precision of the trajectory?"

"Nonsense," I said. "It was pure chance; I didn't aim at him. I'm very sorry." And, although I had no liking for the dog, it was sincere.

Miss Alvaro said no more and was just about to turn and go when we heard Iolanthe's voice through the open kitchen door: "Oh, do stop laughing, you silly goose," and out tumbled the servant girl Marioară, doubled up with laughter, her hands to her face, wiping away the tears. When she looked up and saw me, she controlled herself long enough to say, "I'll never forget that for the rest of my days, never, never," and doubled up again. Her beauty surpassed the superb autumn day, and as she drew a deep breath, straightened up, and gazed at me again, I knew that her door would not be locked that night. Pepi knew it too. He said "Two birds with one stone."

With which Miss Bianca Alvaro also got the message. She turned on her heel and left.

So I was all the more surprised when two days later she spoke to me. "I should like to ask something of you. Will you come to my room for a moment?"

We were alone. She dipped her hand inside her blouse, pulled out a bunch of tiny keys hanging from the chain about her neck, opened a valise, and took out a case wrapped in silk paper. When she'd finally unwrapped and opened it, she held it out to me. "I should be very grateful if you were to tell me whether this ring is valuable or not. I inherited it, but have no knowledge of jewelry. I come from a very poor family. I've heard of such things only in fairy tales."

It was an unostentatious piece, no more than a setting for a single stone. The stone, however, was huge and green; if it were a genuine emerald, it would be worth a little fortune.

"I know nothing of jewelry either," I said. "The best thing to do is to go to a jeweler and then double the price he names you. He'll think you want to sell it and start the bidding low."

"Would you do me the favor of coming with me?" she asked. "I'm from the provinces, a village near Kishinev, and I don't know another soul here in Bucharest I could ask."

I went with her not to one but three different jewelers. The values they quoted varied only slightly and were much higher than I had calculated. This seemed to confuse Miss Alvaro greatly, but she remained reticent. "Thank you very much," she said, as we parted in town—she had already made it clear to me that morning that she didn't want Löwinger's to know about our undertaking, for she had asked that we leave the house separately—"thank you very much, you were as friendly and cooperative as I expected of you."

This drove me to the brink of forgetting my manners. What on earth gave Miss Bianca Alvaro the right to "expect" anything of me at all? What standards had she applied to me and my character, what yardstick of behavior was I obliged to live up to? I for my part gave her no second thoughts whatsoever. By now, I had summed her up and knew which pigeonhole to pop her in. Iolanthe had not been wrong in calling her a lady, but the veneer of her acquired graces couldn't hide her background from me: a drab little Jewish girl from a village near Kishinev—that she was indeed Jewish now seemed fairly certain; Pepi had been prepared to bet on it from the beginning. I couldn't have cared less one way or the other—at all events, I knew her sort. They were a dime a dozen on every village street, all over Rumania; they spent their childhood skipping among mounds of horse dung and flocks of gay sparrows, warbling Hebraic words of wisdom in Jewish schools, chewing Mr. Löwinger's marbled pens and poking their ears and noses with ink-stained fingers, disappearing then to the next town. They returned gangling, cheeky, precocious, and self-confident a couple of years later, unfurled little red flags, and chanted socialistic marching songs; then they went off again. The next time they came back they were unrecognizable—polished, poised, coiffed, and manicured, lugging doctorates on their proud shoulders; they dug themselves in and became dentists, high-school teachers, professors of music, and God only knows what other intellectuals, married similar solid burghers and produced streams of progeny, teaching them to speak refinedly through their noses, packing them off to the Sorbonne to get equipped the better to meddle with the course of the history of civilization. I had witnessed pretty near every stage of these developments in the Carpathian village where I came from, and surmised that Kishinev could not be so very different.

And whereas Miss Alvaro no doubt regarded me as the epitome of a smarmy, once-velveteen-suited, governess-tutored youth, cutely twittering away in French, when the time came, my undivided attention to horses and hunting restricting my vocabulary to a fund of some three hundred words—but not hestitating to entrust me with her priceless heirloom!—I on the other hand couldn't help seeing in her the snotty-nosed Jewish guttersnipe we were always in danger of running over when driving through the dusty village streets. It was on the tip of my tongue to tell her she could think, say, or "expect" what the hell she liked of me for all I cared as long as she left me in peace.

I was even more reserved toward her in the days that followed. Besides, I didn't see much of her. Under Pepi's guidance I had begun to read more systematically and selectively, so my time was taken up, added to which the weather broke at last as the *crivetz,* a wind from the steppes, howled across the open marshlands surrounding Bucharest and hit the city, whistled remorselessly through its street and alleyways, presaging the bitter Balkan winter, discouraging all desire to set foot outside the house. I holed up.

Miss Alvaro wasn't so fortunate; she had to go to her class early each morning, come home then for lunch and disappeared again right afterward, spent her afternoons in some library studying, most probably; and at the dinner table she usually sat with an absent look on her face, seldom spoke, and retired as soon as she finished coffee.

Only once did she take part in a conversation, and that quite heatedly. We were discussing the political situation in Germany. The wrestling troupe had had to cancel a tour in southern Germany and Saxony at the last minute, for the Third Reich authorities had questioned their right to the world championships they claimed, the Nameless One with the Black Mask had been unable to furnish proof of Aryan descent, etc., etc.—the usual story of petty difficulties and preposterous formalities, hardly conducive to showing the "new" Germany in a favorable light. Pepi Olschansky defended the Germans vehemently and ended up by calling the wrestlers "a bunch of loudmouthed fairground barkers," which wounded Haarmin Vichtonen, the Finnish world champion, so cruelly that tears came brimming to his eyes. Radu Protopopescu rushed to his mighty brother's aid and boomed that the Rumanians' sorely tried patience would soon be exhausted if the current megalomania of the "Fatherland" were to increase the already insufferable pretentiousness of its stepchildren living here in their country.

This was just the beginning; the discussion really got under way when Dreher, the putative circus-horse backside, began to question the sincerity of the Nazis' clarion calls in the cause of socialism.

"Do you consider Russian socialism more social?" Olschansky asked.

"That's not the point!" the backside bellowed. "I am debating socialism in principle!"

"Without principle would be nearer the mark," Olschansky answered viciously. "Professing to stamp out poverty but only doing away with the fruits of free enterprise, above all those of the mind. Sacrificing life for an abstract theory. Reducing everything to the lowest possible denominator."

"You've no idea what you're talking about," scoffed Dreher grandly.

Olschansky grinned. "Well, up till now I've always kidded myself that my field of vision at least stretched as far as Sidoli's circus ring."

"What do you mean by that?" Dreher snorted.

"I was attempting to compare our limits of horizon." Olschansky grinned provocatively.

"Explain yourself!" Dreher demanded.

"Oh, do I have to?" Olschansky sighed, looking round at the others. "I don't really think anyone here needs an explanation."

"Well, I *do,*" Dreher barked, and his gray forelock bobbed dangerously in front of his eyes, which looked daggers at Olschansky.

"Since you insist," Olschansky spat back, equally venomously, "I'll put it to you straight: I meant that when one has spent half one's life with one's nose up the ass of the man in front, it's hardly surprising that one thinks as you do."

"Slander!" Dreher screamed. "I know you all believe this ridiculous story that I was once part of a circus number. It's all Cherkunof's doing: he invented it. I shall go to him this minute and demand that he come down and own up right away!"

We had to restrain him from dashing upstairs to get the unwitting sculptor. "Leave him alone!" Iolanthe begged in the midst of the melee. "Dear Mr. Dreher, all these years we've thought of you as a horse's ass and loved you none the less for it. What difference does it make if you're a professor?"

But Dreher was a difficult man to quieten down.

"I will bring proof of my claim," he said, threatening Olschansky. "I will force you to corroborate my evidence and make a public announcement reinstating my honor!"

"If only you knew how little I cared," replied Olschansky wearily. "You could be Lenin himself as far as I'm concerned. You'll convince only fools and small children that that which is taking place in Germany is not an attempt to do something of decisive importance for the history of man. The salvation of the individual within a socialist structure—no more and no less. If you opened your eyes and exercised your brain instead of letting your emotions run amok, even you would be bound to see it."

"You really don't have the slightest idea what you're talking about," Miss Alvaro suddenly commented.

Olschansky fixed her with a stare. "Do you perhaps know more?" he demanded.

"I've just come from there. I was studying in Jena until two weeks ago," she answered.

"They allowed you to study in Germany even though you're Jewish?" Olschansky asked incredulously.

"You are mistaken. I'm an Armenian Christian," she replied, then blushed and bit her lip. After a moment's obvious unease, she raised her head proudly and said, "I won't deny that my parents were Jewish, but the fact remained undetected in Jena. And it has nothing to do with the point in hand."

"In one aspect it certainly does," Olschansky insisted, "in that one identifies Nazism with the Jewish question. One uses it to divert public attention from the very real revolutionary steps being taken in Germany."

"It's my belief—or rather my conviction, based on personal experience—that exactly the opposite is the case. The Nazis are using the so-called Jewish question to cover up far more questionable issues."

Olschansky grinned his provocative grin again; the points of his nose and chin trembled toward each other; he looked for all the world like a demoniacal Punch. "You mention the so-called Jewish question and more questionable issues in the same breath;

an admirable play on words, to be sure. But tell me, do you regard the question itself as a mere red herring, or as being indeed in need of a resolution?"

"The question is of valid importance inasmuch as a small, harmless religious minority is now being held responsible for a thousand years' faulty German policy. And, as though that weren't enough, the Nazis pretend that the golden future they promise their countrymen depends solely on the question's being solved."

"With our extermination," Mr. Löwinger added softly.

"Exactly!" exclaimed Dreher, the professor and former horse impersonator. "That's what's so deplorably retrogressive, so abysmally medieval about their whole ideology: it leads to religious fanaticism; it encourages the insane belief that one has only to exorcise the devil for heaven on earth to set in."

"For God's sake don't you start preaching," Olschansky retorted. "If on the one hand you advocate simple rationalism as the new way ahead—you're a democrat, aren't you? Then you believe in the people's right to self-government? Well, then, won't you concede the Germans the right to remove a few Jews from their ranks if the overwhelming majority are convinced they'll be able to manage their affairs better without them?"

Their futile bantering got on my nerves. I knew Olschansky's devious tricks and maneuvers all too well and wanted to put an end to them. The surest method had always been to cite one of my celebrated quotations, so I cried, "Give the masses what they want! Fifty million coprophile flies can't be wrong: eat shit!"

It made a palpable hit, and nearly everyone laughed; even Dreher made a half-grudging, half-acknowledging gesture toward me. Miss Alvaro was the only one who looked at me in outrage; she was at the point of getting up and leaving. Her place at the table was such, however, that an exit to the right would have entailed asking the whole wrestling troupe to get up and let her out, whereas to the left the frail Mrs. Löwinger had collapsed in a heap. Mrs. Löwinger shook, moaned, and gulped, then grabbed Miss Alvaro's arm and dug her fingers into it.

"What's wrong, for heaven's sake?" Miss Alvaro cried.

Iolanthe sprang to her feet. "God Almighty, she's losing the baby!"

Unfortunately she was right. Mrs. Löwinger was rushed off to hospital, and the next day her mother, red-eyed, told us that all

290 · German Writings before and after 1945

hopes of an addition to the Löwinger family could be buried. When I went to say a few words of compassion to Mr. Löwinger, he looked at me with chill pride in his eyes and said, "I have no regrets; members of our race have no business bringing children into this world."

Soon after this episode, I was flabbergasted when Miss Alvaro stopped me in the passageway, looked over her shoulder in order to make sure that nobody was watching us, and then whispered that she would like to meet me at the Café Corso the next day. She was there before me when I arrived at the appointed time.

"May I invite you to have a drink or something today?" she asked. "I shall be very upset if you refuse."

I accepted and, rather evilly thinking of Olschansky, asked for a *marghiloman,* or what the Italians call a *caffè corretto*—a small cup of mocha coffee with a shot of cognac.

"Do you recommend it?" Miss Alvaro asked. "The thing is, I'm going to ask another favor of you." She smiled shyly, but the smile had a great deal of charm, for she was obviously sure of her ground. "First I must tell you a story," she continued. "The ring you were good enough to help me have valued belonged to an uncle of mine. No blood relative . . ." She hesitated, then went on bravely. "He became critically ill a short time ago, and for this reason I returned from Jena—too late, unfortunately. We had been very close; he had been like a father to me ever since I was a small child. It was because of him that I was brought up an Armenian Christian."

She paused a moment, as though thinking over something she was reluctant to say. "He was Armenian by birth, from a great family in Constantinople. When the persecution of the Armenians began in the twenties, he emigrated here. Of course he had to leave behind the greater part of his estate and arrived with very little, by his standards. But for my aunt, whom he met almost right away, what he had left was a vast fortune; I told you once, did I not, that I came from a very humble family?

"Would you like a little more brandy in your coffee? Or a brandy all by itself? I know I should." She again smiled her small, shy smile. "I never drink, as you surely guessed, but I find myself unable to tell my story without a lift of some sort. I've never told it before, by the way. . . .

"My uncle first met my aunt when he was ordering new spectacles at an oculist's; she was working there. We're not Eastern

Jews at all, not Ashkenazim, but Sephardim, as my name implies, but I'm afraid I can't tell you when my ancestors moved to Bessarabia. Well, as you probably know, among Spanish and Portuguese Jews, especially those who came to Central Europe via Holland, there's a long tradition in oculism, and one of my relatives had continued the practice. This gentleman wasn't exactly a Spinoza, but he seemed to believe in the sovereign rights of the strong over the weak, for he used my poor aunt, who was still very young, quite shamelessly. When she and the Armenian met, it must have been love at first sight. He was probably well aware of her humble origins; he was a man of the world, not only on account of his wealth but through a long family history of intermarriage with the French and Italian aristocracy. However, that she might be Jewish most likely never occurred to him; as I said, their love was spontaneous and unqualified.

"My aunt gave up her job and moved in with him. She was a resourceful housewife and knew how to make life very comfortable, even on their limited means. They became completely self-sufficient and lived happily in splendid isolation for a number of years. Then, when quite unexpectedly both my parents died and there was no one else to look after me, they married in order to fulfill their roles as stepparents respectably.

"I must tell you that my aunt never found the courage to tell him she was Jewish. She knew of the Armenians' general hatred of the Jews, not so much a matter of racial hatred—which would be quite absurd, of course—as a religious rivalry, though none the less fanatical for this. My aunt loved her husband so deeply that she would have done far more than just renounce her faith in order to keep him.

"When I joined them—I was not quite eight years old—she immediately instructed me never, ever to breathe a word that might betray our heritage. I was not with them long before I was sent to an Armenian convent; there, just as had been the case with my aunt vis-à-vis my uncle, my physical appearance aroused no curiosity or comment. Each of the Armenian nuns and the other girls—as indeed my uncle, too—had some facial feature or other that looked just as Semitic to the untrained eye as mine. The only sticky moment was when the teachers found out how ignorant I was in religious matters; they were appalled, but I worked hard and soon caught up with the others. Just as my aunt had done on meeting my uncle.

"I well remember the discussions she had with the priests who came to visit my uncle. They debated for hours the different doctrines of the Monophysites and the Nestorians with regard to the single, double, or composite natures of Christ, or the connection between the vows made for one at baptism and one's own reassertion of them at confirmation. Armenians are extremely devout, and my uncle—who belonged to the United Armenians, the so-called Mechitarists, by the way—positively doted on his church. Can you imagine, he presented his father confessor with a complete first edition of Diderot's *Encyclopedia* because the priest had maintained he daren't possess it since it was on the Index?"

Miss Alvaro took a sip of cognac and then coughed discreetly. "My goodness, that's strong. And I'm not used to it, although I must say I had opportunity enough to get accustomed to it at my uncle's house. He was anything but frugal in that way, loved his food and drink. You know, of course, that Lucullus played an important part in Armenia's history? My uncle jokingly used to say that it was every Armenian's sacred duty to revere his cuisine and his wine cellar, and my aunt used all her considerable guile to make him forget that he could no longer afford to have his salmon sent from Scotland or his wine from Bordeaux. . . . I believe also that their sexual tastes were particularly compatible. . . .

"It broke him when she died last year; he had no desire to continue living without her. Naturally, as a practicing Christian, he did not think of suicide, but there was in any case no need to do so. Only a few months later, although just seventy and in robust health till then, he followed her. His heart simply stopped beating."

She looked at me. "I want to ask another favor of you. As the sole heiress, I inherited not only the ring you saw but the complete contents of my stepparents' apartment. Everything else my uncle possessed—a modest bank account, a few securities, a share in a house, in a word, the remnants of a great fortune, he left to the Armenian Church. I'm very happy; it would have embarrassed me to receive a penny of it. Just the fact that he paid for my education at the convent and later in Germany—quite apart from countless other tokens of generosity—always made me feel, under the covert circumstances, something of a fraud. I have always had a bad conscience that my family concealed our Jewish faith from him. Naturally my aunt made no attempt to have me baptized; she simply let it be assumed that I was a Christian. And perhaps we were in our hearts, but not by right. I often found the conflict hard to bear and was more than once on the point of confessing everything to my priest, then suffered all the more afterward for not having done so. I saw myself as a criminal, not so much before God and my new faith, you understand, but before this wonderful, noble man, to whom I had so much to be grateful for, whom I loved as a father.

"Now to my request: can you understand that I cannot go alone to the apartment? There are the usual things to be done—go through the possessions, make an inventory, pack things up. To be honest, I feel unable to manage alone and know of no one else I might ask. Because of the years I spent in Germany I have grown away from the few friends I made here in my childhood, and of my present acquaintances you are the only one I dare impose on."

Again I was tempted to ask her why, but it hardly seemed the right moment. "May I now buy you a cognac?" I said instead. "From what you tell me, I'm sure we shall find all manner of exquisite beverages in your uncle's flat. We'd better get in training."

The apartment was in a high-rise building not far from Biserică Albă. "How strange," I remarked. "I lived round the corner until not very long ago, up there, on one of the roofs. I probably passed your uncle and aunt on the street many times without knowing that sad circumstances would bring us together one day. By the way, there must be a Russian garden restaurant around here somewhere, with a girls' chorus that starts caterwauling every evening on the stroke of nine."

She didn't know it. "My stepparents moved here only a few years ago," she said. "These buildings are quite new. I wasn't here often—not because they kept me away or anything but they were so happy together that I always was a little shy. I felt I might intrude. They were like the lovers in David Teniers' painting, sitting on top of the hay wagon gazing into each other's eyes, oblivious of the emperors and popes being crushed to death under the wheels below; the *Weltgeist* itself spun a cocoon around their love."

As she said this, Miss Alvaro smiled the little smile that was so becoming to her. I could well imagine her as the prim pupil of the Armenian sisters. The line of her neck was simple and lovely, expressing a modest but defiant pride.

The apartment was on the sixth floor of a building that conceded nothing in hideous barrenness to the one I had lived in myself. We went up in the lift, and Miss Alvaro said, "It's a wonder it's working. I'm afraid this too had something to do with my uncle's premature death: nine times out of ten he had to walk up."

We got out, and again she dipped into her blouse to extract the bunch of keys; I turned my head to hide my smile, as I wondered that her uncle hadn't guessed the origin of his womenfolk from such characteristically careful traits, but then again, as with their physiognomy, perhaps Armenian girls had this in common with Jewish girls also.

She opened the door and we stepped in. It was a typical immigrants' flat: a mixture of old and new junk, purely decorative, impractical pieces salvaged from the ruins of former prosperity standing side by side with the banal indispensables of day-to-day life in incongruous equality, creating that atmosphere of improvised coziness which one suffers gladly only in the conforting knowledge that it's temporary. I had seen the same combinations in the dwellings of Russians who escaped the Revolution with nothing but what they could carry in their two hands. At second glance, I realized that many of the objects here were of some value, however, even though everything was either faded or chipped, and some pieces ruined completely. The modern, practical articles and gadgets had been chosen carefully from the middle-price range, not quite top quality but not quite rubbish either; the housewife's dream—but a nightmare in taste. It was obvious whose hand had sought these out. Miss Alvaro's aunt must have found in them a perfect outlet for her domestic zeal, and the noble old Armenian had obviously given her her head. Everything was clean and pedantically neat; nevertheless, as we stood there for a moment, I became aware of the odors of dust and musty materials, of biscuits moldering in hidden tins.

All the doors stood open: hallway, living room, bedroom, kitchen. One couldn't see much, for the shutters were closed and the windows covered with heavily embroidered but decrepit curtains. Miss Alvaro crossed and opened a French window facing to the west, and raised the shutters. The sun had just set. I recognized my lavender-blue sky, paler now, colder, less sentimental. It had been late summer when I lived in the neighborhood. Now it was late autumn. Golden leaves fluttered down from the trees along the Boulevard Bratianu. Miss Alvaro trembled slightly. And for a few moments we both stood there looking out, breathing deeply, rather like divers, I thought, before braving the deep; but then the city below had much in common with the mausoleum behind us, much the same mixture of modern supertransience and flea-market curiosities. For all its Art Nouveau villas and futuristic glass-and-concrete buildings, Bucharest was as Oriental as Smyrna. The Occident, with its many-splendored towered citadels, was far away, there where the sun, dipping in, blood red, from the swamps and steppes and scrawny settlements of the east, would now only be prewarming the slate and copper roofs before melting them with its farewell blaze.

Miss Alvaro squared her shoulders and turned to her inheritance. "My aunt always spoke of their possessions, especially the furniture and glass and china, as though they were priceless. I'm afraid I'm no judge," she said. "I only want to keep a few things for myself, things that are easily transportable. I've no intention of setting up house in the near future."

On closer inspection it appeared to me that her aunt hadn't boasted; there was a French baroque chest of drawers, an early English grandfather clock, a pair of octagonal Turkish tables with superb inlays of mother-of-pearl, silver and tortoiseshell. The rest was run-of-the-mill stuff: mahogany cupboards; a cumbersome fin-de-siècle bedroom suite, expensive at the time, no doubt; hanging flower baskets; a portable phonograph; a radio. Brocades, gold-thread embroideries, and cashmere shawls were spread everywhere, giving the impression of Oriental luxury. Everywhere too there was evidence of former opulence, surfeit: several solid-silver but aggravatingly incomplete sets of cutlery, dishes and bowls and trays of chipped enamel, fragmentary cloisonné, French and Viennese porcelain sideboard pieces, Bohemian cut glass, but each piece minus a spout, a lid, a handle, with the edges serrated, traces of glue.

I took down one of four leatherbound books with gold stamping that were standing squashed in between pulp novels and department-store catalogues on a bookshelf; it was an edition of Choderlos de Laclos's *Liaisons dangereuses,* early enough still to be signed only "C. de L." Between the pages were a number of religious bookmarks; "Holy Brigitte, Holy Anthony of Padua, pray for us . . ."—tokens of penance for disregarding the Index, most likely.

"The best way to go about it will be to do as we did with the ring," I suggested. "You choose the things you want to keep, then we'll invite three antique dealers to come and make estimates, first separately, then free for all, and may the best man win."

"I hope that one day I shall have the opportunity to show my gratitude," Miss Alvaro replied. "There's just one thing—" She hesitated. "No, I'm sure it's not necessary to remind you again not to mention this business at the boarding house."

I managed not to for about a week. Then Olschansky confronted me: "You're fraternizing with the Alvaro filly. Don't bother to deny it; my information is irrefutable. You meet her in town; you've been observed several times. Why should you deny it? She's not *that* ugly, no cause for shame. Or do you want to shut me out? That's not very nice between friends."

I was obliged to tell him the truth, if only to avoid compromising Miss Alvaro, although I knew immediately that this was but a welcome excuse: I was only too glad for the chance to talk about it.

"You can't imagine what it's like," I said. "We're as complete strangers now as we ever were; apart from what she tells me in connection with her dead relatives, I know nothing about her whatsoever. And she nothing of me, since I've had no call to tell her anything. We still act with the same polite formality as we did on the day she first spoke to me, still keep our distance, partly on purpose and partly because we no longer have any choice. Just think of it: never a personal word, no confidences, and of course, God forbid, no intimacies. It would never occur to either of us to ask the other where or how we were going to spend the evening when we part at the door; our private lives could take place in two different worlds. In reality we simply take separate routes and come straight back here to be under the same roof, sit at the same table twice a day, and watch carefully that no one gets a hint of our relationship, the secret we share—

like partners in crime. Then, when we meet at the apartment the next day, we again negate our other life at Löwinger's, never mention it. As a result, instead of becoming easier with each other, the tension builds. The sense of intimacy I feel with her— and she with me, I'm sure of it—grows stronger by the day, our hearts are continually in our mouths, so to speak, and all generated by a purely vicarious experience, by the exploration of two other, dead people's lives. What we find there grows into a monstrous secret between us.

"I say 'monstrous' because no one should be allowed to delve into another's life in the way we're doing, into the remotest nooks and crannies of intimacy. Each one of us has something we prefer to keep hidden, from ourselves just as much as from others; we shut it away and pretend it's not there. But here we are, Miss Alvaro and I, digging out every last morsel and examining it minutely. We know the lives of these two superb, consummate lovers to the last detail, down to their underwear and toilet articles, their hairbrushes, their soap and eaux de cologne, the racy magazines and jam recipes they read as they reclined on the sofa digesting a good dinner, the dentures they popped into a tumbler beside the bed when they went into their lovemaking routine, less and less passionately over the years, possibly, after decades of experience and experiment, but still with heavenly appeasement; the suppositories they needed to ease the passage of their sumptuous fare, probably giggling and thrusting them up each other's flabby backsides—each day we unearth some new dimension that again adds a new dimension to the intimacy between us. We sold their whole wardrobe, complete with everything from his bedroom slippers to his tails and white ties, from her corsets to a moth-eaten mink stole—his Christmas present in 1927—to a secondhand dealer, so that little chapter's over and done with, thank God. Sorting out their clothes gave us an indelible impression of their physiques. We came to know their collar and hip sizes, the shapes of their feet, their body odors, the peculiarities of the stains their sweat left, the irksome sphincter and bladder weaknesses of the people who wore these shirts and pants, shoes and jackets, dresses, overcoats, dressing gowns and nighties, and pressed the contours of their bodies into them. . . .

"They're ghosts, and because they're ghosts, they take possession of us, enter us like astral bodies. We politely shake hands and take leave of each other every evening, Miss Alvaro and I, but even if the one lies in bed in room number eight and the other in room number twelve at Löwinger's Rooming House, we are in fact lying together in that big double bed near the Biserică Albă, holding each other, making love, taking a sip of camomile tea, then embracing again, lulling ourselves to sleep. We no longer know which is the real existence: that of ardently united lovers, acting as if they are superficial acquaintances who happen to live in the same rooming house; or that of people who are briefly drawn together by chance and who pretend not to realize they are lovers for life. And the next day we crawl a little deeper into the souls of our phantom matchmakers. . . .

"At the moment we're going through all the drawers in the living room. Piles of documents, letters, diplomas, invitations to all manner of festivities, stacks of photos, all dating from Uncle's glorious Constantinople days, of course, before he met the little Jewish girl from Bessarabia. I have a thorough knowledge of the financial status of this Armenian from the Golden Horn,* right down to the last sou, both before and after the momentous day of Mussadegh.† He must have been immensely rich, but the way he ran his business affairs is of a naïveté that would make a bookkeeper weep. Even after he had to emigrate, he should have been in a position to live a life of considerable comfort, but he allowed crooked little lawyers to take him for a ride. The deeper one goes into his papers, the more his innocence touches one's heart, the more one is warmed by his open-handed generosity and his love for the woman who meant more to him than anything he'd lost or still might lose. And all the more intensely, almost violently, does the woman herself take possession of us with her total, heartrending, never-despairing humanity. . . .

"I hope you know me well enough by now to believe me when I say that I'm not normally given to sentimentality. Normally the story of a Jewish woman from the sticks who lives in dread of losing the man who raised her to a certain affluence and security, who gave her a vestige of elegance and social prestige—her efforts to make herself indispensable with her sickly-sweet attentiveness, his slippers toasting by the fireside, the goose crackling in the oven—wouldn't touch me in the least, nor Miss Alvaro, I

---

*Constantinople's historic docks; also used as a synonym for the city on the Bosporus.
†This refers to the persecution and flight of the Armenians from the collapsing Ottoman Empire after the Turks caused a blood bath at Dagh in 1915.

think. But the passion this woman invested in her sole raison
d'être is of such force that one can't help being bowled over by
it; she haunts us with her dedication to the goal of becoming everything for her husband, to replace what he'd lost and possibly
still mourned. All these impressions and feelings are transmitted
to us by ghosts; she's no longer alive, he's no longer alive, they're
both dead, and still their love lives on; you can read it in every
trace: her recipes, with footnotes underlined in red—'Aram
adores this!' 'Special favorite of Aram's!' Or in the lists of presents he made for birthdays and Christmases to come, with shaky
handwritten notes in the margin toting up his bank balance or
the yield of his platry shares. It's so powerful, it so transcends
death, that we feel their presence physically every time we open
a drawer.

"What must the woman have felt when she went through his
papers or sorted his photographs? What did she think when she
saw this evidence of a world that must have seemed like fairy-
land? Wouldn't you think she'd despair of ever filling the gap
when she looked at the pictures of his paradise lost, the thousand
and one nights' extravaganza, the complacent indulgence of im-
measurable wealth? Tea parties at exquisitely timbered villas on
the Bosporus, the guests gliding directly into the reception rooms
in their boats; next to the visiting Sultan of Morocco we see Her
Majesty the Queen's ambassador half hidden by the duchess of
Lusignan's enormous picture hat, the duchess and the hostess
vaguely related by marriage since the days of the Rubenides' re-
gency over Cyprus; another photo shows the same illustrious
party at a sumptuous picnic in Anatolia—the gentlemen in Shan-
tung suits and ladies in white linen draped between chunks of
the ruined pillars of Ephesus, lying on piles of rugs and heaps of
cushions; some have come on horseback, a few of the younger
women already emancipated, sitting boldly astride their mounts;
to one side a spindle-wheeled Daimler, caked with dust, its
demon driver and his heavily veiled passenger posing playfully
beside a camel bearing the whole Kurd family, father, mother,
four children, grandmother with a baby goat and two chickens
on her lap; yet another view of the same slim gentlemen in gray
walking dress, with sloe eyes and tapering noses, mustaches
weighing heavily on their drooping mouths, tarbooshes perched
pertly on their delicate heads; here again the ladies, in diaphan-
ous Neo-Renaissance gowns, diamonds highlighting their hair,

shimmering from their fingers, stout ropes of pearls trussed around their breasts. . . .

"Just think of her, little Myra from Kishinev, who'd been nothing much to write home about in her prime and was now slowly coming apart at the seams—mustn't she have known it was hopeless to wish to appear desirable and elegant in the eyes of the prince charming who had descended to her world? No, her love is too serene, too humble in its pride. It never occurs to her to compare herself to anything connected with him; she no longer thinks of herself at all—solely of him; she has identified herself with him totally. The instinct of her love shows her how to make an incense of adoration from the ghost of his great past; she builds it into a myth and wafts it around him like a golden aura. For his part, he'd have probably thrown all the claptrap out long ago, the now-tawdry brocades, gold-thread embroideries and bibelots, the frayed, smashed, worn-out fragments of former luxuries, the photos of persons reported missing and never found again, the letters and invitations, birth and baptism announcements of people long since dead, superfluous documents, worthless deeds of holding—it's she who dotes on them like an archaeologist sifting through the dust of a pharaoh's tomb; she documents each photograph according to his identification of the people in them and specifies their relationship to him— 'Aimee-Doudou, a cousin of his nephew Dschoudshouoglou-Pasha'—arranges them in chronological order, divides them into annual bundles, wraps them in silk tissue and ties them with silver thread; goes on and does the same with the invitation cards, the stock certificates of Nakhichevanian mining companies that collapsed twenty years ago. She gathers all the tiny splinters of a shattered rose-quartz hookah mouthpiece and beds them on cotton wool in an old cigar box, places one velvet-lined but empty jewel case on top of the other to make a tidy pile. . . .

"But all that may well have been due to some retarded, infantile romanticism of hers; turning a faded world into her dream world. No, I tell you, it's something else. She's building her myth, and she doesn't want it for herself. Far more convincing is the way she made a cult of his Armenian bigotry, the evidence of her studies, her notes on Moses of Khorene and Gregory the Enlightener, the devout little pictures and bookmarkers, the umpteen crosses and rosaries all over the place. And there be-

tween the Bibles and *Lives of the Saints* you find hardcore por-
nographic literature and ooh-la-la pictures from Paris, beside a
heap of rosaries in his night table we hit on an arsenal of connoisseur condoms, with roosters' combs on the spunk bags, or
harlequin heads with baubled jesters' collars. He must have been
a dirty old man, this noble camel driver, and there's not a
shadow of doubt that she kept her end up in his respect—on top
of all the other specters in the house, the image of a lusty devotion to sex bobs up everywhere, culminating in the beckoning
presence of the great, musty, freshly made bed. And there we
stand beside it, Miss Alvaro and I, coolly sorting the wheat from
the chaff amid death's odors of decay. . . ."

Olschansky seemed to have stopped breathing. "Jesus
Christ!" he suddenly hollered, "that's it! I told you you should
write, and you stupidly asked me what. This is it. Exactly as you
just told it, word for word! It's the erotic situation par excel-
lence! It must make the blood rush to your heads, this walk
through the no-man's-land between the realities; you must both
be literally itching for each other in that incubator of a tomb.
Just think of the moment when you can't stand the suspense any
longer, when you fall on each other like cannibals—"

"I think of very little else," I admitted.

"She too, of course. . . ."

"Very likely. Most probably. She gives no sign, of course. . . .
It would have to happen spontaneously, if it's going to happen
at all. Any attempt to force it would ruin everything."

Olschansky grinned. "Still a lot to do?" he asked.

"Hardly anything. We'll be finished tomorrow; the dealer
she's decided on is coming the day after. He's taking the things
she's chosen for herself into storage as well."

"So happy hunting tomorrow, then," Olschansky said.

I lay awake for hours that night. To begin with, I had a guilty
conscience for having betrayed Miss Alvaro's secret. But, then,
what was there for her to be so secretive about, after all? At
worst our cloak-and-dagger behavior. Still, I felt I had sullied
something that had been pure and should have stayed that way;
I was ashamed not so much on her account as on that of her Armenian uncle as I had come to imagine him, and my sense of
guilt grew to the extent that I superstitiously began to believe he
would reach back and punish me. On top of which I felt I'd perhaps laid it on a bit thick; perhaps the suspense I'd described ex-

isted only in my imagination. If Olschansky was so enthusiastic about its literary merits, it probably meant that the reality had already undergone a kind of poetic transfiguration and become pure fiction, all due of course to that powerful imagination of mine. The thought that I could so easily fall for my own hokum made me squirm with discomfort; I pictured myself leering lewdly at her at the supposed right moment and her jumping like a startled rabbit, then withering me with a look of total disgust. My embarrassment would be a fitting punishment for my indiscretion.

I realized too that my feelings for Miss Alvaro had indeed undergone some change, and I analyzed them. I was not in love with her, far from it, but I certainly did want her—especially now, after having described the lurid sparks we threw off—but probably not so much her as a person as the role she played in my little melodrama; any other actress would have done as well, just as any understudy could have stepped in for me. One thing was clear, however: the petite Christian Jewess engendered a mixture of respect and fondness I'd never before experienced with anyone of my own age, only with wise, benign older people. Iolanthe had been right: she was a lady, by no means the simple prim schoolteacher Olschansky saw her as. Her authority stemmed from her noblesse. I resolved to tell him as much: "You once told me about Queen Maria's dignity," I would say. "Try to regard Miss Alvaro as having similar qualities."

This resolution made it easier for me to go with her to the apartment on the final day. Even so, I went reluctantly, as I was convinced that whatever might happen between us was bound to be a disappointment; the tension surely wouldn't build, let alone erupt, to the irrevocable moment of truth, the cannibals' feast; if I hadn't just imagined it and she was really awaiting the onslaught as eagerly as I, we still would have invested too much promise in the fantasy, and the reality could never match it in strength.

We worked silently and swiftly as always, even more resolutely now that the end was in sight. Apart from islands of stacked, covered furniture and overflowing baskets and garbage cans, the apartment was empty.

The love nest was abandoned. We had exorcised the ghosts. The noble old Armenian and his Jewish spouse were dead at last.

I was overcome by a feeling of hollowness, more tormenting than any grief. I stepped over to the window again to look out at the city, over which a gray winter sky merged into twilight. Inadvertently, I peered into the chasm of the street between the building fronts, trying to spot the colorfully lit garden restaurant. Here, during my lonesome, lavender-blue summer evenings, the chorus of girlish voices had risen up to me at the stroke of nine: at precise intervals between then and midnight, they had reeled off song after song, the entire repertoire of Russian evergreens.

Behind me, Miss Alvaro's voice softly asked, "Would you mind answering a very personal question?"

I turned around to her.

"It is very indiscreet of me," she said, flushing slightly with embarrassment. "But I would very much like to find out—I mean, it would help me—"

"Please ask," I said with a throbbing heart. I waited to see how she would ask if I had felt the same feelings as she in these past few days.

"Do you believe in anything?" she asked instead, and now looked me full in the face. "Do you believe in God or something of that sort?"

There we have it, I thought to myself. The crucial question. That's all I needed!

But she wouldn't even let me answer; she went right on: "It's been constantly on my mind these past few days. All the aspects of this legacy must have made you aware of how deeply religious my uncle and aunt were and how strongly the bond between them was forged by their religious feelings. And I cannot help wondering whether my aunt, who denied the faith she was born to and brought up in—our family was extremely Orthodox; it was the only thing that gave them a sense of self and a motive for their existence, an identity and, even more, a raison d'être—I cannot help wondering whether my aunt really forgot all that and traded it for something else. How could she have given herself over to a different faith with the same ardor?"

"Isn't that possible *only* if you have faith in the first place?" I retorted—partly because I noticed that she was less interested in a response from me than in speaking her own mind, partly because I could thereby avoid answering, which would have been difficult for me. "Besides, she did it out of love," I added clumsily.

"Yes, of course, of course," said Miss Alvaro, almost irritated, as though not to be diverted. "That is what they try to

comfort us with when true faith begins to dissolve. The fragments of the old, strict commandments float about in a whey of
general love feelings—that's a condition in which I, too, was led
into temptation. Love as a basic religious feeling and as the highest ethical value to strive for—these are Enlightenment notions.
I wonder whether I am naïve enough for that—no, whether I am
not already too enlightened. Perhaps you're right, and my aunt
succeeded in getting at the very essence of faith—and that is not
the tidings of love!—simply *because* she believed. But *I* believed
too. I was eight when I was torn from my Jewish milieu and
thrust into the Armenian convent. At eight one is truly God-fear-
ing—I mean, in a fundamentalist way. Nevertheless, I was more
than ready and willing to find my God in the new Word that was
proclaimed to me. After all, it was taken from the Old Text and
enriched by the Gospels—expanded by the dimension of love.
And, listen—I have to say something dreadful now. Precisely *because* I often felt that dimension of love to the point of ecstasy
when I was eight and nine and ten and eleven and twelve—the
grand, universal love for God's creation and all creatures therein,
for mankind and every individual—that was the very reason why
I learned that this was the decisive step to the dissolution of faith.
I understood why the Jews crucified Jesus—do you grasp what I
mean?"

She gazed at me almost in despair: "You must not think that
faith is taught with any less fundamentalism in an Armenian
convent than in a yeshiva. My schoolmates took every litany verbatim. They had an almost physical need for all the religious exercises—from matins to evensong and finally the prayers at
bedtime. But none of this had anything to do with faith. They
were marionettes on the strings of their rite. And whenever they
truly believed that they believed, they stumbled once again into
the lukewarm liquid of love, divine love, brotherly love, the love
of God's creatures, for the universe—the love for everything and
anything. And at that point," said Miss Alvaro with a dismal
smile, "the strength of my faith dissolved. At least, that was how
it happened to me."

"And what would have become of your relatives without
love?" I asked tactlessly.

"Oh, please don't misunderstand. My aunt's love was a Jewish love; selfish, jealous, wrathful, greedy, not stopping at any-

thing—not even evil, not even denial, deceit, lies. In that way, she remained unalterably Jewish—far more than I. . . ." She had paled, and seemed embarrassed again. "I'm probably still Jewish only insofar as I long for my God, whom I seek like Jacob, after wrestling with his angels. It's useless. I know that he does not exist, my God—or at least no longer exists for me—the severe, demanding, wrathful, greedy, and jealous God. The God of love may exist. He is an earthly God—an idol, to use another word. But He, the severe God of the Commandments, He no longer exists."

"Doesn't what we've found in your relatives' things prove that he can be resurrected by love?"

All the blood shot back into her face. She vehemently shook her head. For the first time, I saw how rich and fine her hair was. "We didn't just find devotional pictures, did we?" she said, staring right into my eyes. "I know it sounds paradoxical, but the love of my kinfolk would soon have become squalid without their bigotry. Their piety prohibited them from interpreting the tidings of salvation through love as if sexuality were the great, venerable motor of creation and thus the crown of all beauty. Were it not for their piety, they would have joined the followers of Saint D. H. Lawrence, if you get what I mean by that: stigmatized barbarians. But their religion demanded that they view sexual love as something ugly, despicable, something to be concealed—in short, as something sinful. If you remember that, dear friend, then this happy union of what cannot be unified acquires a macabre touch." Her shoulders drooped. "That's exactly what disheartens me so."

"Then you still believe in your severe God of shalts and shalt nots!" I cried in foolish triumph. "He just happens to be named Jehovah!"

"No," she said with no trace of bombast. "I believe in the devil."

"You can't believe in the devil without believing in God."

"Yes," she then said, half turning from me. "I know. That's logical. And if I were occasionally overcome by poetic impulses, like Nietzsche, I would reply, 'But God has grown old and no longer has the strength to stand firm against the devil.' But I'm afraid even the devil has grown senile—or is banality his last and most dangerous disguise?" She shrugged her shoulders and turned away.

She was packing a bag with things she'd decided to keep. I had persuaded her to take a large writing case in red, gold-embossed leather with an Armenian inscription we'd been unable to decipher. She looked up and handed it to me: "I should like you to accept it as a souvenir and a modest token of my gratitude," she said simply.

I leaned forward and kissed her on the cheek, sensed her start and draw back. I took her hand, bent and kissed it also. Her lips were trembling. She quickly turned away and closed her bag.

When I got back to Löwinger's, I lay down on the sofa in my room and was filled with the realization that nothing had changed since my days on the roof above the Biserică Albă; I was in the same melancholic state I'd been in then. The release from the plaster cast hadn't meant rebirth after all; I was being born back into my old wayward self again. There appeared to be no way out, only a flight forward, through enemy lines, the same route Miss Alvaro's aunt had taken to escape the specters of the past: making myths of them.

Olschansky knocked and opened my door before I could open my mouth. As he reached for my cigarettes, he noticed the writing case on my desk. "A trophy?" he asked, with his perfidious grin.

"In a manner of speaking," I answered.

"So it worked out?"

"What?"

"Don't act so stupid; you bloody well know what I mean."

"A lot more happened than you think," I said.

"So, come on, give; did you screw her or not?"

"What? Today? Oh yes, yes, today as well." I didn't lie. In a literary sense it had as good as happened. "Lots of times recently, several times a day. . . ." Reality had undergone transfiguration and become fiction.

He looked at me quizzically. "Are her tits as good as I reckoned them to be?"

"Oh, much better. Go away now; leave me in peace."

"I understand: Monsieur wants to savor his memories. Very well, and congratulations. But I think it was unfriendly of you to keep it to yourself for so long. After all, we belong to the same club, don't we?"

I couldn't sleep that night either, partly because the little dog yapped out in the passage for hours until someone—Cherkunof, presumably—opened his door and let him in. I was wide awake. I decided to write my mother a letter, and got up. The case Miss Alvaro had given me was already filled with my notepaper. The blotting paper on the inside covers were crisscrossed with the impressions of handwriting, and on one of them the lines of a letter showed up clearly; judging by the fine, sloping hand, I guessed that Miss Alvaro's uncle must have written them. I turned the blotting paper over, saw, as I'd hoped, that the reverse side was even clearer, fetched my shaving mirror, and read:

> . . . I beg Your Eminence to restrain our good Father Agop from taking these steps. My wife has proved herself a worthy Christian over so many years—and Father Agop, her confessor and my own, can testify to this—that I venture to suggest to Your Eminence that she couldn't have been a better one had she received the holy blessings of baptism and confirmation as a child. I admit to my sinful comportment in not having confessed to knowing of her origin and uncleansed condition. One of the reasons why I did not do so was that, as an Armenian, I saw in my Jewish wife a sister in suffering. She too belongs to a people that, like ours, was a victim of violence throughout the millenia. Pray let this speak to my favor when I ask Your Eminence's forgiveness. May I appeal to Your Eminence's spiritual understanding that no word of this be divulged to her. Should Your Eminence see your way clear to baptizing her without my knowledge, behind my back, so to speak . . .

I could hardly wait to run to Miss Alvaro and tell her of my discovery the next morning. I knocked on her door several times before she finally opened it. She looked at me with an expression of loathing that took my breath away. "I never want to set eyes on you again. Never." Her packed suitcases were lying on the bed behind her. "I shall do everything in my power to erase you from my memory as quickly as possible, and I shall succeed, don't worry. We Jews have had excellent training in this." Then she slammed the door in my face.

A dreadful suspicion overcame me. I went to Olschansky's room, got no answer, searched the whole house, and finally found him in the bathroom we were allowed to use on a rotation

system worked out with astronomical precision. He was standing naked under the shower with his back toward me, and I saw
the ugly, festering, earth-filled pits all over it.

"You said something to Miss Alvaro," I hissed at him.

He had his face stretched up to the nozzle with his eyes
screwed up and his lips sucked in between his teeth. "I took the
liberty, yes," he spluttered through the cascading water. "If I'd
waited for your permission, she'd still be a virgin."

"For God's sake, don't tell me you have done this to her!" I
was ready to jump on him.

He turned his face toward me, opened his eyes wide, and,
with the most perfidious smile I'd ever seen, said, "I did, yes. But
it was a great help that you claimed to have done so. The argument that good friends and members of the same club must share
and share alike was difficult for a school mistress to reject."

I grabbed his throat. He seemed to think I was joking. He
laughed as he tried to struggle away from me, spluttered water
and soap suds, and groaned. "Don't get so excited, you moron.
What's the problem? Are you going to let some Jewish broad in-
terfere in our friendship?" I let go of him.

Miss Alvaro moved out of Löwinger's Rooming House that
same day; I followed suit some weeks later. It was November
1937. After nearly four years of the Balkans I'd had my fill
and felt homesick for Vienna. I arrived there just in time for
March 1938.*

I never saw Olschansky again. In the flush of my twenty-three
years, I often did battle with him in my thoughts, of course, and
reproached myself equally often. What shocked me most about
the story was that in telling it to Olschansky, I had unwittingly
predetermined the only logical, literary conclusion. But soon, far
more shocking events put it from my mind completely, and by
the time I came to take my strolls along the banks of the lake at
Spitzingsee, twenty years later, in 1957, it was very far away. But
it was still as clear as the pictures of the Eiffel Tower and the
Castel Sant'Angelo one could see through the little lenses in-
serted in the holders of Mr. Löwinger's more expensive pens.

Translated by Joachim Neugroschel

---

*Rezzori was a witness to Hitler's march into Vienna and recounted his experi-
ences in literary fashion here and in *Tod meines Bruders Abel (The Death of My
Brother Abel)*.

The Authors

ERNST JÜNGER was born in 1895. At sixteen, he ran away from home and joined the Foreign Legion, a brief adventure from which his father brought him back to Germany. Jünger described this period in *African Diversions* in 1936. He returned highly decorated from World War I. Jünger joined the new Reichswehr in 1918 and arranged his war diaries to form *In Stahlgewittern. Aus dem Tagebuch eines Stoßtruppführers (In Storms of Steel: From the Diary of a Shock Troop Leader)* in 1920, which immediately made him famous. He entered German nationalist circles and published texts for *Kampf als inneres Erlebnis (Struggle as Inner Experience,* 1922) and *Der Arbeiter (The Worker,* 1932). His publishing of political writings ended with Hitler's seizure of power. *Blätter und Steine (Leaves and Stones),* a collection of essays, appeared in 1934, followed by *Die Marmorklippen (On the Marble Cliffs)* in 1939. Jünger moved with his wife Gretha and two sons to Kirchhorst near Hanover. He was drafted into the Wehrmacht and served as a captain on the Western front. He again wrote about his war experiences, which he revised and published in 1949 under the title *Strahlungen (Radiations).* The first entry was on February 18, 1941, the last on August 13, 1944. In contrast to *In Stahlgewittern,* the war here recedes into the background. By radiations, he said, "is meant the impression that the world and its objects conjure up in the author." In 1945, he refused to fill out his questionnaire; the result was a short-lived disbarment from publishing in the American zone. In 1949, the utopian novel *Heliopolis* appeared, followed by diaries. In 1959, Jünger received the Grand Cross of Merit. Having become a recognized entomologist in the meantime, he collected 40,000 insects. *Subtile Jagden* (*Subtle Pursuits*, 1976) was the literary product of this contemplative passion. His recognition as a writer grew only when he was an old man. In 1982, he received the Goethe Prize of the City of Frankfurt. In 1984, he visited the battlefields of Verdun with statesmen Helmut Kohl and François Mitterand. Jünger died at the biblical age of nearly 103, in Wilflingen.

IRMGARD KEUN was born in Berlin-Charlottenburg in 1905. In 1913, her family moved to Cologne, where she left school after receiving her certificate of general education in 1921. After taking stenography courses, she attended the Cologne Theater School. Between 1927 and 1929, she played several roles—without great success. She returned home and began to write. When *Gilgi—eine von us* (*Gilgi—One of Us*) appeared in 1931, the press had something of a field day. Within a year, 30,000 copies in six printings were sold. In 1932, the novel was made into a movie by Paramount Paris. This was followed by *Das kunstseidene Mädchen* (*The Artificial Silk Girl*—English translation in 1933), her second novel. Both works speak the language of the time. Their female protagonists are self-confident and, as a result of the war, working women who emancipate themselves from the traditional image of women. The success was short: the Nazis placed her on their blacklist in 1933. In 1936, Keun emigrated to Belgium and became acquainted with Stefan Zweig and Joseph Roth. With Roth, she traveled through Europe: France, Vienna, and Galicia (Poland), Roth's homeland. In 1937, *Nach Mitternacht (After Midnight)* appeared; that same year, she traveled to the United States. Keun returned to Germany and went into hiding. After 1945, she remained unknown. She lived to see her comeback at the beginning of the 1980s. In 1981, she received the Marieluise-Fleisser Prize of the City of Ingolstad. One year later, she died.

WOLFGANG KOEPPEN was born in Greifswald in 1906. He grew up in East Prussia. Working odd jobs, he managed to get by, then became artistic director and assistant director at the theater in Würzburg (1926–27). From there he moved to Berlin, where he began work as editor of the *Börsencourier* in 1931 and became acquainted with publisher Bruno Cassirer, who published his first novels. In 1934, Koeppen went into voluntary exile in Holland, but returned in 1938. He was inducted into the Reich Chamber of Literature. Koeppen began to work for film studios, especially for UFA. In 1941, he switched to Bavaria Film Studio in Munich. No traces from this period remain. Munich was his place of residence. Between 1951 and 1954, Koeppen's novel trilogy of the postwar years appeared: *Tauben im Gras* (Doves in the grass), *Das Treibhaus (The Hothouse),* and *Der Tod in Rom (Death in Rome).* It was his literary breakthrough. Not until 1991 did it become known that *Jakob Littners Aufzeichnungen aus einem Erdloch* (1948) *(Jakob Littner's Notes from a Bunker),* one of the first documents about the fate of the Jews under the Nazi dictatorship, also stemmed from his pen. (*Journey through the Night,* by Littner and Kurt Grübler, published in 2000, gives a different account.) From 1958 to 1961, Koeppen traveled through Europe, the Soviet Union (1957) and the United States (1959). He wrote radio essays and especially diaries about these travels, including *Amerikafahrt* (Journey to America) (1959). In 1962, he received the Georg-Büchner Prize; many other prizes followed. Koeppen died in Munich in 1996.

ALEXANDER LERNET-HOLENIA (Alexander Maria Norbert Lernet) was born in Vienna in 1897. According to rumors never entirely substantiated, his father was a Habsburg nobleman. In 1915, he volunteered for the cavalry after passing his school-leaving examination and fought on the Eastern front until 1918. In 1920, he was adopted by his mother's family and assumed the name Lernet-Holenia. His first publications were volumes of poetry, which he brought to press through the mediation of Rainer Maria Rilke. Yet Lernet-Holenia scored his first success as a playwright with his first work, *Demetrius* (1925), for which he received the Kleist Prize in 1926. In 1934, *Die Standarte (The Standard)* appeared. In 1937 and 1939, *Der Mann im Hut* (The man in the hat) and *Ein Traum in Rot* (A dream in red), in which he cryptically criticizes Hitler's ambitions for great power, follow. In 1939, he traveled to the Caribbean and to the United States, yet again dropped his emigration plans. In August 1939, he was drafted into the Wehrmacht. On the basis of personal connections, Lernet-Holenia became chief script editor at the army-film office in Berlin in 1941, which kept him from having to serve at the front. After 1945, he again lived in Austria; his novel *Beide Sizilien* (Both Sicilies) appeared. Lernet-Holenia was active as a translator from English and Italian, becoming president of Austrian PEN, and received several prizes, including the Grand Austrian State Prize. He died in 1976.

GREGOR VON REZZORI was born in Czernowitz, the capital of Bukovina, in 1914. (Rezzori calls it "Chernopol" in his writings.) Although he was expelled from school several times, he passed his high-school-leaving examination and tried his hand in several subjects on the university level, yet gave up everything in 1938 to become a graphic artist in Berlin. Having arrived there, he wrote illustrated novels. In *Greif zur Geige, Frau Vergangenheit* (*Grab Your Violin, Mrs. Past*, 1978), he painted a picture of himself as a writer of trashy novels. After the war, he reported on the Nuremberg trials as one of the pioneers of Nordwestdeutscher Runkfunk (Northwestern German Radio). The four-part broadcast "Analysis of National Socialism" followed in 1948. In 1953, Rezzori enjoyed his first great success with *Maghrebinische Geschichten* (*Tales from Maghrebinia*, 1962). *Ödipus siegt bei Stalingrad* (*Oedipus at Stalingrad*) followed one year later. He received the Fontane Prize of Berlin in 1959 for *Ein Hermelin in Tschernopol* (*The Hussar*, 1960) and was called an "epoch-prolonging author"—which he also had said about himself. As in *Hermelin,* Rezzori allows the vanished Austro–Hungarian province to rise again in *Denkwürdigkeiten eines Antisemiten* (*Memoirs of an Anti-Semite*, 1981) and *Blumen im Schnee* (*Flowers in the Snow*, 1989). *Der Tod meines Bruders Abel* (1976) (*The Death of My Brother Abel*, 1984) is considered his greatest work. In contrast to his reception in the United States, Rezzori is underrated in literary criticism and literary studies in Germany. In 1998, he died in Donnini near Florence, where he had lived since 1960.

ERNST VON SALOMON, scion of a Huguenot family, was born in Kiel in 1902. He attended cadet school in Karlsruhe and Berlin for five years before joining the Freikorps fighters in 1919 and fighting in the Baltic States and Silesia to prevent the loss of German Reich territories as provided by the Versailles Treaty. For his role as an accessory to the murder of the foreign minister of the Weimar Republic, Walther Rathenau, by right-wing radicals, Salomon was sentenced in 1922 to five years in prison and a five-year loss of his civil rights. Salomon described these postwar and prison years in his first novel, *Die Geächteten* (The outlaws), which was published in 1930. This was followed by *Die Kadetten* (The cadets) in 1933 and by *Das Buch vom deutschen Freikorpskämpfer* (The book of a German Freikorps fighter), a collection of material pertaining to the German postwar period, in 1938. In Berlin during the 1920s, he was in the circle around Ernst Jünger and Ernst Niekisch, in whose national-revolutionary journal he published. After Hitler's seizure of power, Salomon retreated from politics and began to write screenplays for entertainment films. In 1951, his autobiographical novel *Der Fragebogen (The Questionnaire)* appeared. In 1972, he died in Stoeckte near Winsen.

ARNO SCHMIDT was born in Hamburg in 1914 and grew up in Lauban (Silesia). He passed his high-school-leaving examination in 1933, completed his apprenticeship as a businessman in 1937, and was drafted into the Wehrmacht in 1940. His first stories were written during the war. In 1945, Schmidt's wife fled to western Germany; he was taken prisoner by the British. Despite their difficult financial situation—the Schmidts received food packages from Arno's sister, Luzie, who had emigrated to the United States in 1939—Arno Schmidt decided in 1947 to become a freelance writer. In 1949, he became acquainted with Ernst Rowohlt. *Leviathan* appeared, followed by *Brands Haide (Brand's Heath)* in 1950. Although few read his novels, Schmidt received the Grand Prize for Literature from the Mainz Academy of Sciences and Literature, which he had to share with four colleagues. For two decades, Schmidt remained something of a literary-insider's tip. In 1952, Alfred Andersch brought Schmidt (as well as Wolfgang Koeppen) to the radio. Schmidt accepted commissions for translations and wrote for newspapers. In 1963, he began work, together with Hans Wollschläger, on a translation of Poe's works, which lasted until 1973. In 1964, he received the Fontane Prize of the City of Berlin; one year later, he received the Literature Prize of the Federal Association of German Industry. At 1,330 pages, *Zettels Traum (Zettel's Dream,* 1970),

Schmidt's first typescript book, is considered his magnum opus. *Die Schule der Atheisten (The Atheists' School)* followed in 1972. He received the Goethe Prize of the City of Frankfurt in 1973. Two years later, *Abend mit Goldrand (Evening with Goldrand)* was Schmidt's last completed work. He died in 1979. In 1981, the Arno-Schmidt Foundation, which manages his estate, edits his works, and awards a literature prize, was founded.

Acknowledgments

Every reasonable effort has been made to locate the owners of rights to previously published works and translations printed here. We gratefully acknowledge permission to reprint the following material:

From *The First Paris Diary* and *The Second Paris Diary* by Ernst Jünger. Klett-Cotta © 1949, 1979 J. G. Cotta'sche Buchhandlung Nachfolger GmbH, Stuttgart © 2001 for the English language translation by Hilary Barr: J. G. Cotta'sche Buchhandlung Nachfolger GmbH, Stuttgart.

Alexander Lernet-Holnia, MARS IM WIDDER. Copyright © 1976, 1997 by Paul Zsolnay Verlag Ges.m.b.H., Vienna.

From Ernst von Salomon, *Fragebogen (The Questionnaire)*, translated by Constantine FitzGibbon (Garden City: Doubleday, 1955) by permission of Sanford Greenburger Associates, Inc.

From *After Midnight* by Irmgard Keun, translated by Anthea Bell, by permission Victor Gollancz and The Orion Publishing Group Ltd.

From DEATH IN ROME by Wolfgang Koeppen, translated by Michael Hofmann (Hamish Hamilton 1992, first published in German as *Der Tod in Rom* 1954) copyright © Wolfgang Koeppen, 1954. Translation copyright © Michael Hofmann, 1992.